THE END OF THE PEASANTRY IN SOUTHEAST ASIA

A MODERN ECONOMIC HISTORY OF SOUTHEAST ASIA

The Australian National University is preparing a multivolume economic history of Southeast Asia, which will for the first time place the remarkable economic changes of the late twentieth century within a broader historical framework. This series is at once a work of pioneering scholarship, since nothing remotely comparable has previously been attempted, and a work of synthesis, since hitherto discrete literatures in several disciplines and on ten countries must be integrated. The series will include several volumes on the economic history of the principal countries of Southeast Asia over the past one hundred and fifty years, and a larger number of volumes integrating the whole region in terms of major themes in economic history. Each volume will be accessible to students and specialists alike, aiming to make coherent a history which has been fragmented or ignored.

The Economic History of Southeast Asia Project has been supported by the Research School of Pacific and Asian Studies of the Australian National University, and by the Henry Luce Foundation.

The End of the Peasantry in Southeast Asia

A Social and Economic History of Peasant Livelihood, 1800–1990s

R. E. Elson

in association with
THE AUSTRALIAN NATIONAL UNIVERSITY
CANBERRA

First published in Great Britain 1997 by
MACMILLAN PRESS LTD
Houndmills, Basingstoke, Hampshire RG21 6XS and London
Companies and representatives throughout the world

A catalogue record for this book is available from the British Library.

ISBN 0–333–55293–8 hardcover
ISBN 0–333–55294–6 paperback

First published in the United States of America 1997 by
ST. MARTIN'S PRESS, INC.,
Scholarly and Reference Division,
175 Fifth Avenue, New York, N.Y. 10010

ISBN 0–312–16596–X

Library of Congress Cataloging-in-Publication Data
Elson, R. E. (Robert Edward), 1947–
The end of the peasantry in Southeast Asia : a social and economic history of peasant livelihood, 1800–1990s / R. E. Elson.
p. cm.
Includes bibliographical references and index.
ISBN 0–312–16596–X (cloth)
1. Peasantry—Asia, Southeastern—History. 2. Asia, Southeastern–-Rural conditions. I. Title.
HD1537.A785E45 1997
305.5'633'0959—dc20 96–43242
CIP

This book is printed on paper suitable for recycling and made from fully managed and sustained forest sources.

10 9 8 7 6 5 4 3 2 1
06 05 04 03 02 01 00 99 98 97

Printed in Great Britain by
The Ipswich Book Company Ltd
Ipswich, Suffolk

For John, Jamie, David and Tony

Contents

List of Tables x

List of Abbreviations xi

Glossary xiii

Preface xvi

Acknowledgments xxiv

Map of Southeast Asia xxvi

1 An Embryonic Peasantry **1**
Material life 2
Techniques of land use 6
Swiddening 6
Permanent field cultivation 9
Dry fields 13
Combinations 13
Non-agricultural production 14
Weaving 16
Commerce 17
Impediments to trade 21
Wage labour 23
Peasants and states 24
State power and village agency 28
Peasant mobility 31
Conclusion 32

2 The Context of Change: Politics, Economics and Demography **35**
Monopoly and mercantilism 35
The phase of liberalism 38
The phase of management 46
The phase of disruption 54
The statist phase 59
Population growth and movement 74
Conclusion 78

3 The Changing Varieties of Peasant Production **81**
Markets, states, demography, commercialisation and growth 81
Spatial expansion of the lowlands: the development of a frontier society 82
The technology of lowland expansion 85
Spatial expansion: into the uplands 88
Intensification of land use 90
Enhanced rice production 96
Diversification of cropping 97
Garden cultivation 103
Fishing 104
Swidden cultivation 105
Village industry in decline 114
Indigenous textiles 115
The development of new village industries 119
Conclusion 119

4 Land and Landholding **123**
Land as a commodity 123
Broader implications 129
Land concentration 131
Landlessness 134
Protective interventions 137
Fragmentation 138
Tenancy 140
The growth of tenancy 143
Tenancy as a social form 147
Land reform 148
Land resettlement 154
Conclusion 155

5 A Revolution in Labour **159**
The 'decline' of cooperative and reciprocal labour in village agriculture 159
The aberration of socialist cooperativisation 166
Technology and labour 167
Labour-saving technology 168
Labour recruitment and control 171
Off-farm employment 173
The division of labour: gender and age 179
Conclusion 183

6 Commerce and Credit **185**
The penetration of commerce 185
Phase I: enclosure, augmentation, elaboration 186
Phase II: transformation 187
Phase III: enmeshment and consumerism 203
Conclusion 211

7 Power and Prosperity **213**
From composite to community 213
The power of the village chief 216
More gradual incorporation 220
The modern consolidation of village power 223
From community to citizenry 225
Patterns of social and economic differentiation 226
Social and spatial mobility 227
Prosperity and its distribution 231
The impoverishment critique 232
The alternative view 235
Conclusion 237

Conclusion 239

Notes and References 242

Bibliography 266

Index 327

List of Tables

2.1 Southeast Asia's population, c. 1800–1990 (thousands) 76
3.1 Expansion of rice areas ('000 ha.) and rice exports ('000 tonnes) in Lower Burma, Siam's Central Plain and Cochinchina, c. 1850–1940 84
3.2 The modern growth of rice production (paddy; in tonnes) 96
3.3 Rubber area and output in peninsular Malaysia, 1910–40 99
3.4 Imports of cotton yarns and piece goods into Burma 116
4.1 Land by type of ownership, Burma 1901–39 ('000 ha.) 136
4.2 Distribution of farms by tenure in the Philippines 142
4.3 Areas let at full fixed rents in Burma, 1901–39 ('000 ha.) 143

List of Abbreviations

AAAG	*Annals of the Association of American Geographers*
AE	*American Ethnologist*
AHR	*American Historical Review*
AJAE	*American Journal of Agricultural Economics*
AS	*Asian Survey*
BAAC	Bank for Agriculture and Agricultural Cooperatives (Thailand)
BCAS	*Bulletin of Concerned Asian Scholars*
BIES	*Bulletin of Indonesian Economic Studies*
BULOG	National Logistics Agency (Indonesia)
BUUD	rural cooperative, predecessor to KUD (Indonesia)
CA	*Current Anthropology*
CAS	*Contributions to Asian Studies*
CrA	*Critique of Anthropology*
CSSH	*Comparative Studies in Society and History*
DC	*Development and Change*
DRV	Democratic Republic of Vietnam
EDCC	*Economic Development and Cultural Change*
EEH	*Explorations in Economic History*
EG	*Economic Geography*
EHR	*Economic History Review*
EKI	*Ekonomi dan Keuangan Indonesia*
FACOMA	Farmers' Cooperative Marketing Association (Philippines)
FELDA	Federal Land Development Authority (Malaysia)
FRIS	*Food Research Institute Studies*
GR	*Geographical Review*
HYVs	high-yielding varieties
JAS	*Journal of Asian Studies*
JBRS	*Journal of the Burma Research Society*
JCA	*Journal of Contemporary Asia*
JDS	*Journal of Development Studies*
JEAS	*Journal of East Asiatic Studies*
JEH	*Journal of Economic History*
JIAEA	*Journal of the Indian Archipelago and Eastern Asia*
JMBRAS	*Journal of the Malaysian Branch of the Royal Asiatic Society*
JPS	*Journal of Peasant Studies*
JSEAH	*Journal of Southeast Asian History*

JSEAS	*Journal of Southeast Asian Studies*
JSS	*Journal of the Siam Society*
JTG	*Journal of Tropical Geography*
KEM	*Kajian Ekonomi Malaysia*
KUD	village-level cooperative (Indonesia)
MAS	*Modern Asian Studies*
MER	*Malayan Economic Review*
MI	*Masyarakat Indonesia*
MJTG	*Malayan Journal of Tropical Geography*
OG	*The Oriental Geographer*
PA	*Pacific Affairs*
PANAMIN	Presidential Arm for the Administration of National Minorities (Philippines)
PEJ	*Philippine Economic Journal*
PhS	*Philippine Studies*
PS	*Peasant Studies*
PSR	*Philippine Sociological Review*
PV	*Pacific Viewpoint*
REPELITA	Five Year Development Plan (Indonesia)
RIMA	*Review of Indonesian and Malaysian Studies*
SJTG	*Singapore Journal of Tropical Geography*
WD	*World Development*

Glossary

adat	customary laws
admodiatie	system of haggling over tax obligations between village chief and government officials (Java)
ahmudan	class of people subservient to the king (Burma)
atap	(roof of) thatched palm leaves
ayadaw	land thought of as absolute property of king (Burma)
bekel	village head/tax agent (Java)
bilek	family room of an Iban longhouse
bobobaing	land which could be held privately, inherited or sold (Burma)
ceblokan/kedokan	system whereby those peasants who had performed work preparatory to the harvest without pay were employed to assist in harvesting the crop (Java)
Chettiar	Indian moneylending caste
cong dien	communal rice land (Vietnam)
dampa	temporary shelters inhabited by swiddeners during periods of intensive field work (Borneo)
desa	village (Malay world)
dusun	component hamlets of villages (Java)
duwa	chief (Burma)
gadai	system under which tenant provided landlord with lump sum in advance, in return for which tenant had cultivation rights until sum repaid (Philippines)
gama/prendes/sagod	system whereby only those peasants who had performed weeding labour without pay were employed to assist in harvesting crop (Philippines)
goung	policing official responsible to district police superintendent (Lower Burma)
herendiensten	compulsory labour (Java)
ijon	Javanese credit system where peasant's crop purchased still standing in the field and harvested by purchaser (Java)
jorong	territorial unit (Sumatra)
jual janji	form of land mortgage (Malaya)
kamnan	head of tambon/village (Thailand)
kampung	local settlement (Malaya)
kepala desa	village chief (Malay world)

ketua kampung	head of a local settlement (Malaya)
kunca	credit system in which repayments made in quantities of rice
kyedangyi	chief village taxpayer (Lower Burma)
ladang	upland swidden (Malay world)
lam	intermediary between traders and upland peoples (Laos)
miang	pickled tea
muban	hamlet (Thailand)
mukim	area of settlement surrounding a mosque (Malaya)
myo	circle of lands under guardianship of *myothugyi*, incorporating surrounding rural settlements (Burma)
myothugyi	chief of township (Burma)
nagari	territorial unit (Sumatra)
numpang	dependent peasants attached to households of peasant landholders who exchanged labour for sustenance (Java)
orang kaya	'rich men'; Iban group leadership
pacto de retroventa	form of land mortgage (Philippines)
padi	unhusked rice
palay	unhusked rice
patta	system of land grants (Burma)
paya	swamp rice fields (Malaya)
penghulu	village/lineage head (Malay world)
pu yai bun	hamlet chief (Thailand)
puesto	variety of premium whereby 'compensation' was provided by a new tenant to the tenant he replaced (Philippines)
ray	swidden (Vietnam)
sari-sari	rural shop (Philippines)
sawah	wet rice field (Malay world)
taikthugyi	chief of a circle of villages (Lower Burma)
tambon	district, commune or collection of settlements (Thailand)
taungok	Government Native Officer (Burma)
taungya	system of conservation involving replanting of cut areas with timber
tebasan	system whereby landholder sold crop while still standing in field to an entrepreneur who organised harvest and sale (Java)
thon	component hamlets of villages (Vietnam)

thugyi	village head (Lower Burma)
tilyadora	large threshing machine (Philippines)
tonarigumi	neighbourhood associations (Java)
tuai rumah	connecting functionary between government and longhouse (Borneo)
volkscredietwezen	popular credit system in the Indies
wali	chief of nagari (Sumatra)

Preface

My introduction, more than twenty years ago, to the world of Southeast Asia's social and economic history took the form of a project that was tightly delimited in time, space and theme. Then, the field was virtually untrodden, except for the deep footprints left by those few giants – Furnivall and Geertz come readily to mind – who had combined boldness of vision, superb synthetic abilities, and elegance and wit with the pen, and employed them to overcome what might otherwise have been a debilitating poverty of data. Practising local history provided me with the opportunity, albeit within a limited compass, to graft the close detail and hard specificities of social and economic change, and the wherewithal to test, question, and perhaps even modify the theories of the mighty. The fact that, two decades on, I now find myself at the other end of the spectrum, wrestling with the problems of attempting a generalised understanding of peasant livelihood over the last two hundred years in this immensely diverse region, but now in the context of a vastly enriched stock of knowledge assembled by a generation of scholars, indicates both how far the field has advanced and how far we have still to travel. The short history of the study of Southeast Asia's social and economic history, then, betrays a pattern of rebounding scholarly concerns, from an initial interest in those things of general and overarching significance to the smaller canvas and scuttling detail of local history, case studies and emphatic limitations of theme, and then – as the very existence of the Economic History of Southeast Asia Project demonstrates – back again.

This latest phase carries with it the perennial difficulties of making useful generalisations over so vast and differentiated an area as Southeast Asia, and over a historical sweep of 200 years or so. Paradoxically, the region's unity is to a considerable extent a product of its jarring diversities, which threaten to cast into shadow those things like fish sauces, shared experiences of colonialism, and female prominence in agriculture and trade, which provide comforting unifying themes. At the level of the simple and straightforward, there are political diversities, manifested today in the form of ten different 'countries' with contrasting political heritages, themselves recently created simplifications of earlier multiple and differing political arrangements. More complex and enduring are geographic differences, with peasant societies inhabiting environments ranging from cool and rugged highlands to humid lowland tropics, and with climates so diverse, even within one 'country', that the annual rainfall in Burma's southern delta area exceeds that in the northern dry zone by a factor of five. In turn, the human endowment in the form of the region's extraordinary and ever-changing cultural diversity dwarfs geography on the scale of complexity.

To compound things further there is diversity and unevenness of the sources. Since a comprehensive assessment of relevant data would exhaust the lifetimes of an army of scholars and their inevitable research assistants, I have had to confine myself in large part to the available English language scholarly literature. Even with this severe constriction, difficulties emerge. A large proportion of the available material, much of it published between about 1950 and 1980, consists of anthropological case studies, often of an ethnographic kind. The abiding preoccupation of such works was the narrow particularity in time and space of the cases they studied; they sought to enmesh the reader in the thick description and analysis of specificities. Many of them, as well, were cast within paradigms of modernisation whose limitations have since been recognised. Their approach was characteristically unmindful of the importance of the historical dimension; only in the last fifteen or twenty years have anthropologists generally come to recognise the need to cast their work with an eye to enhanced temporality in order to site it within diachronic series of processes and changes. More recently, a goodly proportion of the research on rural change has been practised by development economists with the aid of macro-level quantitative data; while this work has provided broad indicators of change (what Benjamin White has called 'monitoring'[1]), it cannot identify with precision the detailed causal sequences of such change; moreover, the values of its practitioners have often led it to conclusions startlingly different from those arrived at by scholars working on local village level studies, whose sympathies are often with the apparent losers in struggles over resources. Historians, as a group, have tended to eschew problems of regional significance and general theory. Perhaps unduly sensitive to the relative backwardness of the study of Southeast Asia's past, they have chosen to burrow into the archival remains of specific eras, places or questions, not often lending their expertise to broader debates about the nature of peasant social and economic change in Southeast Asia except for the occasional snipe at what they see as the more outrageous errors of those who seek to generalise.

Notwithstanding the imposing problems of diversity presented by the region itself and the multiple and sometimes problematic ways in which it has been examined and understood, I am seeking here to analyse from a long perspective the changes in peasant societies and peasant livelihood in Southeast Asia. Whatever the difficulties, the time seems right for an historical analysis which attempts to overcome the boundaries of space, time and theme which earlier treatments, understandably daunted by uncertainty and diversity, imposed upon the region. The most obvious was the preoccupation with specific countries, so that the history of the region became no more than a series of histories of the region's component countries. A second kind of boundedness was that drawn between colonialism and independence or, as it was sometimes conceived, between pre- and post-World War II eras. A third was that which confined analyses to a single theme, such as production or ethnicity or demography. All such restrictions of focus served useful purposes and provided an extraordinary richness of detail, specific analysis and fruitful theorising. But the time has come to attempt to understand the region as a whole, whatever the difficulties presented by its inherent diversity and the fragmented nature of its literature, to bring together the specificities of local projects to create a broader understanding of regional change.

The task I have set myself – indeed, the general theme which sustains this study – is to discover why, over the last two hundred years or so, peasant societies in Southeast Asia organised their productive relations the way they did and, secondarily, how those arrangements affected their social and economic lives. Addressing this agenda, I hope, will provide a sense of perspective on the modern history of Southeast Asia's peasants, a sense of the longer trajectory of their social existence. In his review of the *Cambridge Economic History of India*, C.A. Bayly praised the enterprise which had given it birth but lamented that 'it is difficult here to gain a broad impression of how the Indian economy might have changed over time or how features such as demography, foreign trade, agricultural production and state policy might have acted on each other'.[2] Here I attempt to draw a picture that will provide such an overview of Southeast Asian peasant life. The starting point of my analysis, around 1800, is a conveniently rough date to begin, since the point of the exercise is to show how things changed in general terms and over the long haul as a result of Southeast Asian peasants' collision with 'the modernising West' and a newly and aggressively intrusive international economy.

The way I have organised this book attempts to provide a means of solving the problems that emerge from this central question. In the first chapter, I present a schematic picture of peasant society around 1800 – sometimes a matter of making best guesses based on contemporary data – which serves as a rough base line for measuring change. In the second chapter, in many ways the pivot around which the book turns, I provide a summary of those contexts which proved fundamental in shaping the ways in which peasants have constructed and reconstructed their social and economic life into the modern era. In Chapter 3 I attempt to locate and explain the varieties of peasant production against the background established in the preceding chapter. In the remaining chapters, packaged in themes which I judged most relevant to the major issue, I examine the effects of these changes.

In seeking to provide a sense of why Southeast Asian peasant societies have evolved the way they have, and of the broader implications of those patterns of change, I became ever more acutely aware of the difficulties of generalisation and the grossness of method and result which seems to be its inevitable companion. Given the fact that minds and lives are finite, there is, of course, the ever-present danger of overreaching one's expertise (in my case, grounded in Java) and committing (with varying degrees of gravity) sins of error and omission. As well, many aspects of Southeast Asian social and economic change have been or remain the sites of significant and often unresolved debate; I had not the space, time or skill to resolve them nor, often, even to outline them with the sensitivity to nuance they demand, and I trust that readers will forgive the consequent crudities. The need to generalise sometimes demanded an imaginative (some might say wanton) use of a wide range of sources of differing quality which plays scant attention to their specific context and sometimes attempts to make good their deficiencies through judiciousness alone. Finally, detail, complexity and qualification often had to be sacrificed for the overall goal, with the result that attempts at simplification and regional generalisation may border uncomfortably close to being simplistic, misleading, or just plain wrong. These are the costs of the enterprise, and I can but hope that the usefulness of the outcome outweighs them.

THE CATEGORY OF PEASANT

More than a generation ago, an American anthropologist suggested that the concept of 'tribe' 'figure[d] prominently on the list of putative technical terms ranked on order of degrees of ambiguity as reflected in multifarious definitions'.[3] 'Peasant' is a term that probably ranks higher than tribe on this list of contested understandings, especially when one wants to consider it in an historical dimension. My focus is peasants, by which I mean rural groupings of people whose primary orientation, both economic and social, was towards a broad participation in simple, relatively unspecialised, household-based, subsistence agricultural production, who shared notions of social and economic life beyond their specific community, and who stood in relations of subordination to a more powerful class of claimants outside their sphere.[4] Such a definition, however, is not meant to be precise; it is, in Firth's words, 'suitable only for demarcating rough boundaries in categorization'.[5] While in general my object is 'small-scale producers with a relatively simple, non-industrial technology',[6] it also includes village-based craft workers, agricultural labourers and traders, partly because of the fluidity of occupation in villages and partly – and more important – because these kinds of people shared the same general outlook as rural agricultural producers and shaped their lives around the productive rhythms of the village.

The concept of 'peasant' which underpins this work, then, is essentially one of a fundamental orientation towards and prioritising of the local and the rural, notably a focus on own-production for own-consumption, notwithstanding a general recognition of the legitimacy of claims from the supra-local sphere and of the need for exchange. In this context, even those who did not produce the bulk of their own food from the soil can be claimed as members of the peasant mode of life, because they shared the same understandings of the centrality of own-production and because their social lives were shaped by the multiple sets of local relationships which flowed from that centrality.

What is important here are the relationships and structures which tied people within this locally-focused rural setting, not the demarcation of a narrowly defined group. One's sense of the object of study must be sufficiently rough and broad to accommodate changes in relationship and occupation over time within the village, and how they were perceived from within, as well as developments in relationships with the world outside, what Moerman calls 'the articulation of multisocietal systems'.[7] It must also accommodate different kinds of rural production ranging from foraging to crop cultivation to livestock pasturing and on to manual craftwork. All these things were constituents of peasant life and livelihood. To pursue the definitional task too narrowly and relentlessly may in the end be crippling, distracting and misleading; it runs the risk of missing the larger, longer and broader pattern of change within what became the defining social group of Southeast Asia.

There are those who might object that such a framework is too loose and imprecise. But as Geertz, talking of another context, has remarked, 'essential form may be seen more adequately in terms of a range of variation than in terms of a fixed pattern from which deviant cases depart'.[8] Such a broad perspective allows the examination of groupings which normally escape discussions of peasantries. In the Southeast Asian case, it includes, notably, those peoples whom anthropologists, taken with and further emphasising their boundedness, internal cohesion, and characteristic shunning of larger dominating powers, have often separated from the rest as 'tribal' groups but who, as they became enmeshed in the social and economic transformations which gripped the region in this period, were recast into peasant modes of life.

THE CENTRAL THEME

The concept of peasantry is rooted in time. It is not a fixed, permanent and timeless category, but rather a social formation which appears at certain times and under certain conditions, and which disappears when those times and conditions change. As Shanin has reminded us, 'peasantry exists only as a process, i.e., in its change'.[9] I will argue that, from the early decades of the nineteenth century in some places, and certainly by the latter third of that century in most places, there emerged a peasant formation that was to define the age. Peasants, of course, had long existed in Southeast Asia, providing sustenance for themselves and for their rulers from the soil. Their role in the region's history had been a background one, to provide labour and surpluses to underpin the political and religious activities of their elites, but their importance was not always central to the vitality of the region's states. By around the middle of the nineteenth century, however, long-gestating processes of social and economic change emerged which can be said to have constructed the modern Southeast Asian peasantry. This peasantry was not only large in number and rapidly spreading across and beyond the lowland landscape of Southeast Asia, but it came to carry the burden of production visited upon the region by the rapacious demands of the rapidly expanding international economic system. Wealth, for the colonial and indigenous Southeast Asian states of the late nineteenth and early twentieth century, came from exploiting the fruitful combination of peasant labour and natural environment. If the sixteenth century was the age of commerce, the late nineteenth and early twentieth centuries were the age of the peasantry in Southeast Asia, when peasant labour and production sustained, as never before, the economies of the region.

The peasants who satisfied these demands by producing unprecedentedly large volumes of rice, sugar, coffee, abaca, tobacco and rubber did so without in the first instance losing their essential orientation towards, nor their style of, local subsistence production and local identity and organisation. However, the peasantry's very involvement in such vast production schemes, and others of more modest dimension – whether as landholders, tenants, agricultural workers, craftspeople, or petty traders – set in motion processes which carried the seeds of its social transformation. The new international economy which peasants served, and the strengthening states which first articulated and then managed it, brought them money, roads, and markets, as well as new laws and rules of behaviour, and a stiffening of local power. As well, they provided the conditions for the rapid and sustained growth in peasant numbers. Meshed within these new contexts, the peasantry could not endure as a peasantry. Although the face of Southeast Asia even today remains superficially rural, the trajectory of peasant disappearance is fixed. The progeny of the late-nineteenth-century peasantry still live in the countryside, but not with the permanence, rural focus and sense of local identity their forebears had. They still grow rice, but they grow it more quickly, more often, and according to the template of modern agricultural science, and they grow a great variety of other cultigens as well. They sell the great bulk of what they produce, they produce it to sell, and they purchase the great bulk of what they use. They live in villages, but those villages are administrative creations which look upward and outward, not inwardly oriented local communities. They work outside the village, in a great range of specific and enduring occupations, in rhythms dissociated from those of rural production and at extremes of distance that would both frustrate and bewilder their predecessors. They move about with a facility and alacrity their forebears might both fear and envy. Their culture is not just that of the village but of the nation and the world, relayed to them through schools, newspapers, magazines, CDs, and the electronic media.

The great age of the Southeast Asian peasantry may be dated from around the mid-to-late nineteenth century until the early decades of the twentieth century. In its very success, however, the peasant mode of life showed the first signs of its impending demise. Thereafter came a process of transmogrification that displayed features of social vagueness (for instance, the ambiguities attendant upon the closing gap between urban and rural livelihood and culture) and of social specificity (for instance, the emergence of dedicated wage employment). The peasantry, and its peculiar mode of life, was on a path to disappearance. These changes, and what they meant, are amenable neither to neat periodisation nor precise classification. In some places, where the transformative agency of state and market had been longer at work, they were evident in the early decades of the twentieth century. In some places, they have yet to emerge in more than outline form. But, as I hope to make clear, the trajectory of change in modern Southeast Asia has consigned the peasantry, as a social formation, to the past. To plot this trajectory, and to explain the often intricate reasons for its ascending and descending lines, is the task of this study.

R.E. ELSON

Acknowledgments

The challenging scope of this work meant that I incurred many debts in its writing. I should like to record my gratefulness to the Australian Research Council, which provided the funds to allow me a year free of the responsibilities of teaching to read, think, and write, and to the Faculty of Asian and International Studies at Griffith University for supporting my efforts to bring the book to a conclusion. Librarians at Griffith University, the Australian National University and the National Library of Australia gave me enlightening and wholehearted access to the sources upon which the book is based. Scholars labouring in this and related fields have offered all kinds of advice (sometimes a little too readily for my liking) and encouragement. Chief amongst them was Tony Reid, who has managed the Economic History Project with verve, astounding good humour (even for him) and imaginativeness. Tony organised and orchestrated a weekend-long seminar at the Australian National University which provided me with an extraordinary opportunity to present my ideas at length and witness their refashioning or rejection before my eyes. I thank all those who attended, who participated with an enthusiasm bordering upon relish, and who went out of their way to assist me in all kinds of ways: Colin Barlow, Gillian Burke, Helen Creese, Howard Dick, John Drabble, Pierre van der Eng, Radin Fernando, Jim Fox, Yujiro Hayami, Ward Keeler, Ben Kerkvliet, Roger Knight, Alfons van der Kraan, Paul Kratoska, Thomas Lindblad, Jamie Mackie, Bill O'Malley, Lesley Potter and Ken Young. I am grateful, too, for the help and encouragement along the way of John Butcher and Marika Vicziany, and to Norman Owen, Anne Booth, and Graham Fordham for their insightful and uncomfortably probing comments on earlier drafts. Linda Poskitt deserves special mention for her untiring and cheery support in everything related to the Project, and for being such a kind, generous and hospitable friend. Ken Armitage and Leanne Wood helped pull things together at the end, and Evelyn Ng did everything humanly possible to organise me and quarantine my time for writing. Much the greater part of this book was researched and written in a little office at home; my beloved wife and children rather liked this arrangement, since it meant my permanent availability for more immediately useful and enjoyable pursuits than writing books. I thank them for putting up with me even when they couldn't drag me from the office.

Map of Southeast Asia

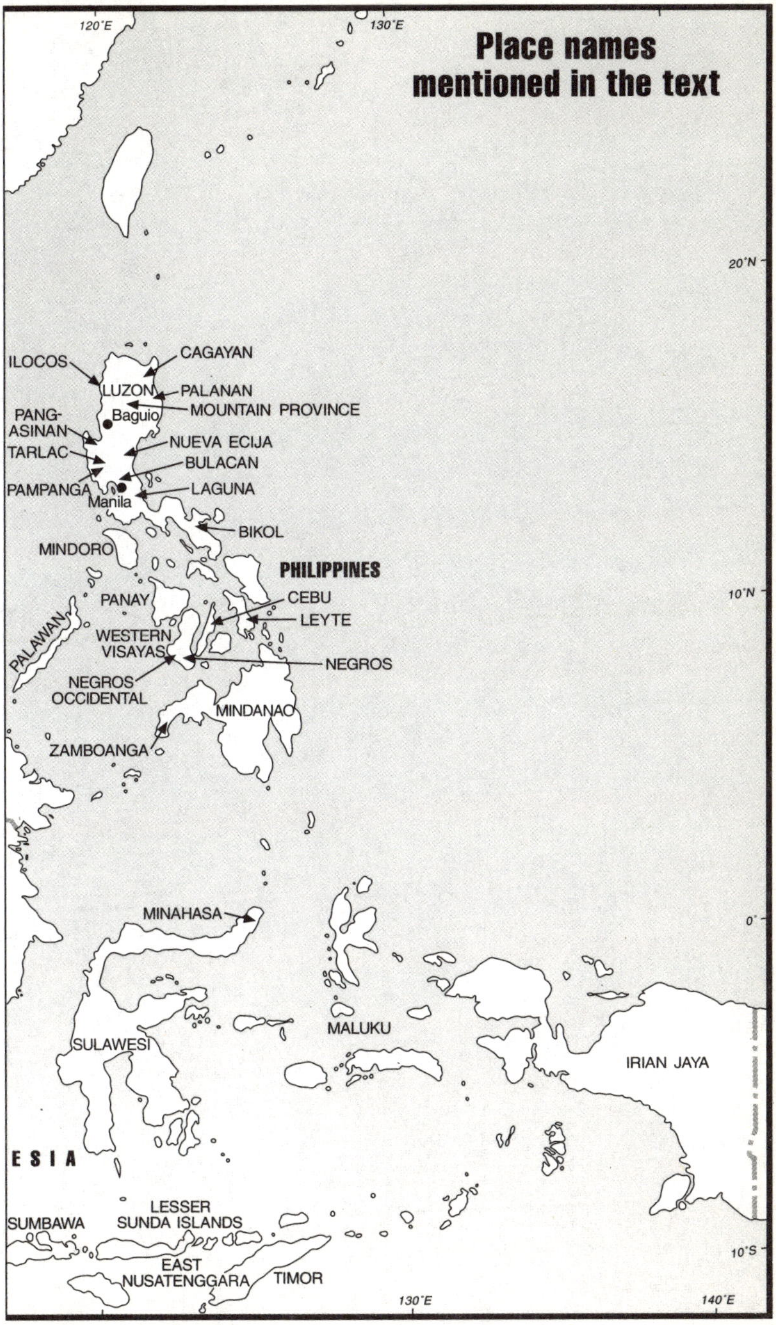

Place names mentioned in the text
120°E
130°E
140°E
20°N
10°N
0°
10°S
ILOCOS
CAGAYAN
LUZON
PALANAN
MOUNTAIN PROVINCE
Baguio
PANG-
ASINAN
TARLAC
NUEVA ECIJA
BULACAN
PAMPANGA
Manila
LAGUNA
BIKOL
MINDORO
PHILIPPINES
PANAY
CEBU
LEYTE
PALAWAN
WESTERN
VISAYAS
NEGROS
NEGROS
OCCIDENTAL
MINDANAO
ZAMBOANGA
MINAHASA
MALUKU
SULAWESI
IRIAN JAYA
ESIA
LESSER
SUNDA ISLANDS
SUMBAWA
EAST
NUSATENGGARA
TIMOR

1 An Embryonic Peasantry

To speak of Southeast Asian peasants today might immediately conjure up images of immensity and profusion: vast landscapes segmented into tiny, brilliantly green rice fields away to the horizon, tightly bunched and dusty villages thronged with legions of people – and their cattle, pigs, chickens and ducks – threading their way evenly about their business, a great bulk and multiplicity of crops to feed surging populations, the busy and fastidious exploitation of nature to the limit of its gifts. Whatever one might think of the aptness of such images in capturing the reality of the contemporary Southeast Asian rural world, there can be no question that they bear little correspondence to peasant life at the turn of the nineteenth century. Then, the ecology of the region remained largely undisturbed; a few foreboding exceptions to one side, the region consisted, from mountain top to often swampy shore, of enormous expanses of unexploited and thickly vegetated land; even as late as 1888, indeed, the Pahang region of Malaya 'had a forest cover that extended from the seashore to the top of all but the highest mountain ranges'.[1] One European spoke romantically in the mid nineteenth century of the 'dense forests' of Borneo and Sumatra: 'trees of gigantic stature, of abundant foliage, and hung with a thousand creeping plants, entangled, fantastic, brilliant with flowers, and equal in their gaudy splendour to the growth of the Brazilian woods'.[2] Such forests and woodlands were home to a great diversity of wildlife: elephants, tigers, rhinoceroses, deer, wild pigs, to name the most obvious; according to one European observer, peasants guarding their crops at night from small watch platforms were 'at the eminent risk at night of being picked off by a tiger'.[3]

The vast lushness of forest vegetation which so impressed Western travellers, as well as the numbers and ubiquity of the wild creatures which inhabited it, convey the main characteristic of the human ecology of the region: its sparse population. To provide but one example, the lowland population of the dry zone heartland of the Burmese kingdom in the late eighteenth century was given at around 1.5 million people, with only about another half million in the rest of what is now Burma.[4] Rural inhabitants, in this imposing natural landscape, were small in numbers and clumped in just a few localised settings. The peasantry which would come to dominate the human space of Southeast Asia and monumentally recast its physical face – that mammoth rural army of sedentary small-scale cultivators, extended across and fastened to the landscape, oriented socially and organisationally to the task of securing its own subsistence from the soil, predominantly through rice cultivation – was but in the early stages of its creation. The interdependent forces that were to shape its preponderance across Southeast Asia were present only in equally embryonic form. In order to trace the origins of this process of social formation, and to provide a point of contrast against which to map the transformations which were to come, I shall begin with a somewhat crude, artificial and synchronic discussion of the material life of the region's rural inhabitants around the turn of the nineteenth century, only then moving outwards to establish the broader spatial, ecological, political and economic lineaments of their world.

MATERIAL LIFE

In the early nineteenth century these meagre numbers of Southeast Asian peasants lived in pockets of spatially diverse rural settlements, usually termed villages,[5] which varied in size from as little as a handful of inhabitants to some thousands but which seem, on average, to have housed around two or three hundred persons. In those lowland reaches where population was relatively dense and the practice of sedentary agriculture long-established, peasants often shaped their settlements as huddled clumps, islands in a sea of surrounding fields. But since dense population and long-established permanent agriculture were exceptional, it was more common, in the lowlands, to find villages ribboned along the banks of rivers ('the Malay clings to the bank of the river; and it is but seldom that you find him settling very far within the jungle'[6]) or the sides of roads, often forming a continuum of human habitation so that the boundaries between communities were vague or haphazard, or, at higher altitudes, hugging the contours of upland spurs or ridges. Whether clumped or linear in shape, villages were seldom single, compact and solitary settlements; usually they comprised some kind of central place and a number of spatially distinct neighbourhoods or hamlets, the members of which were often related by kinship but who often had no close relationship with members of other hamlets comprising the village settlement.

This common preference for clumped or linear settlement is one more indicator of the dominance of the natural environment in which rural inhabitants found themselves, since it was apparently based upon the desire 'for mutual protection against wild beasts and robbers'.[7] A pattern of spatially dispersed or scattered dwellings occurred only very infrequently; it was generally to be found in more isolated or frontier-style places, such as among the Subanu people of Mindanao or amongst those peasants pioneering settlement in the southern deltaic regions of Vietnam, where danger had to be faced alone.

For the most part the dwellings in which peasants lived were small and functionally basic, built rapidly of cheap and easily obtainable products, with walls of woven bamboo or timber planks, in some places 'plastered with clay, and more often with mud or even cowdung',[8] and roofed with palm leaves, long grass or rice straw. Except in east and central Java, the sinified parts of Vietnam and some upland tribal areas, where houses were set on the ground with earthen floors, and for some remote groups of shifting cultivators who customarily built their dwellings in trees, dwellings were built on poles about two metres above the ground, and floored with bamboo slats, providing a space underneath for pigs and cattle, firewood, and a loom. They were often sited without regard for regularity or pattern; according to an 1835 account, for example, the Malay village was composed of 'compounds and houses without order or arrangement, just as their owners liked to build them, some unfenced, some with fences zigzag . . . . None of the houses facing the same way'.[9] Dwellings contained little if any furniture apart from benches and mats used for bedding; they were generally single-roomed affairs divided internally with bamboo partitions. Apart from houses, lowland settlements usually contained rice storage barns, pens for cattle, and religious buildings, in Muslim areas a mosque or prayer house, in Buddhist-influenced regions a wat, in Vietnam a spirit shrine, and in the Catholic Philippines a chapel.

A household usually comprised a nuclear family, with some in-laws and perhaps one or more dependents. The most distinctive physical contrast to this single nuclear household was the longhouse, an aggregation of socially separate but physically connected domiciles, usually the home of clan or lineage groupings of numerous families, sometimes nuclear but often extended, each with its own specific and demarcated quarters; such dwellings might house several hundred people. Some settlements comprised just a single longhouse, other were made up of several. Where lineages and kinship assumed central importance, such as among the Minangkabau of western Sumatra or (with a much looser sense of corporateness) the Iban of Borneo, longhouses might be constructed of richer, more ornamented and more durable materials as a manifestation of their ritual importance.

In some places, villages enjoyed a clear sense of fixed and specific territoriality. Thus, in the delta region of northern Vietnam, villages fenced themselves about with hedge boundaries to separate them from others and to manifest their existence as discrete communities. But behaviour of this kind was unusual in the Southeast Asian peasant world. Much more commonly, village communities enjoyed only weak, insecure and often shifting ties to a defined and particular place; what was of greater significance, as we shall see, was the attachment of people to a particular overlord who could assure them of protection, status and prosperity.

Peasants' clothing was notable for its sparseness and simplicity. In Bali, people generally wore no more than a sarong, and Laotian villagers wore a similar wrapper-like skirt. In Cochinchina, 'the dress of both sexes is nearly alike, and consists generally of a loose vest, with a pair of large, long and loose trowsers'.[10] Although more isolated upland groups customarily wore more elaborate and distinctive dress which proclaimed their identity as well as protecting them from harsher extremes of climate, the predominant item of clothing, especially in the lowlands, was a rectangular piece of cloth, worn around the waist, often drawn up between the legs and tucked in, and usually accompanied by a jacket or tunic or various kinds of scarves. In still more peripheral places, such as the interior regions of Borneo and Sumatra and upland reaches of the mainland, people sometimes wore clothing fabricated from bark, and their basic attire was a loin cloth, sometimes complemented by a tunic, for men, and for women a skirt and tunic.

The major component of peasants' meals was rice (around half a kilogram a day for adults), to which was added a little animal protein – cattle meat, goat flesh, pork, eggs, poultry, fish ('the Burmans could not live without fish'[11]) – together with maize (especially when rice was in short supply), pulses (beans), and roots (yam), and flavoured with salt, shrimp paste ('Balachang, a strange compound of things savoury and loathsome; but in such general use that no one thinks of eating without some portion of it'[12]), coconut, chilli, pepper, assorted leaves, and spices such as turmeric, cumin and coriander; the whole was followed by fruit and its eating accompanied by the drinking of water or, occasionally, rice or palm wine. Peasants prepared their meals in iron or bamboo vessels, on a hearth inside their dwellings; they ate from glazed earthenware or leaves. In eating, 'neither knives, spoons nor any substitutes for them are employed; they take up the rice, and other victuals, between the thumb and fingers, and dexterously throw it into the mouth by the action of the thumb, dipping frequently their hands into water as they eat'.[13] In addition to regular meals, snacking was prevalent; according to a later account, 'one striking feature in all the Burman villages is the number of petty shops for eatables. Almost every house has something displayed for sale in a corner of the lower verandah'.[14]

The bulk of peasants' food came from large-field agriculture, but most of its variety from elsewhere. Most village houses had little vegetable and fruit gardens attached to them, and settlements were generally surrounded and interspersed with different kinds of fruit trees such as coconut, banana, mango, areca nut, and durian. These garden plots and orchards, customarily crammed with an extraordinary diversity of cultigens arranged according to their height, provided most of the essential side dishes for rice; villagers grew vegetables, gourds, egg-plant, pumpkin, sugar cane, sweet potato, fruits and other crops in them. Thus, 'the Dyaks have small gardens, usually the property of women, in which they plant vegetables of different kinds, principally the 'trong,' brenjal of the East, and egg-plant of Europe, sugar-cane, plantains, yams, sweet potatoes, chilies &c'.[15] Such gardens were not dispensable, hobby-like ancillaries to large-field peasant production, but important contributors to peasant diets; as well, it seems likely that their varied produce provided a substantial surplus for barter and commercial interchange. Peasants obtained a significant proportion of their animal protein from the ducks (also useful for controlling ricefield pests) and chickens that visitors always reported wandering through settlements, or from fish reared in special ponds or flooded rice fields, or hooked, trapped, netted or poisoned (with a preparation obtained by pounding tuba roots) in canals, channels, ditches, lakes, marshes or streams. According to Hugh Low, 'during a great portion of the year, the rice-fields, ditches, and water-courses swarm with fish .... Men, women and children are then rarely seen without their fishing rods',[16] while John Crawfurd, travelling near Hue after heavy rains had inundated the surrounding fields, noted 'some persons even engaged in fishing where crops of grain would be reaped in a few months'.[17] In Burma, 'during the rains, when the whole of the plains are more or less under water, fish ascend by the innumerable streams and water ways, to spawn in the comparatively still and shelter of the flooded lowlands, so that the whole country is one enormous fishpond'.[18] Peasants also speared, shot or trapped wild animals and birds in the surrounding jungles.

The labours of subsistence – agriculture, fishing, foraging, repair and maintenance – however intensely practised, was not spaced evenly throughout the year but highly concentrated according to the cycles of cultivation. There was, therefore, a considerable space for leisure activities. For males these included gambling with dice and cards, cock-fighting, kite-flying, wrestling, football, fencing, chess, chewing betel, smoking tobacco ('even babies in their mother's arms are often seen puffing a cigar'[19]) and chewing and smoking opium. Care was also taken to provide time for essential religious observances and village ritual. More communal forms of leisure comprised feasting, theatre, story-telling, pantomime, dance, orchestral music, and singing. Women, their available time foreshortened by ancillary tasks in the home, had much less time than men for formalised leisure.

TECHNIQUES OF LAND USE

Land was central to peasants' lives. It provided them with the food that sustained them, and the rhythms of its cultivation profoundly ordered their lives both materially and spiritually. In a context where 'any conspicuous display of wealth usually drew the extortionate attentions of the local officials',[20] land and its working was the single major target of peasant investment. But given the multiformity of ecologies in evidence across the region, the different purposes and requirements which agriculture was called upon to serve, and the varying stocks of resources available to peasants in different settings, the techniques employed to make land productive were characteristically diverse. In early nineteenth-century Java, Crawfurd distinguished four techniques of cultivation: upland swiddening, called *ladang*; dry field perennial cropping; rainfed flood cultivation, and artificially irrigated fields.[21] His categorisation, with some emendation, provides a useful means of simplifying and surveying the variety of productive techniques in force in those limited parts of Southeast Asia where peasants – or those who would become peasants – lived.

SWIDDENING

Today, swidden cultivation finds its most common expression in Southeast Asia's shrinking stock of heavily wooded uplands. In the early nineteenth century, however, it was also the dominant form of agriculture in the many regions of forested lowland which were still in evidence in Southeast Asia, notably in large stretches of the Malay peninsula, in Sumatra and in Lower Burma. In swiddening, peasants cleared scrub and felled the trees on a designated stretch of land (chosen for religious reasons as well as for its location and perceived agricultural potential), and burned the resultant vegetation, spread across the field, when it had dried. They fenced the fields they had cleared in this way against attacks from pigs, deer and other animals, and planted out their crops on the scorched earth. Once one or more seasons of use had exhausted the fields they had claimed, cultivators simply abandoned the land to nature's repair, shifted their activities to another site and repeated the process of clearing, felling, burning and planting.

Some swiddeners made repeated and cyclical use of the same large stretch of territory; their villages, accordingly, remained in the same place for perhaps a hundred years and more. Thus, according to one writer, numerous Karen villages in what is now Thailand 'have been in the same location for a century or longer',[22] and much the same was reported of some villages of the Kachin of northern Burma.[23] Similarly, the Lamet of Laos 'are as a matter of fact permanent, and several of their villages are very old. Now and again a village is moved, or part breaks loose to form a new village, but this happens at such long intervals of time that one can certainly not classify the Lamet as nomads'.[24] In the outer islands of what is now Indonesia, 'most of the indigenous, traditional swidden cultivators . . . have permanent villages and fixed, delineated village territories'.[25] Such settled peoples generally took a more deliberatively conservationist approach to their cultivating; for example, they characteristically left belts of trees to act as seed reservoirs and allowed long periods of fallowing to permit regeneration of the forest before they cut it over again. Thus, the Karen 'seldom remain more than two seasons in one spot, and all through the jungles are found abandoned Karen hamlets, where rank weeds and young bamboo-shoots supplant the cultivated fields'.[26]

Peoples of a more pioneering cast regularly abandoned their villages and established new ones in their continuing search for more fertile land for reclamation and cultivation; the Mnong Gar of central Vietnam transferred their habitation about every seven years, measuring time in relation to the use of a particular piece of land for swiddening. Thus, explains Condominas, 'we have eaten the forest of the stone-spirit Goo . . . designates the year 1949'.[27] The Malays of Temerloh were said to have been constantly moving, combining shifting cultivation of *paya* (swamp rice fields) with commerce in the products of the forests. According to one European observer, the Negritoes of Luzon were often 'wandering and unsettled, seldom remaining long enough in one place to form a village. They sometimes sow a little maize or rice, and wait its ripening, but not longer'.[28] Sometimes, movement was less frequent; the Hmong of Laos shifted their settlements only when they had exhausted the land within walking distance of their habitation. In northern Siam, notwithstanding the constant shifting from one site of cultivation to another, settlements might occupy the same residential site for a couple of generations. This pattern of pioneering swiddening contrasted strongly with patterns of circular swiddening practised from a stable base; in the case of the Iban peoples, it manifested itself in a spreading migration northwards across the Bornean forests.

Whether swiddening was stable or pioneering in type, the land cleared for cultivation was usually deemed to belong to the household which had cleared it, and so it remained until such time as it had obviously been permanently abandoned. Occasionally, however, one household might allow another to use its secondary jungle provided the same right was extended to itself at some future time; 'after all, in the sparsely populated areas where swidden farming was practiced, there were usually plenty of potential swidden plots, and any man who wanted to do the heavy work of clearing, burning, and planting was welcome to any plot'.[29] More broadly, swiddening communities had quite clear understandings of the domain to which they laid claim for swidden agriculture, whether it was in use, used, or to be used in the future.

Since their fields often lay far from their houses, swiddeners commonly built temporary shelters – 'no mean shed, but a substantially built, well thatched house'[30] – which they inhabited during the months of intensive work in clearing, planting, guarding the crops from animals and harvesting, returning to the main habitation only in the off-season. With the Iban, these shelters (*dampa*) were semi-permanently inhabited scaled longhouses, abandoned and dismantled only when the land surrounding them was played out; 'in this intermittent way, dampa follows dampa, until a return is made to the main long-house'.[31] Where settlements were closer to fields, villagers built shelters in their swiddens as places for rest and guarding posts, and sometimes for overnight stays, and used them as temporary rice barns at harvest time.

Swidden farming was extremely arduous. The strenuous and grinding task of felling, slashing and burning fell to able-bodied males, although women and older children often assisted with light clearing. Usually, discrete households performed the tasks of clearing, planting, cultivating and harvesting their own fields, although other households might often assist them when work needed to be concluded rapidly, themselves receiving such assistance as required, all on a strictly reciprocal basis. Since swiddening required no hoeing, ploughing or harrowing of the land, planting began as soon as the rainy season was imminent. Peasants interplanted rice (and different varieties of rice) with other vegetables, pulses, tubers and fruits in the same field – cucumber, onions, leafy vegetables, tobacco, beans, cotton, pepper, sweet potatoes, chillies, peanuts, eggplant, sesame, sorghum, gourds, millet, taro, yams, cassava, maize, fruit trees. Men and women shared the job of planting, often employing reciprocal labour among households. Men led the way across the cleared and burned field poking seed holes with dibble sticks; women followed, placing seed in the dibble holes, while children sometimes covered the seeding sites with earth. Weeding was done periodically once crops had begun to sprout; it was normally the work of women, except in those times when the demand for such labour required men to participate as well. Within about five months of planting, the rice crop was ready; it was reaped with a sickle in some places such as Cochinchina, but in others stalk by stalk with a small finger knife or sometimes with the hands alone, a technique partly attributed by one observer to the fact that 'the grain is often, from perhaps an intermixture of different sorts, not all ripe at once'.[32] Non-rice crops were harvested as they matured which, in the case of root- and tree-crop cultigens, sometimes meant that a swidden remained productive for many years after it had been abandoned for the purpose of rice cultivation. The crop remained the property of the household which had cleared and planted the fields on which it grew; they harvested it as a unit, men and women alike, although in some places reaping was deemed to be the work of women alone.

The growing season – and the success of the harvest – was strictly conditioned by the timing and availability of rainfall. This absolute dependence on the elements meant that swiddeners could usually reckon upon a single growing season, one crop a year. Consequently they were often affected severely by food shortages immediately before the harvest, while the results of the harvest itself were often unpredictable and sometimes a cause of scarcity. Nonetheless, in some places the moisture available in the soil at the onset of the dry season sometimes allowed a second crop on swiddens; thus, in the Ilocos region of Luzon, a cotton crop could be planted after the mountain rice crop.

PERMANENT FIELD CULTIVATION

In quite different ecological settings from those where their fellows practised the shifting patterns of swiddening, peasants applied themselves to permanent field cultivation, characterised by the continuing (if sometimes seasonally intermittent) exploitation of specific stretches of land. Such sedentary cultivation was of three general kinds. The most important, if only in terms of the numbers of people it sustained per unit of land, was wet-rice cultivation, which preponderated in lowland areas with dense populations and reliable supplies of water, and which was therefore still quite localised, relatively restricted and, in spatial terms, inconsiderable. In early nineteenth century Java it seems that around 70 per cent of cultivated land comprised wet fields, there called *sawah*, but this pattern of predominance was exceptional for the region as a whole. Wet-rice growing was practised intensively and on an expansive scale in only a few thickly peopled pockets of the region, such as central Java's lowland valleys, the royal heartlands of the Burmese dry zone, the Central Plain of Siam, the northern delta region of Vietnam, and west Sumatra's fertile highland valleys.

Wet-rice cultivation relied either on seasonal flooding or rainfall, or on artificial irrigation. Some localities were entirely dependent upon flooding; Siam's Central Plain did not receive sufficient rainfall for wet-field cultivation and prospered instead on the lowland flood surge from its great rivers. Similarly in Lower Burma, 'the heavy floods . . . during the monsoon place the whole country except the hills more or less under water'.[33] In the Philippines, 'during the rainy season, the incessant fall of rain on the mountains causes the rivers, both large and small, to overflow and to become torrents, that rush down upon the plains, covering them with water, and depositing the broken earth and slime which they have gathered in their course'.[34] Other places, among which must be numbered the greater part of the Javanese wet-rice environment, relied directly on heavy monsoonal rainfall which peasants impounded in their dyked fields. Land inundated by the gravity flow of flood or rainwater needed no special techniques for distributing water. Artificially irrigated fields, however, were fed from streams dammed for the purpose with logs, brushwood, earth and stones, or from specially constructed channels or (much less common) tanks and reservoirs; their watering normally required the use of a variety of irrigation tools such as scoops and wheels. Accordingly, artificial irrigation was comparatively rare, not just because of the labour and maintenance it demanded but also because the efficient collection and distribution of water required a certain level of organisation and cooperation within and outside the village which was not always available or forthcoming; thefts of water and village disputes over its distribution were not unknown. Its major sites, not surprisingly, were those core areas of the major wet rice regions where history and environment had combined to control the flow of water, and it was also to be found in lesser centres such as small stretches of hinterland Malaya where the practice of irrigation appears to have been introduced by those Minangkabau who had been emigrating from west Sumatra since the fifteenth century.

The cultivation regime of wet-rice production began with burning off or ploughing in the stubble from the previous harvest and the weeds which had subsequently sprouted. This practice, together with the random droppings of grazing animals, was virtually the only artificial fertilising the fields enjoyed; 'none of the Indian islanders ever apply any kind of manure directly to the land'.[35] Peasants generally employed cattle to plough and harrow their fields, dragging in turn a shallow iron-tipped plough – 'which only scratches the ground to the depth of six or eight inches'[36] – and a rough harrow. However, in marshy areas such as Lower Burma and parts of Luzon and Malaya, and in some upland areas where environmental conditions kept fields wet all year round, the plough was rarely used, and peasants used their cattle to stamp in old growth and puddle the muddy ground. Those who could not afford to buy or hire draught animals – not an insignificant number of people – had to do the best they could with hoes; the hoe was also necessary where land had not been sufficiently cleared to admit use of the plough.

For the most part, wet-rice fields dependent upon flood or rainfall produced just one crop a year; in the dry season, cattle were left to roam the fallowing fields, providing themselves with fodder and the fields with manure. Such was the case in Lower Burma while, according to one observer of the Penang region, 'the Malays here have not attempted double cropping . . . . Most of the Malayan wet land rice requires so long a period to reach maturity, that there would be a deficiency of water for a second crop were an attempt to be made to grow one'.[37] But in areas of dense population where irrigation facilities allowed it, cropping was continuous. Around 1814, the city of Yogyakarta in central Java was 'surrounded in every direction, for many miles, by an extensive cultivation chiefly of rice by irrigation, of which one crop follows another with little interruption throughout the year'.[38] Elsewhere in Java, 'in the richer lands, and those which have a perennial supply of water, the land is . . . scourged by the *perpetual* succession of a double harvest of rice',[39] or 'very generally one crop of rice and a green crop'.[40] In the region around Ava in Upper Burma, 'three crops of rice are generally produced yearly, and always two. The best crop is obtained with the assistance of the periodical rains . . . . The next two crops are obtained by the assistance of irrigation from the lakes';[41] alternatively, peasants might also grow one 'crop of rice in the wet season, and a crop of pulses in the dry',[42] as well as vegetables, tobacco, maize, and sesame. In Bali, two crops of rice could be obtained in a single year through the use of irrigation water from lakes, while 'of rice, in Cochinchina, they are almost certain of two plentiful crops each year, one of which is reaped in April, the other in October'.[43] In some parts of the Philippines, the collection of water in reservoirs in the wet season allowed two crops of rice in a single year. In Bulacan around 1820, for example, second cropping was said to be commonplace, with vegetables and fruit crops succeeding rice, while second cropping was also familiar in Pampanga around the same time.

The contrast between flood/rainfall wet-rice and artificially irrigated rice often went hand in hand with a contrast between broadcasting – simply dispersing seed upon the land prepared by ploughing, puddling or hoeing – and transplanting, where seedlings were grown in special beds, uprooted and then laboriously replanted in the flooded field. Broadcasting, much less demanding of labour and time, enabled a much larger area of land to be sown; as well, it was best suited to flood-prone areas where water levels could not be sufficiently controlled for transplanting and where the use of floating rice varieties was common. Crawfurd noted that while transplanting was practised around Ava, it was something 'contrary to the usual practice of the lower country, where [rice] is sown broad-cast, and not afterwards removed'.[44] Similarly, in the 'western part of the island of Luzon', mountain rice was broadcast on ploughed fields.[45]

The household was the basic unit of labour in wet-rice cultivation, with family members assisting with the various tasks of cultivation. Within the family, many roles were, in a broad sense, gender or age-specific. Men prepared the fields, ploughing, harrowing, bunding, and guarded the emerging crops from the unwelcome intrusions of wild animals and birds, sometimes with strings tied across the fields, with fences, and with scarecrows. Where transplanting was practised, women inserted the rice plants (in some places employing a pronged hand tool for the job) which men had uprooted from the seedling beds into the finely mushed fields; they also weeded the crop and harvested it, commonly with a finger knife (apparently, as was the case with swiddeners, because of uneven ripening, and perhaps, too, to compensate for low yields by capturing every panicle) or, in areas with fewer resources of labour, with a sickle, and carried it to the village. Women outside the household who assisted in the work of the harvest customarily received around one-fifth of what they harvested in payment for their labour, but sometimes as much as one-half, an indication, perhaps, of a keen shortage of labour in many rural areas. Again, where labour was in short supply, harvesting was often shared amongst men, women and children. Threshing was usually left to men who flailed the harvested stalks or trampled them with their own or their cattle's feet. Thereafter, women winnowed the grain, and (when it was needed for food) pounded it with hand or lever stampers with a hollowed log as a mortar. Children often assisted their mothers in planting and weeding, and were also responsible for simple tasks such as tending animals, collecting firewood, fetching water (often employing large bamboo tubes for the task), guarding crops, caring for younger siblings (especially during field labour time), and helping carry harvested rice from field to threshing area.

The division of labour by gender, however, was generally quite loose. Men sometimes performed 'women's work' while, in some places, women performed the lion's share of cultivation work as well as more general household tasks. According to one observer of southern Vietnam, 'the labours of the field are ordinarily their [women's] portion. They guide the plough, and handle the spade and mattock; from morning to evening they wade in the water transplanting rice. They carry provisions to the market. They cultivate and they manufacture the cotton and silk for the use of their families. They often take the principal part in commercial affairs'.[46] Other visitors to Cochinchina shared this view: 'almost all kinds of labour are performed by women, whom it is not unusual to see guiding the plough and sowing the seed'.[47] According to another, the women in Cochinchina 'plough, harrow, reap, carry heavy burdens, are shopkeepers, brokers and money-changers'.[48] In Laos, 'the women do all the really hard work . . . . They plant the rice, they gather the harvest, they husk and clean it, they cook it and they help to eat it, and this is one of the few things they do on an equality with the men'.[49]

Since different phases of the agricultural production process required the application of large amounts of labour within a limited time, it was common for different households within a settlement to pool their labour for particular tasks like planting and harvesting. This labour sharing, however, was essentially reciprocal; what one household lent another was expected to be paid back in equal measure at the appropriate time. Beyond these reciprocal labour relationships there was also informally contracted labour, often involving payment in cash or kind for the work performed.

DRY FIELDS

Perennial dry fields were often located in the neighbourhood of wet-field cultivation, but in many regions, the Malay peninsula for example, they were the dominant setting for agriculture. Dry fields were solely reliant on rainfall and not otherwise watered. Generally situated on sloping land or in foothills or uplands, they were used to produce wet season crops of rice, maize, tubers and other crops such as indigo, sugar cane, cotton and coffee; they commonly required a short period of fallow after being put to use for four or five years at a stretch. In such environments, peasants tended to focus their productive activities on garden cultivation, and correspondingly needed to find non-agricultural sources of income to maintain themselves. In perennial dry field cropping, as in dedicated wet-rice growing, the seemingly random intercropping of a great diversity of cultigens, so much a feature of swidden cultivation, was notably lacking; in its place was a much stronger sense of crop specificity.

COMBINATIONS

The different techniques of production I have surveyed are pure types; in practice, of course, many peasant producers, notably those on the frontier of land exploitation, combined them in different ways to secure their livelihood. Thus, while the peasants of Pahang were chiefly wet-rice cultivators, they also collected jungle produce, particularly when their crops did not produce the expected bounty. Given the generous availability of land, and that yields per unit of labour invested were similar for swidden as for wet-rice, many peasants maintained swiddens to supplement the produce of their established wet-rice fields or, where they lacked technically sophisticated irrigation facilities, moved from one technique to another as circumstances dictated. As populations in specific sites thickened, there was a sense, too, of an evolutionary progression from less complex to more labour-intensive and intricate methods of production; pure swidden systems, perennial dry-field cultivation and mixed swidden/wet-field or dry-field/wet-field cultivation complexes might eventually be turned into dedicated wet-rice paddies; in much of the Minangkabau uplands, for example, permanent cropping had been established in the place of shifting cultivation by the early nineteenth century. It would be misleading, however, to see such development as a simple chronicle of population-determined social and technical progression, of inevitable movement from primitive/sparsely populated/swidden complexes to sophisticated/densely populated /wet-rice ones; in the Philippines, for instance, intricate forms of wet-rice agriculture which depended upon marvellously constructed terracing were to be found among the thinly distributed upland peoples of Luzon, notably the Ifugao. In all this it is as well to bear in mind that there was by no means an 'ancient and stable adjustment between man and land. Instead it was perpetually in a state of flux and adaptation'.[50]

NON-AGRICULTURAL PRODUCTION

Notwithstanding the centrality of agriculture to the peasant world, domestic industry was also well developed in rural Southeast Asia at this time. Skills of a commonplace character, such as basic carpentry ('everyone is able to build his own house of bamboo'[51]) and straightforward weaving, as well as the plaiting of mats and baskets, were practised everywhere. The production of lacquer ware and the processing of indigo for use and sale was common, as was the manufacture of sugar from cane and of tobacco for smoking and chewing. The wearing of ornaments – bracelets, necklaces, armbands, hair combs and beads, ear adornments, rings, chains, belts, and even decorative weaponry, often worked in precious metals – was very prevalent, and sustained the labours of many village craftspeople. More highly developed industrial skills of limited marketability were more sparsely distributed, and their practitioners normally brought their talents to bear only when specifically commissioned for a particular piece of work. In Laos, for instance, village silversmiths manufactured their artistic wares at the orders of 'the princes and wealthy classes';[52] in Malaya, craftsmen fashioned pottery only according to order. Some villages developed particular, acknowledged and distinguishing expertise in specific branches of industry. Some became well-known for their residents' distinctive skills in dyeing and weaving, others for the mining and smelting of iron, others for blacksmithing, usually of specific products such as swords or gun barrels, others for pottery, knife manufacture or carpentry and woodcarving, others again for salt-making or rattan weaving. In places remote from centres of population, a number of individuals within a settlement might possess certain essential proficiencies such as blacksmithing, basketry or cloth weaving; upland areas sometimes produced their own iron tools and brass ornaments from metals imported from the lowlands, and they also fabricated pots, lacquerware, mats and baskets, as well as clothing. Village industry was not conducted, as Gourou claimed for a later period and different circumstances, simply for the sake of a 'supplementary income' which 'merely helps the field-worker, underfed by the earth, not to die of hunger'.[53] It was, rather, an essential part of the village world, providing many of the goods peasants required for life and livelihood.

Forest foraging and hunting provided a further fertile source of goods. In the off-season period, for example, peasants sometimes left their settlements for periods of time to hunt elephants for their ivory and rhinoceroses for their hides and horn, to catch birds for their feathers, to gather turtle eggs and edible birds' nests, and to collect timber, *atap*, palm sugar, and rattan. Swiddening's major function was to procure food subsistence, but it served broader purposes as well. Clearing virgin forest not only secured cultivable land but also materials for housing and other construction, for tools, mats, baskets, and even for lighting. The unclaimed forest environment where swiddeners made their homes and which often abutted the fields of settled cultivators was also a rich reservoir for consumption. Its resources served as important supplements to the yields of swiddening, through hunting, fishing ('the mountain streams [have] fish in abundance'[54]) and foraging in the forests for bamboo, herbs, wood, bark, gums, resins, oils, leaves, wild vegetables and tubers. Thus, the Iban consumed 'pork, fish, and the flesh of deer, and other animals which are pursued by the chase',[55] while '[the Chin] is an expert tracker and has an intimate knowledge of the ways and habits of all game'.[56] Villagers employed bows and arrows, as well as poisoned darts, to kill game, they fixed traps and snares as well, and sometimes they set dogs to capture animals ranging from tigers, pigs and monkeys to birds. Such fruits of the forest, as we shall see, were important not just for peasants' own use but as essential items of commerce.

WEAVING

Perhaps the most commonly noted of all these industrial activities was weaving, which supplied the locally different but essentially simple clothing requirements of the region. Notwithstanding the long tradition of cloth imports from India, and the evidence of lively commerce and local specialisation in raw cotton, spun cotton and textiles, it was common for village communities to spin and weave their domestic clothing from cotton they had themselves cultivated, as well as to prepare the dyes needed to colour their cloth. Virtually every Western observer commented on this industry: 'Every family has its loom, which is worked by the women, and employed in weaving coarse sarongs and salendongs', wrote one;[57] another commented that 'every woman can make all the clothes necessary for her family'.[58] In Java, cotton yarn was spun 'from the cotton produced, in great plenty, in the interior parts';[59] 'large quantities of [Javanese calico] . . . are manufactured by the women, both for home use and for exportation . . . a month at the least is required to clean, spin, and weave a piece of cloth four feet wide and twelve feet long'.[60] Again, 'the women spin, manufacture, and dye, all the cloth necessary for their own consumption'.[61] Indeed, some places such as Aceh had become so esteemed in the production of textiles that they exported them to other parts of the region in great quantities.

By the early years of the nineteenth century, European manufactured cloth was beginning to made significant inroads upon domestic manufacture in the region, especially in the lowlands, taking advantage of the fact that, because of the huge investment of labour in cotton cultivation and cleaning, as well as in spinning and weaving, domestic cotton goods were 'always high-priced'.[62] According to Anderson, 'all classes [of people] now wear cotton manufactures of Great Britain',[63] while Crawfurd remarked that 'British piece goods can be sold cheaper, even in the interior of the country, than the domestic manufacture', and that Burmese headwear was 'now most commonly made of English book-muslin, or English or Madras printed handkerchiefs'.[64] Nonetheless, places more distant from the centres of commerce, such as the uplands or the further hinterlands, continued to provide their own yarn and cloth from locally grown cotton, and to dye it with material obtained from the jungles. Thus in Laos, 'every house has its native loom, and the garments are for the most part home-spun. Cotton is very plentiful and cheap . . . and native dyes are used'.[65]

COMMERCE

Notwithstanding the long heritage of romantic literature on the self-sustaining village, the range of agricultural and industrial skills which peasants possessed was no guarantee of self-sufficiency. The diversity of such skills, indeed, was in large part premised upon the fact of exchange. While it was true that the surplus production available for sale from both agricultural and non-agricultural sectors in village Southeast Asia at this time made up only a relatively small proportion of overall production, commerce was an essential if in some cases only episodic feature of peasant life; no peasant community produced all it needed or consumed all it produced. Some places along the east coast of Sumatra, for example, were unable themselves to grow sufficient rice for their needs and had to import it from elsewhere. In the uplands of Laos, the Lamet did not produce their own clothing and relied on the neighbouring Tai Lu to supply their needs. In the Cordillera of northern Luzon, 'some mining or gold-trading communities grew no food of their own at all'.[66] Other groups produced far in excess of their own requirements; thus, 'cotton is grown by the Sea Dyaks sufficient in quantity for their own use, and to make cloths for exportation'.[67] Sometimes, too, food shortages required people to sell off their goods (gongs and jars in the case of the Iban) to buy the food they needed. Trading, too, was an important way of earning income, usually of a supplementary kind; in times of want, for example, women might leave their settlements to pursue commerce by buying up and reselling goods, sometimes at a considerable distance from home. Commerce, then, was quite well developed even if its importance and regularity was subdued; thus, remarked one observer of the Philippines at the turn of the nineteenth century, 'the circulation of the country's productions and effects of all kinds among the inhabitants of the provinces . . . is tolerably active and considerable'.[68]

Despite the proportionately small surpluses available for disposal by villagers, and the common resort to barter as a means of exchange, the use of money was widespread among peasants, usually in the form of silver, tin, copper or lead coins or lumps of varying, often very small, values, and sometimes even in cowry shells or rice itself. 'Coins', noted Crawfurd, 'either native or foreign, have long been used by the more improved [tribes]'.[69] In the Philippines, copper money was reported to be scarce (although people were aware of its use and value), so that 'the natives are in the habit of employing cigars as money, to represent the smaller coins; and all over the Philippines a cigar is actually the most important circulating medium, each representing a cuarto'.[70] The scarcity there of copper coins also led to forgeries. Burma had no system of regular coinage; the lumps and fragments of metal – silver, copper, lead – had to be weighed at every transaction. In Laos, 'before the French occupied the country, Laotic and Siamese coins, consisting of small copper and silver billets were used, as well as Burman weights and even cowries to a certain extent'.[71] Notwithstanding this confusing and erratic diversity, it is clear that the general notion of money as well as its use and usefulness were well-established amongst the region's villagers.

Commerce had local, regional, inter-regional and international dimensions. At its most basic, trade involved no more than simple barter transaction between neighbouring communities: salt exchanged for eggs, cloth for ironware, jewellery or handicrafts for rice, cattle for gongs. Thus, in Upper Burma, 'the commerce for the necessities of life, as food and clothing, is rather a barter than buying and selling. The inhabitants of the places abounding in rice or cotton go to exchange their commodities with those, the produce of whose fields is gingili, tobacco, indigo, etc. In all the villages of Ava rice is the ordinary commodity bartered for fish, vegetables, and other things necessary for food'.[72] Amongst the Negritoes of upland Luzon, 'those nearest the Spanish settlements carry on a little commerce, receiving wrought iron, cloth, and tobacco, but oftener *dollars*, in exchange for gold-dust, &c., or for wax, honey, and other products of their mountains'.[73] Barter between Malays and the hinterland Semang people of the Malay Peninsula was described in the following terms in the early nineteenth century:

> The usual method of barter prevailing between the Malays and these aboriginal tribes is for the former to bring their commodities, consisting chiefly of coarse cloths, tobacco and knives, to any open space in the vicinity of the places known to be the resort of the Semangs, and retire to a convenient distance as soon as they have deposited them. The Semangs then approach, and, having selected such articles as they either fancy or require, bear them off, leaving in their room whatever they may deem an equivalent: this consists chiefly of elephants' teeth, gharu, dammar, canes, rattans etc; of which, from their ignorance of the value which they bear in the market, they always leave an ample return.[74]

Much of this localised commerce was informal, but it was also catered for by local rotating markets; there, trade was nearly always carried on, and the items of trade carried, by women. Sometimes villages possessed a little shop of their own to facilitate exchange within and outside their communities. Peripatetic petty traders also serviced this local commerce; peddling was the common method of commercial interchange between upland and lowland and centre and periphery. Thus there were itinerant boat traders in Lower Burma, 'travelling up and down the great rivers, and turning into their various smaller branches, visiting the interior villages which lie out of the regular route of traffic'.[75] The boat traffic of the Irrawaddy carried rice, fish paste, salt and goods of European origin from the delta to Ava, and sugar, cotton, oil and petroleum downriver. The east-flowing rivers of central Sumatra serviced the trade needs of the west Sumatran highlands. Throughout the region traders, often Chinese and often acting as agents for port broker/merchants, gathered local produce in exchange for money, cloth, ironware and other produce. Sometimes they themselves went deep into the interior, contracting with peasant producers for their agricultural produce, sometimes providing advances on crops before they were harvested, and exchanging them for the supplies which villagers needed. Thus, Malay traders 'always come to the [Iban] villages to trade when the harvest has been gathered in'.[76] Similarly, in the Philippines, 'there is another species of speculation peculiar to the rich Indians and Sangley Mestizos, an industrious race, and also possessed of the largest portion of the specie. This consists in the anticipated purchase of the crops of indigo, sugar, rice, etc. with a view to fix their own prices on the produce thus contracted for, when resold to the second hand'.[77]

At the regional level, more developed and permanent markets, focussed on towns, had long served as the apex for trade; according to one writer, the towns of Upper Burma and the Shan states 'have held bazaars every five days since the time of Marco Polo'.[78] Such market places offered a wide variety of goods for sale: snacks and staple foodstuffs, tobacco, betel, mats, resins, gambier, coffee, cloth, pots, oil, tools, weapons, cotton, ornaments and trinkets, jewellery, livestock. Peasants might bring to these markets the vegetables, fruit and rice they had grown, the firewood and jungle products they had collected, the fish they had caught, and the craft-wares they had fabricated, to sell or to exchange for what they wanted for themselves or as items to break down for resale to others in their locality.

In the uplands and deep interiors there were trading posts for the interchange of goods between these commercially peripheral regions and lowland centres; uplanders often took themselves to lowland markets, and traders from such centres often ventured into the wild to procure what they needed. In Malaya, for example, swiddeners sold the materials they had collected from the forests, notably rattan and gharu wood, to local Malay middlemen who had advanced them money in expectation of receiving their goods and who passed them on down the chain of traders. The contents of such commerce included gold, opium, chewing tea (*miang*), pigs, deer, elephant tusks and rhinoceros horns, stick-lac, teak, sappan-wood, hides, cutch, tiger skins, woven blankets, woven tunics, beeswax and other forest produce such as rattan, benzoin, and valuable woods, which villagers exchanged for salt, rice, pickled and dried fish, iron, weapons, glassware, guns, gongs, yarn and cloth, metal pots, and tools. Upland and interior peoples, indeed, sometimes resorted to slave raiding to procure items which they might exchange with the lowlands. It should not be thought, however, that this kind of trade was purely an exchange of primitive for more sophisticated products; in 1837, the Lawa near Chiang Mai were mining iron, making and selling swords and muskets, and growing large amounts of cotton for export.

International commerce, the next rung of commerce in size and sophistication, saw, for example, Cochinchinese sugar, cinnamon and cotton exported to China, while 'the Chinese of Junan . . . bring to the Burmese capital, in great boats, several of the commodities of their country, as wrought silks, paper, tea, various kinds of fruit, and other trifles, and they return laden with cotton, raw silk, salt, birds' feathers, and that black varnish which . . . is distilled from a tree'.[79] Indeed, Burmese trade with Yunnan, 'employing caravans of up to seven thousand mules and horses',[80] and based around the exchange of Burmese cottons for Chinese silks, was highly significant. Burma also imported areca, silks, nankeen, porcelain, tea, sugar, muslins, linen, pottery, muskets, looking glasses, articles of iron and brass, woollen cloths, and exported lac, cutch, isinglass, vegetable oil, petroleum, and teak. Further to the east, 'nine or ten Chinese boats leave Bangkok for Lakon [Nakhon Phanom] monthly, each bringing goods to the value of between 9000 and 10 000 rupees every trip. This implies an import trade from Bangkok, chiefly in English goods, of 90 000 rupees a month'.[81]

International commerce was largely the domain of rulers and their circles; it often assumed quasi-monopolistic forms and remained tightly restricted. At this stage in the region's history, commerce was amongst the major sources of the state's money income, and sometimes the greatest source. Apart from collecting taxation on internal commercial traffic – usually by means of revenue farms established on toll-gates – the ruler also dominated, indeed, often monopolised a state's international trade; the Southeast Asian king was typically the state's greatest trader, the revenues from commerce providing him with substantial funds to control manpower and administer the state, preventing, incidentally, the evolution of an independent class of merchants. Royalty kept the communications lines with the interior open, organising construction and maintenance work on roads, building overnight shelters, and working to ensure that traders were protected from the attacks of bandits.

Where its reach was felt, international commerce of this kind had often affected patterns of peasant production, sometimes deeply; thus, the Chinese and European demand for pepper had seen an elaboration of village pepper production in Minangkabau in the sixteenth century during Southeast Asia's great age of commerce, exchanged via merchants for cloth, salt and specie. But in the late eighteenth century, the volume and value of interstate commerce was – in comparison to what was to come – relatively small. Moreover, while there is clear evidence of a resurgence of the region's trade from around the middle of the eighteenth century, it was not – with a few exceptions, such as the forced cultivation of coffee in Java and the American promotion of pepper production along Aceh's western coast – primarily based around large-scale, dedicated and spatially expansive peasant production. In Siam, for example, the expansion of the China trade prompted by the gradual relaxation of imperial bans on private Chinese international commerce allowed the early Chakkri rulers, linked with indigenous Chinese merchants, to develop a profitable commerce with China, but although Siamese rice was a component of this trade, exotic collectables were its staple. Generally, while in some cases the major Southeast Asian export to China was food, especially rice, more commonly the contents of commerce took the form of exotic luxury produce for the markets of China, India or Europe – gems, precious woods, cardamom, ivory, gold, gums, precious oils – collected in the outer regions of kingdoms and exported by Chinese or Indian merchants under royal sponsorship and supervision. In return, traders brought cloth, firearms, silver, saltpetre, building materials. The great majority of the region's small cultivators were hardly involved in, or commercially affected by, such commerce. Their production was essentially geared to feeding themselves and their society's elites, and not to commerce.

IMPEDIMENTS TO TRADE

It would be misleading, then, to give undue emphasis to the relative importance of commerce to peasant life and livelihood at this time. Whilst the dimensions, ubiquity and liveliness of peasant commerce were worthy of note, it remained true that, for the most part, village communities themselves produced much the greater proportion of the items they consumed, and that 'only a small proportion of locally produced commodities ever entered the stream of commerce'.[82] Moreover, peasants tended to produce themselves a much broader range of items than would later be the case; the specialisation that is consequent upon elaborated exchange was not a common feature of their agricultural or industrial practice.

A major impediment to a more expanded practice of trade was the region's limited transport infrastructure, which rendered the movement of goods expensive and risky. Although some places like Java had extensive road systems, they were often impassable in the wet season, and often required substantial (and expensive) repair after rain and flood had demolished surfaces and washed away bridges. Larger-scale trade between villages and other units, therefore, was generally restricted to the dry part of the year – the post-harvest period – which was, in any case, the time when villagers had most to trade. In such circumstances, commerce of this kind took on the form of a periodically recurring or seasonal activity. Most parts of the region, moreover, were seriously deficient in roads; given the nature of their economies, in which the large-scale and regular movement of bulk goods had no place, rulers had little use for them except for military purposes. As one moved away from commercial centres, roads declined in quantity and quality and gave way to narrow tracks and paths; there were, for example, few roads in northern Siam, while those in the Philippines were few in number and of poor quality. In some places, indeed, the nature of the terrain was such as to make inter-regional trade virtually impossible. Throughout much of the region, accordingly, canal and riverine transport was much more important than road traffic. In Lower Burma, for example, according to Crawfurd, 'the internal traffic is almost wholly conducted by water communication; there are hardly any roads'.[83] Because of these deficiencies in land transport, vehicles like carts and wagons were few and beasts of burden an expensive alternative for bulk carriage. In Laos, crudely constructed carts, drawn by men, were sometimes used to transport rice, and elsewhere there was land transport by ox, mule and horse (sometimes in the form of large trains) and by elephant. But the great majority of the items traded by land were carried on the backs of men or women, using poles or frames.

There were, as well, other encumbrances to trade. One was the large amounts of taxes – sometimes over a third of royal revenue – levied on the movement of goods through toll-gates farmed out by rulers, which often militated against the elaboration of commercial links. Closely associated with royal taxes on commerce was the king's role as the major state trader, which often saw him exercise a monopoly on some products and invoke bans on private trade in others, not to mention the time taken by people collecting required items as tribute, all of which tended to impede domestic commerce. In northern Siam, as a result of such policies, 'the regions whose forest products were demanded for export in great volume had hardly any local trade'.[84] A third check on the volume of trade was the continual threat of banditry and attack by wild animals, especially tigers, and a fourth the disruptions caused by episodic warfare. All these things served to make the land transport of goods a costly and potentially disastrous undertaking and to restrict its widespread use.

All this – the lack of infrastructure, royal taxes and monopolies, the lack of demand, reliability and certainty in markets, the huge costs involved in commerce, not to mention the inhibiting effects of small populations – served to limit rural-based commerce severely. Relatively speaking, there was little incentive to produce for the market because of restrictions on the marketability of produce, and little specialisation of labour for commercial ends.

WAGE LABOUR

For some peasants, the options of working one's own fields or procuring one's income through industrial production or commerce were either unavailable or insufficient for their livelihood. There was, accordingly, some restricted scope for wage work where demand allowed it. In Minangkabau, for example, men were employed in the iron-working industry for wages. In Malaya, similarly, peasants sometimes worked at tin mines in the period following the rice harvest, while in Java landless workers secured paid employment in the Chinese sugar mills around Batavia. Closer to home, there were plentiful opportunities for employment within the village in such tasks as harvesting for which workers might be paid in money or in beads or, most commonly, with a share of what they had harvested, or for agricultural work outside the village. Thus, 'the [rice] reapers are for the most part composed of the idle and vicious part of the population, who go abroad over the country to engage themselves in this employment, which affords a livelihood to the poorer classes; for the different periods at which the varieties of rice are planted and harvested, gives them work during a large portion of the year'.[85] Hired agricultural labour, indeed, was commonplace in lowland sites. On the north coast of Java, for example, paid workers from Kudus came to help harvest *padi* in Demak; equally, hired agricultural labour was in evidence in the regions closely surrounding Manila.

Wage labour, however, was of a very circumscribed kind. In a general context where labour was generally scarce and valuable, and its exploitation managed within webs of personalised social obligation, there was not a well-developed sense of individual freedom to pursue wage work. Those without independent access to land, craftwork or commerce to secure their livelihood generally found their most secure salvation as dependent clients of more prosperous and powerful villagers, and spent their time assisting in field labour, in servile tasks, and as replacements for those whose labour the state demanded by way of taxation. Where peasants indulged in wage labour, they usually did so to earn supplementary income outside the normal cropping routines of the village, and such activity did not imply those notions of specialisation or permanency of employment which denote a fully-fledged wage labour regime. For the most part, wage labour was thought of as insecure, poorly rewarded, demeaning and difficult. Those who sought to employ wage workers usually encountered great difficulty in recruiting and managing their workers, and found it necessary to employ a system of generous advance payments to attract them and enduring indebtedness to retain them.

PEASANTS AND STATES

No discussion of peasant life and livelihood is complete without its being placed in the broader context of peasants' relationship with the state. 'States', at this time in Southeast Asia's history, were multiply-occurring and sometimes, to use Leach's word, interpenetrating[86] sets of shifting relationships which revolved around the personality and power of regionally or locally autonomous rulers. Through informal and hierarchically structured bonds, such rulers could reach down to peasants and make claims on their produce and their labour. In return, a ruler/patron promised peasant communities administrative coherence, security, prestige, religious legitimation and prosperity.

Because of the inherent institutional weakness of these vertically shaped structures of allegiance, and their tendency for cyclical collapse, not to mention the often 'wobbly balance'[87] between central and local bases of power, politics was an often tense and fragile set of arrangements. Power lay with those who could demand the greatest followings, and control of manpower – the greatest single source of wealth – was all the more important given its scarcity. Control of people, this 'precious resource',[88] the key to a ruler's power and prosperity, meant that a ruler's special interest was to enhance the number of people directly tied to him, and prevent others from establishing potentially competitive groupings of vertical alliances. Throughout Southeast Asia, there was constant competition for manpower, and constant fluidity within the population as people transferred their allegiance from one patron to another who might offer them a better and more secure life. In Siam, for example, enduring tension characterised the competition between the claims of the king and those of courtly and local power holders for control of the populace, to such an extent that commoners were tattooed with the name of their lord. In Cambodia, similarly, every free man had to be registered with a patron to whom he rendered services and from whom he received status and protection. In Burma, such competition meant the enhancement of that class of people, called *ahmudan* ('those who shoulder tasks'), who were subservient to the king, and limits on the numbers of slaves and other dependents who served as clients to other people. In other words, 'the throne aimed at the radical subordination of the principal elites – princes, ministers, governors and headmen – to the person of the ruler'.[89]

Naturally, then, the ruler's power was strongest where he was able to manipulate – by marriage, by bribes, by the threat of force, by the lure of status, by an efficient intelligence-gathering service, by religious legitimation, and sometimes by the antagonisms which flowed from his fostering of competition for his favour – the subordinate heads of vertically-shaped congeries of followers, especially through the mechanism of prebendal property. In these core areas of power, the ruler commanded through a system of royal officials. Beyond that centre, the state's representatives tended to be existing potentates – sometimes identified in the literature as a gentry class of a hereditary kind – who had realised the fortune that might come their way from attaching themselves and their followings to a centrally powerful figure. As the ruler's ability to control and supervise this ever more broadly based pyramid of relationships weakened with distance, so did his power, fading away in the end to the weakness of transient tributary relationships and then off into nothingness.

Where skilful rulers succeeded in establishing and consolidating their power, they fed upon their peasantries, imposing taxes on rice production as in central Java, or household/capitation taxes as in Burma and Vietnam, and demanding substantial taxation in labour, including the raising of military levies. But given the essentially shaky nature of the state's control – exemplified by the fact that the great proportion of taxation levied was siphoned off by the layers of officials through whom it passed – the burden of taxation needed to be set off against some manifest benefit for the subject peasantry; of itself, 'heavy taxation almost inevitably led to a declining tax base'[90] as peasants took their leave of too grasping a patron.

The state's relationship with its peasantry, then, needed some substantial reciprocity to endure and prosper. In Southeast Asia, that was most commonly found in providing peasants with secure access to land. In other words, peasants' holding of established village land was premised on their ability to provide revenues to the state in cash, kind or labour. In such places, land, perhaps because of the investments of time, labour and memory already devoted to it, and, more generally, the protection afforded its use by the state, had taken on a value far beyond that which it enjoyed in its unreclaimed state. Those people most willing and able to service the state's taxation obligations were rewarded with the largest and most fertile tracts of land; equally, those unable to do so were relegated to the ruck of villagers, earning their livelihood as dependents.

This principle in turn affected styles of peasant tenure. In regions where state control was more directly and effectively exercised, and competition amongst competing power centres less intense, the state held the upper hand over against peasants. Stamford Raffles, Lieutenant-Governor of Java during the British interregnum, expressed his understanding of the situation in Java thus: 'In the neighbourhood of despotic authority, it may naturally be expected, that the constant and undefined demands for the public service, and the corresponding demand on the land, led to continual changes in its distribution. In some cases, one half of the inhabitants of a village were kept in constant readiness for the Government employ, while lands were divided among the remainder: these were alternatively changed at the end of each year'.[91] In other words, with prized land in short supply and demands from above relatively intense, peasants rotated the use of their land amongst each other, and correspondingly the taxation obligations to their lord that were a condition of its use. In Upper Burma, where the exercise of royal power was of comparable intensity, local chiefs assigned lands to as many people as possible to enhance the local community's ability to tolerate the impositions in labour and produce made upon it. In northern and central Vietnam, the relatively heavy centralisation of power through the exercise of mandarinal officialdom meant that the state was always seeking to secure and enlarge the area of communal rice land (*cong dien*) within villages against attempts by village and supra-village elites to restrict such land for their own private use; when that state was strong – increasingly the case through the early nineteenth century – the area of communal land within the village was large and parcelled out amongst that segment of the village population inscribed on the tax rolls; when its reach was less pronounced, village and supra-village leaders tended to seize upon such land and turn it to their own private purposes.

Accordingly, the best measure of the intrusive power of the state was the disposition of village land. Where the state was stronger, the ability of villagers to make their own arrangements concerning the distribution of land was proportionately prejudiced, with limitations on the ability of individual villagers – and power holders outside the village – to enhance their individual holdings. Equally, where the state's reach was tenuous or irregular, localism held sway. In Vietnam, then, the state-structured north and central regions saw a proliferation of communal lands, and only the usufruct, not ownership, of privately held land could be pledged as security for loans. By contrast, on the distant frontier of southern Vietnam where the power of central authority was often feeble, communal lands were much less in evidence. Again, in many parts of Minangkabau, there were strict limitations on individual peasants' ability to dispose as they wished of their land, while in the 'highly peopled provinces of Java, where the population begins to press on the good land, the cultivator exercises no such [individual] rights over the soil, and I hardly know of any privilege which he possesses in regard to it, except the liberty of abandoning it'.[92] By contrast, in the western and eastern corners of the island, distant from royal control, an individual proprietary right to land was acknowledged. In those areas of Burma which fell under the king's effective sway, large portions of land were thought of as the absolute property of the king (*ayadaw*), part of which he allotted as appanages or as grants to crown service people, and which were wholly inalienable. Other lands which fell outside this domain, called *bobobaing*, could be held privately, inherited and (usually in the form of irrigated paddy land) were capable of sale or mortgage. In Lower Burma, however, because land was so relatively plentiful, and state power relatively weak, peasants could claim land in allodial property simply by clearing it and putting it to productive use; they could mortgage it, sell it, and hand it on to their heirs in the next generation. Crawfurd, speaking generally of lowland Burma, found 'no community of property' amongst Burmese villagers, 'each individual being the exclusive proprietor of his own fields, and tilling them at his own risk and cost'.[93]

This generalised pattern, crudely hammered from the exquisite complexity of the state–peasant–land nexus, indicates a broad relationship between landholding and obligation to the state. It indicates, too, in some places at least and in a way not often recognised in the literature, that in tandem with or alongside the state-moderated sector peasants could control (and dispose of) individual holdings in ways which did not differ greatly from the usages flowing from contemporary conceptions of ownership. We see as well the existence of localised shortages of certain kinds of land, presumably irrigated and close to markets (a feature enhancing its value), and the vitality of markets in land, often conducted in cash.

STATE POWER AND VILLAGE AGENCY

The success of the state in drawing resources from the village was naturally reflected in the manner in which power was exercised within the village itself. Where state power was most intense, village leaders were often no more than tax-farming agents of their superiors. The central Javanese *bekel* often obtained his position as village head by undertaking, for a fee, to wring the optimum taxation from a village. 'I believe', remarked Raffles, 'it will be found, that in the central districts, almost every Bakalship has its price, varying from twenty to thirty Dollars'.[94] This directness of agency between supra-village authority and the village itself sometimes became the occasion for violence because of disputes between a newly appointed bekel and the man he had displaced. The rejected bekel might gather his followers and fight back against the new bekel, 'and in such frays, which are of daily occurrence, many lives are lost'.[95] In circumstances where supra-village intrusion was so much in evidence, peasants often identified themselves with their local patrons rather than their village peers; thus it was that 'though for the purposes of mutual protection, a number of cultivators are assembled together in one village, there exists no community of property among them, and it may even happen, that cultivators who live as next-door-neighbours in the same village, are frequently as distinct and unconnected, as those who live twenty miles off'.[96] Thus, the personal bonds between power holder and follower might cut across what passed for the territorial integrity of the village.

Notwithstanding instances of sustained and successful intrusion into the affairs of villages, Southeast Asian states were characteristically weak. This state of affairs was manifest in the prevalence of tax-farming as a major means of raising domestic revenue rather than more direct forms of taxation such as land tax, and in the difficulties which states encountered in mobilising their peasantries for compulsory labour. In Siam, for example, a considerable number of commoners customarily managed to evade the reach of royal corvée, and in Vietnam many villagers successfully evaded inscription on the tax registers. Most villages, then, were at a somewhat distant remove from the state's direct and effective grasp. Village headship, while often alleged to be the result of village election, was usually the preserve of the most wealthy and powerful families of the village, usually those linked to its founding members. But state weakness meant that the position of village chief was often not clearly formalised. European officials arriving on the scene sometimes found it difficult to identify such an office at the village level. In Malaya, for example, the *penghulu* was sometimes thought of as enjoying a general nurturing role amongst villagers, without any necessary attachment to or authorisation from higher authority. In Burma, the lowest level of formal administration was the hereditary *myothugyi*, or chief of a township, responsible for a circle (*myo*) which incorporated surrounding rural settlements, sometimes numbering in the hundreds; the locus of village leadership was considerably more hazy. In Vietnam, village authority tended to be focused on a collectivity, the council of notables, rather than a pre-eminent village leader. Within the Minangkabau 'village', penghulus were the heads of differing village clans, and the penghulus as a group formed a ruling council. This was a pattern repeated elsewhere, an indication, perhaps, that villages were conglomerations of settlement rather than tightly integrated and corporate communities designed for the efficient delivery of service to supra-village authority – or, to put it another way, that they had created they own sense of community and interests quite separate from those of the state, something exemplified in concepts of village justice and policing. In these circumstances, the role of the village chief was to act as some kind of defensive intermediary between the interests of villagers and those of supra-village authority, a role he customarily exercised through his power to allocate land amongst villagers and thus satisfy the demands of the state.

Further out on the periphery of the state's influence, village 'independence' was more pronounced still. According to one scholar, 'Malay society on the Pahang frontier was a fluid pool from which important power centers bubbled up in one period engulfing others and in another declined and were swallowed up by new emerging centers'; the state, such as it was, was so weak that 'the mass of cultivators were neither bound to the land nor obligated to give a share of production to a ruling class'.[97] There, rulers enjoyed nothing more than token tribute. Further out again in the remote uplands, the state's influence was barely visible; shifting cultivators were usually never more than wishfully incorporated by larger lowland state systems. In the hill country of central Vietnam, for example, 'there was no political superstructure or recognized permanent leadership beyond the village'.[98] Indeed, the Lamet of Laos apparently had 'no real chief as such'.[99] Equally, the 'rich men' (*orang kaya*) among the Iban were in no sense chiefly leaders. In these circumstances, village headship blurred into non-existence; leadership tended to be found in the group of elders rather than in a specific individual, and their influence seems to have been grounded in their ritual knowledge or their powers of conciliation rather than their ability to command and enforce material or political sanctions, although they were not above employing the honorifics bestowed on them by lowland rulers for their own purposes.

Like the state sphere above it, village society, especially in permanently cultivated and densely populated regions, was stratified, but the erratic reach and essential weakness of state structures generally meant that state-based power was only weakly available to village elites. Village leaders in regions where state power imposed itself more heavily upon villagers had to balance the exercise of their power against the reality that its too vigorous use would alienate the followings upon which wealth ultimately rested. In such places, those with the closest connections with state power endured the tensions between seeking their own particular interests and sustaining those of the state, between accumulating land and the followings to work it and ensuring that villagers were sufficiently rewarded for performing state exactions that they would not flee to the succour of other patrons. In places where state power was less manifest, the sanctions which might have assured privileged access to village resources were weaker still. Overall, then, the resources of the village tended to be shared relatively evenly; as far as we can judge, the greater proportion of villagers held land, or at least enjoyed, as dependents or as traders or craftspeople or even hirelings, an assured level of living.

Under these circumstances, landholdings remained relatively small. The size of farms in Lower Burma in 1861–2 was said to be around three to four hectares, and in more heavily settled territories it was certainly much smaller. In a context where – to use Crawfurd's exaggerated phrasing – land was 'of no more exchangeable value than air or water',[100] size of holding was a function of a household's ability to work it effectively; in the relative absence of enduring and powerful supra-village authorities to underpin large village-level holdings and provide sanctions to police the workforce needed to exploit them, sustained large landholding did not develop to any notable extent. A further impediment to land accumulation was the custom common throughout the region (albeit less strongly maintained in places where Muslim or Sinic influence ran deep) of equal distribution amongst all heirs, male and female. Consequently it was difficult for a single family to enhance its holdings continually at the expense of others. At the same time, families had to ensure that they were sufficiently large to be able to service the obligations contingent upon the amount and quality of the land they held, so there was a constant tension between the imperatives of large and small families. In the Minangkabau region, indeed, 'land seems to have been continually circulating, acquired and alienated as the size of families changed for better or worse'.[101] It seems likely, therefore, that there was a constant generational circulation of land and elite status. Family size was an important variable in the attainment of prosperity, but could itself become the source of impoverishment as a result of the custom of equal inheritance.

PEASANT MOBILITY

The fluidity of social relationships indicates a related and important feature of Southeast Asian peasant life at this time, the extraordinary mobility of peasant populations. This phenomenon has seldom been accorded its due weight in Southeast Asian history, partly because observers have been entranced by the 'tradition' they have wished to see. Thus, asserted Crawfurd, 'migrations . . . except in extreme cases, are not frequently resorted to. The tombs of their ancestors, which in Java are held in high veneration, attach the peasantry so much, that nothing short of extreme oppression will compel them to forsake them; and advantage is not infrequently taken of this superstitious attachment, for the purpose of raising the rents to an exorbitant height'.[102] A similar dismissive tendency sometimes appears in the work of scholars, so that some have viewed peasant migration 'as a rather desperate move, involving as it did the abandonment of laboriously irrigated fields and the severance of links with one's extended family'.[103] Nonetheless, the logic of circumstance dictated that movement happened frequently and continuously. Thus, 'the Burmese household is movable and when people disliked the Myothugyi they could easily migrate to another township'.[104] In the words of a British administrator, 'flitting is easy . . . . If the local magistrate is so blind to his own interests as to oppress his people, there is another wiser man few score leagues away who is ready to welcome them'.[105]

The desire to escape from intolerable burdens imposed from above was just one of the reasons for movement. Political volatility and warfare was another prime cause, and its effect upon people's mobility was evident in the delta regions of the Irrawaddy and Chao Phraya in the eighteenth century, and in the depopulation of Kedah and Pattani as a result of the Siamese invasions of 1821 and 1832 respectively. In addition to periodic subsistence crises caused by drought, flood or similar catastrophe, the desire for a better life, or to sustain a existing mode of life, was also a strong incentive for movement. Sometimes, spurred by resource shortages occasioned by population growth at home, villagers left their homes spontaneously and struck out for the great frontier – that is, the area just beyond the habited and cultivated region – later to be joined by relatives or others attracted to join them in developing their new lands; 'people spread here and there, taking up land like a puddle of slowly flowing water that extends an arm and swells to roundness before bursting out again in some new direction'.[106] Where unreclaimed land was in abundant supply, upland swiddening villages might divide as their populations grew too large for convenient access to fields. In this way there were great surges of peoples into areas which were uninhabited or only sparsely peopled, such as the penetration of Javanese into western Java in the sixteenth and seventeenth centuries and thereafter, bringing with them wet-rice cultivation into what had predominantly been a swidden regime, the movement of Minangkabau to Jambi and to the Malay peninsula, and of Bugis from south Sulawesi to central and northern Sulawesi and to the Malay peninsula. Since at least the mid eighteenth century, large numbers of Karen have moved out of their original hill habitats and resettled in lowland Burma. Some also moved eastwards into what is today Thailand, where they settled in both upland and lowlands. And there was, as well, the continuing migration of the Iban into the valleys of the Rejang river in the early nineteenth century and thereafter.

Sometimes, too, expansion resulted from the direction of states which sought to buffer themselves against their enemies or expand their economic or military potential. Perhaps the most dramatic example was the southward migration of Vietnamese, often in the form of settlements established as military colonies. Allied to this was the royal sponsorship of military colonies in the second part of the nineteenth century in upland areas abutting the coastal plain, a process which brought Vietnamese in dominating contact with the hill groups, where they dispossessed the uplanders and used their labour for their own purposes. To the west, a centuries-long Burman policy of deporting defeated neighbouring populations and settling them in the basin of Upper Burma led to a considerable expansion in both the core and the fringes of settlement. Again, in the late eighteenth century, the Burmese court colonised parts of the Irrawaddy delta area with Burmans in order to dampen Mon rebelliousness. On a smaller scale, and in order to secure the east against possible Vietnamese attack, the Thai king in 1837 commissioned the digging of a large canal in a marshy plain east of Bangkok, named the land of 100 000 Stings; once the task had been accomplished by 5000 hired Chinese labourers, the king encouraged noblemen to settle prisoners of war there. Across the whole region, as well, the extension of settlement came also from the work of renegades escaping from the retribution directed at them for their unsuccessful political or other escapades. And the northern uplands of Siam and Burma had still to receive groups of Chinese and Tibeto-Burman peoples – Hmong, Yao, Lisu, Lahu, Akha – who were to move in through the nineteenth and twentieth centuries.

CONCLUSION

This brief and generalised survey of Southeast Asia's peasantry around the turn of the nineteenth century permits us to point to several key elements of how they lived and produced. For the greater part, peasants were grouped in small settlements in a vast and sparsely-populated rural landscape. Their livelihood was centred around the production of the bulk of their food supplies, and as much as they could manage of the other necessities of life. For what they themselves needed and could not themselves produce, and to dispose of that relatively small proportion of their overall production surplus to their needs, they traded both locally and further afield. By far the greatest number of them lived from the land which they had themselves inherited or reclaimed from the forests and which they considered their own; it took most of their labour time and provided the great bulk of their income. That small number within peasant society without direct access to land lived through trade or through the products of their industry, or as dependents or – much less frequently and subsidiarily – hired labourers. Most peasants lived in close association or, better, propinquity, with states, and provided them with wealth in the form of produce and labour; the press of state power, however – certainly in comparison with what was to come – was, one or two notable exceptions to one side, relatively light and erratic. This state of affairs was a function not just of the bureaucratic and infrastructural primitiveness of Southeast Asian states, but also of the variety of options open to peasants to move from place to place and from patron to patron as circumstances allowed or dictated.

There was, then, a considerable degree of fluidity about peasant life, and this was reflected both in peasants' ready geographical mobility and in the relatively fluid social stratification to be found within villages. There were no enduringly powerful figures at the level of the village who could enforce their will or the will of states without due regard to the wishes of their constituencies and, accordingly, no development of deep divisions of wealth, land and status within the village. The Southeast Asian peasantry, then, was a curiously shapeless and paradoxical category; while its members made up much the greater part of region's small population, they were, in an important sense, still a world to themselves. They were at once steadfast yet restless, constant yet unsettled. In a very real and important way, they were about to bid farewell, had they known it, from this ill-defined condition and to begin to undergo a process that was to shape and define them in very different ways from those they had hitherto known and accepted.

2 The Context of Change: Politics, Economics and Demography

Before we can begin the task of charting changes in peasant life and production over the two centuries since 1800, we need, in addition to a general sense of the setting of peasant life and livelihood around the turn of the nineteenth century, an outline of the broader context which shaped those changes. There are two components of this context which are of particular importance for my purpose, and to which I shall devote this chapter. The first is a schema of the economic and political developments which conditioned the manner and speed of changes to peasant livelihood. For the most part, those developments were themselves a function of the mostly burgeoning power and reach of the state in Southeast Asia, first in its colonial (and quasi-colonial) and later in its independent mode, as it sought in various ways to enhance its dominion over people and to integrate them with a commerce which was now of global dimensions. The second, in important senses a condition of the first, was the onset of continuing and rapid growth in population in the region, which was to have a fundamental impact on the nature and function of the peasantry itself. This chapter, then, seeks to periodise the years since 1800 according to a variety of phases through which various states passed as they constructed the broad contours within which the transformation of peasant life and livelihood took place, and concludes with a summary discussion of the nature and extent of population growth throughout the region. This context in place, we shall be better positioned to assess the broad outlines of social and economic change among Southeast Asia's peasantry over the last two hundred years.

MONOPOLY AND MERCANTILISM

Around the turn of the nineteenth century, the prevailing style of Southeast Asian commerce was monopoly. The Western commercial presence in Southeast Asia, relatively weak in terms of the numbers of its representatives and the reach of their influence during the great 'age of commerce' which the region had enjoyed through the long sixteenth century,[1] had moved by the late eighteenth century to a position of ascendancy in the international maritime commerce of island Southeast Asia. Its practice had long been similar to the tactics of indigenous and regional participants in trade; it had sought to establish its own monopolies where its power and influence were sufficient for the task and, for the rest, adopted the pose of suppliant agent to indigenous power, seeking to channel to itself some part of the wealth which flowed from the exercise of indigenous royal prerogative. By the turn of the nineteenth century, the military power of the West was sufficiently decisive for it to have things much its own way in the region's commerce.

The age of commerce had run on the wheels of Southeast Asian spices and pepper. The new age of international trade, however, was to be based not on exotic products kept in artificially short supply but on the abundance of tropical agriculture, providing the world with mild drugs, condiments, industrial crops, staple foods and, less important for our purposes, minerals. The late eighteenth and early nineteenth centuries were a curious and indecisive transition period between these two great ages. Notwithstanding such developments as the stunning growth of Acehnese pepper exports, and the resurgence of regional commerce resulting from the reappearance of Chinese shippers, planters and miners, Southeast Asia's agricultural economy lay relatively sequestered from any impetus for dynamic change; the momentous effects of the social and industrial revolution taking place in Europe had not yet begun to exert the fullness of their influence upon the region. Accordingly, the first decades of the nineteenth century were times of continuity; they were notable chiefly for the continuing impact of monopolistic mercantilism and its local variants, and especially for the European embellishment of mercantilism by the adduction of forced agricultural labour in the Philippines, in Java and, a little later, in west Sumatra. These were the only places in the region where European powers had substantial territory and people at their disposal; they sought to gain from them, first, by 'reducing'[2] them to a state of settled and malleable subservience and then by mobilising them en masse for the productive purposes of the state. Thus began what might be called an age of peasant production, when wealth flowed not from trade in valuable exotica but from the international sale of the bulked products coursing like a great flood from the vast exertions of millions of peasants on their own lands.

In the Philippines, the Spanish authorities from 1781 introduced a system of monopoly tobacco cultivation and marketing in the south central lowlands of Luzon under which peasants grew tobacco for compulsory delivery at fixed prices to the government. The government graded and processed the tobacco into cigars, cigarettes and snuff, and thereafter offered it for sale throughout the Philippine islands. Growers received advances on their crops and whatever balance was due to them after their tobacco was received and graded; factory workers, most of them women, were responsible for completing an assigned quota of production every ten-hour workday. Those who cultivated or traded in tobacco outside the monopoly area were subject to severe penalties. Within five years of its introduction, the monopoly had been extended to cover the whole of Luzon, although in many places peasants included in the monopoly were allowed to grow tobacco for their own consumption. The thrust of the monopoly was a forced and partial commercialisation of peasant life in the areas it affected, since it 'required the peasantry to pay in scarce specie what it had previously grown for free or obtained by barter'.[3] From 1797, with the expansion of the production region to the felicitous environment of Cagayan in northeastern Luzon, where tobacco had long been grown commercially, production surged, especially after the imposition of forced compulsory cultivation in 1830. Indeed, the government sought to enhance production still further by enticing farmers from Ilocos to labour-poor Cagayan to grow tobacco. By 1839, the government had gone beyond its original scheme of tobacco sale within the monopoly areas of the Philippines and had begun exporting excess tobacco to Spain; in time, tobacco became the colony's third most valuable export.

In what remained of the Dutch empire in the East Indies at the turn of the nineteenth century, the late eighteenth century decline into ineptitude of the former vast power of the Dutch East Indies Company led to a period of colonial indecision and disarray, complicated by the effects of the Napoleonic dispensation in Europe which saw the Netherlands fall under the sway of France and the jewel of its Asiatic possessions, Java, conquered by the British in 1811. The years of uncertainty which succeeded the return of Java to the Dutch from 1816 were ended by the purposeful plan of Johannes van den Bosch, appointed Governor-General of the Dutch Indies in 1828, which sought the reconstruction of the Netherlands – and Java – from the profits of tropical export goods produced by the forced labour of the Javanese peasantry. In the years after 1830, as conditions permitted – and whim dictated – peasants in all but the traditional heartland of Java were set to cultivating coffee, sugar, and indigo, as well as a number of subsidiary crops, for compulsory delivery to the Dutch government in the Indies and subsequent sale on the markets of Europe. From 1847, a variant of this forced cultivation system was visited upon the peasantry of west Sumatra, obliging them to cultivate and deliver large quantities of coffee (in which there already existed a profitable indigenous private sphere of production and commerce) to the Dutch at low prices; at the same time, Dutch monopolies on the sale of cloth and salt served as an important means of promoting coffee production through which peasants might purchase these vital goods. In Java, the effects of forced cultivation were complex, but they delivered peasants more thoroughly into a regime of regulated labour on export crops and infrastructure development and into a money economy, stimulated trade and specialisation, and brought a new stiffness to the administration of the countryside. The entrapment of Minangkabau peasants into forced coffee cultivation, by contrast, maimed the 'dynamic, market-oriented society of the pre-colonial era'[4] and brought social and economic stagnation in its wake as the Dutch sought to blunt economic specialisation and control and limit alternative channels of commercial production and trade, notably rice exports, as a means of enhancing the delivery of low-priced coffee.

By the mid nineteenth century, however, monopoly as a mode of economic organisation was in serious decline as its productive limitations became more obvious to both Spanish and Dutch. In the Philippines, the increasing financial difficulties of the colony found the government unable to meet its cash payment obligations to peasant tobacco growers. Without the capacity to ensure supply and quality, and hampered by endemic corruption and smuggling, the system finally collapsed. In Java, similarly, the Cultivation System went into decline from around 1850 as it became obvious, following a series of food crop disasters through the mid and late 1840s, that forced cultivation on so large a scale was beyond the administrative capacity of the Dutch colonial state to manage effectively and productively.

THE PHASE OF LIBERALISM

Dutch and Spanish attempts at the imposition of schemes of monopoly production were possible because of the unusual territorial sway which those colonial states exercised over their dominions. Elsewhere in Southeast Asia, the wind of European liberalism – or rather, that privileged version peddled by Britain – was blowing more gustily. By 1819, Britain had established its presence at three small settlements, at Penang, at Melaka, and at Singapore; these were essentially transit ports, distributing the goods of Europe and India to the region and to China, and collecting regional produce for export to Europe, India and China. The British sought, through the establishment of these free ports in the region of the straits of Melaka – the Straits Settlements, as they came to be called – to break down the force of monopoly and attract merchandise freely from all parts of the archipelago. Even the Dutch and Spanish territories were not impervious to the blandishments of free trade; thus, the Spanish decision to open Manila to Asian vessels in 1785 and European-flagged shipping in 1789 – 'the crucial economic breakthrough in the eighteenth century', according to one commentator[5] – and Raffles's liberal reforms during the British interregnum in Java and the succeeding efforts under resumed Dutch rule to promote the cultivation of export goods by the Javanese through production incentives. Indeed, 'without the income from foreign trade, the [tobacco] monopoly [in the Philippines] would have had . . . little chance for success'.[6] Correspondingly, from the late eighteenth century the Spanish colonial government had begun to encourage (still, albeit, under monopoly) the production of indigenous goods for export such as textiles, pepper and indigo; Manila's role gradually changed from international entrepot to a service conduit for the production of the Philippine hinterland, a role which the establishment of foreign merchant houses in the 1820s enhanced. For Spain, long complacent in the ease of riches disgorged by its galleon traffic, the new age of commerce had finally – and belatedly – begun.

The emergence of this liberal revolution, of which Singapore was 'the spearhead of an expanding international system, of which industrializing Britain was the principal practitioner and preacher',[7] must have taken indigenous commercial circles by surprise. It was based upon the notion that free trade in itself would bring greater popular prosperity and thus enhance the wealth and stability of a kingdom. Rulers saw its force, and the threat it represented to their prerogatives; the arguments of the liberal free traders 'would not strike a responsive chord with a monarch to whom the stability and prosperity of the kingdom rested not on the prosperity of the amorphous entity, "the people", but on the control that he and his officials had over their labour and produce'.[8] They sought to resist it by indulging in a series of actions which are best described as exercises in introspective state strengthening and centralisation.

Thus, in Siam, the throne rejected the advances of British missions in 1821 and later (in 1826) aimed at opening the kingdom to free British commerce and began to look all the more interestedly at ways of developing its own capabilities against the threat. A major factor in the early nineteenth-century indigenous development of Siam was the immigration of large numbers of Chinese. This movement, which had been taking place in considerable numbers at least since the fourteenth century, accelerated with the coming to power of the half-Chinese Taksin (1767–82) and the subsequent establishment of the Chakkri dynasty; between six and eight thousand Chinese were arriving annually around 1830. Skinner has remarked, in referring to the period 1850–1917, that 'the development in Siam attracted and, indeed, was to a large degree made possible by, emigration from south China'.[9] But his statement is even more germane for the decades leading up to the mid-century; indeed, around 1830, contemporary sources indicate that Chinese made up perhaps more than half of the population of Bangkok. While the early Chakkri kings had meant Chinese immigration to enhance royal trade by creating infrastructures, producing goods and supplying commercial and shipping expertise (and in so doing had given the incoming Chinese 'the most unbounded encouragement, and granted them privileges which render their condition infinitely preferable to that of the natives of the country'[10]), the effects were much more broadly felt within the Siamese economy. Freed from corvée and granted freedom of movement, Chinese immigrant labourers set to work creating the wherewithal of economic expansion, notably the canals necessary for agricultural development and transport. This in turn allowed Rama II to halve indigenous corvée demands and promote a more single-minded approach to agricultural production by Siamese peasants. No longer were they 'a people who are compelled to devote one third of the labour of their manhood to the service of a highly oppressive government'.[11] Indeed, 'by the mid 1820s, there was a sufficient level of production above subsistence . . . for the king to think in terms of large-scale internal revenue collection'.[12] The changing nature of the Siamese economy allowed Rama III to introduce extensive tax farming 'as the major form of revenue collection in the kingdom',[13] and to abandon royal trading as a direct source of revenue. While much of the weight of revenue farming fell upon Chinese consumers of alcohol, gambling and opium, it also tapped the escalating economic activity of the Siamese themselves.

Despite the success the Siamese enjoyed in enlivening and expanding their economy, they were unable to deter the British for long. In 1855, their sovereign signed a treaty with John Bowring which destroyed the exclusivity of royal trade and effectively opened the country to the winds of world commerce. The Bowring agreement, however, was not a radical change of direction for the Siamese state; it simply accelerated the process of Siam's economic reorientation which was, in any case, the inevitable result of the thickening of productive activity since the 1820s. This trend expressed itself most forcefully in the rapid extension of rice cultivation, bringing into play those 'immense tracts [which] remain to be recovered from the jungle',[14] and the accelerated development of the export rice industry. Once the barriers to commerce with the wider world outside had been beaten down, the favourable terms of trade which rice enjoyed (fuelled by the effects of the Indian mutiny and the Civil War in the United States which disrupted the supply of rice needed in Europe) and Siam's comparative advantage in its production compared to, say, sugar or sesame, ensured that rice would become 'more than [Siam's] primary domestic staple and replace practically all other crops as its principal money-earning export'.[15] Correspondingly, the commercial links with upland peoples which had delivered exotic produce for the China trade faded in relative importance. Over the next eight decades – abetted from the 1880s by technological developments in shipping, local milling and telegraphic communications – Siam's rice exports grew at an average rate of increase of around 13 per cent per annum, a performance described by one writer as 'phenomenal for prewar economic development in an uncolonized country and . . . unmatched in world agricultural history'.[16] In turn, the rapid growth of rice production for export stimulated the development of a mechanised rice milling industry, first concentrated in the capital and expanding upcountry especially after the turn of the century; mainland Southeast Asia's first steam-powered rice mill was constructed in Bangkok by an American in 1858. Even as early as 1865, rice exports comprised more than half of Siam's total exports.

These developments went hand in hand with both structural changes to Siamese society and a rapid extension of the rice frontier. The result was something already evident in places like Java and Luzon: the creation of a new kind of peasantry with new functions. Chinese immigrants continued to arrive, and in rapidly increasing numbers, pushed by disintegrating political and social conditions in southern China, pulled by the opportunities for work on the railways and docks, and in sawmills and ricemills in Siam, and their movement facilitated by steamship transportation between south China and Siam. In 1882, there were 17 000 arrivals; by 1893, that number had swollen to 28 000, and by 1905 to 46 000. Their presence allowed King Chulalongkorn to abolish slavery – according to Bowring, 'the condition of a large part of the population of Siam'[17] – and to substitute a capitation tax for both regular and irregular corvée. The ending of slavery and corvée had three important consequences for peasant production in the last decades of the nineteenth century: it provided Siamese peasants with the freedom and mobility to pursue rice cultivation as a full-time occupation, it forced them to produce commercially to obtain the money to satisfy their new desires for imports and their new tax obligations, and it provided, in the form of emancipated slaves and especially their children, a work force eager – or at least required – to make its own way and find its own means of livelihood. Subsequently, the amount of land devoted to rice grew quickly, especially in the delta regions to the south of the old capital of Ayutthaya, an area which previously had been 'largely an uninhabited wasteland of jungle grass'.[18] There, peasants in large numbers established their farms, usually ranging in size from about eight to thirty hectares. Canal construction provided both transport and enhanced flooding, prerequisites for development, and was essentially the product of private rather than state-sponsored exertion. Capital came in the first instance from the private moneys of the king and nobles; later, peasants wishing to take up land along the new canals were encouraged to subscribe either money or their labour to finance production, and, towards the end of the century, the task was entrusted to private companies, of which the most famous – or notorious – was the Siam Land, Canals and Irrigation Company, established in 1880. That company's great work was the development of the Rangsit canal complex on virtually uninhabited lands east of Bangkok, a site of feverish land speculation in the 1890s as peasants (as many as 100 000 of them) flocked from more northerly reaches of the Central Siam plain to carve out holdings, and where royal and aristocratic Siamese invested heavily. There, as we shall see, unlike elsewhere on the Central Plain, landlordism, large landholding and tenancy were commonplace from the very beginnings; the nature of land sales made for a new pattern of dispersed housing on plots rather than the clumped or linear patterns of settlement common elsewhere.

Under circumstances where free and unencumbered rice production was dominant, revenue farming became ever more important for the Siamese state; the reforms made to it by Chulalongkorn in 1873 were designed to bring it under greater royal control and make it a more efficient conduit of state revenue. By the end of the century, revenue farming was responsible for raising 'almost half of [Siam's] government revenue';[19] moreover, by providing most of the finances needed to restructure and free the labour force, it allowed Thai peasants 'to produce for the capitalist markets without being much shaken by the forces of capitalism'.[20]

Things went less successfully as far as Burmese sovereignty was concerned. The British swept up the provinces of Arakan and Tenasserim in 1826; the imposition in those places of British-sponsored security, as well as the encouragement to trade (including the rapid development of a shipbuilding industry), brought a rapid expansion in agriculture; production of rice increased by one-third within a year of Britain's taking of Tenasserim, and population grew rapidly as people moved in from Bengal, south India, Malaya and – to a lesser extent, Lower Burma – to share in the bounty. The pattern was repeated on a much grander scale in the region of the Irrawaddy delta in 1852 when the Burmese crown proved obdurate in the face of demands that it ease its monopolistic powers over commerce. In opening these places to 'free commerce', the British facilitated a momentous and profitable expansion in rice production for export, a much enlarged if not altogether new direction, the success of which was based on the same factors as those propelling expansion in Siam. Thousands of peasants flocked from Upper Burma to settle on and take possession of land in the unreclaimed regions of the Irrawaddy delta; indeed, Lower Burma's population reportedly doubled between 1852 and 1861.

The rapid development of rice production was stimulated by the liberal land, tax, and production policies followed by the British, who provided infrastructural development (notably the construction of embankments to prevent flood damage), easy access to land (to create a vast class of smallholders), low taxes, and access to new markets, further enhanced as the deployment of steamers and the opening of the Suez Canal brought speedier transport to Europe, allowing rice to be milled in Burma (to save shipping space) and still arrive in Europe in good condition. Indeed, as was the case in Siam, the expanding volume of rice exports was itself responsible for the development of a mechanised rice milling industry, the only way to handle the rapidly burgeoning volume of rice produced. Export rice milling was originally dominated by Europeans, but later and increasingly came to be managed by Burmese themselves, often financed by European capital (though European influence in terms of processing power remained disproportionately high in relation to the number of mills owned). Originally centred on Rangoon, the milling industry, like that of Siam, gradually spread through the whole country, a process which accelerated after the turn of the century; there were about 30 mills in 1875, around 100 in 1900, 500 by 1925 and 700 by 1940. As in Siam, enduringly favourable terms of trade for rice in relation to the goods peasants wished to purchase were a bulwark sustaining production at high levels; as in Siam, the result was an 'extreme monocrop dependence',[21] an economy focused almost entirely on the production and export of rice.

Meanwhile in Upper Burma, the same efforts at indigenous royal consolidation which had been in evidence in Siam were being practised. Already suffering from the loss of the delta rice bowl and vital access to southern ports for sustaining international trade, King Mindon sought to increase his leverage over provincial officials, began a process of military modernisation along Western lines, reasserted, enhanced and developed his royal monopolies over trade, reorganised his administration and increased agricultural production. An important part of his strategy was to keep rice prices low, a manoeuvre made difficult by the loss of the delta, and he sought to do this by importing rice – notably from the British-held delta – and subsidising its sale. He also tried to enhance production by expanding and improving irrigation facilities in the Dry Zone. However, the gradual collapse of the administrative infrastructure of Upper Burma, as well as the swelling leakage of peasants to Lower Burma, led inevitably to agricultural decline; moreover, the silting of rivers and canals – caused, according to one historian, by the deforestation resultant upon the sale of extensive timber leases to the Bombay Burma Trading Corporation after 1862[22] – removed large areas from agriculture. The long drought of 1883–5, also attributed to deforestation, was the final and crushing calamity for indigenous Burmese rule.

A third site where the liberal phase had an momentous impact was in the region of French Cochinchina. As in Siam and Burma, indigenous fears of the West had led Vietnam to self-imposed isolation, coupled with anti-Western xenophobia and an intense effort at centrally-controlled development. Such strategies proved unsuccessful in containing a process of French nibbling which began with the seizure of six provinces around Saigon and ended with their having consumed the whole of Indochina by 1893. From their early footholds, the French organised the construction of canals to enhance drainage and improve transportation to the north and east of Saigon. To the west and south, in the region of the trans-Bassac, the marshy topography was less amenable to simple methods, and the French proceeded with a thoroughgoing recasting of the swampy landscape, dredging a vast series of canals to irrigate, drain and desalinate the land. The opening of these lands, together with the French policy of expanding rice exports, brought huge numbers of Vietnamese peasants from central and eastern Vietnam to carve out settlements on the reclaimed land, much of it in the form of large holdings which had been ceded or auctioned off to French or Vietnamese collaborator interests. French encouragement of commercial rice production was almost immediately rewarded by success. 'The frontiers of rice cultivation doubled between 1865 and 1867 and were extended by almost a third between 1870 and 1878. In 1860, only 57 000 tons of rice were exported from Cochinchina. By [1880], rice exports had increased dramatically to 229 000 tons, and 522 000 hectares of rice land were under cultivation'.[23] As in Bangkok (but not in Burma), Chinese quickly came to dominate the export rice milling industry centred in Cholon.

A fourth site where liberalism promoted the further development of production was Luzon. There, the late eighteenth century tendencies towards opening to the larger world were consolidated in the first half of the nineteenth century. The Chinese mestizo elite, under pressure from the gathering numbers of Chinese immigrants who successfully reclaimed the commercial space lost as a result of Spanish restrictions on Chinese immigration in the 1750s ('These China shopkeepers [in Manila] have nearly driven all competition, except with each other, out of the market – very few mestizos or Spaniards being able to live on the small profits which the competition among themselves has reduced them to'[24]), moved out from its urban base and its erstwhile concern with commerce to become owners and managers in commercial export production in the provinces: cattle raising, sugar, rice. At the same time, peasants moved rapidly and in increasing numbers into the unreclaimed jungles and grasslands of the lowlands. This movement of population – 'the most outstanding feature of transformation'[25] – originated from the southern regions around Manila and, more spectacularly, from the Ilocos region to the north. It filled in the central plain of the island, so that the province of Nueva Ecija, which had been virtually empty at the turn of the nineteenth century, became first a major supplier of meat for Manila through cattle ranching and, after that industry declined after serious outbreaks of rinderpest and foot and mouth disease in the later nineteenth century, an important producer of rice by the early twentieth century, continuing to expand its cultivated area into the 1930s and beyond. But where the tobacco monopoly was strongly maintained, and where distance from the Manila markets effectively prevented the development of other kinds of cash cropping, the result was economic stagnation or decline. Cagayan exemplified this ossification most starkly; around 1800, more than half the province's tribute payers had left in search of opportunity elsewhere.[26]

Elsewhere as well through the nineteenth century the effects of liberal policies on production for export were being felt. In Java, the effective abandonment of the government-sponsored system of forced cultivations by the 1860s led to legislation which allowed private enterprise greater scope and security to invest in plantation agriculture and saw in particular a rapid expansion in the reach and influence of the Western sugar industry. In Minangkabau, the forced coffee system – long in decline through a combination of crop disease, land shortages and the disappearance of incentives for peasant production of the crop – was abandoned in 1908 and replaced by a system of free production and direct taxation. The removal of the ban on rice exports from the region in 1912 soon saw west Sumatra regain its position as rice exporter, and release from the forced delivery system brought a spectacular growth in cash crop production.

The decisive feature in all these developments was the desire of states, for whatever reason, to encourage a vast increase in the peasantry's production of simple bulk goods for sale on global markets: coffee, sugar, rice, abaca and similar items. The result of this marriage of potential to opportunity was a rapid, even savage, expansion of production of these basic goods across much of the landscape of lowland Southeast Asia. Peasants began to gush across what had previously been sparsely peopled areas, breaking out of the locally confined pockets of dense sedentary population, bringing swamps, floodplains, and forests under the plough and hoe, and creating, through their efforts, a radically new ecology. 'The Java we know today covered by rice fields' one scholar has remarked, 'was mainly the achievement of the nineteenth century peasantry'.[27]

In a variety of places, however, liberalism had little impact on the development of peasant production. Colonial ignorance and impotence meant that for the most part upland peoples were left to themselves, except when their activities – such as Karens cutting over teak for swidden cultivation in Burma's Pegu Yoma hills – threatened resources which the state claimed for itself. In those few lowland areas where indigenous power still held out against the forces promoted by European intrusion, markets remained subordinate to royal whim. However, remaining apart, or exerting a measure of purely self-interested local dominion over people and production, were conveniences that could not long be sustained.

THE PHASE OF MANAGEMENT

The distinguishing feature of this third phase was the emergence of the modern state, in controlling sovereignty over a territory with specified borders, in command of its currency, in close, enduring and busy contact with those it now called its subjects, and allied in profitable partnership with the agents of Western capital in their various manifestations.

Perhaps the most immediately obvious achievement of such new states was the rounding out of their political sovereignty. In Siam, this meant a gradual process of incorporation of former tributary states and 'tribal' peoples into the Bangkok-based state, subservient to Siamese taxation and, as well, a cultural process of 'becoming Tai'. In the central highlands of Vietnam, from the late nineteenth century the French adopted a policy of 'pacification' which entailed the imposition of monetary taxation and corvée (mainly for road building) on uplanders, the establishment of military outposts, the creation and supervision of markets and, gradually, the imposition of a provincial administration (with law courts), and the beginnings of plantation agriculture on land which uplanders had thought their own; 'by 1930 the presence of towns such as Dalat, Ban Me Thuot, and Kontum, the proliferating estates where wild forests gave way to neat rows of coffee, tea and rubber seedlings, and the network of roads . . . attested to the success of the French penetration'.[28] In Sarawak, the Brookes brought a significant measure of restriction, territorial delimitation and even fixedness to mobile swiddening groups such as the Iban. In Laos, only with the coming of the French – notwithstanding the minuscule numbers of officials they provided (there were just seventy-two French officials stationed in Laos in 1904) and French unwillingness to consider the region in its own terms – did Lao peasants and uplanders begin to experience 'a relatively stable national political structure'.[29] In the Philippines, the process of establishing a nation-state meant not just bringing the populations of the remote south under the American flag but also making them into 'real' citizens, stable, socialised, subordinate. Thus, remarked a former governor of Zamboanga district,

> Placing the wandering Christians, Moros, and Pagans permanently upon homesteads by the government will do more to civilise them and add to their prosperity and that of the government than any other measure that can be undertaken for the development of these dependent people . . . . The dependent people of the various Moro and Pagan tribes . . . must be taught the advantages of a permanent home, the benefits to be derived from the legal possession of land, its proper cultivation, the maintenance and education of a family, the making of an honest living, respect for the rights of others, and obedience to the law.[30]

Elsewhere the same process was in train, creating a Netherlands East Indies in the archipelago on the basis of treaty and, where necessary, unforgiving war, and then attempting to tie it together economically through Dutch control of interisland shipping (notably through the Koninklijke Paketvaart Maatschappij), a British Malaya on the peninsula (incorporating northern polities which had previously been tributaries of Siam), and Burma (now populated by 'Burmese' rather than by Burmans, Shans, Karens and others) as an appendage of 'India'.

The most eloquent manifestation of the modern state's coming to be in Southeast Asia was its now confident ability to tax most of its subjects directly and regularly. Whereas in the past, revenue had come from the profits of trade and from the device of revenue farming – the latter, as I have already noted, had played a key transitional role in financing the gestation of the modern state – states now had sufficient vigour and competence to make more direct claims of their subjects, make them regularly, and make them stick. Accordingly in Siam, for example, the opium revenue farm was abolished by 1908–9, while the gambling and lottery farms were ended in 1916–17; elsewhere across the regions, revenue farms of different kinds suffered the same fate around this time. As Chulalongkorn remarked in 1907, 'now . . . we collect these taxes and administer these monopolies ourselves, leaving only a few unimportant ones to Chinese farmers. The Chinese turn increasingly to private enterprise, of which rice milling is an example, and become further separated from involvement in governing administration'.[31] Taxation collection was increasingly centralised and monetised; moreover, as time went by, the state began to extend its reach by broadening the taxation base. In 1905, indeed, the Siamese government had been sufficiently confident of its power to institute a steep increase in the land tax, and did it so successfully that it nearly doubled its revenue from this source. In Java, a new land rent ordinance proclaimed in 1907 ended the old *admodiatie* system of haggling over tax obligations between village and government officials; the new system demanded a thorough cadastral survey of village lands. In Minangkabau, as we have seen, the ending of compulsory coffee cultivation saw the introduction of monetary tax in 1908.

This new dispensation was premised on the rationality of the new economic rules which had pushed themselves to the fore through the nineteenth century, and which demanded that wealth flow from the sale of the fruits of the labour of the rapidly proliferating peasantry. We have already noticed this adjustment in Siam, where slavery and corvée made way for full-time productive work in export crop production. In Kedah, too, the ending of corvée 'became one of the major incentives for the accelerated land colonisation during the last quarter of the 19th century. For the first time the peasant had more time and security for his agricultural pursuits'.[32] In Java, compulsory labour (*herendiensten*) was replaced by payment in money, although progress on this front was slower in the less developed outer regions of the Netherlands Indies, while in Vietnam, as well, corvée duties were gradually subsumed into monetary taxes by the early twentieth century.

The elaboration of the taxation system was possible because of the creation of new and more efficient administrative frameworks. State bureaux were staffed by newly recruited or recently transformed officials, now trained in the narrow ends-means rationality of Western thought, valuing such things as Western concepts of disinterested law, legality and policing above the apparent arbitrariness of indigenous models, occupational specificity, professionalism, and eager to know about and intervene helpfully in the lives of the great masses. One sign of this change was the 1916 regulation which required peasants in northern Siam to adopt surnames so that they could better be supervised and assessed. Another was the fact that in Malaya, lower level officials took over the supervision of planting schedules in the place of religious figures. For one scholar, writing in this case of Burma, the tenor of displacement of one order by another was expressed in 'the abandonment of the golden palaces of the kings at Mandalay as the centre of the state for the great utilitarian pile of brick in Rangoon known as the Secretariat'.[33]

This more elaborate and efficient administrative machinery expressed itself in numerous other ways. One was in the development of formally decentralised power structures like municipal councils in places such as the Philippines, Burma, and Java. Another was the creation of direct lines of authority connecting the centre of power to the village. A third was the gradual development of the notion of land as a commodity, premised upon the state's enjoying the competence and authority to function as assigner, guarantor and, as necessary, protector of rights in property; this function, as we shall see, entailed not only the provision for orderly distribution of new land to peasant colonisers but, more complex and important, the translation into modern terms of existing customary tenurial rights.

Control of this kind, too, required the elaboration of communications infrastructures which, around the turn of the twentieth century, were still rudimentary. In 1912 in Cambodia, for example, there were only 430 kilometres of all-weather roads; from 1922 to 1924 alone, 400 kilometres of such roads were built. In the Philippines between 1909 and 1934, the American government 'augmented the colony's 400-odd kilometres of "approximate first class" roads with over 7500 kilometres of new 'first-class' highways'.[34] In Laos, by 1938 the French had built 2258 kilometres of main roads and 2569 kilometres of secondary roads. In Burma by 1935, there were 2000 miles of surfaced roads, with another 7000 miles of unsurfaced roads. Elsewhere, however, where water transport was the dominant mode of movement and flooding commonplace, as in Siam, roads were less important. In 1934, the only road capable of carrying cars from Bangkok led to the airport, and though by 1936 there were 3587 kilometres of roads in the kingdom, only 125 kilometres of them were serviceable in all weathers; in 1939, Bangkok housed most of the 4500 motor vehicles registered in Siam. In other places more peripheral to state concerns, developments of this kind were marginal; in Sabah, for example, there were less than ninety kilometres of metalled roads by 1927.

Railways captured more neatly than roads the developmentalist ethos of the new states. Even though the Siamese were more taken with the potential of the railway to tie the kingdom together and facilitate the maintenance of its sovereignty than with economic development, construction of links such as that between Bangkok and Chiang Mai, completed in 1922, had the effect of promoting commerce between these centres. In Malaya, by contrast, railways aimed not so much at political integration as to cater more efficiently to the needs of mining and export cropping; the first lines serviced the developing tin industry on the west coast, while ancillary lines later provided a grid for the rubber industry's use. By 1907, Burma had already been provided with a main trunk line of railways. Such developments in themselves allowed for the expansion of economic activity; new local roads and railways facilitated the growth in the number of Chinese-owned rice mills up country from Bangkok which could then transmit locally milled (and thus less bulky and lighter) rice to the city.

A final manifestation of the state's ability to manage came with the proliferation of plantations. Though they existed before the turn of the twentieth century – developing most notably on the east coast of Sumatra, in Java and on the island of Negros – their successful operation was essentially predicated on the existence of the kinds of state control which I have discussed above. Among the earliest of them, those established to produce tobacco on a rotational swidden basis in east Sumatra from the 1860s, were based upon contracts for land use made between Dutch interests and local indigenous hierarchies who claimed 'to have the right to dispose of all land within their jurisdiction';[35] they were worked by what became a huge imported force of indentured labourers, first from China and then from Java, the fulfilment of whose contracts was subject to state sanction. The Negros sugar industry, founded upon the injection of large amounts of indigenous capital from the failing textile industry centred on the western Visayas, grew with extraordinary rapidity from the 1860s on the basis of a consolidated hacienda system of plantation and the injection of large amounts of cheap plantation labour. In Java, the Western sugar industry adapted hesitantly then readily to the private arrangements which succeeded the Cultivation System, while new European-managed plantations multiplied on unoccupied lands held on long lease from the state. In Malaya, struggling efforts to promote coffee plantations gave way after the turn of the century to the seemingly miraculous boom in rubber production. In Cochinchina, around 30 000 hectares were under plantation rubber by the early 1920s, and this area expanded rapidly through the 1920s.

The administrative enhancement and authoritative competence of the new states pointed to a much more intrusively well-meaning form of governance than Southeast Asians had ever known before, an attempt to provide for a desired level of prosperity by intervening in the life of ordinary people. One measure of this development was the investments made or sponsored by governments to enhance agricultural production, both for domestic consumption and export, notably through irrigation improvement. In Malaya, where Wan Mat Saman, Kedah's chief minister, had dug his famous drainage canal in 1885 and 'transformed what was a useless swamp land into another vast area for rice cultivation and soon attracted a large number of settlers'[36] who grew rice for consumption and also for sale to Chinese padi brokers, the Krian irrigation scheme was initiated in 1889 and completed in 1906. It aimed to secure a more predictable environment for rice cultivation and to expand the cultivable area, partly to provide for greater domestic production of rice to lower the huge bill for rice imports for Chinese miners. To be sure, this early initiative went against the general policy grain of easy reliance on importing cheap foreign rice but, by the early 1930s, with Malaya producing just one-third of the rice it needed for its own consumption, the government sought more broadly to expand commercial rice cultivation by financing drainage and irrigation works. By 1932, the heightened interest in padi planting had brought increases in the areas of sawah cultivated and in yields, and 'between 1932 and 1940, a total of 160 dams were constructed and more than 186 000 acres of rice fields in the F.M.S. [Federated Malay States] benefited from them'.[37] In 1939, the government established a minimum floor price for paddy. These efforts, however, were ultimately unsuccessful; enlarged production areas and enhanced yields did no more than keep pace with a rapidly growing population. In Vietnam, as we have seen, the French shifted mountains of earth – 'annually . . . between six and ten million cubic meters a year between 1893 and 1930'[38] in Cochinchina – to drain land, to construct canals and to consolidate and raise dykes. In Siam between 1907 and 1931, the area irrigated by state-sponsored works rose from 21 900 hectares to 344 300 hectares. Between 1914 and the end of World War II, works were carried out in the north, in the northeast and on the Central Plain to improve irrigation, drainage, and flood control which brought direct benefit to 651 820 hectares. In Java, too, from around the turn of the century the government directed and funded the construction of a series of technical irrigation schemes such as the Pekalen–Sampean scheme in east Java to improve the reliability and quantity of water supplies. In central Luzon, large-scale and publicly funded irrigation schemes were undertaken from 1907.

To improvements made in irrigation and water control were added some small scale and perfunctory efforts to improve and implement advanced technologies in agriculture. In Java, a research station for rice and dryfield crops was established in 1905 – its work had little impact on rice production in the colonial period, though it laid the groundwork for later great advances – and an agricultural extension service in 1911. A Bureau of Agriculture was established in the Philippines in 1901 to conduct agricultural research and 'to make Filipino farmers aware of modern agricultural techniques'.[39] In Malaya, a padi experimental station was created in Melaka in 1926, and a soil section set up in the Department of Agriculture in 1927; the focuses of attention were rice varieties, fertilisers and plant husbandry. Mechanisation and pest control research received little attention. In Siam, an experimental farm was established in Rangsit in 1916. In Indochina, a seed laboratory began operation in 1916. Although Burma established a separate Department of Agriculture in 1906 and its first experimental farm at Mandalay as early as 1907, efforts to improve seed stock met little success; by the early 1930s, improved seeds were employed in only 8 per cent of Burma's padi land. With so little new knowledge to distribute, agricultural extension services remained weak. The failure to increase rice yields across the region was in part attributable to this limited commitment to technological improvement and its diffusion.

Such efforts at popular improvement, however, were always subject to apparently more consequential concerns. The well-known refusal of the Siamese government to undertake the ambitious plan of irrigation recommended by the Dutch irrigation engineer, Homan van der Heide, was simply the most notorious example of the reluctance of governments to commit themselves to the high levels of irrigation expenditure needed to develop agriculture to its full potential in the face of greater perceived demands for administrative development, political order and consolidation, and defence. Thus, in Siam, for example, the pattern of government expenditures between 1905 and 1938 was one of concentration on state consolidation: almost half went on defence and the administration of the various regions, 10 per cent on the Royal Court, and another 7 per cent on metropolitan administration. By contrast, 'expenditures on economic development projects, such as irrigation, railways and highways and on human resource development accounted for only about 16% of the total'.[40]

Limited and perhaps grudging though it was, state intrusion on behalf of popular welfare marked a new departure in the behaviour of states. There were limited interventions of other kinds as well in the name of the good of the people. In 1913, for example, the British colonial government proclaimed the Malay Reservations Act (revised and strengthened in 1933) which was designed to protect Malays against the loss of their land to non-Malays and foreigners; by 1931, the area reserved had grown to almost half a million hectares. As well, governments in the region began edging towards imposing their will on hitherto free domestic and international markets. In 1911, the Netherlands Indies imposed a temporary ban on rice exports, a step it repeated in 1914 and 1918. In Malaya, a government alarmed by a rice import supply crisis of 1918–21 consequent upon crop failures in Siam and Burma attempted to promote domestic production by establishing a minimum price for rice, and a guaranteed price system was reintroduced in the 1930s. In the Philippines in 1936 the government established a Rice Commission, a body which fathered a National Rice and Corn Corporation which aimed, without immediate success, to secure fair prices for producers and a reliable consumers' supply. In 1938, the Siamese government formed the Thai Rice Company to buy up peasants' paddy, apparently in an effort to break Chinese control of the rice industry. Similar in kind to these interventions was the attempt by the British government in Malaya to impose restrictions on rubber production under the Stevenson plan and which had the effect of penalising rubber smallholders relative to plantation owners.

Related to these market interventions was the emergence of the notion that Southeast Asian peasants were crippled by usury and in need both of government protection against private credit providers and government-sponsored credit provision and savings opportunities if they were to progress. In Java, for example, the Dutch established local savings banks – more than 7000 of them in villages by the end of the colonial period – and took on the task of regulating pawnshops, as well as providing specialised rural credit. With these good intentions, however, marched ignorance of peasants' credit practices and a plethora of inappropriately designed delivery structures. Thus, post office savings banks in Burma were largely staffed by Indians and accordingly ignored by Burmese; in Malaya, 'it took one day for an Ijok peasant to borrow from the Malay agent of a chetty, it took him three and a half months to get a government loan, besides necessitating a journey to the district headquarters'.[41] Cooperative societies were set up across the region from the turn of the century; they attracted little support amongst peasants, partly because of their regimentation, and most collapsed into insolvency as a result of corruption and neglect. In the Indies, state-sponsored village banks were not geared to provide production credits for agriculture. Government-operated pawnshops were never able to shuck off their earlier history of being farmed out to Chinese as revenue-raising devices. In Vietnam and elsewhere, well-to-do peasants obtained cheap credit from government-sponsored credit establishments and then lent it out to poorer people at much higher rates of interest, effectively hijacking the system.

Notwithstanding the neatness that periodisation imposes, it would be wrong to think that enhanced state power reached concertedly and evenly across the region. Despite the best efforts of lowland colonisers and 'pacifiers', much of the uplands retained its peripheral relationship with the newly strong centres. And even in the lowlands, state-building progress was equivocal. In Laos, for example, the French searched in vain for an existing political vehicle upon which to base their intended closer control; they found instead that 'there was no central state . . . in a position to carry out such change'.[42] While they attempted reforms such as the abolition of bondage of varying kinds, the imposition of direct (head) taxes and a more useful (to them) allocation of corvée, their achievements remained limited.

THE PHASE OF DISRUPTION

This third phase was itself marked by three distinct periods: the Great Depression, followed by the Japanese invasion and occupation of the region, and then a protracted period of recovery complicated by the ideological and practical complexities of ending colonialism and establishing new independent indigenous states.

The Depression struck Southeast Asia with great suddenness: prices began to drop from 1930, especially in rice, as producers attempted to compensate by producing in larger quantities. In Rangoon, the wholesale price of paddy per one hundred baskets had stood at 195 rupees in 1926 and 160 in 1929; already by the first quarter of 1930 it had fallen to 138 rupees, a year later it stood at 77. By 1932, the Singapore price of rubber had fallen to one-fifth of its level in 1929. In the great Java sugar industry, disappearing markets and eroded prices saw production fall from just under three million tonnes in 1930 to just over half a million tonnes in 1935, and two thirds of the factories cease operation. In short, the prices of all primary export products fell rapidly and precipitously; as a result, prices for products aimed at the domestic markets – vegetables, maize, baskets, mats, woven textiles – also fell. Some sense of the economic effects of this slide in prices may be gained from the fact that the average value of Burma's exports between 1926–30 and 1931–5 declined by 32 per cent and imports by 45 per cent. The result for peasant producers was a proportionately rapid decline in their incomes. The Philippines evaded the full harshness of the Depression, essentially because of the protection which Philippine exports, notably sugar, enjoyed in the American market. The crisis, indeed, engendered a short-lived boom in the Philippine sugar industry as producers sought greater market share as they looked to the time when import quotas would be imposed. When that time arrived in 1934, the sugar-sustained economy of the country slumped.

Governments cast about for ways to ease the crisis. They sought, for instance, to contrive production regulation schemes to limit output. The International Rubber Regulation Scheme introduced in mid 1934 set quotas on production; their calculation and operation saw the burden of restriction fall on smallholders rather than plantations and a sharp decline in the planting of new rubber. In Malaya, the government installed a temporary import duty on rice and padi in order to stimulate and diversify domestic production; in the Indies, the authorities sought to protect producers from low rice prices by restricting rice imports both through licensing importers and taxing imports. As well, there were direct efforts to ease the plight of Indonesian peasants caught up in the Depression, notably by reducing levels of land taxation (though not sufficiently to compensate for price deflation).

The period was marked by an upsurge in crime and popular unrest. Governments, alarmed by the turn of events, made their first half-serious efforts at land reform. In Burma, however, efforts by the quasi-independent nationalist Burmese government at agricultural reform in the late 1930s – aimed principally at protecting Burmese from losing their land to non-Burmese and non-agriculturalists and improving the security of tenants – were rebuffed by political opposition, the lack of appropriate administrative skills and structures, and, in the end, the outbreak of World War II. In the Philippines, even less was achieved because of the interlocking of political power and large landholding. However, a more characteristic response than rebellion for most Southeast Asian peasants in this 'harsher and puzzling economic climate'[43] was a renewed interest in subsistence production to provide their own requirements directly.

The war broke upon Southeast Asia just as the economies and peoples of the region were climbing slowly out of the worst effects of the Depression. From the end of 1941, the armies of Japan swept across Southeast Asia, into the American-held Philippines, through Indochina and down through the Malay peninsula to the Netherlands Indies, and west across Thailand and Burma. They came professedly as an army of liberation, to free the region from European colonialism and to uplift its peoples by incorporating them into a Greater East Asia Co-Prosperity Sphere. For peasants, however, the period was one of uninterrupted turmoil.

Paradoxically, martial activity contributed little to the upheaval; for the most part fighting was restricted to the initial period of invasion in 1941–2, and the Allied liberation campaigns in the Philippines and Burma in 1944–5, and apart from the scorched earth policies of retreating Allied and Japanese forces which notably affected transport facilities, and the bombing of cities like Bangkok and Manila which pushed urban dwellers out into the countryside, it had little social significance. Of much greater and more lasting consequence were the social and structural changes wrought by the Japanese presence and the policies they employed. Existing hierarchies of authority, and the legitimacy they had for whatever reason enjoyed, were cast down; rules of right behaviour were suddenly and radically changed. Moreover, the period of Japanese dominance completely disrupted the primary-export oriented base upon which the economies of Southeast Asia had been constructed. In east Sumatra, for example, the Japanese takeover resulted in a rapid decline in plantation production, with large areas of plantation land handed over to squatter/smallholders; 'a quarter of a million hectares of old tobacco estates . . . were parcelled out among the population . . . farmers from less fertile areas in the hills moved down into the old estate lands'.[44] The foreign trade which had sustained those economies had suddenly evaporated. Finally, the exigencies of a state of war meant that the Japanese were most strongly concerned with mobilising Southeast Asians to assist in attaining their victory. All these dramatic occurrences involved the framing and implementation of policies which deeply touched peasantries everywhere.

The new wartime economic dispensation placed a premium on the production not of goods for commercial export in an international economy (except where these were necessary for the Japanese war machine) but of basic food and clothing for Southeast Asians themselves, for the Japanese armies and, where possible, for the Japanese homeland. Each region, as far as possible, was to be self-sustaining in the necessities of life. Under the new economic rules of the game – characterised by a lack of economic incentive and the rampant inflation associated with the use of Japanese-occupation money – local self-sufficiency implied policies of forced deliveries and rationing, and often resulted in the destruction of existing local marketing and distribution networks. In the Philippines, the Japanese banned rice imports and installed a system of monopoly rice purchases from peasant producers for its resident army and non-agriculturalists. In Burma, they confiscated food and transport facilities (cattle, railways cars, railway lines). Notwithstanding Malaya's already-serious deficiency in rice – which the Japanese took some measures to remedy in 1943 by introducing quick-maturing non-photosensitive japonica varieties from Taiwan ('the first successful adoption of double cropping with rice in West Malaysia'[45]) and by encouraging the cultivation of a wide range of fruit, vegetables and root crops – the peasantry was similarly afflicted by forced deliveries for negligible cash returns and requisitions of rice supplies surplus to rationed requirements, as well as brutality for those caught evading the regulations. Much the same policies were in force in the Netherlands Indies. The Thai government, for its part, found itself forced to direct exports of its rice surpluses to Japanese-dominated regions, an important factor in the decline of Thailand's rice exports from 230 000 tonnes in 1941 to 117 000 in 1942, 83 000 in 1943, 50 000 in 1944 and just 33 000 tonnes in 1945.

Apart from requisitioning foodstuffs, the Japanese also sought to deploy indigenous labour on a large scale to assist its war effort. Large numbers of Burmese were corralled into forced labour projects. In November 1944, the number of labourers recruited or coerced into service for the Japanese in Java stood at over 2.6 million, while the number of Javanese mobilised at one time or another during the war years was probably of the order of 10 million; around 160 000 of them were sent to labour on projects in other parts of Southeast Asia, about 15 per cent of whom perished. In Thailand, young men drafted into the police and military in the period immediately prior to the Japanese arrival remained in the city as guards – depriving their communities of their labour in the rice fields. Within these countries, the Japanese diverted large amounts of labour (sometimes as much as half the available work time) to defence projects and other schemes aimed at improving wartime economic performance. Japanese brutality and hunger for labour also had the effect of driving lowlanders into mountains or interiors, sometimes to join resistance movements, themselves displacing upland or hinterland swiddeners.

All this had damaging implications for food production in Southeast Asia. Rice harvests declined seriously in the Philippines under the impact of wartime dislocation, which included the flight to rural areas by many urban workers whose employment had been destroyed through the interruption or cessation of commerce, the rural spoiling of anti-Japanese forces like the Hukbalahap, the proliferation of black marketeering, a disintegration of irrigation systems and a decline in cattle stocks through requisition and death. 1944–5 brought perhaps the most serious subsistence crisis in modern Philippine history; the area harvested in rice in 1945–6 was almost 30 per cent lower than that harvested in 1940–1. Much the same could be said of Burma, where huge areas of rice land on the Burma delta fell into disuse and reverted to scrub; in the period 1941–8, more than 1.2 million hectares of paddy land were abandoned in Lower Burma. In 1945–6, the rice crop was just over one-third of the normal crop. In Vietnam, well over a million people perished in famines in the north and central parts of the country (the effects of which were exacerbated by compulsory delivery of rice quotas to the authorities), 'while surplus rice from the south was shipped to Japan or used for fuel'.[46] In Java, food cropping was disrupted by forced labour requirements and rice requisitions, declining official buying prices, poor transport facilities, the extensive deforestation carried out for shipbuilding and fuel which increased flooding and siltation, and commercial networks were shattered by Japan's anti-Chinese activities. Only about three-fifths of Aceh's rice fields were planted in 1945. The disintegration of production and commerce throughout the region resulted in widespread shortages of the basic necessities of peasant life: rice, sugar, salt, dried fish, kerosene, cloth, cash.

Meanwhile, industries based on export cropping went into serious decline. With the Japanese unable to transport or absorb all the rubber that Southeast Asia customarily produced, production was halted in some areas, although damage to plant stock was not severe with only about 6 per cent of Malaya's rubber trees cut down. With Taiwan's sugar production capability, the sugar industries of Java and the Philippines were dispensable; in 1943 in Java, only half the previous season's cane area was planted out, and the surplus land put to rice. In the Philippines, the Japanese sought (unsuccessfully) to convert sugar land in central Luzon to cotton production.

The aftermath of World War II required an enormous effort to recover from the economic damage wrought by the war years: the clearing of large amounts of agricultural land which had suffered neglect, the rehabilitation of irrigation works, the resettlement of the many refugees who had fled to cities for succour, the rehabilitation of heavily damaged transport facilities and infrastructures, the recovery of cattle stocks, the stabilisation of supplies and the reining in of prices which had surged in line with high post-war demand.

The recovery was uneven. Virtually all of Malaya's rice land was again under production by 1945–6 (although pre-war levels of production were not attained until 1948), but in Cochinchina even a year later only 70 per cent of the available rice land was being cropped, while in Burma food production in 1946 was around three-quarters the prewar volume and as much as a quarter of Lower Burma's rice area remained uncultivated as late as 1950–1. In the rubber industry, by contrast, smallholders were able to take up production much more rapidly than the estates; in Malaya, they provided 85 per cent of production in the early part of 1946 and 55 per cent during that whole year, a proportion that had fallen to 40 per cent by 1962.

To these difficulties were soon added those attendant on the complex processes of decolonisation and political independence. In most parts of Southeast Asia, the turmoil of the occupation period was succeeded almost immediately by domestic turbulence, arising in some places from Southeast Asians' refusal to acquiesce in the reimposition of European colonial hegemony and elsewhere from the confusion, division and disarray arising from the unaccustomed experience of political independence. In Indonesia, for example, the four-year-long struggle for independence from the Netherlands was intermingled with domestic revolts of an embryonically revolutionary or religious kind, and followed by a long period of corrupt and ineffective governance. At the outset in Java, strongly egalitarian and anti-authoritarian sentiments were directed most fiercely at incumbent officials, notably at the village level; many fell from grace and position and some lost their lives in the political unrest subsequent to the Japanese surrender. Outside Java, and notably in Sumatra, hostility was directed at aristocratic elites whose authority had been buttressed by the Dutch; it was often fanned by hopes that the revolution would end taxation and redistribute land. Throughout the struggle for independence, production remained low and commerce disabled. In central Luzon a long period of rural unrest succeeded the American confirmation – in undisturbed power and authority – of an uncontrite collaborator elite. In Burma, independence from Britain in 1948 was achieved against a background of political assassination and popular regional and communist revolts. The government proceeded to nationalise the lands of Chettiars (who had fled before the Japanese) and redistribute them to Burmese, to outlaw absentee landlordism, to place a maximum size of 50 acres on holdings, and to restrict rights to alienate land. The Malayan 'Emergency' brought limitations on movement, commerce, and even the cultivation of food where authorities judged it might easily fall prey to the guerillas; these controls helped to delay the expansion of irrigation in the peninsula. The turbulence of revolutionary change was most in evidence in Vietnam; the anticolonial struggle there became a proxy Cold War battle, and the country was effectively divided into two, first between the revolutionary Viet Minh controlling the rural areas with the French doggedly hanging on in the cities, and thereafter between the northern-based communist government and the US-sponsored right-wing government in the south.

THE STATIST PHASE

The countries of Southeast Asia emerged at different rates from the periods of instability and disruption which had been their lot since the early 1930s. The states which issued from the post-war struggles for identity and independence tended to have strongly held and fiercely asserted – if not well analysed and understood – views about their dominant role in society. Their peoples and their economies were meant for their service, not for the benefit of some foreign power. In particular, there was a sense of aggrieved paternalism about the way they shaped their economies, proclaiming that the evils perpetrated on them in the past could be righted only if the state took to itself the role of protector and nurturer of its subjects who had long been left to fend for themselves as best they could in a hostile and foreign-dominated environment. These new or newly-confident states, then, took a much more intrusive and proprietorial role in their respective economies and how they might best operate to serve – and be served by – their own subjects.

In the most general terms, there were two approaches to this nationalist/paternalist task, both usually expressed in the ambitious solemnities of two-, five- or eight-year development plans. The first was that of state or state-sponsored capitalism based upon a corporate re-ordering of society. It manifested itself in a limited free market with strong state control, and occasional ventures into the nationalisation of strategic industries and the establishment of state monopolies on the export of important primary products. The second alternative was state-sponsored revolution, based on a variety of Marxist or Leninist understandings of social progress, which sought fundamental reshaping of the societies and especially the economies subjected to it.

The approach of the first variant was paradoxical. These states controlled economies which were essentially structured around the production of primary crops; they sought both to protect and extend them, and their producers, but at the same time to milk or manipulate the revenues they provided as a means of securing rapid industrialisation and damping down incipient unrest, notwithstanding a general context of declining commodity prices for primary exports. In Indonesia, for example, exchange rates were controlled to advantage the consumers of Java and served to disadvantage the export producers, including smallholders, outside Java; infrastructure for smallholders remained at very low levels of development, which served to keep marketing margins high. This balancing act resulted in a serious bifurcation of aims and policies which in the end served no-one well.

There were pressing economic – not to mention political – reasons for the state's interest in enhancing rural productivity. Malaya, for example, found itself hard up against its perennial problem of rice supply, having to import up to 40 per cent of its rice needs at an annual cost of about US$50 million, and aimed early at the goal of rice self-sufficiency, to be achieved by 1963. Similarly, Indonesia was forced to import ever greater supplies of rice to sustain its population, at a serious cost of its foreign reserves. At the same time, the political sensitivity of rice price policy as well as the need to maximise state earnings for other ends led to a paralysing and demoralising lack of definition in policy. From the end of World War II to 1954, the Thai government installed a monopoly on rice exports, purchasing rice from peasant producers at prices which were a fraction of export prices. Elsewhere, states sought to stabilise or control prices, not always successfully or consistently, by manipulating buffer stocks. In the Philippines, rice price policy in the 1950s and early 1960s 'seemed to have wavered, supporting the producer at times by restricting imports and the consumer at other times when prices rose to the point that political pressures became intolerable'.[47]

Nonetheless, and in spite of the fact that crop production dominated the economies of these countries – in Thailand in 1947, for example, '84 per cent of the working population were directly engaged in production of rice which occupied more than 90 per cent of cropped land'[48] – the major attention of Southeast Asian states was not on the rural areas but the cities, which they saw as the sites and agents for the kinds of rapid heavy industrialisation of the import-substitution kind which would make them modern and rich. Under these circumstances, the countryside was to serve the city. Thus, the mechanism of the rice export premium implemented in Thailand in 1956 was an effective tax on the rural areas and a guarantee of cheap rice prices (and thus labour) in the cities. Again, Burma, in the period 1952–3 to 1959–60, invested just 9.4 per cent of its total capital expenditures on agriculture. The concentration of resources on urban manufacturing rather than rural agricultural development also expressed itself in differential and discriminatory access to credit.

By the late 1950s and early 1960s these policies were in disarray, crippled by political instability, bureaucracies swollen in size and ineptitude, rampant corruption, decaying infrastructures, rapidly increasing levels of indebtedness, rural and regional unrest, stagnant primary exports, and a secular decline in the prices which primary commodities – still the sustaining element in all economies – fetched on international markets. For our purposes, the important concomitant of such policies had been neglect of the rural areas, partly through lack of resources and political will, but mainly because conscious policy decisions to put resources elsewhere had resulted both in the failure to develop the irrigation sector and in a serious running down or neglect of rural transport and irrigation infrastructures. Indonesian rice production declined by 13.6 per cent between 1960 and 1964, and widespread problems of malnutrition became evident, especially in Java. The situation in southern Vietnam was the most obvious case of escalating disarray, notably after the intensification of war from 1959 onwards which produced such disruptive fruit as the strategic hamlet programme launched in 1962.

In Thailand, it was 1957 before a network of all-weather highways connected Bangkok to regional capitals and these capitals to each other; as late as 1965, Thailand boasted just 12 276 kilometres of roads, only 5452 of them all-weather. Laos lagged even further behind; only in 1955 was the railway connecting Vientiane to Bangkok completed. The Lao elite, feeding ever more insatiably on American aid – it was in the mid 1950s the largest per capita recipient of such aid in the world – permitted itself the nationalist luxury of abolishing the old French head tax; other agricultural taxes remained minimal, and leaders generally ignored questions of agricultural improvement. It was not until 1958 that the government required its citizens to register their land holdings. The results everywhere of indifference, impotence and decay were conditions in rural areas of a kind similar to those found in the Philippine countryside in 1957:

> The typical barrio, then, is one which is characterized by too many people dependent upon the available land base, uneconomic units of farm land, large families with the majority of children under ten years of age, persistent poverty due to restricted base, poor land use, a one-crop economy, a lack of credit facilities other than private loans with usurious interest, a lack of communication between barrio citizens and government rural service agencies, a rising rate of illiteracy, a lack of public sanitation and sanitary facilities.[49]

It would be wrong, however, to perceive this period as one of total neglect. The limited efforts of governments to support their rural subjects – partly motivated by the fear of communist rural insurgency – meant that they sometimes sought to develop roles and tasks which had been adopted only embryonically in the pre-war period. Thus – occasionally in the guise of a nationalist drive against the Chinese minorities which dominated rice trading – they sought to establish credit institutions (sometimes claimed to embody enduring indigenous values of harmony and cooperation) to free their peasantries from the dragging chain of credit dependency. In Thailand, the government sought to promote peasant cooperative associations, partly as a means of means of reducing Chinese dominance in rice marketing. In the Philippines, bodies were established in the 1950s to facilitate farmers and larger cooperative endeavours obtaining credit. In south Vietnam in 1957, a presidential decree established a National Agricultural Credit Office, supported with American aid. States also sought, with varying degrees of seriousness and an almost total lack of success, to institute reforms in prevailing patterns of land tenure. Most such efforts lacked conviction; they remained the occasion for the venting of rhetoric rather than the execution of policy.

Agricultural development itself was pursued with a greater general seriousness from around the mid and late 1950s. In Thailand, for example, the

Chainat dam which Homan van der Heide had proposed a half a century before was completed in 1957; its aim was to increase the area of irrigated land and generally provide more stable cultivation conditions for wet season rice farming. In the country as a whole, state-directed irrigation works expanded the area of irrigated land from 375 000 hectares in 1949 to 1 445 500 hectares in 1967. In Malaya, the FELDA (Federal Land Development Authority) scheme, established in 1956, had by 1974 provided for the development of more than a quarter of a million hectares of land and its settlement by 30 000 peasants, most of them cultivating perennial export crops in the form of rubber or oil palm. About the same time – and partly a function of the need to capture rural votes in the elections leading to independence – the government began to devote greater attention to the smallholder rubber industry, assisting peasants to plant new higher-yielding clones, expanding the area of production and providing education on production and processing techniques. Throughout the region, efforts to improve agricultural extension were intensified; 'in the old days', remarked one village leader in Thailand's Central Plain, 'we had many varieties because we planted what we liked, but now the government is the manager who tells the district officer, the *kamnan* [village chief], and the hamlet headman to plant good varieties'.[50] In Indonesia, well-intentioned but less than concerted efforts by the state to improve rice production, such as the 1952–5 Kasimo plan and a later scheme, the Padi Centra Programme (1959–62), which aimed to improve yields through rehabilitating irrigation and providing cheap credit, fertiliser and improved seeds, met with little success. One commentator asserted flatly that 'the various [Indonesian] programs for food self-sufficiency should probably be regarded as mainly symbolic, since the real planning and resources which would be necessary to make them succeed were never accorded them'.[51]

It was only around the early and mid 1960s that governments gained the will and, to some extent consequentially, the capacity to focus more single-mindedly on enhancing agricultural production. From about that time, the capitalist states of Southeast Asia began to adopt – through the very gradual and piecemeal adoption of export-oriented industrialisation focussed around labour-intensive manufacturing – economic policies the focus of which was growth as such rather than redistribution. At least in the first instance, this move necessitated a systematic development of rural agriculture, incomes and employment, much of it of a protected import-substitution kind.

Generally speaking, improvements in this sphere involved huge new investments to rehabilitate, enhance and expand existing irrigational and associated infrastructures, which had been allowed to disintegrate in the period of disruption. The push for improvement was perhaps best exemplified in the first five-year plan of Indonesia's New Order (and, much assisted by the revenues from the oil boom, continued and refined through succeeding plans), enabling double cropping of rice or cropping of rice with second (that is, non-rice) crops on a much more extensive basis. Closely associated with infrastructural development came a set of administrative and technological improvements in the conduct of agriculture, notably the development of short-stalked, photoperiod-insensitive, quick-growing, highly nitrogen-sensitive and high-yielding varieties of rice, such as IR-8, first developed in the Philippines in 1962, subsidies to enhance the sale of fertiliser, and a surge in agricultural mechanisation, notably the use of hand tractors. For the most part, irrigation improvement and technological development were the mutually dependent components that together made up the Green Revolution. Irrigation improvement certainly extended the area of land cultivated; but much more important was the fact that two or more rice crops could now be planted on the same land within a single year.

Irrigation improvement in Malaysia saw the area planted in rice expand from 377 000 hectares in 1955 to 760 000 hectares in 1979. The most spectacular manifestation of this development was the construction of the huge Muda irrigation scheme in northwest peninsular Malaysia between 1966 and 1970 which, together with the Kemubu rice intensification project, commenced in 1968, provided the country for the first time with the large-scale capability for double-cropping rice. In the 1930s, less than 200 hectares of rice land in Malaya had been double cropped in rice; in 1963 the percentage of rice land being double cropped was just 5.5 per cent and in 1966 only 12 per cent. By 1971 this figure had risen to 45 per cent and by 1976–7 62 per cent, by which time more than one-third of all Malaysia's rice land was planted to new varieties. The New Economic Policy which resulted from the race riots of 1969 can only have helped to confirm and strengthen the new policy of fundamental support for Malay peasants. By 1980, Malaysia was 92 per cent self-sufficient in rice and, by the mid 1980s, 92 per cent of the Muda area was being double cropped in the new varieties.

Philippine farmers were first provided with the new rice varieties in 1966, and the first substantial planting of IR-8 took place in 1967. By 1970–1, 67 per cent of the irrigated areas had been planted to the new varieties, as opposed to 45 per cent of the rain-fed lowlands. Their introduction brought some immediate but not enduring improvements, so that the government sought to consolidate the situation with the introduction of the Masagana ('bountiful') 99 production programme in 1973, which aimed to increase rice yields from a countrywide average of 36 cavans per hectare to 99 cavans per hectare. The programme bundled together new rice varieties, agricultural extension services, the availability of fertiliser and pesticides, the provision of credit, pricing and marketing support, and irrigation improvement, all trumpeted in a vast publicity campaign. By the mid 1970s, two-thirds of the rice land in Philippines was under the new varieties.

Even before the emergence of the New Order in Indonesia, the government had adopted a modest and limited production program first trialed in 1963, the Bimas (mass guidance) programme. Bimas combined enhanced agricultural technology with improved irrigation and cultivation, greater access to fertilisers, pesticides and credit, and intensive moral sustenance and technical advice from agricultural extension teams. Thereafter, the programme was rapidly expanded and adapted, employing the new varieties from 1967. However, a variety of difficulties with the scheme and the plethora of sub-schemes and ancillary arrangements which spawned from it, most notably the inflexibility of the package of seeds, fertilisers, pesticides and credit provided to peasants, the problem of credit repayment, and bureaucratic deficiencies, rigidities, and corruption, brought its abandonment in 1970. The successor programme, 'Perfected Bimas', relied more heavily on farmers' individual incentive and allowed them more choice over what they received in the form of agricultural inputs and credits, and newer intensification programmes – Inmas, Insus (a form of group farming) and Supra Insus – were put in place over the next two decades. By the mid 1970s, new varieties accounted for one-third of the rice planted, and by 1979–80, two-thirds. The result of these strategies was a massive increase in Indonesia's rice production, so that the country achieved its goal of rice self-sufficiency by 1984 (even if that success was accompanied by a decline in non-rice second cropping as non-irrigated land was provided with irrigation and used to produce rice in the dry season). Production rose from 11.67 million tonnes in 1968 to 26.92 million in 1987, and yields from 2.14 kg/ha to 4.01 kg/ha in the same period. The major component of this growth was not the extension of land area but rather its more intensive use, with many parts of Java growing three rice crops in a single year. Between 1969–70 and 1988–9 in Indonesia, the irrigated area annually rehabilitated through public investment averaged 123 000 hectares, while newly irrigated areas funded from the same source grew at an annual average of 59 000 hectares.

Some parts of the Southeast Asian lowlands did not share proportionately in this bounty. In Thailand, the Green Revolution had a less immediate and pervasive influence, essentially because the flood environment of the deltaic central plain did not allow for the degree of water management most conductive to the new varieties. By 1970–1, less than 10 per cent of the Central Plain and less than 3 per cent of the whole country's rice land was under the new varieties; by the mid 1970s, this figure had grown to only 7 per cent. Moreover, government continued to tax rice production in contrast to the situation in such places as Malaysia and Indonesia, where subsidies to producers were increasingly in evidence. In the turmoil of Cambodia in the mid and late 1960s, there were no substantial improvements to agriculture; yields in the 1960s remained of the same order as two decades previously. But aspects of state-centred policies were in evidence, as where the government nationalised exports in 1963 and attempted in 1967 to introduce direct rice purchases from the peasantry in order to eliminate the middleman and to seal off the seepage of rice going to the Vietnamese insurgents.

Despite the extraordinary overall success of agricultural intensification, there were numerous problems along the way. Costs incurred by the enormous demand for fertiliser (between 1956–60 and 1971–5, the amounts of fertiliser imported into Malaysia grew by a factor of two-and a half, those into Indonesian by a factor of almost four) soared after the 1973 OPEC oil price hike and were reduced only with the development of facilities for domestic production. More important, however, were environmental problems occasioned by the new varieties and their use. Perhaps the most immediately obvious was the decline of fish populations as a result of pesticide use, but the removal of genetic diversity in plants, the continually stable conditions occasioned by a non-stop regime of wet rice cropping, and the destruction by pesticide of natural predators brought disasters such as the brown planthopper attacks in Java in the mid 1970s, which occasioned great crop losses (1 144 000 tonnes in 1977 alone) and a partial return to old varieties. Such problems were (at least temporarily) overcome by the introduction and rapid spread of new resistant varieties (IR-36, then IR-64), and the adoption of integrated pest management schemes.

Increased production could not have occurred without the elaboration of physical and administrative infrastructures. In Indonesia, the development of roads outside Java allowed new land to be put into production. Moreover, the building of regional road networks such as the Trans-Sumatra Highway greatly enhanced people's ability to move and to trade, and provided a degree of economic integration both regionally and nationally not previously experienced. In the country as a whole, road length increased two-and-a-half times between 1967 and 1985, and the quality of roads also improved significantly. Their use increased at an even greater rate; between 1968 and 1986, the number of registered buses in Indonesia grew from 20 000 to 257 000, the number of registered trucks from 93 000 to 882 000, and the number of registered motorcycles from 308 000 to 5 119 000. In Thailand, where the first development plan of 1961 had allocated over one-quarter of total expenditures to improving provincial and inter-provincial road networks, there were just 15 697 kilometres of roads, 9103 kilometres of them of the all-weather variety, in 1969. By 1980, these roads extended 28 151 kilometres, of which 22 403 kilometres were hard-surfaced, reached into most villages, and were under ever-greater use with the growth of motorised transport. 'There is', remarked one scholar, 'a wave of motorization spilling over Thailand that is going to put river and rail as means of transport into the shade'.[52] In the Philippines, road length grew from 37 153 kilometres in 1960 to 72 820 in 1971, although many roads were of poor quality, and animals and humans used extensively for short-haul transport. The Second Malaya Plan (1961–5) saw more than 3000 kilometres of roads built in the countryside, an eightfold improvement of what had been achieved under the first Plan. There were, as well, correspondingly large improvements in grain storage capacity.

The development of administrative reach was especially expressed in the creation of a multiplicity of local level state-sponsored organisations which acted as channels for the delivery of political demands, credit, and the new technologies (and knowledge about them) and for the transfer of produce out of the village. In Indonesia, rapidly burgeoning village 'cooperatives', latterly known as KUDs, assisted in distributing fertiliser and in rice procurement; village units of the Bank Rakyat Indonesia (People's Bank of Indonesia) sprouted to provide local credit. At the upper reaches of the state machinery, stable procurement, pricing and marketing were managed by state boards like BULOG. In Thailand, similarly, state-sponsored local rural organisations acted as channels into the villages for the conveyancing of improved seed varieties, machinery, credit and fertiliser. In addition to these bodies, the state created more extensive and intensive research facilities and provided greatly expanded extension services.

All this represented – and itself further facilitated – a massive increase in the control of the village by the state, characterised by increasingly effective penetrativeness as well as a national standardisation of the mechanisms of administration and management. In Sumatra, for example, Law 5/79 abolished the old *nagari* as the basic territorial unit; its component parts, called *jorong*, were now designated as villages (*desa*). The position of chief (*wali*) of the nagari was likewise consigned to the past and replaced by a Java-style village chief (*kepala desa*) whose role was specified by law. The corollary, of course, was that villagers themselves tended to lose control over their own institutions as the state pressed down with its directions, its seeds, its credit and its machines, attempting to sweeten its message through training programs and 'symbols, songs, [and] slogans'.[53] Peasant participation in agricultural development programs, at least in the earlier stages, was often the result of coercion or at least browbeating from a bureaucracy unsympathetic to the difficulties faced by peasants in implementing the program.

The state's role in promoting this programme of agricultural intensification is evocatively described in an account of village organisation in one part of Thailand:

> In both villages, the four principal ministries with statutory activities at the district level have a number of schemes. These include: housewives' groups and pre-school centres run by the Community Development Department (CCD); agricultural extension by the local agricultural extension officer of the Department of Agricultural Extension (DAE); activities associated with the village primary schools; health stations close to each village; frequent training programmes and intermittent 'advice' at village meetings; and administration of national programmes, such as the Rural Employment Generation Programme (REGP), and ideological training. The *tambon* council is instrumental in the administration of these programmes, but initiatives, final decisions, and budget allocations are made by district or provincial officials. Some other government agencies have occasional activities at the village level: the Land Development Department has carried out a soil survey of Ban Mai; the military hold occasional 'development' training programmes in both villages, the latest being the Army Reserve programme in Ban Dong and the National Defence Volunteers programme in Ban Mai; BAAC is the major institutional credit institution in both villages; and in Ban Mai, ALRO plays an important development role, both in land reform and in infrastructural development. Government is also active in road building and electrification, infrastructural development that affects both villages.[54]

The other side of this coin was the growth of a plethora of similarly intrusive but frequently oppositionist non-government organisations; by the end of the 1980s, there were more than 100 NGOs working on rural development projects in Thailand alone.

The tightening grip of government upon rural areas was felt not just in the rice heartlands but further out on the periphery, where states had previously done little. This development was expressed in two major and often interconnected ways. The first was the attempt to stabilise peripheral populations as permanent field cultivators and provide them with 'civilisation', something designed to make them more accessible to the state, to curtail the 'waste' and 'damage' caused by their swidden style of production, and to quarantine the environment for more productive purposes such as lumbering and hydroelectricity schemes.

The second was the movement into the periphery of large numbers of former lowlanders. In south Vietnam in the mid 1950s, for example, Ngo Dinh Diem attempted a heavy-handed assimilation of upland peoples into Vietnamese culture. He coupled this with efforts to colonise the highlands with Vietnamese immigrants (many of whom had fled from the north after the 1954 Geneva agreements) in order to develop the region and to assist in sedentarising its people. By 1960, over 60 000 settlers, mostly Vietnamese, had been settled in the upland regions. The problems generated by these policies were compounded by rebellion sprung from a violent ethnonationalist backlash, and the inclusion of the region in the wider war, involving troops and especially devastating American bombing. Uplanders became refugees in great numbers, moving away to escape the war or placed in resettlement camps; 'an estimated 200,000 highlanders died during the Vietnam War, and an estimated 85 percent of the villagers were forced, one way or another, to flee as refugees'.[55] After 1975, the consolidation of communist rule brought little change to the thrust of these old policies; like their predecessors, the communists wanted to settle the uplanders down, to 'civilise' them and to exploit their environment by moving large numbers of lowlanders – especially from Ho Chi Minh City – into special economic zones. In Laos in the 1960s and early 1970s, huge numbers of 'tribal' people – over half a million – were resettled into areas not under the control of the communist Pathet Lao. In Thailand, where uplanders had escaped taxation, conscription and registration, a Hill Tribes division of the Department of Public Welfare was established in 1959; its brief was to transform the 'tribes' into sedentary villagers and citizens of the Thai nation. The basic forestry law was amended in 1960 to limit swiddening to land already cleared or owned; as well, the government began establishing public services in the uplands, notably schools and health facilities, partly in response to fears about national security. By the mid 1980s, there were reportedly '168 various government agencies under 31 Departments as well as 49 international donor and non-government organisations conducting hill tribe and minority group development efforts'[56] in Thailand. Quite apart from these state-sponsored moves, there was increasing encroachment on upland areas by timber workers and road builders. In

Sarawak, the government established land settlement schemes to persuade the Iban to settle down as commercial rubber growers. To the Subanu people of Mindanao, the expansion of Christian settlements brought markets, schools, taxes, police, land laws, and new forms of local political organisation while, throughout the islands more generally, PANAMIN (the Presidential Arm for the Administration of National Minorities) sought to consolidate uplanders into sedentary farming communities.

The remainder of Southeast Asia throughout this period was driven along a revolutionary path. In Burma, following the army's final seizure of power in 1962, the state led its subjects into an extended period of quasi-socialist and highly nationalist self-seclusion – the period of the 'Burmese Way to Socialism' – and of state-strengthening. It nationalised all trade and managed it through a series of state enterprises (thereby stimulating an extensive black market), it abolished (unsuccessfully, as it turned out) private credit and, after 1973, peasants were required to fill government quotas on rice at a fixed and low price. The result, as far as rice production was concerned, was stagnation and decline. Peasants were at first effectively denied the high yielding varieties of their peers elsewhere in the region (Burma had only 7 per cent of its rice land in high-yielding varieties by 1974–5). They were also shackled by the wasteful and inefficient practices of the past, with most land in Lower Burma still only rainfed and much of it ecologically unsuited to short-strawed HYVs. These factors, together with peasants' easy access to unsupervised government credit, and their lack of incentive to produce for a government purchasing monopoly (something which seems to have led to a considerable return to broadcasting as a means of lowering costs) consolidated Burma's reputation for low rice productivity. The result, in a context where peasants could gain more by selling their crop to insurgents or black marketeers, or stockpiling it for domestic barter purchases, was an intensification in the decline in rice exports already evident in the 1950s, from 1.8 million tonnes in 1963 to 0.3 million tonnes in 1968. Only in the late 1980, as high yielding varieties began to spread, taking up just over half the rice area in the mid 1980s, and when government loosened its central controls on trade, did the situation show much improvement.

In socialist Vietnam, the path followed was one of agricultural collectivisation. On the heels of a programme first of rent reduction and then of land reform and the creation of peasant work-exchange arrangements, collectivisation began in 1958. Within two years, with great haste and little preparation, almost nine-tenths of the peasant population and 70 per cent of cultivated lands had been organised into cooperatives, mostly low-level ones; by 1971, 96 per cent of households were reportedly in cooperatives. The major incentive to join, apart from political pressure, was that state subsidies for basic goods needed by peasants was channelled through the cooperatives. However, peasants' incentive to produce – built around the earning of work points – remained low, and their attention disproportionately invested in the tiny tracts of land granted them by their cooperatives for their individual use, which provided them with more than half their household income. According to one account, 'most of the people involved were usually trying as best they could to get around the attempts of the government to make them do things they did not want to do'.[57] There were, as well, continuing problems in the administration and discipline of the cooperatives. Attempts to force cooperatives to deal directly with the state rather than participating in horizontal commercial interactions with each other usually failed. There were enduring difficulties, tensions and conflicts between the management committees of cooperatives and the brigades which actually carried out production.

Notwithstanding continuing efforts at reform, notably the 'New Management System' which emerged in 1975 and which gave much greater power to management committees over brigades, and despite the widespread introduction of high yielding rice varieties (31 per cent of total rice land was under the new varieties by 1975), by the late 1960s the DRV was not producing sufficient food to feed itself and relying on imports, notably from the Soviet Union. The cooperatives, in one view, were 'ex cathedra central government policy, justified by reference to historical necessity and inherent ethical value', rather than being based upon 'close attention to local variation and a respect for the incentives actually operating upon both immediate producers and producing organizations'.[58] Conflicts between state interests and those of the rural order were such that by the late 1970s the very programme of collectivisation was beginning to fray and then unravel, with peasants being allowed to farm 'idle land' individually. By 1981, a policy of decollectivisation was under way; the productive relationship between cooperative and producers was being expressed in terms of output contracts, whereby individual households provided the state with a contracted amount of rice produced on holdings allocated to them and were allowed to market any surplus freely. Further liberalisation in the direction of enhancing private landownership, production, labour contracting and marketing was undertaken in 1988, allowing peasants to dispose as they wish of their after-tax production and giving rise, not incidentally, to the redevelopment of significant inequalities in rural areas. These changes stimulated a rapid growth in production, from 14.4 million tonnes in 1980 to 18.2 million in 1985 – something unattainable under previous social conditions, notwithstanding the introduction of modern rice technologies – so that by 1989 Vietnam was once again a net exporter of rice: indeed, the world's third largest.

In the south of the country, meanwhile, the movement to collectivise agriculture had begun around 1976 and reached its apogee in 1978. But problems of administration and legitimacy, and massive non-compliance in Mekong delta regions – by 1986, only 6 per cent of farmers there were members of agricultural cooperatives – compounded by low official procurement prices, corruption and state attacks on private commerce, were even more serious than in the north, and resulted in a substantial decline in production. In 1979, the Sixth Plenum of the Communist Party Central Committee recommended a slowing of the pace and a new emphasis on family production. Land reform in the south was not carried through properly either. All these administrative and ideological difficulties, it needs to be said, were exacerbated by the presence and devastation of warfare: the absence on military service of males from villages, the bombing of the countryside which damaged irrigation systems, the ecological damage caused by the American policy of defoliation (of almost ten per cent of south Vietnam's area), the destruction of roads, and the salinisation of rice fields caused by the destruction of sea dykes.

In Laos, the movement into socialist agriculture was much more gentle, a result, perhaps, of the serious damage done to the economy by the flight of capital, entrepreneurs and merchants after the 1975 communist takeover and the subsequent prohibition on private commercial activity, and a reflection, too, of the relative weakness of the state to impose its will upon its subjects. At first, the formation of cooperatives was merely encouraged, so that by the end of 1976 low-level cooperatives boasted only a few thousand members, most of them in the zones which had been liberated before 1975. A collectivisation campaign begun in 1978 resulted only in disrupting production; as in Vietnam, the serious lack of incentives for those who had previously held land was a fatal flaw and led to their abandoning the cooperatives en masse, leaving them as organisations wholly dependent upon state largesse. The campaign was suspended in 1979, to be replaced by reforms of a more liberal character. Accordingly, the number of cooperatives fell by nearly half between 1979 and 1980, and private capitalist enterprise was accorded formal recognition; contracts rather than some form of compulsory sales to the state were regarded as the key economic link to the peasants. Cooperatives, then, 'quickly and easily dissolved back into peasant society'.[59] Unlike in Vietnam, state and party were never sufficiently strong to reach down effectively into the majority of villages and cooperatives; state managers and party cadres enjoyed no local power bases from which to coordinate and enforce their plans.

The most extreme example of the radical approach to development was that of Cambodia's Khmer Rouge regime. It came to power in 1975 following a period of civil war and prolonged American bombing of the countryside which had sent a considerable portion of the peasantry scurrying to the relative safety of Phnom Penh and other urban areas. Unfortunately, given what they had in mind, the leaders of the Khmer Rouge 'knew very little about "the people" and distrusted them en masse'.[60] A systematic inversion of old ways and values saw the creation of violence and chaos which destroyed the country. Ascribing the highest value to their conception of 'peasantness', and sure in the knowledge that the laws of history were on their side, they outlawed the use of money and the practice of religion, moved vast numbers of people (in the months after April 1975, between two and three million) from urban areas into the countryside, attacked any semblance of intellectual pretension, abolished postal services and newspapers, and forced everyone to wear peasant clothing and eat their meals in communal settings. Communes and work groups replaced villages, and property and labour were collectivised. Family ties and orientations were discouraged or destroyed. This intensely-driven state, guided by its belief in the superiority of revolutionary thinking over the old order of private acquisitiveness, imposed a regime of immediate food self-sufficiency, set fancifully high targets for rice production (so as to purchase the technology for industrialisation), and proceeded to minimise the possibility of attaining them through an ignorant commandism that, for example, saw fields aligned in exact squares to replicate the pattern of the state's coat of arms, never mind topographical considerations. There were attempts to provide double cropping through the construction of dams and irrigation works, but the central strategy for increasing rice production involved mobile production brigades as well as forcing people to work unprecedentedly long hours in the fields.

With the defeat of the Khmer Rouge forces by the invading Vietnamese in 1979, many peasants returned to their villages to find devastation; there were no draught animals, seed stocks or even tools; many males had disappeared during the years of turmoil. In the main harvest of that year, only 700 000 hectares, less than a third of the 1960s level, of rice land was planted, and the product, 285 000 tonnes, was just one-fifth of 1960s levels. The result was a thoroughgoing famine, said to have cost half a million lives. The Vietnamese-backed People's Republic of Kampuchea returned the village to its erstwhile position, abolished communes and mobile work teams, and permitted, alongside gentler forms of collective agriculture, private production and commerce. By the mid and late 1980s, social and economic reform allowed for the private tenure of land and encouraged a broader practice of private commerce and rice production again approached levels of self-sufficiency. Nonetheless, the legacy of war – social dislocation, large areas mined, the destruction of irrigation systems, continuing insurgency – were hefty impediments to further progress.

POPULATION GROWTH AND MOVEMENT

As we have seen, the context for peasant livelihood was profoundly shaped by the development of new kinds of state power and new ideas about how that power should be exercised, all in a context of the region's ever firmer and broader incorporation into global trade. But a transformation of similarly monumental proportions, as far as the peasantry was concerned, was the rapid and sustained rise of population. While there are many substantial difficulties in arriving at accurate notions of the population of Southeast Asia around 1800, the figures we have, in some cases illuminated and cleaned by scholarly insight and perspiration, give us a good sense of orders of magnitude.

Even in the early nineteenth century, the population in some parts of lowland Southeast Asia was already growing rapidly. This was perhaps most notably the case in lowland Java where, from around the middle of the eighteenth century, the establishment of a peace of hitherto unknown dimension and duration, the relative absence of serious epidemics, and a period of unusual prosperity and economic expansion saw the beginnings of a era of burgeoning of population. Similarly, in that other area of the region where population was, in relative terms, already thickly concentrated, the Red River delta, population began to grow at a faster rate than hitherto, so that by the first decades of the twentieth century it was already 'saturated with humanity',[61] with rural population densities as high as 1650 people per square kilometre in 1931.

Elsewhere, the rate of population growth did not begin to climb until the first few decades of the nineteenth century. On the eve of Luzon's nineteenth-century economic transformation, the population of the central plain was only about 139 000, with less than 8000 people in the upper reaches of Pampanga. In the century after 1818, however, the population of the Philippines overall grew from 2 026 230 to 10 314 300, and between 1918 and 1975 to 42 070 660, with the rate of growth increasing steadily all the while. Much the same story of rapid and escalating growth could be told about the Central Plain in Thailand, while in Cambodia in the late 1960s the population continued to increase, notwithstanding stagnant rice production. Robequain estimated that the population of Cochinchina grew by about 60 000 each year between 1913 and 1929, two-thirds of which he attributed to natural increase.[62] The population of what is now West Malaysia grew from 2.4 million in 1911 to 6.8 million in 1970. In Laos, continual population growth meant a 50 per cent increase in the average size of villages over the first half of the twentieth century.

Rapid and continuing population growth in upland areas was a much later development – for the most part becoming noticeable only in the twentieth century – perhaps because it was only around the turn of the twentieth century that state power imposed a measure of peace and, often, sedentary modes of existence in these peripheral places. But once growth had begun, it continued unrelentingly and at high rates. Between 1947 and 1970, for example, the population of Thailand's seven northernmost provinces grew from just over 2 million to 3.8 million; by contrast, in the ten years before 1947 the annual average rate of growth had been just 0.4 per cent. In both uplands and especially lowlands, efforts to restrict family size enjoyed encouraging success, but the age structure of populations ensured a continuing growth in population over coming decades even through growth rates showed signs of falling.

The reasons for the high and continuing rates of population growth in Southeast Asia remain a matter of controversy. But it seems likely that the initial stages of growth everywhere were prompted by the imposition of enduring peace and stability on an ever widening scale by the new states which developed through the nineteenth century; stability and the ending or recurrent warfare lowered mortality and allowed a normally high rate of fertility – in a context where labour was scarce and land was regarded essentially as a free good – to remain virtually unchecked. The lowered mortality provided by peace was enhanced only later – notably in the decades after World War II – by improvements in environmental conditions, especially sanitation, more widely available and effective health care, improvements in the specific prevention of disease, notably the use of drugs, and in communications. In Thailand, for example, malaria was virtually eliminated from the lowlands in the 1950s, while diseases such as malaria, cholera, whooping cough, tetanus and smallpox were successfully combated in the uplands. In addition, there were improvements in mortality rates flowing from generally improving standards of living resulting from crop commercialisation, and perhaps in fertility as well. As a consequence, 'national crude death rates fell by an average of close to 20 per thousand in the four decades following the war, as annual population growth rates climbed to rates unprecedented in human history'.[63] The late conversion of many Southeast Asian states to fertility control programmes eventually began to affect rates of population growth, but

Table 2.1 Southeast Asia's population, c. 1800–1990 (thousands)

	1800	*1850*	*1880*	*1900*	*1930*	*1960*	*1990*
Burma	4 600		9 129*(a)*	10 491*(b)*	14 667*(c)*	25 886*(d)*	35 308*(e)*
Laos (incl. NE Thailand)	1 200						
Laos					944*(c)*	2 177	4 202
Siam (minus NE)	2 800						
Siam/Thailand		5 500	6 200	7 320	11 506*(f)*	26 258	54 532
Cambodia-Champa	1 500						
Cambodia			1 100*(g)*	1 500	2 806*(c)*	4 740*(h)*	6 682*(i)*
Vietnam (north and centre)	7 000			11 409*(j)*	12 447*(k)*		
Vietnam (south)			1 679	2 969*(b)*	4 417*(c)*	15 917	
Vietnam				14 378*(l)*	16 864*(c)*	30 172	64 412*(m)*
Malaya (incl. Pattani)	500						
Malaya				2 339*(n)*	3 788*(c)*	6 279*(o)*	
Malaysia						7 908*(p)*	17 567*(q)*
Brunei				22*(n)*	30*(c)*	84	261*(q)*
Sumatra	3 500			4 500	8 255	15 739*(r)*	36 507
Java	5 000			29 000	41 718	62 993*(r)*	107 581
Borneo	1 000			1 300	2 169	4 101*(r)*	9 100
Sulawesi	1 800			2 500	4 232	7 079*(r)*	12 521

	1800	*1850*	*1880*	*1900*	*1930*	*1960*	*1990*
Bali	700			800	1 101	1 783(*r*)	2 778
Lesser Sunda islands	900			1 400	2 359	3 775(*r*)	7 386
Maluku	400			500	893	848(*r*)	1 858
Irian Jaya						700(*r*)	1 649
Indonesia				40 150	60 727	97 019(*s*)	179 379
Philippines	1 835	3 858(*t*)	6 174(*u*)	7 635(*v*)	15 984(*w*)	27 088	60 685
Total	32 735						423 028

(a) 1881; (b) 1901; (c) 1931; (d) 1973; (e) 1983; (f) 1929; (g) 1875; (h) 1958; (i) 1981; (j)1906; (k) 1931–2; (l) 1901, 1906; (m) 1989; (n) 1911; (o) 1957; (p) includes 1957 figures for Malaya; (q) 1991; (r) 1961; (s) estimate for 1961; (t) presumably 'Christians'; (u) 1876; (v) 1903; (w) 1939.

Rounding and omission of small territories mean that columns do not always add correctly.

Sources: Reid, *Southeast Asia*, vol. 1, p. 14; J. Russell Andrus, *Burmese economic life* (Stanford: Stanford University Press, 1948), pp. 22–3; Ng Shui Meng, *The population of Indochina* (Singapore: ISEAS, 1974), pp. 30–6; David Feeny, *The political economy of productivity: Thai agricultural development, 1880–1975* (Vancouver: University of British Columbia Press, 1982), p. 147; Adas, *Burma delta*, p. 42; Jean Delvert, *Le paysan cambodgien* (Paris: Mouton, 1961), p. 434; B.R. Mitchell, *International Historical Statistics: Africa and Asia* (New York: New York University Press, 1982), pp. 43–7; Graeme J. Hugo et al., *The demographic dimension in Indonesian development* (Singapore: Oxford University Press, 1987), pp. 31, 42–3; Charles P. Trumbull (ed.), *Britannica Book of the Year 1995* (Chicago: Encyclopaedia Britannica, 1995), pp. 630, 764–9; personal communication from Norman G. Owen.

the impetus provided by squat age pyramids ensured that growth would continue well into the twenty-first century.

To natural population growth must also be added the effects of the movement of peoples on a large scale into areas that were still only sparsely inhabited. Sometimes these were on a scale that had no immediate or even medium-term impact. The movement of tribal peoples southwards from 'China' into the hilly country of Burma and Thailand was one example; thus, Tibeto-Burman peoples such as the Lisu, Lahu, and Akha, as well as the Hmong and Yao from southern China, apparently began to enter Thailand around 150 years ago. The Hmong, inhabitants of Thailand for around a century, continued to move in a spreading southerly direction. Similar movements were evident in the modern era; the Haw, for example, took flight from Yunnan in the early 1950s, moving first into Burma, and then into Thailand by the mid 1950s. As uplanders grew in numbers, they moved to new and virtually uninhabited areas, and increasingly into the lowlands as well. Movements of much greater dimensions than these, however, were to be found in the lowlands of Southeast Asia. I have already noted the great procession of people from the northern region of Ilocos into the central Luzon plain, notably into what was to become Nueva Ecija, beginning a process of migration and colonisation that was to last for more than a century after 1815. Similarly, as the population in Thailand's Central Plain grew relentlessly, many peasants moved to the regions of the north to seek a better life, and those in the lowlands began even to penetrate into the highlands in search of land. The same pattern of spreading, swelling populations was in evidence everywhere.

CONCLUSION

All these developments, notably the emergence of stronger and more determinate states, the integration of massively enhanced small-scale production into huge and integrated international markets, and the extraordinary growth of populations, combined to create something quite new in Southeast Asia's history, a vast society of petty cultivating rural inhabitants who pushed out the frontiers and spread themselves inexorably across the previously empty landscape and who themselves became the defining characteristic of the region.

What this amounted to was no less than the effective creation of a dominant and (from the point of view of the state) more clearly defined and controlled Southeast Asian peasantry. By the turn of the twentieth century – the heyday of peasant production in Southeast Asia – the human and natural ecology of the region had been definitively transformed, and with it the essential economy of the region. Where trade, especially in precious commodities, had been the foundation of the old age of commerce and had provided the conditions for a heavily urbanised region where large-scale production was limited to a few discrete parcels of territory, international commerce now fed upon the expansive activities of millions of Southeast Asian peasants, producing mammoth quantities of rice, sugar, rubber, tobacco, abaca and numerous other primary export items on small farms for consumption both in Europe and in Asia. However, the essential nature of peasant production and peasant life remained. Notwithstanding that peasants, now in great numbers and often in vast, newly-tamed locations, produced huge surpluses for the international market, their primary social and productive orientation remained local, rural and directly self-providing; their productive activities in the service of international commerce remained ancillary. Indeed, the states of the region did all they could, for their own reasons, to confirm and endorse this identity.

It was paradoxical but inevitable, however, that the combination of forces that had created the social and economic ascendancy of the Southeast Asian peasantry by the early decades of the twentieth century – the waxing state, the ever more consuming reach of international capital and commerce, and the undeniable trajectory of demographics – were already at work to destroy the social formation they had conspired to create and enhance.

3 The Changing Varieties of Peasant Production

Around the turn of the nineteenth century, the productive activities of Southeast Asia's peasants were limited in scope, output volume and specialisation by low market demand, relative isolation, poor infrastructures, and simple technologies. Much the greater part of what they produced was aimed at meeting their own subsistence requirements, and the methods of production they employed were primarily geared to that end. Over the succeeding two centuries, however, the transformative potencies of state strengthening, global commerce and demography wrought change – sometimes elaborative, sometimes gradual, more recently radical and rapid – to peasants' productive patterns. This chapter seeks to describe and explain the evolving varieties of productive arrangements to which Southeast Asia's peasants, under the impact of new demands and restraints, resorted over the long stretch of these years.

MARKETS, STATES, DEMOGRAPHY, COMMERCIALISATION AND GROWTH

The political and economic changes of the nineteenth century linked the region, directly and indirectly, to a new kind of world economy which thirsted for regular supplies of bulk foods and stimulants and, later, timber and industrial raw materials, all of which Southeast Asia, with its natural environment and population, was well-positioned to provide. The new order, as well, sometimes created new specialisations and markets within the region itself; in Malaya, for example, the development of mines and plantations occasioned the massing of large numbers of non-food producing labourers who had to be fed; on a much less substantial scale, the growth of the teak extraction industry in northern Siam similarly promoted the partial commercialisation of rice production to feed those involved. In mid nineteenth century Java, local rice deficits resulting from the compulsory production of export crops were made good by imports of foodstuffs from elsewhere in the island. In east Sumatra, the demands of plantations for nipa shingles for tobacco barns saw coastal peasants clearing mangrove swamps and growing nipa palm to fill the need. Infrastructural improvements within each country, as well as burgeoning links across and beyond the region as a whole, also contributed to a growing commercialisation. Markets, of course, meant incomes for producers, partly devoted to acquiring some of the vast range of consumer goods which international trade suddenly made available and partly to meeting the demands of the more intrusively effective taxing power of expanding states. Both were incentives to increase production and to direct a greater proportion of output towards the market.

The desire of governments to enhance and control domestic food production led them increasingly to intervene in production; the Dutch in west Sumatra, for instance, introduced timetables in the mid nineteenth century to ensure all cultivable land was planted, and planted simultaneously.[1] In the face of all these seductions and pressures to promote production and surplus, peasants moved more and more into a world where commerce was central rather than peripheral or episodic and where expanding production was directly translatable into personal reward. As well, the expanding contours of peasant production were in part a response to the accelerating growth of population which had began in lowland sites from the later eighteenth century. Demographic enlargement, as I have noted, served not only to increase the volume of production but helped to contrive a new pattern of rural social and economic organisation, with vast numbers of small peasant farms proliferating across the landscape, employing the great proportion of the region's economically active population. Twentieth-century labour force statistics from Indonesia, for example, indicate that the proportion of agricultural workers of the total labour force remained at around 70 per cent until the 1960s, and the proportion was almost certainly a little higher in the nineteenth century. As late as 1950, nearly 90 per cent of Thailand's labour force was engaged in agriculture. In sum, the direction of this combination of forces was a prodigious increase in the volume of agricultural production, an enhancement of the specialisation with which peasant agriculture was practised, and a much more compelling enmeshment of peasants in commerce.

SPATIAL EXPANSION OF THE LOWLANDS: THE DEVELOPMENT OF A FRONTIER SOCIETY

The lowland wet-rice field, while contained for the most part to tightly localised settings, was a major site of peasant production in early nineteenth century Southeast Asia. Over the succeeding two centuries, the sites and practice of peasant wet-rice production changed radically. For the greater part of the period, change expressed itself in the simple – but extraordinary – extension of cropping across the valley floors of Southeast Asia: the gradual reclamation of the eastern and western salients of Java, the settlement of the central plain of Luzon, the clearing of forest land along river valleys in the Malay peninsula, the expansion of the cultivated area in the north Thailand plain, to name just a few examples. The outstanding cases of this momentous process, of course, were to be found in the Central Plain of Thailand, the Irrawaddy delta region and the trans-Bassac in Cochinchina. In these places, as I have already noted, lateral development involved the reclamation of forest, scrub and swamp to make sites amenable to the cultivation of wet-rice, fed by rainfall (as in Lower Burma and Cochinchina) and by flood (as in Thailand). What developed were endless panoramas of fields devoted to rice, to the virtual exclusion of other forms of field agriculture. Up to 1914, in the words of one writer, 'the period of expansion . . . is characterized by a steady cash demand, at constant or rising prices, for a seemingly infinite amount of rice, to be grown on seemingly unlimited land'.[2] Burma's obsession with rice was such that in 1940 two-thirds of the country's arable land was planted to rice, four-fifths of which was located in the delta area. Through this process, Lower Burma took shape as a very different and more highly specialised society from Upper Burma whose productive diversity ensured it a 'more constant economy'.[3] In the three decades after 1870, the rice area of Lower Burma expanded at an average rate of 4 per cent. The picture in Siam's Central Plain and in southern Cochinchina was similar: the relentless establishment of rice monoculture on flat landscapes stretching forever into the distance.

The process of lateral expansion of wet-rice cultivation expressed so spectacularly here was paced differently across the region, depending upon the press of population, state policy or the attractiveness and availability of markets. It usually involved peasants leaving those old core pockets of wet-rice growing which were themselves often equipped with year-round irrigation facilities or at least the means for regular and predictable cropping, and encroaching, step-wise, on the frontier. In Kedah, for example, the canals developed by the indigenous administration after 1870 (notably the Wan Mat Saman canal) 'became the baselines from which pioneering peasants moved out to reclaim the swamps; and each of these became the baseline from which subsidiary canals were constructed making more areas of swamp accessible'.[4] In their new sites, peasant pioneers moved through a rapid cycle of evolution of productive technique from dry-land farming to bunded wet-rice cultivation, often employing a mix of techniques in the process as occasion allowed or dictated. Thus, according to Bowring's description of the Philippines, 'the sowing of the dry rice usually precedes

Table 3.1 Expansion of rice areas ('000 ha.) and rice exports ('000 tonnes) in Lower Burma, Siam's Central Plain and Cochinchina, c. 1850–1940

Year	*Lower Burma*		*Siam's Central Plain*		*Cochinchina*	
	area under rice	*rice exports(a)*	*area under rice*	*rice exports*	*area under rice*	*rice exports*
1850						
1855	402			59(*b*)		
1860	539			110	215	57
1865	658			98		
1870	795			112		
1875	1 094	693		212	349(*c*)	
1880	1 377	812		215	522	284
1885	1 623	965		319	743	
1890	1 969	1 002		435	854	439
1895	2 333	1 250		480	1 026	525
1900	2 765	1 522		668	1 174	719
1905	3 048	1 976	1 088	885	1 407	495
1910	3 247	2 093	1 152	913	1 528	1 003
1915	3 384	2 009	1 312	947	1 766	
1920	3 607	2 103	1 536	1 061	1 752	840
1925	3 878	2 450	1 744	1 403	1 880	935
1930	3 933	2 732	1 888	1 543	2 214	804
1935	3 992	3 058	1 920	1 522		1 530
1940	4 019	2 934	2 256	795	2 300	1 467

(a) rice exports for Burma as a whole; (b) 1857–9; (c) 1879

Source: Cheng Siok-Hwa, *The rice industry of Burma: 1852–1940* (Kuala Lumpur: University of Malaya Press, 1968), p. 25; Aye Hlaing, 'Trends of economic growth and income distribution in Burma', *JBRS* 47 (1964), p. 95; James C. Ingram, *Economic change in Thailand 1850–1970* (Stanford: Stanford University Press, 1971), pp. 38, 44; Robert L. Sansom, *The economics of insurgency in the Mekong delta of Vietnam* (Cambridge, Mass.: MIT Press, 1970), pp. 258–62. For the years 1865–1935, the data provided for Lower Burma's rice area and exports refer to the average for a five year period; for example, 1865 refers to the period 1865–9; the same applies to the statistics for Siam from 1860 which, for example, refers to the years 1860–4.

that of the water rice, and takes place at the end of May. It is usually broadcast on the hills, requires to be hoed and weeded, and is ripened in from three to four months and a half. It is harvested ear by ear'.[5] Indeed, in areas of relatively small or slowly-growing populations such as the lowlands of Laos, this mixing of cropping systems endured into the modern period, beginning to decline in the region around Vientiane when, finally, even that frontier began to close and areas which had been used for dry rice cultivation began to be taken up for wet rice.[6] For the most part, however, the bounty that fed peasants (and the export trade) came from lowland fields inundated by seasonal rain or flood, and which produced but one crop (rice) a year.

THE TECHNOLOGY OF LOWLAND EXPANSION

At its most intense, the work of the rice peasant in such sites was gruelling, but the production technique simplicity itself. The reclamation of rice land from Lower Burma's swampy forests was 'a monument to the sustained effort of millions of peasants working only with bullocks or buffaloes and the simple, locally-made ploughs and implements they had evolved in their own way over the centuries'.[7] The technological bareness of the process was reflected in the words of a foreign observer of Siam's development: 'when a system of irrigation is properly developed, and there are further facilities for communication, especially by canal, the wealth of Siam from this source [rice production] will receive a still further increase'.[8]

In Siam, the simplicity of method was exaggerated by the common practice of seed broadcasting rather than the transplanting in evidence in most other places. The practice sprang in the first place from the undeveloped nature of the environment of much of the floodplain north of Bangkok. The short period of time between the first rains which softened the soil for ploughing and the arrival of rapidly swelling floodwaters was insufficient to allow for the growth and transplanting of seedlings; moreover there was no way to control the rapid rise of water levels between October and November with the precision required for transplanted rice, nor to provide a continuing water supply through the season. Much of the rice planted was perforce floating rice, which demanded broadcasting. Accordingly, peasants simply broadcast their seeds on the ploughed fields, even though many had been accustomed to transplanting in the regions from which they had migrated, a turn of events somewhat perversely described by one writer as 'the only important technical innovation made by

Thai farmers during this period'.[9] There were other forces at play as well in the choice of this technique. The first was an initial shortage of labour as well as a continuing one of capital. Transplanting, with its investments in seedbed construction, transplanting, water control, irrigation facility construction and maintenance, and weeding was much more expensive in labour and capital than broadcasting, which required no weeding or irrigation maintenance. A final reason contributing to the popularity of broadcasting – and perhaps the most important given the general trends of declining real wages and rising rice and land prices – was the insecurity of tenancy and the absentee nature of landlordism on the frontier, notably at Rangsit, which encouraged low capital risk. Notwithstanding that transplanted rice was less wasteful of seed, easier to harvest, capable of fertilisation and more predictable and productive, 'broadcasting was the economically preferable, rather than simply the easier, mode of cultivation'.[10] Accordingly, in the early 1920s, around 70 per cent of the rice harvested in the Central Plain came from broadcast seed. Aside from a brief period during the Depression when some peasants attempted to take advantage of very cheap and abundant labour to increase yields (and thus compensate for much lowered prices) by converting to the transplanting technique, broadcasting retained its importance in the region until the end of the 1960s when major irrigation works brought greater regularity to water control. Elsewhere in Thailand, where this constellation of conditions did not obtain, transplanting remained supreme; thus, 'only a negligible portion of the north-eastern rice fields are sown by broadcasting seed'.[11]

Apart from its technological simplicity, a second notable feature of this expansion of rice cropping was its enduring fixity. While frontiers remained for further reclamation, and while the prices peasants gained for their produce remained sufficiently high and wages sufficiently low to allow producers to turn a profit without considering efforts to raise the productivity of labour, there was, of course, no need to develop newer ways of proceeding. States, like peasants, felt little temptation to improve things. Most failed to invest significant sums in technological improvement, especially in irrigation. Thus, in west Sumatra, 'the Dutch made no direct engineering investment in irrigation during the nineteenth century .... All planning, construction, operation, and maintenance of irrigation systems was left in the hands of the farmers themselves,'[12] while in the Philippines, some notable exceptions to one side, irrigation was 'almost unknown'[13] until about 1850, and the country had to wait until the early 1950s for significant and rapid growth in irrigation facilities.

Technological stagnation was evident in other spheres as well. As I have already noted, efforts by government instrumentalities before World War II to improve seed varieties and distribute them widely were limited. Equally important, peasants made little use of fertiliser, apart from the custom of burning off or ploughing in stubble from the previous crop; 'throughout the [Philippine] Islands rice lands in general receive no more fertilizer than that which nature gives them'.[14] In some places peasants used manure for seedbeds or house gardens but not on their fields; elsewhere, the droppings of cattle (sometimes, as in Kelantan, mixed with coconuts and areca nuts), chickens and ducks, gathered from under the houses where these animals congregated, and even bat guano, were applied to fields, but often only sparsely, irregularly and casually. For the most part, however, fields were left fallow in the dry season so that they could regain fertility; according to one account 'the exposure of the soil to the air and sun allows bacterial action to go on'.[15] There was in any case no large supply of natural fertiliser; Lower Burma, for instance, had few cattle and no horses. And, until the 1960s and 1970s, the use of commercial fertiliser of any kind was virtually unknown, and peasants used no inorganic fertilisers at all. Only in north Vietnam does human nightsoil seem to have been employed; it was collected and applied with a care that verged on scrupulosity; its value was sufficient to support a village of manure scavengers near Hanoi who collected nightsoil, mixed it with earth and sold it to villagers within a wide radius. Peasants in northern Vietnam also used green manure (azolla) in their fields, especially those expected to provide two crops a year. Lowland Southeast Asian peasants clearly knew the benefits of fertilising; their reluctance to use it was in some places a result of environmental conditions such as the flood fields of the Central Plain of Thailand, but elsewhere and more important because they judged its inflexible input cost too high in a context of uncertain returns. By the 1930s, a pioneering study of rice cultivation claimed that 'much of the paddy land of Burma, Thailand, Indo-china and British Malaya has lost its original fertility. Little or no manure or fertilizer is applied to the paddy crop in these countries, and no system of crop rotation is practised on an important scale'.[16]

The result of this enduring primitiveness, rational and appropriate as it was in the circumstances, was that in most places growth in production resulted purely from the huge lateral expansion of the cropping area which, in Thailand for example, grew in at a rate of around 3 per cent per annum in the period 1913–75. Similarly in the Philippines, 'the expansion of cultivated area . . . provided the major source of the production growth of Philippine agriculture . . . at least up to the 1950s'.[17] The rice yields of Cochinchina saw no sign of increase through the colonial period; indeed, they were lower than in any comparable rice producing centre worldwide. Where the scope for simple lateral expansion began to falter, and where water control systems began to deteriorate through siltation and lack of maintenance, the result was productive stagnation or, as in the case of Thailand through the 1920s and 1930s, a significant fall in rice yields.

Notwithstanding the extraordinary development in lateral cropping, the incentives provided by states and markets and the impulse created by population pressure to its practice were not always and everywhere operative, nor operative to the same degree. In Malaya, for example, as I have already indicated, for most of the early decades of the twentieth century the colonial government was content to rely on cheap overseas rice grown in nearby countries and provided few pressures or incentives for Malay rice producers to increase their production to help meet the country's labourers' need for rice. Elsewhere, markets operated inefficiently and infrastructure was poorly developed; thus Lao lowland peasants found little attraction in producing at more than subsistence levels, and urban dwellers in Vientiane and Luang Prabang were dependent upon Thailand for the rice they needed. In other places, colonial governments imposed the forced cultivation of non-staple export crops and opposed, purposely and otherwise, commercial rice growing. We have, for example, already noted in west Sumatra the ban imposed by the Dutch on rice exports in the late nineteenth century, meant to stiffen peasants' resolve to plant coffee for delivery to the government, which saw rice production decline in coffee areas and fields abandoned in places outside them. And, as we have already seen, the period of warfare and occupation in the early 1940s was severely disruptive to food production, what with forced deliveries of rice, the absence of male labourers, off fighting or working as virtual slaves, and the failure to maintain irrigation systems.

SPATIAL EXPANSION: INTO THE UPLANDS

We have seen that as part of the process of lowland expansion, settled valley rice farmers commonly employed subsidiary swidden cultivation in the forested areas close by their ricefields; in Perak in 1930, almost one-third of the rice area was cultivated under a swidden format. With the passage of time and the lumping of populations, such subsidiary cultivation declined as swidden areas were brought under more intensive and permanent forms of cultivation. But in some lowland sites where resources were coming under ever greater strain as available frontiers closed, pressure was mounting to find new fields of exploitation. Notwithstanding its salvific benefits for rice production (which we shall presently explore), agricultural technology often did not save enough land, or save it quickly enough, to prevent proliferating lowland farmers from expanding productive activities into new and unfamiliar environments. Peasants' use of nearby uplands had long been a feature of their productive systems; thus, some peasants in the lower Tonkin delta put higher land to cotton in the dry season, and harvested it at the onset of the rainy season, while Bikolanos grew abaca on the well-drained slopes of southeastern Luzon. But as population grew inexorably in the lowlands, the pattern of lowland exploitation of higher lands became much more pronounced. In Java, dryland cultivation, mostly in the uplands, developed steadily through the nineteenth century and accelerated towards its end, so that by 1920 there were 3.3 million hectares of land under dryfield cultivation, most of it in upland rice but also producing cassava and maize. The result, somewhat paradoxically, was that the proportion of land under sawah in the twentieth century was much lower than it had been through much of the nineteenth century, with dry fields and house gardens today comprising more than half Java's cultivated land.

More recently, the process was perhaps most notable in postwar northern Thailand, where lowland farmers, pressed ever more tightly by rapidly rising numbers, shrinking farm size and declining agrarian resources, and with little alternative employment available, began in increasing numbers – said to number a quarter of a million – to encroach upon the slopes and practise swidden cultivation. Swidden, for them, was usually a supplement to their livelihood, but a most crucial one, nonetheless; 'the great majority of them have no choice but to cultivate a swidden to produce what they can, usually rice for partial subsistence at least'.[18] Their encroachment on the uplands gave them access to land which was otherwise unavailable to them. These 'reluctant swiddeners'[19] cultivated crops like rice (available earlier than lowland rice) for their own subsistence, as well as vegetables, maize, tobacco, soybeans, and peanuts as cash crops, prompted by spiralling demands for such crops from population centres and their ability to meet that demand through the existence of improved transport infrastructures. In some villagers, local pressure on resources was such that some peasants moved as much as a hundred kilometres away and began swiddening on neighbouring slopes. Lowlanders also took to the hills as collectors rather than swiddeners, notably in the *miang* (pickled tea) industry of northern Thailand; living in small hamlets scattered through the rugged hills, they picked and processed tea from the naturally occurring miang groves. The miang industry was 'a magnificent opportunity to redeem a secure and respected place in lowland society',[20] providing some peasants with the income they needed to purchase lowland paddy fields. In Laos, lowland farmers were wont to use upland swidden for periods of three to five years, sometimes in a supplementary mode to lowland farming, sometimes not. In the Philippines, too, lowlanders moved inexorably into upland regions to practise swiddening, creating a source of potential conflict with upland groups over the use of resources, forcing uplanders to move, at least partially, to permanent-field cultivation, and sometimes provoking them to other responses; Ilongot resistance to the encroachment of lowland Christians into the Sierra Madre in the later 1930s saw around thirty settlers killed.

The task of upland exploitation was facilitated by the accelerating commercialisation of upland areas for timber extraction and mining; by opening up these previously isolated regions, these industries were the thin end of the wedge for subsequent penetration by lowlanders. The result of lowlander farming in dry upland environments was nearly always environmentally damaging; characteristically their farming practices – sometimes resulting in the shortening of the swidden cycle to one crop in three years – usually left the land exhausted and prey to weed invasion, while they themselves moved on to exploit new sites. And, of course, it could also be devastating not just to the environment but to the upland peoples themselves: 'according to popular sources, about 14 000 Negritos inhabited Panay in 1849. But by 1900 there were less than a thousand Negritos, and today only a "handful" of uncertain ethnicity remains'.[21]

INTENSIFICATION OF LAND USE

Spatial expansion of productive activity was just one aspect of the elaboration of agriculture in this age of the peasantry. The second aspect was the development of more intensive modes of cropping. For much of the period since 1800, the characteristic feature of lowland wet-rice cultivation in Southeast Asia was the wet season cropping of rain- or flood-watered fields. The lateral expansion I have already described was, indeed, no more than a spatial elaboration of this simple technique. Authorities often claimed that more intensive cropping would damage the soil, as well as being of dubious economic benefit. Accordingly, the great rice deltas were cropped just once a year, while in Malaya, rice double cropping was a practice 'unknown before the [Second World] War'.[22] and, indeed, off-season cropping of any kind was most unusual thereafter.

Some limited areas, as we have seen, notably the volcanic valleys of south central Java, the Tonkin delta of northern Vietnam and the core region of the Burma Dry Zone, had long enjoyed the facilities for double- and second-cropping. Raffles, for example, had remarked of Java that 'such is the fertility of the soil, that in some places after yielding two, or sometimes three crops in the year, it is not necessary even to change the culture'.[23] As a result of further improvement – and considerable government investment – in irrigation facilities in Java from round the turn of the twentieth century and thereafter, the cropping ratio [that is, the area harvested as a percentage of the available area] increased from 103 per cent in 1900 to 147 per cent in 1940; by the late 1930s, nearly two-thirds of Java's wet-rice fields were served, at least partly, by 'technical' irrigation systems. In the Tonkin delta, according to Gourou, 'just about all lands bear two crops per year, so that there is not a moment in the year when some kind of agricultural work is not going on'.[24] 'Few are the lands', he went on, 'which bear only a single crop: major river bed lands, where the summer flood stops all work; high rice fields with soil so poor that a dry-season crop would not pay; middling high rice fields with a soil too argillaceous to support dry crops and which cannot be irrigated to grow a fifth-month rice crop; low rice fields inundated all summer. On all the rest of the Delta at least two crops are grown, either two rice crops, or a dry crop and a rice crop; but sometime three crops are raised . . . and in exceptional cases four crops'.[25] He estimated that of the 1 100 000 hectares of rice fields in the delta, 500 000 of them were double cropped in rice,[26] and 'that secondary crops occupy a maximum of 250 000 hectares: 100 000 hectares of cultivated lands where rice is not grown . . . 150 000 hectares of rice fields occupied by dry crops in the dry season'.[27]

Apart from these places, however, and with a few other exceptions, intensified rice double-cropping or second cropping of other produce following wet season rice was not possible. Notwithstanding its fabled fertility, some parts of Java remained significantly dependent on dry field cropping in the second half of the nineteenth century – the regions of Pacitan and southern Banten were perhaps the most important examples – and the greater part of the island's rice crop before the turn of the century was grown on rain-fed sawah which was unsuitable for double or second cropping. In Vietnam, there was hardly any double cropping outside the region of the Tonkin delta until after the end of World War II. In addition to the problem of water supply and control, there were other inhibitions to double cropping; one was that there was often insufficient time to prepare the land properly and plant and harvest two separate rice crops; another, already noted, was the belief that uninterrupted rice cropping depleted the land for subsequent crops.

In the two decades after the end of World War II, there were some improvements in the area of irrigation which led to an intensification of cultivation. In Malaya, for example, irrigation facilities in some regions such as Sungei Kulim were improved and expanded to allow for a greater incidence in double cropping; by the mid 1960s around one-tenth of Malaya's rice area was double cropped. In west Sumatra after 1950, limited irrigation enhancement saw the transformation of a marginal amount of rainfed sawah into irrigated sawah. But many places could not boast even this modest development. In the early 1950s in central Luzon, there was insufficient irrigation to allow the 'great majority of farmers' to cultivate second crops.[28] This deficiency was a major reason why rice yields in the Philippines remained stubbornly fixed at approximately 1.2 tonnes per hectare in the period from early 1920s until towards the end of the 1950s. In southern Vietnam, remarked Gourou, 'the Cochinchinese rice fields are for the greater part flooded by rain water impounded by the field dikes; they receive no other irrigation. Irrigation would be of service only if it were desirable to have a harvest during the dry season'.[29] There was, consequently, no dry season cropping in villages like Khanh Hau, although 'part of the village land [could] produce two crops of rice a year'[30] by capitalising on early rains. In Laos, lowland peasants could grow only one rice crop a year. In north-eastern Malaya, wet-rice cultivation remained reliant on seasonal rainfall, and peasants employed permanent lowland dry rice cultivation on a large scale.[31] Rice productivity in Thailand after the turn of twentieth century went into a period of gradual decline, partly, as already noted, from the failure to invest in irrigation technology to unlock the potential for second cropping on the Central Plain and partly, too, because cultivation was expanded beyond the prime rice-growing areas into more problematic and marginal ones. As late as 1980, 90 per cent of Thailand's total cultivated area remained without irrigation; in 1985, only 16 per cent of the country's 24.3 million hectares of cultivated land were subject to irrigation and the remainder depended directly upon rainfall.

The rate of change in the intensification of land use began to accelerate from the 1960s. In retrospect, the major reason for the extraordinary development to follow was that throughout the region the limits of lateral expansion in peasant agriculture had finally been reached. In Java, for example, the area harvested in rice between 1953 and 1963 fluctuated between a low of 3.65 million hectares and a high of 4.39 million hectares; the corresponding figures for the regions outside Java were 2.38 million hectares and 3.19 million hectares. The general tendency for rice production and yields showed a similar flatness. There and elsewhere, the age of frontier expansion which had transformed the landscape, sustained lowland peasant agriculture and the export markets it served, and provided the essential condition for the rise of the Southeast Asian peasantry, had finally passed.

The answer to the challenge presented by the closing of the frontier – in many places by the 1960s one of feeding and employing the vast and still-swelling army of Southeast Asian peasants as much as using their toil for economic benefit – was the installation of technologies which were essentially land saving or replacing: in short, the so-called Green Revolution outlined in the previous chapter. The Green Revolution's importance was that it not only provided for a huge enhancement in the irrigation facilities available for cropping, increasing not just the total area available for rice growing but also the incidence of double-cropping, but that it also increased substantially the yields of this more intensive use of land. As a result of such improvements, cropping ratios in Java grew still further to 155 per cent in 1970 and 200 per cent in 1990. In west Sumatra before the advent of the Green Revolution, 'all sawah . . . was only single cropped to rice, and usually no unirrigated crop was grown in the sawah. Yet by 1985, the cropping index for all sawah had risen to 1.48',[32] and nearly all sawah was planted to the new varieties; with irrigation improvements, 'the area of sawah rose by almost 50 per cent over the decade to 1983' with the percentage of irrigated sawah rising from 47 in 1973 to 72 in 1983'.[33] In Kedah and Perlis on the Malay peninsula, the area subject to double cropping rose from 14 228 hectares in 1968 to 102 460 hectares in 1972 – a sixfold increase. By 1974, the area planted in off-season rice in Kedah made up 43 per cent of that region's planted paddy area. In West Malaysia generally, whereas less than 1 per cent of paddy land had been double cropped in 1957, around one-third was double cropped by 1970, with the new high-yielding varieties taking up about half the total rice land, and by the early 1980s the off-season paddy area had grown to two-thirds the main season area. Much of the improvement was attributable to the Muda and Kemubu schemes.

In 1978, peasants in the village of Ban San Pong in northern Thailand were putting their irrigated riceland to three crops a year (two rice crops and a catch crop), 'a practice a few households had begun ten years earlier on an experimental basis'.[34] Overall in Thailand, according to Feeny, the growth in rice production after 1950 was 'not primarily accounted for by the growth of land and labor inputs. Whereas in the earlier period . . . area grew faster than output, in the 1950 to 1975 period, the reverse was true'.[35] The story in the Philippines was similar; with the closing of the agricultural frontier in a last flurry of expansion which saw an augmentation in the area of cultivated land by 50 per cent between 1950 and 1960, activity was thereafter concentrated on more intensive cultivation. The proportion of rice land under irrigation rose from 24 per cent in 1959 to 45 per cent in 1969–71 and continued to rise thereafter through the National Irrigation Administration's programme of construction and rehabilitation of irrigation works. By 1971 about half the lowland rice fields were planted to the new varieties, by 1980 75 per cent and by 1985 85 per cent. Progress, however, was slower in upland regions; 'Mountain Province started experimenting with planting the IRRI varieties only in 1974'.[36] In the Mekong delta region of southern Vietnam, the area occupied by the new varieties 'grew from 500 hectares in 1967 to approximately one million hectares in 1975'.[37] Everywhere, the great bulk of production increases came from improved productivity. Intensification spread, too, to areas where it had never been practised before, such as Sabah.

The Green Revolution was a complex package involving not just irrigation improvements and new rice varieties but also the use of large quantities of chemical fertilisers and pesticides. Fertiliser had been employed in relatively small amounts – and often only on seedbeds – by some farmers in the 1950s and early 1960s, but from the mid 1960s, its employment in large quantities proliferated because of its indispensable role in rice growing with improved varieties. In the Philippines, for example, its use on rice lands grew from around 53 000 tonnes in 1966 to nearly seven times that amount – 344 000 tonnes – in 1979. In Indonesia in the decade after 1976, fertiliser consumption for food production grew by a factor of four to nearly four million tonnes. In West Malaysia, too, fertiliser use had become general by the late 1960s. Equally, the dousing of crops with pesticides expanded dramatically; as I noted in the previous chapter, the creation of a stable, genetically restricted and continually cropped environment inevitably invited depredation from pests, a problem not just in long established wet-rice areas but one particularly prevalent in newly doubled-cropped areas such as Sabah.

The final plank of the Green Revolution platform was the growth in use of labour-saving technologies of mechanisation which were, in general, all of a piece with the predominant strategy of land-saving. Until recent decades, mechanisation played virtually no part in peasant production; early twentieth century observers in the Philippines, for example, had remarked that 'rice will perhaps never be grown in oriental countries with the aid of machinery, as labor is cheap and carabaos and cattle will for some considerable time, form the motive power used in producing the cereal'.[38] Around 1960, mechanisation was at very low levels. In Malaya, in that year, only 32 tractors and 26 rototillers were employed exclusively for growing rice; indeed, only about 5 per cent of rice farms 'employed mechanical power at some stage of production'.[39] The subsequent introduction throughout the region of mechanical aids to production was essentially designed to save time previously spent on field preparation and other tasks in order to take advantage of the new potentials of multiple cropping. Accordingly, mechanisation in a variety of forms gathered pace. In the Philippines, for example, the number of two-wheel power tillers was estimated to have grown from 3 437 in 1966 to 57 802 in 1980, for the most part taking the place of buffaloes in readying the land for planting. Tractor ploughing became more popular in Thailand, with large numbers of machines imported in the 1960s – in 1968, there were said to be 25 000 of them, ploughing more than half the annually cultivated area – although it was much less common in the northeast. Farmers without the means to purchase mechanical tillers had to take recourse to hiring in contract tractor ploughers. Similarly, the growing use of rotary weeders was a response to the fact that weeding was much more necessary in an environment where fertiliser caused weeds as well as rice to grow quickly. Sickles, required to harvest the crop more efficiently and quickly so as to allow the land to be put back into use again, rapidly took the place of finger-manipulated harvesting knives.

Mechanisation worked in similar land saving ways in areas which were not suitable for double cropping. Thus, in 'Ban Ping' in northern Thailand, by 1960 peasants were hiring in tractors to plough distant flood fields which they then broadcast before the onset of the flood. This mode of ploughing, under the conditions then obtaining, gave farmers access to land which would otherwise have been denied them. Within a few years, when the process of levelling and clearing had been completed and the risk of flood had abated, peasants dispensed with the use of tractors and employed hand ploughing and transplanting; 'the tractor was no longer worth its costs in cash, yields, and autonomy'.[40] Similarly, elsewhere in non-irrigated areas, mechanisation allowed the ploughing of hard-baked soils without the need to await the first substantial rainfall to soften the ground, delivering a more regular and predictable environment for cultivation. Again, tractors were increasingly employed in upland area for ploughing fields where weather conditions made for a short planting season and where soil had become hardened as a result of deforestation.

There was more limited use of labour-saving technology as well. In the Philippines in the early twentieth century, steam threshers were in use (although they seem then to have been much less popular than threshing done by cattle-drawn rollers or cattle treading), and from the late 1970s mobile light threshers became commonly available. But, increasingly throughout the region, such technology played an important role in freeing household labour for the cultivation of non-rice crops.

The alacrity with which Southeast Asian peasants took to mechanisation – at all levels of society, to the extent that it offered the chance of heightened rewards – should not surprise; as one writer noted (though not in this context), 'the margin of return is so small that it seems safe to conclude that all farmers try to increase production in all years and will adopt any method or new practice which will help them do so'.[41]

ENHANCED RICE PRODUCTION

All these measures brought an extraordinary increase in rice production to Southeast Asia. Between 1965 and 1985, rice yields in the Philippines doubled; by 1976, the country had achieved rice self-sufficiency and, 'for the first time in this century',[42] had become a rice-exporter. In West Malaysia, total rice production increased more than two-and-a-half times and yields rose by two-fifths in the period from 1956 to 1970; in the Muda region itself, rice production tripled in the decade after 1965. In Java, production of sawah rice increased by almost three-quarters between 1972 and the end of the 1980s; by the mid 1980s, as we have seen, Indonesia had achieved its long-sought goal of rice self-sufficiency.

Table 3.2 The modern growth of rice production (paddy; in tonnes)

Year	*Indonesia*	*Malaysia*	*Philippines*	*Thailand*
1946–55	10 180(*a*)	743(*a*)	2 768	6 546
1956–65	12 159	971	3 747	8 177
1966–75	18 738	1 679	5 060	13 182
1976–80	25 695	1 862	7 221	16 400

(a) 1950–55

Source: Randolph Barker, Robert W. Herdt, with Beth Rose, *The rice economy of Asia* (Washington, DC: Resources for the Future, 1985), p. 45.

Not all parts of lowland Southeast Asia were in a position to put this bundled technology in place, nor to employ all its features. In much of central Java, partly because of the tiny size of many fields and the poverty of their owners, draft animals remained in common use to the exclusion of mechanical ploughing. In Cambodia – to say nothing of the devastations and dislocations caused by continuing civil war and revolution – the annual flooding of the central plains prevented the kinds of water control needed for the new short-stemmed rice strains; the result was that 'at present, less than 10 per cent of Kampuchea's agricultural production teams have access to land with sufficient water control to implement the Green Revolution technology'.[43] Moreover, those areas beyond the flood zone were regions of poor fertility and unreliable rainfall. As a consequence of these limitations, in 1982 just over four per cent of the rice crop area comprised IR-36. Cambodia remained essentially a region where only one rice crop a year could be planted.

DIVERSIFICATION OF CROPPING

Thus far I have discussed two major aspects of peasant agricultural production, the spatial expansion of the area cultivated, in both lowlands and uplands, and the later intensification of productive activity, notably in rice-cropping, with its resultant substantial yield increases. A third was the developing diversification in non-rice production which moved through a number of phases. An important manifestation of this diversification was the increasingly common use of lowland dry season fields for second (and sometimes third) crops. This kind of production was essentially subsistence oriented in the first instance although, increasingly, considerable quantities of produce like cotton, tobacco and soya beans were produced and exported elsewhere. Lao peasants, for example, planted cucumbers, fruits, vegetables and sometimes manioc and corn on their dry season rice fields on those occasions when sufficient water was available. In Ilocos, rainfed wet-rice land was sometimes second cropped in garlic, egg-plant and tomatoes, while in Ilocos and the Cagayan valley peasants often planted tobacco in succession to crops of rice or maize; it was 'the major commercial crop in each region'.[44] In Nueva Ecija as well, dry season cultivation of tobacco and vegetables expanded. In some parts of lowland northern Thailand, peasants planted tobacco ('the second most important agricultural product of Upper Siam'[45]) in their rice fields during the dry season, although it grew best, and was cultivated most commonly, in the light riverbank soils along the upper reaches of the Chao Phraya and its tributaries after the flood. The area devoted to sesamum expanded after the turn of the century so that it accounted for 16 000 acres by 1920,[46] sometimes being cropped in dry season rice fields. The practice of second-cropping was much more common, of course, in areas of heavy population. In 1874 in the east Java region of Pasuruan, for instance, 60 per cent of the wet rice area was put to dry season second crops; by 1914, that figure had risen to 100 per cent. One notable variant of this rotational use of rice fields, of course, was the forced cultivation system in Java. In this context, the method employed was to plant sugar cane or indigo in irrigated fields in place of rice, rather than as a dry-field successor to it, usually one year in three.

A second development, already adverted to under the rubric of spatial expansion in the uplands, was an extraordinary increase in what might be called dedicated field cropping, that is, the assignation of land for the continuing cultivation of non-rice crops. The impetus for the development of this kind of production came from different sources. In Java, large areas of upland west Java were planted in coffee under forced cultivation from the early eighteenth century, and this form of coffee cultivation intensified across Java around the turn of the nineteenth century and especially after coffee was incorporated into the forced cultivation system in 1832. Later in the century, under the press of increasing population on land, upland dryfield cropping of root crops, maize and pulses came into its own. In other circumstances and times, as in the expansion of abaca production in nineteenth century Bikol to service gathering world demand for rope and cordage, the impetus was entirely commercial. It was perhaps most strikingly exemplified in the development of rubber, especially in Malaya, which rapidly gained peasant favour as a smallholder cash crop from the first decade of the twentieth century.

Smallholder rubber growing was stimulated in the first instance by the rubber boom; as the consumption of rubber world-wide doubled in the first decade of the century, the price rose until it peaked in May 1910 at 12s. 9d. a pound. World consumption trebled again in the next decade, although increasing supply saw the (still highly profitable) price halved. The first notable reaction to the early twentieth century price boom was a tendency for Malays to develop land through rubber planting and then sell it off to European entrepreneurs (much as they had done a decade or so before with coffee trees during a short-lived coffee boom); one Malay in Perak succeeded in selling off twelve acres of rubbered land for $8000 in 1910. Of much greater and enduring importance in Malaya, however, was the enormous increase in rubber smallholding by peasants (as well as by Chinese and Indians) from about 1910. Since such smallholdings were usually in close proximity to Western estates, they benefited both from the demonstration effect exercised by those plantations as well as the infrastructures established to serve them. By 1930, well over one-third of Malaya's rubber land was in the form of smallholdings as against plantations, and those smallholdings accounted for just under half Malaya's production of rubber.

Table 3.3 Rubber area and output in peninsular Malaysia, 1910–40

	Plantations		*Smallholdings*	
	planted area ('000 ha.)	*output ('000 tonnes)*	*planted area ('000 ha.)*	*output ('000 tonnes)*
1910	173	?	46	?
1920	539	?	344	?
1930	763	238	483	218
1940	843	337	547	216

Source: Colin Barlow, 'Changes in the economic position of workers on rubber estates and smallholdings in peninsular Malaysia, 1910–1985', in Peter J. Rimmer and Lisa M. Allen (eds), *The underside of Malaysian history: pullers, prostitutes, plantation workers . . .* (Singapore: Singapore University Press, 1990), pp. 26–7.

There were three major reasons for this development of peasant commercialism. The first and most straightforward was new international demand for rubber. The second was that rubber could be grown easily and simply without the adduction of much capital. All that was needed were a few trees, a knife, coconut shells for collecting latex, buckets, a pan for coagulating, and simple rollers for transforming the coagulated latex into sheets. Once this process was completed, the rubber was dried in the sun and passed on to local rubber dealers. The third reason was that rubber cultivation could so easily be combined with prevailing and subsistence-oriented modes of production; 'the growing of rice . . . remained the floor of the peasant economy'.[47] It was a simple addition, not a change which had structural ramifications for village society, and meant that smallholders could profit from the rubber market when prices were high, but have a good measure of protection from it when things turned sour; thus, when prices dipped as they did at the end of the post World War I boom, peasants could simply turn their full attention once more to subsistence rice production or – as they later did during the Depression in the Netherlands Indies – actually increase their latex production to compensate. Equally, when rice shortages occurred, peasants could take refuge in their rubber as a means of stabilising their incomes.

From Malaya, smallholder rubber spread rapidly elsewhere in surging patterns of planting which reflected periodic price booms. In southeast Kalimantan, *hevea brasiliensis* 'revolutionised much of the economic life in the southern part of the province, in particular in Hulu Sungai where the indigenous population, mostly enterprising Banjarese, almost to a man took to cultivating rubber gardens'.[48] The Iban began planting rubber in the 1920s. By the end of the 1920s, smallholder rubber comprised nearly 40 per cent of Malaya's rubber area, despite the deleterious effect on smallholders of the Stevenson scheme (1922–8) to restrict production. At the same stage, smallholders held 57 per cent of the Netherlands Indies' rubber area (which, unaffected by Stevenson, had enjoyed an extraordinary spurt of expansion in the mid 1920s), 96 per cent of that in Sarawak, nearly 38 per cent of British North Borneo's (where its development was enhanced by an already existing railway system) and all that in Siam. Much of this cultivation was integrated into prevailing modes of swidden production, notably in Sumatra and Borneo, where rubber was planted on abandoned swiddens and harvested years later. By the late 1930s, more than three-quarters of a million Indonesians were cultivating over half a billion rubber trees in Sumatra, Kalimantan and Sulawesi, which occupied an area of nearly 700 000 hectares.

In some cases, indeed, rubber came to dominate peasant income; 'a very large number of Malays own small rubber holdings', remarked one British official, '[but] . . . some unfortunately are wholly dependent on rubber. It was they who suffered so seriously during the slump'.[49] In the late 1920s in Negeri Sembilan, British officials reported that, because of rubber, it was becoming 'increasingly difficult every year to persuade sawah owners to plant up their [rice] land and to take an interest in its efficient cultivation',[50] including the upkeep of the rice infrastructure. Indeed, the much less arduous nature of rubber production compared with rice cultivation, as well as its profitability, led many Malays to purchase their rice requirements from the proceeds of their rubber sales rather than producing it directly themselves. Where such trends emerged – and they were not evident everywhere rubber was planted – they signalled a substantial change in peasant behaviour and outlook, from one characterised by a subsistence mentality to one of more specialist production in return for the prices paid out by international markets. This turn of events also brought increasing pressure from European plantation interests, notably in Malaya, to curb smallholder production, not just to ease competition but also to keep Malay peasants planting rice, not rubber.

There were two notable developments in smallholder rubber production in the post World War II era. The first, as I have already noted, was the development in Malaya of new high-yielding clones which were first planted in the late 1950s and which, through the Smallholder Replanting Scheme, helped to lift smallholders – or at least those able to take advantage of the scheme – from a position of threatened obsolescence. The second was the development of farms devoted almost entirely to rubber production, especially on newly established government land settlements, and thus no longer intertwining commercial and subsistence production. In West Malaysia the establishment of these farms, together with the replanting of old stock, meant the smallholder planting of more than 300 000 hectares of rubber between 1952 and 1962. Between 1952 and 1973 the area of smallholder rubber grew from about 654 000 hectares to around 1 104 600 hectares, although the number of smallholders grew much less quickly as holdings grew in size. These technological and administrative developments, however, were not in evidence everywhere; in Indonesia, for example, notwithstanding a continuing rapid expansion in area and innovations such as the nucleus estates program, designed to extend plantation technical and management expertise to smallholders, yields remained stagnant, a reflection of enduring traditional cultivation and processing practices.

Dedicated smallholding, of course, was not restricted to coffee and rubber. In response to a rapidly increasing world demand from the late nineteenth century for vegetable oils for cooking, for margarine, for soap and other uses, the commercial smallholder cropping of coconuts expanded rapidly. Already by 1917 in Malaya, smallholders held just under two-thirds of the 180 000 acres under coconuts. By 1935 the coconut acreage had tripled to 606 000 acres, a figure that remained relatively constant to 1961, and of which more than 80 per cent was held in smallholdings of less than 100 acres. Elsewhere, especially in areas which had difficulties providing themselves with sufficient food, such as north Sulawesi and Maluku, copra became an increasingly important item of commerce. The staggering figure of one and a half million hectares of land was under smallholder coconut in the Indies, mostly in its eastern sector, by the eve of World War II. By the late 1930s in the Philippines, coconuts had come to occupy more than a quarter of the total cultivated area. Palm oil production lagged behind the development in rubber, but it was a crop of the same kind. In Malaysia, with high levels of profitability, the area planted to oil palm grew very rapidly from the 1960s, so that by the mid 1980s Malaysia supplied more than two-thirds of world exports of palm oil and oil palm occupied an area greater than that under rice.

Commercial tree crop cultivation, notably rubber, was the great model of market-motivated diversification from food staple production. From around the turn of the twentieth century there was a imposingly expanding array of other varieties of commercial cropping. In east Java, for example, from the last decades of the nineteenth century peasants contracted with European entrepreneurs to cultivate and deliver cigar tobacco. In west Sumatra, a cash cropping commodity boom in gambier, coffee, and tobacco, as well as rubber, followed the release of the region from forced cultivation in the early years of the twentieth century. Such developments, however, were dwarfed by the scale and breadth of expansion and diversification which took place especially after World War II with the gathering enhancement of markets and transport networks and, in some places, the growing availability of mechanised ploughing. In Thailand, where monocultured rice remained easily ascendant into the 1950s, the post-war era brought a swelling expansion of cultivation into upland areas – not suited to wet-rice production, and hitherto not much used for agriculture – where an enormous variety of new crops were grown on dry lands cleared from forest. The chief crops involved were maize, kenaf, mung beans and cassava.

Through the 1960s and after, maize production – much of it exported as feed for animals – expanded spectacularly on the northern reaches of the Central Plain. By 1970, the area under maize was 829 280 hectares as against 285 600 in 1960 and 36 000 in 1950. Kenaf's history was of even more impressive proportions: first grown commercially in 1947, 4960 hectares in 1950, 140 320 in 1960, 420 960 by 1970, although its expansion was not later sustained. Similar histories of growth were recorded by mung beans (40 640 hectares in 1950, 52 320 in 1960, 238 880 in 1970), and cassava (around 14 000 hectares in 1950, 71 520 in 1960, 224 480 in 1970). The later growth of pineapples for canning and export was such that exports rose from 162 000 tonnes in 1981 to 370 000 tonnes in 1990. Non-rice crops whose production had previously been localised spread into other regions with improvements in transport. Overall, the area of land occupied by non-rice crops increased four times between 1950 and 1965; 'whereas in 1950 only 12 per cent of the total area sown was devoted to non-rice crops, by 1967 their share had grown to nearly 35 per cent'.[51] Production in many of the villages that supported this more diversified agriculture was increasingly heavily commercialised, with double cropping and the sale of virtually all produce outside the village. 'By the late 1980s', remarked one commentator, 'the most peripheral areas were producing crops for urban and export markets'.[52] A similar pattern of elaboration of dry land commercial cropping was evident elsewhere as well. In parts of upland Java in the 1970s, peasants began to concentrate on the cultivation of cassava rather than rice in order to meet an increasing demand from urban areas, taking advantage of Green Revolution inputs of fertiliser. Ironically, the incomes of cassava producers increased to such an extent that in the 1970s and after they increasingly took to consuming purchased rice rather than the cassava that had hitherto served as their major food source. There was, as well, an expansion of maize cultivation and sometimes the substitution of staples like cassava and maize by more high-return commercial crops like cloves, coffee and vegetables.

The general pattern that emerged, and which became increasingly pronounced in the decades after World War II, was one of decline in rice cultivation as a percentage of all cropping and a concomitant increase in other crops, often but not always produced primarily for sale. The pattern was evident even in the nineteenth century in such heavily populated regions as Java where peasants were forced relatively early to press against the margins to procure what they needed to survive (although later reversed in Java with the great expansion in rice production from the 1970s). In Java, the preponderance of rice in the diet began to decline from around the mid nineteenth century, so that by the period 1916–24, rice made up made up less than one third of the average food intake, with the balance coming from second crops.[53] In the early 1950s in Malaya there developed a tendency towards a greater mixing of produce, especially rubber and copra, to enable peasants to acquire the income they needed. Elsewhere the most potent thrust towards greater diversification came somewhat later, in Thailand reducing rice's proportion of the annually cropped area from around nine-tenths in 1950 to a shade over six-tenths by 1978. Notwithstanding the still pre-eminent position of rice in peasant cultivation, the general trend was for it to become gradually less important as a food source for peasant sustenance and less widely grown throughout the region.

GARDEN CULTIVATION

Perhaps the most immediately evident case of crop diversification was found in the gradual elaboration of garden cultivation. As we have seen, it had long been common for peasants to devote areas of land around and in the vicinity of their dwellings to gardens which produced the vegetables and fruit that served as accompaniments or desserts for the main meal of rice and provided some opportunities for local commerce. With increasing pressure upon land, however, as well as in response to commercial opportunities for the sale of produce to the growing population of nearby towns and cities, horticulture of this kind became more intensive, elaborated and diverse. It was prominent early in colonial settings in cooler upland areas – favourable for the cultivation of crops like potatoes, onions, cabbage, cucumber and lettuce – close to clusters of European population; Batu, near the east Java town of Malang, was just one such example, Baguio, in the Philippines, another. While a portion of the fruits of this kind of production remained reserved for the grower's own use, its commercial value and importance for peasant producers multiplied, notably in the post-World War II period, with the increasing assurance of regular and good prices, much increased marketing opportunities, infrastructure improvements and more rapid and voluminous traffic. Consequently, the proportion of goods sold, and the land and resources devoted to garden cultivation, increased greatly; often production assumed the form of straightout market gardening. The diversity of cultigens in these gardens was often extraordinary; they produced such crops as cabbage, pumpkin, lettuce, tomato, watermelon, celery, onions, cucumber, mushroom, carrot, gherkin, spinach, garlic, yams, manioc, squash, egg-plant, beans, maize, taro, peppers, ginger, turnip, peanuts, bananas, coconuts, papaya, oranges, grapefruit, mango, jackfruit, and guava. Although in some upland and hinterland areas garden cultivation was conducted according to a swidden regime, it was a highly land- and labour-intensive form of agriculture, with a continuing turnover of crops – as many as five or ten in a single year – which called for heavy inputs of fertilizer, reliable supplies of water and a ready availability of labourers.

FISHING

Given the predilection of Southeast Asians for fish, their harvesting was always of the greatest importance to peasants. 'Every Filipino is more or less of a fisherman', opined one Western observer at the turn of the twentieth century;[54] in Tonkin, similarly, remarked Gourou, 'every peasant is also a fisherman . . . who is happy to fill out his slender meal with a few fish, shrimp or shellfish'.[55] Fish and shrimp were caught in rivers, streams, canals and flooded rice fields, with traps, nets, lines or by draining. They were caught everywhere and at all times of the year; 'there is no time in the year when at least some fish are not available, nor is there any time in the year, even the busiest, when the family does not want fresh fish for its menu'.[56] Increasingly, too, it appears, peasants farmed fish in bunded rice fields or tanks or ponds filled from canal or rainwater in villages or in brackish ponds along coastlines.

Except for those villages where fishing was the major occupation, either throughout the year or in the off-paddy season, or where it was carried on with commercial zeal and techniques by 'one or more professional fishermen, who are past masters in the art of discovering and catching fish',[57] fishing was never more than a short-term, part-time activity. It was something done in the time left over from other pursuits; thus, 'when a lull from the pressure of other activities permits, members of the family are likely to be seen fishing'.[58] Nonetheless, its importance was such that 'every farm family devotes part of its time to fishing – fish is the most important source of protein in the peasant's diet – and the peasant family eats some fish at every meal'.[59]

In more recent times, however, inland fishing came increasingly under threat. In the uplands, widespread commercial logging often caused siltation in water courses and drastically affected fish supplies. In the lowlands, growing population intensities put ever more pressure upon inland stocks; overfishing of freshwater supplies left stocks depleted and unable to recover in the numbers previously available. As well, the Green Revolution, with its potent cocktails of chemical fertilisers and pesticides spread onto fields and washing into water systems, also had a damaging and depleting effect on freshwater fish supplies.

SWIDDEN CULTIVATION

The same kinds of imperatives and opportunities to change that affected permanent field cultivators were also gnawing at the swiddening peasants of Southeast Asia, although much more slowly, and less intrusively and effectively. There were important reasons for the more measured rate of change. One was that pressure of population against resources was felt much later among more peripheral groups, partly because they were granted the fruits of Westernised medical intervention much later and more gradually than their wet-rice growing fellows in the lowlands. Perhaps more important than this was that swiddeners received little attention and almost no control from the lowland-based centralising states – notwithstanding vague discouragement of what was seen as a wasteful and environmentally damaging practice in places like the Federated Malay States around the turn of the twentieth century – until very late in the period. One writer, discussing Java's uplanders, makes the point tellingly: 'swidden agriculture persisted in Java's highlands not because it was necessary there but because the absence of state control made it possible'.[60]

The result of this curious stability has been a vast if unmeasurable increase in the rate of swiddening across Southeast Asia over the last two centuries. Dobby, from his vantage point in the late 1950s, estimated that swiddeners cleared perhaps two million hectares of land each year across the region, leaving as much as fifteen to twenty million hectares either under cultivation or regenerating after recent use. In Burma, he put the number of swiddeners at around 2.5 million, cultivating annually around three million acres in upland Burma and leaving twice that amount subject to the eroding rains each year. In Thailand, he estimated their numbers in the north and northeast at around one million, while around six million people were engaged in shifting cultivation in Sumatra.[61] Through the 1950s, as well, swiddening remained important for most of the people of Laos, while one scholar calculated recently that 'even today approximately one million Lao farmers practise some form of slash-and-burn cultivation . . . lowland Lao as well as hilltribe shifting cultivators'.[62] Around 1970, shifting cultivation was said to be still commonplace in north Sulawesi, with just 10 per cent of cultivated land under irrigation.[63]

Nonetheless, as change came to swiddeners, the same features of spatial extension, production intensification and crop diversification which I noted in the lowlands were equally in evidence. As numbers grew, mostly by natural growth and to a much smaller extent by the entry into Southeast Asia of groups from southern China, a much greater proportion of land was put to swiddens, and the supplies of primary forest of which pioneering swiddeners customarily had availed themselves disappeared. The typical pattern of swiddening among primarily subsistence cultivators such as the Lua' and Karen, as we have seen, was for a short cultivation-long fallow cycle. There was, of course, considerable variety in this; in the central Vietnamese highlands, some groups cultivated for just one year, other for as long as ten years, but generally they allowed fallowing periods of around twelve years. The Kayah pattern was for a series of croppings and short fallowing on the same piece of land until its exhaustion required the exploitation of a new section of forest.

A long period of fallow allowed the forest to recover from cultivation, but it required the ever less available luxury of vast amounts of land. Consequently, as population grew, as lowlanders themselves began to push into upland and hinterland more relentlessly, and as loggers drove into forest areas, armed with government concessions ('nearly half of Sarawak's forests, 4.9 million hectares, are leased out as logging concessions'[64]) and often followed by destructive lowland 'truck swiddeners', increasing pressure was placed upon available land resources. 'It takes', remarked one observer, 'only a few additional land users to upset the delicate balance between man and land in this self-replenishing system of agriculture'.[65] The adoption of taungya-like systems of conservation – involving cultivators replanting the areas they had cut, and, as we shall see, most commonly practised in Burma for the production of teak – required too much time to be effective in the context of increasing population and more intensive land use. The outcome, then, was generally either an increase in the cultivation period, a contraction of the fallowing period, or both. The Buhid of the Philippines, for example, with the territory at their disposal whittled away by encroaching lowlanders, found themselves forced to adapt their swiddening routines by sharply reducing fallowing periods. A similar situation was occurring with Karen swiddeners, so that 'by 1975 the secondary forest had largely disappeared from an estimated 70 per cent or more of the Karen swiddens in the Mae Sariang district'.[66] The Mandayas of Mindanao faced similar competition from encroaching lowland Bisayans, and 'either reverted to dry rice cultivation by moving into the forested interiors or [became] part of the rural proletariat, working for minimal wages from Bisayan landlords on land they once possessed'.[67] In some places, there remained alternatives; among the Banjarese of south Kalimantan the practice developed of swiddening *imperata* grasslands by means of cutting and burning the grass, ploughing the soil, and cropping the fields thus created for a number of years in succession.

Much less commonly, increased pressure upon resources brought an intensification of cultivation in the form of permanent field wet-rice cultivation and, of course, permanent and stable settlement. In some cases, of course, upland groups like the Ifugao had long practised elaborate forms of terraced wet-rice cultivation, but elsewhere as well in the Philippines the practise of settled wet rice cultivation was becoming more common. The Kalinga of Mountain Province in Luzon, for example, appear to have moved in an evolutionary line through hunting and swiddening to the development of settled wet-rice, although not to the total exclusion of their earlier practices. While the inhabitants of some Kalinga areas had employed irrigated rice terraces for centuries, such fields in the more northerly regions had been established only in the recent past; 'indeed, rice fields are still being newly constructed everywhere in the Kalinga area'.[68] Irrigated rice fields there were capable of producing two rice crops a year (and were not used for any other crop); no fertiliser was employed. By one account, it was 'highly probable that rice did not become a regular staple in the Kalinga diet until it was grown in irrigated terraces'.[69] As swiddens were recast into rice terraces, newly cut swiddens were no longer used for the cultivation of staple rice but rather to grow protein-rich vegetables, 'at a time when the original source of protein – meat from wildlife and domestic pigs and carabaos – [was] becoming scarce from the pressure of population growth'.[70] The Ata, a mountain Negrito group in Negros Occidental, were forced by increasing immigration from the lowlands and the deforestation of their region, and the consequent loss of game, fish and wild fruit and vegetables and sources of carbohydrates, to move to swidden and then, finally, settled plough agriculture, even engaging in second cropping. On the island of Mindoro, 'the Mangyan have increasingly adopted the life in permanent settlements, each of which is connected to the town and regional centers of Mindoro'.[71] In Borneo, the process of 'stabilization' of shifting agriculture began perhaps a century ago.

In some cases, it manifested itself in the development of permanent wet-rice fields and the breakup of the longhouse into a pattern of separate nucleated dwellings; in others, as we have seen, it involved a movement into the cash-crop cultivation of items like rubber and pepper which, because they remained an integral part of the swidden regime, permitted the longhouse pattern added longevity. In the uplands of the mainland, some Karen people, as they moved to lower latitudes from the hills, took to wet-rice and constructed their villages around their new lands, while still employing supplementary swiddening. Mostly, however, the Karen adapted to the increasing pressure of population by constructing paddy fields in the hills. Lua' mountain swiddeners had apparently been practising settled wet-rice agriculture from at least the 1880s, and probably earlier. Other groups, for instance the Lua' and Karen of eastern Mae Sariang district, had come to irrigated rice production only around the 1950s, having been taught the techniques by northern Thai farmers. Some hill Chin were reported in the mid 1970s to have begun cultivating wet rice in terraced plots. In the highlands of central Vietnam, swidden cultivators took to permanent wet-rice cultivation where the availability of suitable land and water permitted it, even employing the new high yielding varieties of rice in the late 1960s; some, indeed, took to wet rice cultivation to the exclusion of other cultivation regimes. In Laos, the Khmu people gave indications of a greater proclivity for settled wet-rice cultivation in the 1950s.

The major cause of this apparently evolutionary development, as I have suggested, seems to lie in necessity, another word for the press of population. 'At present and in the recent past in the Mountain Province', remarked one scholar, 'densely populated regions can be correlated with irrigated rice cultivation, and conversely, those areas having sparse populations can be correlated with dry rice farming'.[72] At the same time, many peoples retained apparently superseded regimes as supplements to sedentary regimes as long as possible. According to one scholar, 'the low labor expenditure to prepare soil for planting and to control weed growth makes shifting cultivation attractive to peasants and, therefore, wherever they have a choice of agricultural techniques to achieve subsistence, they would choose shifting cultivation'.[73] Other scholars agreed that the labour productivity of swiddens, other things being equal, was superior to that of wet-rice. According to one, it took twenty-five people days to produce the same amount of rice from a paddy field as a swidden would provide from nineteen people-days.[74] Another made much the same point, and argued that even peasants accustomed to wet-rice cultivation will continue to practice swidden agriculture where the opportunity presents itself – a tactic bolstered by the fact that each regime produces crops at different times.[75] Thus the Moi of Vietnam employed a combination of shifting and sedentary cultivation, together with hunting. In one Kachin village in north Burma, one anthropologist noted four complementary techniques in use the 1940s: orthodox forest swiddening, grass swiddening using hoes, terraced wet-rice cultivation using cattle for ploughing and harrowing, and terraced wet-rice hoe cultivation.[76] Similarly, among the Pwo Karen, hunting and gathering retained some importance. In Sumbawa, peasants practised swidden cultivation – taking up over a third of the island's area in so doing – as well as wet and dry field permanent cultivation, at the same time continuing to hunt game on the grasslands fired for the purpose. On Mindoro, the Buhid still fished, hunted and gathered in addition to their major agricultural occupation; indeed, gathering took on commercial overtones to supply farmers unable to provide for their needs in grass, bamboo, rattan and similar goods.

In all this, adaptability remained supreme; thus, Lao peasants turned to swidden to supplement normal wet-rice agriculture when there was insufficient land available or when cropping patterns were disrupted by war or migration. Indeed, some groups constantly changed their cultivation regimes to suit new circumstances and opportunities; the Hmong, for example, as they moved from the hills to the valleys, combined both swidden and paddy cultivation, as well as changing their planting techniques and their crops. Such compromise between permanent field cultivation and swidden created its own problems; because peasants' attachment to irrigated fields necessarily inhibited their mobility, local swiddens tended to fall prey to over-use.

The same pattern of evolutionary response to population pressure and its corollary, resource depletion, was evident amongst groups which were primarily hunter-gatherers. While the trapping and hunting of game such as rats, snakes, birds, monkeys, lizards, deer, pigs, tigers, panthers, and even elephants remained an important source of nutrition for some upland groups such as the Lamet of Laos, the Kalinga of Luzon and groups on the Vietnamese central highlands, in other places its importance was ebbing, mainly as a result of the thinning of game through forest clearing, logging and over-hunting. Gathering – 'in general, the items collected are roots and leaves of various sorts, bamboo shoots, herbs and bark for medicinal purposes, wild fruit, frogs, small lizards, insects of several varieties, paddy crabs, ant larvae, honey, mushrooms, firewood, weeds for pig food, and even snake at times'[77] – underwent a similar decline. The Ayta of the Philippines 'through time . . . have relied progressively less on hunting and gathering, and more on agriculture,'[78] so that, in a context where the use of gun rather than bow and arrow and the very act of swiddening reduced the availability of game, they are 'today entirely dependent upon carbohydrates derived from swiddening'.[79] Similarly, the Batak of Palawan still practised hunting and gathering on forest reserve land, but also took to swiddening and even the sale of forest products in return for lowland rice. In northern Thailand, too, hunting was in decline and the reserves of big game had virtually disappeared.

The major thrust of all these efforts was to produce greater amounts to feed the growing consumption needs of the communities involved. Another and increasingly popular adaptation to the changing circumstances of swiddeners was to respond to the more tenacious intrusion of markets expressed in the extension and elaboration of the economic circuits of the lowlands to upland and hinterland zones. An early example was the introduction of the taungya forestry system into Burma in 1856, where swiddeners were induced for a payment to plant teak, together with their customary crops, on land they had burned over. Such adaptations sometimes resulted in new patterns of swidden cultivation, of which the most spectacular example was probably the development of opium cultivation to meet lowland demand. In some cases opium growing was mandated by the state; thus, in Laos, the French colonial regime, as part of its opium monopoly, required the Hmong to expand the production of poppies and produce opium by way of taxation. Similarly, the French attempted to counteract the shortage of imported opium during World War II by encouraging the upland Hmong of Laos and Tonkin to produce more opium. Elsewhere, accelerating lowland and international demand was sufficient to fuel expansion. By the mid 1960s in Thailand, an estimated 17 920 hectares of land was devoted to poppy cultivation.

Opium was an exceptional upland crop because it could continue to yield in the same site for ten years and, where land fertility allowed, sometimes as long as twenty. This in itself had seriously damaging effects on the land, which frequently became choked by grass as a result of the long period of use. A poppy growing community combined its cultivation of poppy fields with swidden cultivation, usually rice or maize interplanted with beans, gourds and the like. Poppies were generally grown in dedicated hoed fields, and the pods tapped mostly by women. Happy only at altitudes of 1000 metres or so, the opium poppy produced a high value/low bulk commodity which was exceptionally suited to peasants living long distances from markets. Apart from that portion of it consumed locally, the product was delivered to government or – much more common, especially with the passage of time – sold to traders, often Chinese, for smuggled distribution in the lowlands and further afield, and sometimes for sale to other highlanders in return for the rice needed by opium growers. These circumstances almost inevitably led to a increasing reliance on poppy growing to the exclusion of other forms of agriculture, especially food production. Some poppy growers, indeed, came close to becoming purely commercial producers of opium, mostly reliant on others for tools, basic goods and food. In one Hmong village in Thailand, only 17 per cent of the cultivated land was in padi; the remainder was under poppies. The commercial success of these people was evidenced in the ornamental silver neck rings commonly worn by the Hmong and Yao. It was also reflected, as among the Hmong, in the rapid growth in their numbers, something which gradually began to upset the environmental balance.

Commercialism was dominant amongst poppy growers, but it also proved its attractions to other swiddeners. They could provide the burgeoning lowland townships nearby with the fresh vegetables their inhabitants increasingly craved. They could also produce crops like rubber, tobacco and pepper without changing the rhythm and structure of swidden cultivation regimes; indeed, in one sense, cash cropping lived in symbiotic relationship with subsistence swiddening. In south Sumatra for example, peasants simply planted their rice swiddens with rubber trees; once the land had been exhausted for rice, the rubber trees were left to themselves, to be returned to and tapped when they had sufficiently matured. Thus, 'the ability of the swidden cultivators in the Outer Islands to engage in export-crop production is not an anomaly . . . but is related integrally to the character of their systems of swidden agriculture'.[80] The money swiddeners earned brought them the things they needed from the 'outside world': tobacco, salt, textiles, a wide range of consumer items.

The demands of swidden-based cash cropping sometimes had radical effects upon patterns of cultivation and upon the environment. It generally led to a closer specialisation in certain crops, as well as the devotion of larger areas of land to cash crops rather than subsistence, and these practices often meant a shortening of fallow periods. Thus the short-cultivation-short-fallow pattern typical of northern Thailand, associated with permanent-field tree crops. Again, amongst the Iban, the use of portions of land for rubber reduced the quantity available for food cropping, and gave rise to a tendency to shorten fallow periods to compensate for shortfalls in food production. In one Thai village, 'by careful planning and a few additional weedings',[81] peasants could use their recently cropped rice swidden for a second cash crop, employing whatever moisture remained; intensity of this kind was reflected in a pattern of swiddening that reduced the period of fallow to five or six years. For peasants under these circumstances, 'swidden [was] no longer seen as an integral system, a ritually sanctioned way of life largely self-contained and traditional the year round'.[82]

There were, as well, other kinds of 'cash cropping' which developed in response to the commercial demands of lowland inhabitants. In East Nusatenggara, peasants raised cattle in the plentiful dry grasslands of that region. Farmers also involved themselves in pig farming and poultry raising, while in south Kalimantan, swampland villages took to the commercial production of duck eggs. Some highlanders tended livestock to slaughter as meat for lowlanders; others offered their cattle as draught animals for lowland ploughing. Large numbers of cattle were also driven from Thailand's northeast to the central plain to work on rice cultivation. Equally, lowlanders sometimes put their livestock, such as elephants or buffaloes, on agistment in the highlands, their upland carers reimbursed with cash (for example, an equal share of the profits) or a share of the progeny. Both these arrangements were testimony of the increasing difficulty of finding pasture for cattle in the lowlands.

Where, for whatever reason, the development of more intensive or commercially-oriented cultivation proved impossible, the result was usually the failure of a harried environment to cope with increasing numbers. I have already noted a 1980s estimate that varieties of swidden cultivation were still being carried on by around a million Lao agriculturalists, while another estimate put the annually swiddened area at just under 300 000 hectares. One observer was 'doubtful if any significant areas of pioneer shifting cultivation now remain' among the Iban areas of Sarawak.[83] In Thailand, by the end of the 1960s around two-thirds of the forests standing at altitudes of more than 1000 metres 'had been cut over both by "hill tribe" people and by lowland Thai'.[84] Freeman, writing of the Iban, noted that 'if virgin rain forest is felled, fired and farmed for *one season only*, and then allowed to recuperate, adequate regeneration takes place. Furthermore, if thereafter the resulting secondary jungle (*damun*) is brought into cultivation at sufficiently rare intervals (i.e., about every 12–15 years), and *never for more than one season*, the land may be utilized virtually indefinitely without serious degradation taking place'.[85] Once, however, the population expanded beyond the ability of the available land to sustain it, environmental damage, sometimes of lasting proportions, inevitably followed. While Freeman's view that successive cultivations on sites of secondary jungle growth could result in significant damage and a third cropping would leave the land permanently degraded has been vigorously contested,[86] it was increasingly clear that the upper limits of the land's carrying capacity in the swidden mode were approaching.

Subject to the gathering attacks of both lowlanders and uplanders – not to mention the depredations of commercial timber concerns – the forest areas of post World War II Southeast Asia entered a period of rapid and catastrophic decline. In some places, indeed, serious damage had been clearly evident long before this time. By 1910, it has been estimated, the Philippines had already lost half its original forest cover of 30 million hectares to grasslands and arable land. In Luzon, the clearing of the forests in and on the flanks of the Central Plain through the late nineteenth century created grasslands, locust plagues, the diminution and disappearance of many water courses and lakes (and with them the opportunity to cultivate other crops in dry season), flooding and drought and general aridity. Panay, as a result of progressively more intensive shifting cultivation, had virtually no woodlands left. Perhaps the most thoroughly devastated of all the islands of the Philippines was Cebu, harried by deforestation and slope-aligned ploughing; according to one estimate, 'since man began farming on Cebu some 699 000 000 tons of soil have been lost'.[87] More generally in the Philippines, by the 1960s around three quarters of the farm land suffered some kind of soil depletion, while a sixth of the land was covered in deep rooted grass (*cogon*) which 'the Filipino has found . . . almost impossible to convert . . . to agricultural lands, or to any other economic asset'.[88] But damage of this kind was commonplace across the face of the region in contemporary times. By the late 1970s, Indonesia was losing annually an average of 550 000 hectares of forest, Thailand 325 000 hectares, Malaysia 230 000 hectares, Laos 120 000 hectares, and the Philippines 100 000 hectares. In Thailand, the proportion of forested land fell from around 75 per cent in 1913 to less than 30 per cent by 1980, and less than 20 per cent by 1989, with much of the loss attributable to the rapid growth of upland cropping. In Indonesia, the swiddening of land for both food and cash crops was thought to be a major cause for the presence in the 1970s of around 30 million hectares of grasslands. In Java, the continual denuding of forest land, especially in east and central Java, and, more recently, the expanded cultivation of upland heavily-hoed dry-land vegetable gardens on steep slopes, brought with it erosion and landslides, and consequent flooding and silting of the lowlands.

The declining forests were just one reason why the apparent tendency towards permanent cultivation was generally applauded and much encouraged by states. Only the stronger states were able to impose a measure of their will with greater effect than hitherto; in Thailand, for example, new swiddening was outlawed; in Indonesia, the government proscribed swidden in some places and relocated some peoples to the lowlands to enforce this ban. By contrast, in Laos after 1975 governmental efforts to curtail swiddening by installing terracing or resettling people to the lowlands had little effect, and its 1987 closing of the forest was similarly inconsequential.

VILLAGE INDUSTRY IN DECLINE

The final aspect of the productive life of the peasant was village industry. As we have seen, it was formerly the case that many villagers were involved in crop processing as well as producing a wide range of industrial goods for their own consumption and for trade. Many of these industrial skills – simple carpentry and tool making, food processing such as the production of soybean cakes or coconut oil, basket and mat weaving – were widely shared amongst the community; others, like metal working or paper making or pottery, remained the specialised preserve of the few, and were often concentrated within single villages which had become well-known for their skills in producing specific articles. In Tonkin, indeed, the majority of petty village industrialists in the 1930s were to be found in specialised villages. In some cases, villagers practised their industry within the village itself, either for local or for wider sale; in other cases they worked outside the village. In nearly all cases, however, industrial activity had long been a part-time activity, and most of its practitioners had also been involved in farming. The general pattern over the last 200 years – apart from periods of scarcity and disruption when the absence of things like matches and kerosene saw a revival of ingenious home industry – was one of the decline of industry of this sort, or at least its increasing local specialisation, and its replacement by new kinds of industry of a different order.

In the sphere of toolmaking, home industry – spread far and wide amongst Southeast Asians through the hill peripheries as well as the lowlands – was gradually supplanted by imports. Around the turn of the twentieth century in Java, it was reported that the previously common practice of villagers purchasing iron and steel to fabricate their own tools was falling into disuse as they took to purchasing European-made tools available in nearby township shops. In the Minangkabau region, the iron-smelting industry diminished when faced with the competition of cheap European iron. In central Borneo, 'smelting disappeared when inexpensive iron bars became available from traders'.[89] In northern Thailand in the mid 1950s, village blacksmiths were fading away in the face of the competition provided by cheap tools manufactured in Japan. Handicrafts suffered a similar fate. In Malaysia, villages which previously wove their own fish traps and baskets now bought them from Chinese traders. Their production was increasingly centred in specialist villages which supplied the general market. Again, a 1926 report from Java remarked that European export firms were purchasing woven hats at local markets, or their agents were advancing money or textiles to weavers against future deliveries of woven goods.

These changes were gradual ones, and felt less rapidly and strongly in areas dispersed from the centres of commercial activity. Thus, in the late 1950s, 'such highly developed arts as gold and silversmithing are found in all Lao towns outside of Luang Prabang as well as villages'.[90] In northern Thailand in the early 1950s, such skills as carpentry, tile-making and hat weaving seem to have enjoyed a continuing vitality, while metal working (using metal from the lowlands or the reliquiae of war) and mat and basket weaving endured in the Vietnamese central highlands. Metal-working (of tools, spears, axes), often from lowland scrap, retained its importance among the Kalinga of Luzon, bark was still used for blankets and clothing, pottery, broom, bag and shield manufacture and basket weaving were still carried on, and even the manufacture of sugar cane presses from hardwood. In the Ilocos region, industries such as potting, wine manufacture, different kinds of fibre-making, salt-making, and wood and silverworking were evident. Even in the lowlands of southern Vietnam, tool makers and carpenters were still sufficiently in demand to enjoy incomes higher than most of their peers in the village. In these situations, the old practices endured: production to fill specific orders only and not for a generalised market, and the mixing of the major occupation, small-scale industry, with agricultural work.

INDIGENOUS TEXTILES

The best known example of industrial decline was that of the indigenous textile industry. From about the early nineteenth century on, it entered a period of gradual but nevertheless almost complete decline. In Java, from the 1810s on, first the British and then the Dutch imported increasing quantities of cheap machine textiles which found a ready sale in Java. Even as early as 1832 it was remarked of Siam that 'cotton-twist is daily getting into more use . . . . The article being now so cheap, the women find it not worth their while to continue spinning it, and as they discontinue the manufacture, the consumption of foreign twist will continue'.[91] Textile imports rose sharply as large-scale rice cropping intensified in the last half of the nineteenth century. By the early 1860s, Mongkut remarked that most peasants in the Central Plain preferred to purchase cheaper foreign cloth rather than weave their own. The British consul in Bangkok was understating the situation when he remarked in 1885 that 'the manufacture of native hand-woven cotton cloths has of late years decreased considerably, the imported goods, though not so durable, being far cheaper'.[92] A later British observer was more blunt: 'Lancashire and Bombay practically supply the clothing of the whole people',[93] while another noted that 'cotton goods are among the most valuable imported. The people are year by year demanding more clothing, as the fashion for wearing foreign cloth extends gradually over the whole interior'.[94] As Homan van der Heide remarked, 'when rice became a general product of commerce, people more and more applied themselves to cultivation alone and in consequence gradually commenced to neglect other such occupations, as did not prove to be as profitable or easy as rice growing'.[95]

In the Minangkabau region, too, imports crushed the production of everyday clothing, and indigenous weaving became devoted to luxury goods, a development that brought with it the virtual disappearance of cotton and indigo production. According to a Dutch official travelling in the region in the 1870s, 'the noise of spinning and weaving could be heard everywhere in the highlands fifty years ago. But we can seldom hear it now'.[96] In Malaya, village weaving suffered a comparable decline. The first annual bulletin of Kedah state (1906–8) remarked that the availability of cheap cloth imports from Birmingham and India had brought an end to the manufacture of native handwoven cloth; 'in the 1930s the British were able to find only one weaver in all of Kedah.'[97] According to a post-war commentator on Burma, 'although looms were to be found in many Burmese homes at the time of the Japanese invasion, a large proportion were seldom used and it was chiefly a few old women who continued to spin and weave at home'.[98] Burma's import statistics, recording huge jumps in yarn and piece goods, reflect the decline in indigenous spinning and weaving prevalent across the region.

Table 3.4 Imports of cotton yarns and piece goods into Burma

		cotton piece goods (millions yards)		
year	*cotton yarns (million pounds)*	*grey and white*	*coloured*	*total*
1876–80	5.4	31	13	44
1886–90	10.1	45	26	70
1896–1900	14.3	52	32	85
1906–10	13.1	60	60	120

Source: Hlaing, 'Trends of economic growth', p. 105.

For the most part, the domestic weaving industry turned towards regional specialisation in an attempt to secure a market niche; 'thus, the Ilokan provinces of north-western Luzon are notable for their production of cotton cloths, mostly of a coarse but quite serviceable sort, and for some production of silk fabrics'.[99] Such cores of the industry were often based upon locally specific products to give them a uniquely parochial flavour, such as the sinamai cloth woven from abaca fibre in southeastern Luzon. In Burma, the weaving industry (employing imported yarn) became localised in central and upper Burma, with different places specialising in different products.

The industry's decline was much slower in more peripheral areas. In the 1920s, for example, Hmong women were said to be heavily occupied with weaving and embroidery; while 'in more isolated communities in Laos the importance of domestic weaving has never faltered. Among the Black Tai, for example, cotton is grown, harvested, spun, woven and dyed by each family'.[100] In Thailand's northeast in the 1930s, 'nearly every house . . . except for Najor Rajasima, has its own loom under the house; and nearly every farmer wears habitually the clothes which his wife and daughters make for him'.[101] In Thailand's uplands, hand looms were still in popular use in the 1950s. More recently in Sumbawa, peasants continued to grow cotton on their swiddens and weave it into cloth. But almost everywhere, the story was one of decline, disappearance and displacement, whether observed in some places already in the nineteenth century, or evident only in more recent times. Among the Kalinga people, local weaving was being replaced by cotton imports from the lowlands by the late nineteenth century, although its practice continued into the present. In Laos, while women's traditional dress was 'invariably hand-loomed',[102] and men's working clothes also woven at home, men's better clothing was in a Western style and town-purchased, while women's apparel, especially amongst the young, were increasingly Western-influenced; the blouse became popular and was usually manufactured in Hong Kong. Under circumstances like this, many household looms fell silent. In the lowland parts of northern Thailand, the process was much slower than in the Central Plain because of poorer integration with marketing and transport networks, but was headed towards the same end; by the 1950s in the north, 'spinning and weaving . . . has all but vanished'.[103] One observer found just one operating loom in eleven villages.[104] In the northeast, the development of railways linking the region to the capital brought in a flood of textiles and concomitantly a fall the region's production of silk and cotton. In the Vietnamese highlands, while the women of the villages continued to weave for everyday use – items like skirts and blankets – people purchased an increasing proportion of their textile needs. And while cotton continued to be grown and dyes manufactured in the village, 'most thread and dyes now are purchased in local markets'.[105]

From time to time the industry made something of a comeback. In the 1930s in west Java, the invention of a more efficient loom and the growing competition presented by Japanese cloth saw a remarkable recrudescence of cottage-style weaving, but its longevity was never tested because of the onset of war. In the late 1930s in Burma, nationalist fervour encouraged a growing new interest in peasant domestic weaving of traditional garb. In Thailand, the exigencies of World War, in this context a shortage of imported cloth, 'brought out a few of the old spinning wheels and looms, and some cotton thread was spun at home by old women (young women today do not know how to weave), but the end of the war and the return of cheap textiles quickly banished the loom again. The day of cloth weaving is gone for village women'.[106] In Laos, the weaving industry which had virtually vanished in the face of foreign competition through the 1950s revived strongly after 1975 in a context of restrictions on foreign imports, so that 'as published in a study in 1980, 75 per cent of households surveyed in Vientiane province were engaged in some weaving'.[107] In Indonesia in the 1970s and after weaving made a strong resurgence once more as the government attempted to develop industrially; it was, however, no longer a peasant industry.

It is worth noting in all this, too, that the import of cotton goods affected not just the domestic cotton weaving industry but also, in Vietnam and Siam especially, the silk weaving industry. Gourou noted that 'fine cotton goods of European manufacture . . . for a great many have replaced silk; so that these imports have perhaps damaged silk producers and manufacturers of coarse silk goods more than they have damaged weavers of common cotton goods'.[108]

To what did all the people released from these labours with the decline of local industry turn their hands? One reaction, noted in the Philippines, was a greater engagement of women in agriculture, rising 'from about 51 per cent in 1902 to 61 per cent in 1918 and to 71 per cent in 1938. Much of this increase was derived from females leaving household tasks and entering agriculture per se.'[109] Another, in diametrical opposition to the first, was an enormous surge in the numbers of people finding off-farm work: in new kinds of village industry, in commerce, in services, in extra-village labour. The transformations which had destroyed one form of work were even better at creating employment spaces for others in what had become a more complex and interactive economic setting.

THE DEVELOPMENT OF NEW VILLAGE INDUSTRIES

As some kinds of village industry died or faded, then, others arose. In Siam around the turn of the twentieth century, for example, Homan van der Heide noted the development of such new industries as boat building, industrial rice- and saw-milling, and brick, tile and lime manufacturing. According to Homan van der Heide, 'the various industries above mentioned are giving employment to many people, and more or less are taking the place of those industries which were killed by foreign competition'.[110] Elsewhere bullock-driving or commuter transport became profitable pursuits. Expanded production of crops for commercial sale multiplied the processing industries needed for their preparation; kenaf, for example, had to be cut, bundled, submerged in water for 10–12 days to loosen the bark, and then beaten, washed and dried; abaca, coconuts, tobacco, cassava and numerous other export items similarly were subject to relatively simple but labour-absorbing processing. The preparation of foodstuffs for local and wider sale also developed strongly. Industrial change came from enhanced competition (as in the metal-working industry), new demands (as in the growth of the transport sector) and also the availability of new technology. A sewing machine, for example, could make a man into a village tailor. A knitting machine could transform a villager into a cottage labourer, turning out cheap piece goods for urban merchants and shopkeepers. New technology, however, could also displace, as pedicab drivers in Vientiane (mostly immigrants from villages of northeastern Thailand) found when confronted with the taxi. Overall, however, it can safely be concluded that as the wider economy grew in sophistication, reach and liveliness, both inside and outside the village, its ability to accommodate the displacements it had created correspondingly strengthened.

In the 1950s, an anthropologist remarked of the village which he had studied that 'this is not a society in which specialization is well-advanced or particularly important'.[111] This may have been true in comparison to what he knew in the West. But compared to the situation of the early nineteenth century, there had clearly been a significant change in both the pattern of village industry and the types and demands of the employment it provided, a theme which I shall explore in greater depth in a later chapter.

CONCLUSION

For the greater part of the period since the turn of the nineteenth century, the dominant productive pattern of the region's peasants was one of pushing back the frontiers of sedentary cultivation, so that what had been mere pockets of dense population and perennial cultivation engulfed much the greater part of lowland Southeast Asia. This unprecedented expansion was achieved by a simple extension of existing technologies across the region's face. Through the nineteenth century in Java, the process was already in train; whereas, according to Raffles, just one-eighth of Java's land area was cultivated in the 1810s, by the later nineteenth century that figure had risen to one-fifth, and was nearly one-half by 1920, the limits of lowland extension. Elsewhere in the region, albeit lagging behind pace-setting Java by half a century or more, peasants were multiplying across what had been an empty landscape. By the beginning of the twentieth century, the region and its economy became truly and deeply 'peasantised'. 'Burma', remarked an eminent geographer, 'is best described as a country of villages'.[112] Much the same could be said for the great part of the region. Southeast Asia's lowlands were dominated by myriads of petty peasant producers, each farming a small area of land in rice once a year or absorbed in farm work predominantly associated with the production of rice. In a context of continuing rapid population growth, such a pattern could not last.

Salvation for lowland agriculture, such as it was, came from three general directions. The first was the elaboration of water control mechanisms which had two major effects: it increased the amount of land where the flow of water could be controlled, and where more reliable ('irrigation is of primal importance for obtaining a dependable crop of rice'[113]) and remunerative methods of cropping could be introduced. Much more important, it allowed such land to be cultivated more intensively. The second was the introduction of modern technology, in the form of new varieties of seeds, fertilisers and pesticides, and machinery which allowed for a more efficient practise of agriculture. The combination of all these things allowed not just for production to keep pace with population but, as new technology took root, to provide for a vast increase in yields. The third element in the transformation was a diversification in agriculture, occasioned by ever intruding markets, new machines, and the improvement of infrastructures to bear goods for exchange cheaply, rapidly and efficiently. It involved not just the proliferation of non-rice second cropping of produce, but also the employment of large tracts of land for dedicated cash cropping, most notably in tree crops such as rubber, greatly extended dry land cropping in such crops as maize and kenaf, and more intensive and more heavily commercialised small garden agriculture. All these developments helped ensure that food could be produced or purchased in sufficient quantities so that famine was never a significant problem in the region. In those times and places where famine did manifest itself, it almost always emerged in the form of a price famine where the adequacy of food supply was not matched by the means to procure it.

Much the same problem of thinning resources afflicted uplanders, especially as their numbers began to grow much more rapidly after World War II. There, too, patterns of change were of roughly the same kind: an expansion of the swiddened area across the region's forests, an intensification of agriculture which saw a greater proclivity to exploit forest lands by tightening the cycles of cropping and fallowing, and a diversification (and, sometimes, a subsequent specialisation) of cropping to accommodate the demands of the ever expanding circles of commerce. More important, as expanding numbers and ever more scarce resources in both upland and lowland brought the two sectors in collision, there emerged amongst swiddeners an acceleration of the evolution to more intensive sedentary cropping. This development, much applauded by the state, was a significant step in the direction of social homogenisation. Uplanders, too, were now becoming peasants, though at vastly different rates across the region: steadfast in their focus on own-use production, yet growing in numbers, increasingly incorporated by the state, increasingly affected by the reach of markets, increasingly defined.

4 Land and Landholding

The dominant theme of the nineteenth century was the emergence across the Southeast Asian landscape of a colossal horde of peasant producers, filling up the valleys and expanding through the hill country in their search for the land which was their primary resource. Land and its use structured their lives in fundamental ways. The labour it demanded to make it productive, the rice and other food it yielded, the power relationships spun about its allocation and use, all were defining characteristics of rural life. The land was, therefore, at the heart of the processes of peasant change. Movement, settlement and exploitation, in the contexts already outlined, created new relationships with the land, between peasants themselves and between peasants and their masters. This chapter seeks to establish how the changing context of social and economic life transformed not only conceptions of landholding and access to land, but also more fundamental appreciations about the place of land in peasant life, and to analyse the implications such changes carried for Southeast Asia's peasantry.

LAND AS A COMMODITY

Perhaps the most important single change related to land use was the gradual evolution of land from a necessary – but plentiful and thus essentially valueless item – into a prime commodity. What mattered most at the turn of the nineteenth century was not land but the problem of making it productive; that is, the control of labour. But that conception was, first gradually, then rapidly, superseded through the course of the century. The transformation in attitude took place at different paces and for somewhat different reasons across the region. It was already identifiable in those places which, even in the early part of the nineteenth century, were both heavily settled and under relatively tight control by the state, notably Java and the delta area of northern Vietnam. In such areas of dense and settled populations, the notion of land as a commodity was already strongly rooted. In early nineteenth-century Java, for example, there is clear evidence of individually-held land, of landlessness, and of the custom of sharecropping and even land hire. There had also developed the notion that the holding of land was a privilege for which the state could exact taxes in produce, money and especially labour. As I have already suggested, there appears to be a close correlation between population density, state control and communal landholding. 'Are the communal holdings', asked Gourou with more than a hint of rhetoricism, 'remains of an ancient land regulation which did not admit of private property? Are they, on the contrary, created by the state to the detriment of private property which, occupying all the territory and tending to transformation into large landholdings, threatened to arouse social disturbances?'[1] Putting things that way indicated the correct answer. Accordingly, in both these places there developed the notion of communal land, that is, land distributed widely amongst village inhabitants as a means of increasing the stock of labourers and taxpayers to meet the demands of the state, and who were themselves rewarded by their access to land: 'Very fortunately, many poor peasants are able to supplement their resources a little from the communal lands; these are inalienable, and are divided among the inscrits [that is, the persons inscribed on the tax rolls], usually once every three years'.[2]

It was, thus, in the interests of the state in these regions that there be a significant amount of communal land. Even as late as the 1930s, communal land took up a considerable portion of the cultivated land in the Tonkin delta: 'according to the cadaster figures they would occupy 2300 square kilometres, or more than one-seventh of the total area of the Delta, and more than one fifth of the cultivated area'.[3] While in Vietnam the amount of communal land allocated to villagers remained quite small ('In most of the villages each listed person receives only a very small area of communal land, a few sao [1 *sao* = 360 square metres]'[4]), and significant sections were set aside for ritual expenses and, to a lesser extent, to support the needy, the fact that a household might have a number of inscribed persons meant that 'it can obtain with its shares a piece of property which enables it to live well above the level of the rural proletarian'.[5] It is instructive to note in this context that the southerly elongation of the Vietnamese state, and the relatively weaker exercise of state power in the south, meant that communal land was much less in evidence, and a much weaker institution, than in the north. In Java, muscular state power usually went hand in hand with communal holdings; at various times in the first half of the nineteenth century, the amount of communal land expanded to accommodate the high points of demand from the state. In the princely territories of central Java, for example, landless peasants sometimes came in possession of land as a means of compensating them for their labour. Again, the operation of the Cultivation System, at least in its early years, saw a resurgence of communal holding as a means of maximising the labour of villagers in the service of state-sponsored production.

The state's disposition towards communal land as a means of social control placed reins upon the exercise of untrammelled power by wealthy and influential figures both inside and outside the village. Periodic state-enforced land reforms in Vietnam, for instance, such as that of 1839, served to remove holdings from private hands and make them available to the broader village community in the form of communal lands. Nonetheless, there was a certain paradox at work in the sense that the presence of communal lands gave village authorities in charge of their allocation an opportunity to enhance their power; Gourou noted that 'those who are in power, their families, their friends will receive the best shares, that is to say the most fertile rice-fields, the best watered and the closest to the village . . . in villages rich in communal land we see families adopt several children in order to obtain, when these have reached their eighteenth year, a larger number of shares of the communal rice-fields . . . . Sometimes also, in villages rich in communal land, the notables list more persons, that is more men between eighteen and sixty, than there really are: thus the common land will be divided into a larger number of parts and the extra parts will be kept by the notables who will pay for the listed person's card relating to these shares'.[6]

It would be misleading, however, as I have already intimated, to see the Tonkin delta and the region of central Java as typical cases. Intrusive and relatively powerful states where varieties of communal landholding were entrenched were much the exception in Southeast Asia around the turn of the nineteenth century. In much of the lowland regions of Southeast Asia, typified by sparse population, weak political control and low levels of peasant production, notions of communal land had not arisen; there was always sufficient land to move into, and no real power to stop peasant emigration. As a consequence, notions of property rights of any kind were virtually unknown; land, like air, water, and forest, was there for the taking.

The practice of communal tenure implied some sense, albeit a weak one, of land as a valued commodity. But this concept could, in the end, no better survive the changes that were to come than the undeveloped notion of land as a free gift. As we have already seen, what developed in Southeast Asia from around the last decades of the nineteenth century was an altogether new kind of state structure which, for the sake of economic development, wished to impose order and security upon property relations and to increase the state's collection of revenue from expanded production, notably in the form of a more precisely and accurately assessed land tax.

The result of this development was a slow but nonetheless inevitable decline in the incidence of communal landholding in the stronger states. In Java, with the encouragement of the colonial state which, from about the 1860s as it fell more completely under the sway of liberal ideas, increasingly saw village communal tenure as a cause of economic stagnation, communal landholding was increasingly transformed from forms which saw it regularly redistributed amongst villagers to forms of fixed-share holding. In Vietnam, as the French began to impose their new view of society, communal land similarly went into decline.

In less strongly institutionalised states, land began to attract a value, and a concomitant need for it to be protected, as its fruits entered more fully and regularly into the circuits of commerce. In Thailand's Central Plain, although land sales were legally recognised before this time, the process of modern land-property formation dates from around the 1860s, as the rice industry, fed by rising international demand, began to grow. In 1861, the king recognised by decree the notion of private ownership of land. Thereafter, peasants could lay claim to new lands and their ownership was recognised by a certificate of possession issued them by the Department of Lands. Equally, those paying tax on their land received certificates which served as evidence of ownership, and land began to acquire a value which encouraged a development of the practice of buying and selling. It was not, however, until the turn of the century, with the establishment of the Land Registration Department, that such instruments of ownership became formalised into land titles which, by means of surveys, clearly and unambiguously indicated the dimensions of the land over which ownership was claimed. These developments heralded the fact that the changing economic and political context had given land-as-such a value which it had never before possessed; thus remarked one commentator at the time, 'the most generally recognised means of investing money is, or was until house property in the capital and banking took the public fancy, the buying of, or lending on, rice fields'.[7] Moreover, with Chulalongkorn's labour reforms, the option of offering oneself as security on a loan had disappeared; 'as the value of rice fields increased, it became more common to offer land as security for loans'.[8] The fury of private land speculation which gripped the Central Plain around the turn of the twentieth century sent land prices spiralling, especially on the newly reclaimed areas to the east of Bangkok. Poorly administered registration procedures, however, caused endless disputes over land, often between squatters and land purchasers, through the last decade of the century.

In Burma, we have noted, as the rice export economy grew quickly over the last half of the nineteenth century, the British sought to establish a smallholder rice economy by encouraging peasants to develop and take up new holdings – apparently they averaged 6–12 hectares compared to the 3 or so hectare size of farms before the development of the rice industry – in the unclaimed vastnesses of the Burma delta. While native title to land upon which one had settled and cultivated had always been observed, now the issuance of a taxation assessment by the British authorities on the land was specific evidence of ownership; it could be transferred or borrowed against. The government also introduced a system of land grants (*patta*) prior to clearance. In 1872, the office of settlement officer was introduced; his task was to map and mark out landholdings and set rates of taxation. In 1900 a Land Records Department was established. In Cochinchina, the French began a gradual process of converting customary tenures into registered titles from the 1860s, while a little later the British began a similar process in Malaya. In the Philippines, formal land tenure laws took shape in the late nineteenth century, a development which 'saw the bulk of the principalia-owned haciendas established or expanded at the expense of the public domain and smallholder neighbours'.[9]

Only around the turn of the twentieth century, however, were governments across the region in a position to create apparatuses which could oversee the process of credentialling land holding and guarantee it as well; they generally adopted variants of the Torrens land registration procedure, based on centralised records and cadastral surveys, pioneered in South Australia. From that period, customary notions of tenure were gradually replaced by permanent titling based upon land surveys. In Malaya, where some states were already gradually establishing formal land regulations, such as the Perak General Land Regulations of 1879, the Torrens system was adopted in Selangor in 1891 and later came to form the basis of the land legislation of the Federated Malay States. In Siam, the severity and frequency of land disputes in Rangsit and other commercial rice producing areas on the young delta led to the government's adoption of the Torrens system from 1901. In the Philippines, the ruling Commission followed suit the following year with a Land Registration Act 'which provided for the systematic registration of land titles under the Torrens system',[10] and in 1903 passed a homesteading act – never very successful in attracting people to take up land – which allowed people to claim plots not exceeding sixteen hectares and also foreclosed the opportunities for new large-scale plantation agriculture. Strangely, and for reasons which still await investigation, the Dutch, though they conducted cadastral surveys in Java and Bali and issued tax certificates there which doubled as proofs of ownership, made no such efforts to formalise landholding titles across the Indies.

Notwithstanding the fact that its introduction was dogged by ignorance, delays in cadastral surveying and corruption, a general tendency for reclamation of new land to outpace the titling process, and indifference and avoidance, the Torrens system signalled the unfolding of a new basis for economic activity in the region. Land was now a good; its dimensions and ownership could be precisely identified, its value calculated and secured against, its ownership guaranteed and transferable. Equally, the state could be clear about just what was not 'owned'. Slowly, customary rights of tenure began to be converted into title – predictably, the upper echelons of society moved more quickly in that direction than their fellows – with both the certainty and limitations that conveyed.

The same processes outlined here were evident wherever increasing commercialisation and a stronger state structure developed. In the Minangkabau region of west Sumatra, for example, individual private property gained ground at the expense of ancestral lands; the process of individuation was reflected in the increasing tendency for nuclear families to form and live as units, alongside or in place of the longhouse system. A similar movement from longhouse to nucleated residence was evident elsewhere as well. In the course of these developments, land had become, in a certain sense, 'the only form of wealth',[11] the basic good that could be secured with certainty and whose ownership was backed by the power of the state. Money, by contrast, remained insecure; 'a peasant cannot keep large sums of money about, for in this country for all that it is quiet and pacified, there is a certain lack of security; it is not a good idea to have a large reserve of piasters in one's house for this is a way to expose oneself to attacks of "pirates"'.[12]

It should not be thought, of course, that the new instruments of land registration were immediately and everywhere effective. In the Philippines, for instance, 'despite the introduction of cadastral surveys in 1910, land registration was very slow and bureaucratic. In 1936, it was estimated that only 27.6 per cent of the total land area of the country had been surveyed, leaving some 21.4 million hectares out of the total 29.6 hectares still unsurveyed'.[13] Thailand's story was a similar one: 'up to 1985 only 15 percent of the 152 million rai [1 rai = 0.16 ha.] of agricultural land carried title deeds; some 46 percent was covered by a certificate of utilization or other papers; and the rest had no legal papers whatsoever'.[14] In one northern Thai village, for example, most land was not titled until the government requested that application for title be made in 1957. In Sabah, the North Borneo Company's efforts to impose a new system of land registration in place of customary usage were generally and successfully ignored by landholders. However, to lay undue emphasis on this pattern of slow and irregular implementation – what better might have been expected at the time? – is to miss the institutional significance of the changes that were taking place, manifested, for example, in the tensions aroused by the increasing demand by lowland swiddeners for land titles for their plots and, among the Pwo Karen, the gradual development of separate household dwellings at the expense of longhouses together with the emergence of the notion of individual paddy holdings in place of communal avail of swidden.

BROADER IMPLICATIONS

These developments, and the contexts which had given them birth, affected all peasants, but they had a catastrophically dislocating effect upon those peoples – often peasants in the making – who did not lead settled existences. In the first place, the very acts of surveying and titling tended to concretise the locality of settlement with a permanence, fixedness and exactness never before contemplated. States now knew, with precision in those places where surveys had been conducted, who owned what land and could all the easier claim the residual and unclaimed as their own, for their own purposes. They now had a better sense of who belonged where, and could more easily police and curtail movement. They could now restrict access to resources, such as nearby forests, which had previously been construed as in some sense belonging to villages and communities.

These new ideas about land inevitably collided with those long held by upland and hinterland swiddeners. For the Moi, for instance, 'for the duration of its use the *ray* is the private property of the one who has cleared it; once abandoned, it reverts to the community'.[15] The Karen held to a similar notion. The Iban, similarly, had established a household's ownership by the very act of felling virgin forest growth; 'thereafter, the land belongs to the *bilek* family[16] responsible for this first felling, and it has full discretionary rights over the usufruct of the secondary jungle which springs up within a few months of the harvest'.[17] The fruit of the harvest, too, remained the ownership of the household cultivating it. Generally, then, claims to forested lands were asserted simply by their first clearance, and remained in force until such time as the land had been finally abandoned.

As far as shifting cultivators were concerned, the new state-sponsored 'rational' land policy not only ignored their situation – for example, it frequently gave no legal protection to abandoned rotational swidden – but effectively sounded the beginnings of the end of their mode of life. In Thailand, where the 1954 Land Code gave legal protection only to permanently cultivated land, 'swidden cultivation is . . . regarded by law as very harmful to the economy of the nation and is indirectly prohibited . . . . A person who practises swidden cultivation starts his business by committing a crime as soon as he moves onto the land'.[18] What states prized and guaranteed was permanent settlement; what they disliked was random movement, vaguenesses in possession, the difficulty of taxing people customarily on the move, and the 'damage' swiddeners visited upon an environment for which the state had other and more lucrative purposes. Such attitudes meant that, as population grew rapidly and resources thinner and more contested, competition for land between lowlanders and hinterland and upland dwellers was almost always resolved in favour of the former. Thus, in the Philippines, conflict over lands emerged between lowland Bisayans (who had begun growing hemp in the foothills and who claimed legal title over this land) and the upland Mandaya, whose customarily-held style of land was unsurveyed and untitled and hence indefensible. In northern Luzon, similarly, the hunter-gatherer-swiddening Agta people found land which they thought lay at their disposal whittled away through either purchase or confiscation by the settled farmers of Palanan. In Borneo, the state placed limitations on the movement of the Iban and the areas which they could cut for their swiddens. Since most remaining primeval territory was already the 'property' of existing Iban communities, 'this means that when a bilek family wants to gain access to new land, it can do so only by attaching itself to an established community'.[19] In North Borneo in the 1950s, the combination of a desire for government control and declining land resources for shifting cultivators saw the development of land resettlement schemes to sedentarise Dusun and Murut peoples and turn them into wet-rice cultivators. In many places where swiddeners were resettled into sedentary-style villages, they continued their old practices of swiddening and collecting forest products for use and sale in the sites of their former habitation, sometimes abandoning their new residences to return permanently to their former abodes.

Notwithstanding the essential incompatibility of state understandings of land law and those of swiddeners, the importance of specific ownership gradually began to impinge upon swiddeners in the form of a strengthening notion of personal ownership of swiddens and a necessary evaporation of ideas of joint village possession of the whole swidden area available for shifting cultivators. In other words, the commercial aspects of land ownership inevitably made their mark. This expressed itself, for example, in 'a change in the nature of land ownership customs'[20] in the direction of permanent and individualised holdings – and competition for holdings – in places where long-term tree crops such as rubber or pepper were sited within swiddens. Similarly, as swiddeners in increasing numbers became sedentarised and established permanent wet-rice cultivation sites, notions of individual ownership, and concomitant conceptions of rights of rent, mortgage and sale of such sites came to approximate those in the lowlands.

There were also efforts at appropriating government understanding to defend the status quo; Banjarese in south Kalimantan, for example, took to planting fruit trees in fallowing forest so that such land might be classified as fruit grove (and thus land privately owned) rather than 'jungle' (and thus government domain).

LAND CONCENTRATION

The emergence of these new conceptions had radical effects upon the distribution of landholdings. Land that was now titled and circumscribed, that was now a thing of value and an object of investment, necessarily became an object of exchange. The necessary result was a gradual polarisation of landholdings across the face of Southeast Asia: on the one hand between a small number of people owning relatively large holdings and the great mass of holders with land sizes of just one or two hectares or less, on the other hand between those who held land and the growing army of those who did not.

This result was produced in a number of ways. One was through the conscious exploitation of new land laws by those who knew them and knew how to turn them to their own advantage; the result was the dispossession of many peasants who had settled and cleared land and had come to think of it as their own. In the Philippines, for example, many peasant squatters who had cleared land and made it productive found their right to ownership successfully challenged in the courts by hacenderos who had already laid claim to large territories and were sufficiently versed in the law and politically connected to defend their claims; 'smallholders were powerless before the fact that most lawmakers and national leaders were landed principalia'.[21] Again, according to a scholar of Vietnam, 'perhaps the most effective institutional lever employed to transfer land ownership into French hands was the colonial land register'.[22] In Burma, wealthy persons could subvert the smallholding intention of the law and could acquire land simply by laying claim to it and paying taxes on it for the requisite twelve years. Even in backwoods Temerloh in Malaya, 'those most closely connected with the administration, those with a more cogent sense of the implication of the registration process were able to use the new system of land registration to consolidate their economic position'.[23]

Another way, closely allied to the first, was the simple exercise of privilege. It was this that saw large quantities of newly valuable land in the Central Plain of Siam – especially those areas which developed so rapidly in the last two decades of the nineteenth century – held by the king, the royal family, noblemen and officials. During the rubber boom in the early part of the twentieth century in Malaya, good political connections allowed budding entrepreneurs favoured access to land on which to grow rubber. In Java around the mid nineteenth century, the strengthening of the indigenous administration by the Dutch for their own economic and political purposes allowed officials to usurp land as they wished; in Demak and Grobogan, for example, by 1850 village chiefs and elites held almost one-third of the available wet-rice land and supra-village chiefs a further one-fifth. By 1930 in Vietnam, as a result of the long-standing sale and concession to French settlers and Vietnamese who collaborated with the French, 'the total area of land transferred to French citizens [including Vietnamese] via piecemeal appropriation was approximately 104 000 hectares in Tonkin, 168 300 hectares in Annam, and a truly spectacular 606 500 hectares in Cochinchina'.[24] Moreover, in Vietnam, asserted Gourou, 'the large holding can be formed to the detriment of the communal lands through the paid complicity of the village authorities'.[25] The pervasive power of the state was such that one writer on contemporary affairs was moved to remark that the existing system 'favours (because it does not forbid) government officials acquiring choice land'.[26] Such exercises of power, of course, were not confined to the state apparatus and its functionaries. In northern Siam in the early twentieth century, peasants sometimes raised accusations of witchcraft against persons marrying into a landholding household. In upland northern Luzon, too, some village elites in the mid and late 1950s were said to have capitalised on ritual obligations by providing carabaos to poorer members of their kindred in return for their land when such animals were required for ceremonial slaughter.

A third means of land alienation was the development of commercial relations themselves. With commercialisation, peasants required greater sums of capital to invest in their farms; in order to secure this, they had, formally or informally, to use their land as security. When, as often happened, they were unable to service their credit obligations, they were forced to sell or give over their land. The well-known technique of *pacto de retroventa* in the Philippines was a mechanism whereby a peasant effectively alienated his land to a creditor in return for capital. While the agreement stipulated that the owner had the right to buy back the land within a certain time, he was seldom able to amass the necessary capital to do this, with the result that he lost his land forever. A similar institution was also to be found under other names across the region. In Thailand, for example, the sale of land, with a guarantee of the right of repurchase, became commonplace on the Central Plain from the late nineteenth century, and it began to make inroads in the north from the 1960s onwards. In Malaya, the similar mechanism of *jual janji* was increasingly in evidence; it was according to one scholar 'the major means of dispossession of the Kedah peasantry'[27] in the early twentieth century. In Lower Burma, many of the thousands of poor peasants who had come to the delta, especially from Upper Burma, gradually managed to gather the resources to purchase their own land; many of them, however, lost it just as rapidly through their inability to service their obligations to moneylenders for the credit upon which its operation depended. As the Lower Burma land frontier gave out in the early years of the twentieth century and as population continued to grow, the proportion of landless agricultural workers increased rapidly; by 1911, they made up 35 per cent of agriculturalists in Lower Burma, in 1921 40.4 per cent, and in 1931 52.1 per cent, compared to just 18.2 per cent in 1881. In Vietnam, smallholders' failure to meet their credit obligation was also central to the emerging pattern of landownership: 'the moneylender acquires land at low prices, either by what is termed sale with right of redemption, or by loans of money at heavy interest. The peasant, if he is unable to return the money, loses his land. The lender is within the law, from the point of view of French law, since he has an incontestable title; but were it not for the zeal of certain officials, the moneylender could not come into possession of the security, and the complaints of the people could be heard'.[28] Furthermore, such developments were not just phenomena of the early stages in the commoditisation of land; they continued through the twentieth century. Thus, according to a recent observer of rural Java, 'land concentration by wealthy villagers and urban investors has occurred and is accelerating because of a very active land market that transfers control by sales of land from small, marginal farmers to those who have capital, by renting land from small farmers to large farmers, and sharecropping of land from the large farmers to marginal farmers and landless villagers'.[29]

These kinds of problems were exacerbated as more expensive technology developed and as land became more productive and more valuable. Especially from the 1960s onwards, as the technology of the Green Revolution found more widespread application, a greater concentration of landholding and an increase in landlessness became more evident or, to put it another way, there was 'some consolidation of sawah holdings in the hands of the more productive farmers'.[30] Overall, it was the differential access to the newer and more productive technologies which advantaged the already wealthy; by comparison, poor and marginal landholders were either less able to take advantage of the new developments and thus less able to compete, or, should they attempt to compete, more likely to attain such states of chronic indebtedness that there was no escape short of parting with their land.

The growing value of land also had an inhibiting effect upon potential peasant purchasers. The more expensive land became – a function of its increasing scarcity as well as its ability to produce higher returns with the application of modern technology – the less likely it was that poorer peasants could purchase it. For the same reasons, those who had lost their land were generally precluded from buying it back again, what with high costs and high interest rates.

Finally, there was the problem of an inexorably growing population. In one village on Siam's Central Plain in the 1920s, many farmers had more land than they could use: an eight hectare plot of land, for example, might only be partly cultivated by the owner and the remainder rented out or used for pasturing animals; twenty years later, such wantonness was no longer possible with the rapid expansion of population. In northern Thailand, the land under rice cultivation expanded from less than 300 000 hectares in 1950 to 400 000 hectares in 1963, but the average size of holdings declined from 1.4 hectares in 1950 to just over one hectare in 1963. As the frontier – at least of easily reclaimable and readily usable land – closed everywhere across the region in the decade or so after 1950, as the upward mobility which easy access to land had earlier afforded finally ended, and as population growth continued unrelentingly, the landless or near landless proportion of the village population began to expand.

LANDLESSNESS

In some places of heavy population and declining local resources landlessness – by which I mean absence of ownership rights – was already evident in the early part of the nineteenth century. In Java, for example, as I have already pointed out, there are many references to land shortages at that time to which people made accommodations such as the alternate use of land shares. But this was a pattern of limited application across Southeast Asia as a whole at this time. By the early part of the twentieth century, however, landlessness was reported in many lowland regions where commercial production had become commonplace. Perhaps its most spectacular expression was to be found in Lower Burma; there, land alienation became an acute problem in 1915–30, when over 500 000 hectares were lost to peasant owners because of debt. In the early 1930s, nearly half the agricultural land of the delta region was owned by non-agriculturalists (a rate which reached 67 per cent if only the five major districts are included), and Chettiars held 50 per cent of this land. Around the same time in Upper Burma, by contrast, 85 per cent of land was owned by people engaged directly in agriculture.

Around the 1960s, landlessness was a defining feature of life for a great number of lowland peasants. By that time in Java, perhaps as many as 60 per cent of households were landless or near landless, without access to land or perhaps renting or sharecropping it. In central Luzon, 'by 1971 over half the households . . . were landless'.[31] Local studies of particular villages across the lowland areas of Southeast Asia provided the sharp detail of the general trend. In one village in the Philippines, for example, the proportion of landless households mounted from 31 per cent in 1966 to 43 per cent in 1974 and 63 per cent in 1980. In the mid 1950s, 58 per cent of the households in one village in Leyte in the Philippines were reported as landless. In another Philippine village, this time in Laguna, around half the households were made up of landless labourers. The same reporters described a village in west Java where one quarter of the village households were landless with another quarter cultivating no more than 0.1 hectares of land each and dependent for the bulk of their livelihood upon agricultural wage labour.[32] In one Malay village, 'only 199 of the 399 adults in the village owned any land at all, and among them holdings varied from .094 acre to about 32.75 acres',[33] while it was already the case in the mid 1950s that 'less than one half of the padi land of north Malaya [was] owned by the farmers who cultivate[d] it'.[34] In Thailand, too, the problem of landlessness was deepening; around Chiang Mai in the north, the rapid growth of commercial agriculture from the early 1950s had apparently caused 'a concurrent development of three phenomena: first, a large part of the village population became landless householders; second, an increasing number of villagers were cultivating on smaller and smaller farms; and third, ownership of greater proportions of the riceland around every village tended to be concentrated in fewer hands'.[35] The movement of population from the centre to the north only exacerbated these problems. By the late 1970s, varying estimates put the number of landless rural households in the whole country between 10 and 25 per cent.

As I have noted, this process spread only gradually across the landscape, so that some accounts of a roughly contemporary kind still remarked on the prevalence of landholding. One scholar, for example, reported of a northern Thai village in the early 1960s that 'throughout the history of Ban Ping, there has never been a class of landless farmers'.[36] In Thailand's northeast around 1970, 'the overall lack of pressure on land [was] reflected in the lack of concern over land titles and the general absence of dispute over land ownership'.[37] In Luzon's Ilocos region, 'almost all farmers

Table 4.1 Land by type of ownership, Burma 1901–39 ('000 hectares)

Period	*Total agricultural land*	*Area owned by agriculturalists*	*Area owned by non-agriculturalists*		*Percentage of land owned by non-agriculturalists*
			resident	*non-resident*	
1901–05	4 734	4 076	251	407	13.9 (18.1)(*a*)
1905–10	5 810	4 917	330	563	15.4 (21.4)
1910–15	6 816	5 806	381	629	14.8 (21.5)
1915–20	7 054	5 930	347	776	15.9 (23.2)
1920–25	7 234	5 913	390	931	18.3 (26.3)
1925–30	7 484	5 984	438	1 063	20.0 (28.2)
1930–35	7 630	5 461	514	1 656	28.4 (40.6)
1935–39	7 850	5 210	588	2 028	33.4 (47.5)

(a) bracketed figures are percentages of land in Lower Burma owned by non-agriculturalists. The first bracketed figure relates to the years 1901–2.

Source: Cheng, *The rice industry of Burma*, pp. 143–5.

own the land they till. Few are tenants of absentee landlords'.[38] In Laos, the only pocket of notable landlessness was around Vientiane, 'where demographic conditions [were] such that there was a small but significant group of landless peasants';[39] before 1975 in Vientiane province, it was estimated that about 70 to 80 per cent of peasants worked land they owned, of sizes between one and five hectares; the largest holdings were about thirty hectares. Landlordism, therefore, was not generally significant. In Cambodia between 1955 and 1965, nearly all farmers owned their own land, although by the 1960s, local landlessness was becoming more obvious, resulting in a significant movement of poor peasants to the capital. But notwithstanding the lagged spread of the phenomenon outside the most heavily populated areas, there could be no doubt about the direction and inevitability of change.

PROTECTIVE INTERVENTIONS

Some governments made some efforts to contain these apparently relentless tendencies towards enrichment and impoverishment. In Burma, authorities introduced the so-called patta system, which offered secure title to land and exemption from land taxes in exchange for an undertaking that the land would not be mortgaged; in general, however, only already prosperous people took advantage of the scheme which was wound up in 1907. Around the same time, a number of abortive legislative schemes sought to protect Burmese peasants from alienation of their lands. The most notable example of protectionism was the creation in Malaya of reservations for Malays. Under the Malay Reservations Enactment introduced in 1913, no title to land of any kind within a reserved area could be transferred to a non-Malay. This was an attempt by the British government to prevent the wholesale appropriation of Malay land by Chinese and others, and was designed, for political as well as economic reasons, to preserve the Malay peasant economy in its 'traditional' rice-growing form, and to allow Malays to develop at their own pace, segregated from the harsher economic winds of open competition. New regulations in 1933 sought to strengthen the enactment by closing loopholes which, for example, had earlier permitted Chinese to control land in reservations through the use of a power of attorney or to come into the enjoyment of reservation land offered as a security for a loan. Notwithstanding its well-meaningness, the reservations scheme failed to take account of the fact that 'the Malay population did not itself command the financial resources to create a Malay economy, and with non-Malay finance excluded the government was the only remaining source of capital for Malays in reservation areas'.[40] A different kind of defensive accommodation was provided by various state-sponsored efforts to allow peasants to buy land through the encouragement and support of cooperatives. In Thailand, for example, the government established such land purchasing organisations, but with little success; in 1950, there were just 820 families collected into 21 such groups, in possession of only 3000 hectares of rice land.

FRAGMENTATION

The processes of transformation I have described involved not just increasing land concentration but also the phenomenon of land fragmentation. Fragmentation involved not only the division of land shares into ever smaller plots (for a variety of reasons including topography and the need to spread risk), but also the reduction of the land area held by most landowners. In the first of these senses, fragmentation was most evident in long settled and heavily populated regions; Gourou, for example, noted 'the remarkable parceling of the rice-fields' in Tonkin; 'there are at least sixteen million parcels'.[41] In the second, for our purposes the more important sense and the one with which we shall be concerned, fragmentation was the evitable result of the combination of land concentration, population growth and increasing commercialisation. In one village in southern Vietnam before 1958, for example, 35 per cent of the village's rice land was held by one landowner, while a quarter of the village's households owned less than one hectare. In another southern village in the late 1950s, just under half the landholders owned less than two hectares each, while two-thirds held less than four hectares; that minority holding ten or more hectares, comprising just over ten per cent of landholders, held almost two-thirds of the village land. By 1973 in Java, nearly 60 per cent of farms were less than half a hectare in size, while the bottom 40 per cent of farms occupied only 12 per cent of the total area in farms.

Sometimes fragmentation resulted from the sale of parts of existing holdings; one report of a northern Thai village around 1970 noted a growth of smaller holdings through subdivision as the limits of the frontier were reached. But a major cause of fragmentation lay in the predominant custom of equal inheritance of holdings in a context of a closing land frontier. 'The equal sharing of the estate among all the children makes for a great development of parceling in this country of large families,' remarked

Gourou.[42] The widespread fragmentation of land in West Malaysia was also attributable in significant measure to equal inheritance. Generational change, then, usually implied a subdivision of a holding among heirs, both male and female. The result, over time, in some places was a complex fragmentation into tiny shares; Gourou, for example, cited the example of the village of Nhi Chau in the Red River delta, where there were thirty-two parcels per hectare.[43] For a time, and in various places, there were techniques for avoiding such situations. In Burma, for example, while the frontier was still open, it appears to have been commonplace for joint inheritors to sell their interest to a single family member and move on to reclaim their own piece of new land. Something similar was reported in Malaya. Sometimes, too, the land might be rented out and the proceeds divided amongst the heirs. Sometimes, again, heirs chose to rotate the use of the inherited land amongst themselves. Sometimes, a single inheritor rented in the shares on the other inheritors. In some cases, as well, the custom of equal inheritance might be ignored in favour of the perceived greater good of retaining the integrity of the holding. Strategic marriages were also a method of consolidating land amongst landholders to avoid the fragmentation which would otherwise result from generational change. In addition, apart from the fissuring caused by inheritance, generational problems also arose from time to time: in Laos, according to one writer, the partitioning of land or plain misfortune 'can easily lead to this generation's rich peasant family being next generation's poor family'.[44]

Notwithstanding attempts to restrict the effect of inheritance, and the fact that farms in newly reclaimed commercial rice areas were often much larger than those in longer settled regions – some in Lower Burma as large as 160 hectares – fragmentation both of land plots and of ownership continued and intensified. Malaya's 1960 agricultural census revealed that more than three-quarters of all farms were less than five acres [2 ha.] in size, and one-third were less than two acres [0.8 ha.]. In 1970, the average size of paddy-growing farms in West Malaysia was 3.1 acres. According to one assessment of a local area in West Malaysia, 'the most conspicuous feature in landholding in the villages studied was subdivision and fragmentation'.[45] In the village of Bang Chan in Thailand's Central Plain, the size of land shares in the mid 1950s was just over half what it had been in 1910. More generally, in Thailand between 1950 and 1963, there was similarly a fall in the average size of holdings. In northern Thailand, according to one local study made in the 1970s, 'many smallholders (under 10 rai and especially 5 rai and under) own increasingly small and marginal plots which cannot regularly meet their own subsistence needs'.[46] In Indonesia, according to the 1973 agricultural census, just under 60 per cent of rice farms (only those of 0.1 hectares and larger were counted) were less than three quarters of a hectare in size, just over 10 per cent were larger than two hectares in size, while 'the average wet rice farm area per farmer is only one-half a hectare'[47] and average farm size in decline. According to the 1960 census, 9.1 per cent of Philippine rice farms were less than one hectare in size, almost one-third were between one and two hectares in size, with 24 per cent between two and three hectares. More generally in the Philippines, average farm size shrank from about 3.5 hectares in 1960 to just 2.8 hectares in 1980. In the Pangasinan region, average farm size was around one hectare in the early 1960s, but getting smaller all the time. In Burma, too, the average size of holdings dropped while the incidence of land fragmentation increased; between the 1930s and the 1960s, the average size of Burmese farms was halved.

TENANCY

It is evident from all this that the image of the typical peasant as a sturdy landholding producer, focused on and occupied by the production of the household's means of subsistence, is misleading. Emerging state power, more elaborate commercialisation and population growth combined to ensure that a great part of Southeast Asia's agricultural land fell into a variety of arrangements which are most conveniently labelled as tenancy.[48] 'Almost all the large holdings and a large part of the middling holdings are exploited by tenants and sharecroppers who work approximately one half of the cultivated area of the Delta', remarked Gourou in the 1930s of the Tonkin delta; 'many of the small landowners are tenant farmers also'.[49] In the Philippines, the 1965 census revealed that 46 per cent of farms were tenant operations. In Malaya, the 1960 agricultural census reported that almost 50 per cent of rice farms were tenanted, either wholly or partly. In addition, share tapping (as distinct from tree rental) of rubber farms was very common. 'Many, and perhaps most, Malay peasants', remarked one scholar, 'do not gain access to land by becoming land owners. Instead farmers depend on a complex system of leasing and borrowing, and a great many Malay peasants achieve their livelihood by combining agriculture on hired land with supplementary labour of various sorts'.[50] In the delta region of Thailand, where the proportion of landless had reached 46 per cent by 1950, 'the bulk of commercial rice . . . comes from great estates cultivated by a changing stream of tenant farmers supervised by a rent collector for the absentee landlord';[51] the tenancies were often terminated annually, giving 'no encouragement to settled village life'.

In the Philippines, tenanted land as a proportion of all farm land grew steadily through the late nineteenth and twentieth centuries. In central Luzon, for example, 38 per cent of all farms were tenant-operated in 1903; by 1948 that figure had risen to 60 per cent. In that year the census revealed that 85 per cent of farms larger than 24 hectares were in the possession of absentee landlords, while in the province of Pampanga, 88 per cent of all farms were tenanted. Increasingly, land fell into the hand of speculators – 'in essence, a capital migration'[52] north from the Tagalog areas – who acquired land bit by bit in small pieces; 'financing and credit mechanisms replaced the axe and plow as the means to acquire land'.[53] Homesteaders without sufficient capital often borrowed too heavily, were forced to sell their land or pass it over to their creditors, and found themselves working as tenants on what they had previously owned. By the early 1960s, three-quarters of Pangasinan's peasants were landless tenants. In 1968, the emerging pattern of land acquisition was that the largest owners had come into the possession of multiple small parcels of land, a significant contrast from the vast contiguous stretches of land in the old haciendas.

The same process, albeit of more limited scope, was at work in Siam. By 1910, most rice land in the Rangsit region on Siam's Central Plain was in the hands of absentee large landholders and worked by tenants. A major reason for this development was that many immigrants, far from home and the support mechanisms they might otherwise have relied upon, had to seek credit to operate their holdings. Their inability to service their obligations frequently led to the loss of their land and, equally, the growth of a class of larger landholders who rented out their acquired agricultural land to tenants. Accordingly, the levels of tenancy in this highly commercialised centre were higher than anywhere else in the country, with land increasingly concentrated in fewer hand and fewer farms, and the growth of a permanent class of people who relied wholly on their labour to make ends meet. In time, the phenomenon of landlessness and the practice of tenancy which it fathered spread elsewhere in the plain and beyond. In northern Thailand by the 1930s, sharecropping was 'commonplace'[54]; by 1968, two in five farmers in the Central Plain rented at least some of the land they planted.

In Burma, the pattern was similar but much more pronounced; indeed, as we have noted, the exigencies of the Depression saw vast amounts of land fall into the hands of Chettiar moneylenders and led to a situation in which 'over half the land in Lower Burma was owned by people who did not, personally and continuously, either work the land or supervise and direct the cultivation of their holdings'.[55]

Table 4.2 Distribution of farms by tenure in the Philippines

	1903		*1918*		*1938*	
	no.	*percent*	*no.*	*percent*	*no.*	*percent*
owners	658 886	80.8	1 520 026	77.8	804 766	49.2
part owners	–	–	–	–	254 637	15.6
cash tenants	14 678	1.8	61 996	3.1	17 111	1.0
share tenants	132 103	16.2	256 517	13.2	547 954	33.5
labour tenants	817	0.1	6 259	0.3	–	–
non-rentals	8 969	1.1	110 478	5.6	–	–
share-cash tenants	–	–	–	–	8 652	0.5
farm managers	–	–	–	–	1 587	0.1
TOTAL	815 453	100	1 955 276	100	1 634 726	100

Source: Donald E. Douglas, 'An historical survey of the land tenure situation in the Philippines', *Solidarity* 7 (1970), p. 69. See also Norman G. Owen, 'On using the Philippine census', in Norman G. Owen (ed.), *Compadre colonialism: studies on the Philippines under American rule* (Ann Arbor: Michigan Papers on South and Southeast Asia No. 3, Center for South and Southeast Asian Studies, University of Michigan, 1971), pp. 117–18.

Table 4.3 Areas let at full fixed rents in Burma, 1901–39 ('000 hectares) (*a*)

	Area let at full fixed rents		*As percentage of total occupied area*	
Period	*All Burma*	*Lower Burma*	*All Burma*	*Lower Burma*
1901–05	854	774	19.9	27.6
1905–10	1 064	1 009	18.3	30.2
1910–15	1 243	1 188	18.2	32.0
1915–20	1 376	1 336	19.5	35.0
1920–25	1 576	1 512	21.8	37.5
1925–30	1 904	1 779	25.4	41.6
1930–35	2 398	2 221	31.4	50.8
1935–39	2 851	2 594	36.4	57.2

(a) table does not include areas let on share rents. Around 1930, these made up around 1 per cent of all rented lands in Lower Burma and about 67 per cent of all rented lands in Upper Burma.

Source: Cheng, *The rice industry of Burma*, p. 157.

THE GROWTH OF TENANCY

Lack of land and shortage of capital were the major reasons for the growth of tenancy. For the landless, the only means available to farm land for their family's sustenance was through tenancy. For those with marginal holdings, tenancy was the only way to enhance their access to land. Peasants strapped for cash were sometimes forced to rent out their land and regain access to it through a sharecropping arrangement; 'this is one of the few sources of large-scale credit available to small landowners, and the alternative would probably be outright sale'.[56] Alternatively and ironically, shortage of the capital a peasant needed to cultivate his own land could force a peasant to rent it out to his creditor; in one peasant's words, 'land is in the name of the poor but in the hands of the rich'.[57]

The major form of tenancy that developed in Southeast Asia was share tenancy. In the crudest sense, tenants provided their landlord with an agreed proportion of the crop in return for the use of the land. However, the arrangements made were generally much more complex than this, and changed in relation to a wide range of circumstances. In the earliest forms of tenancy practised in the Philippines – a major site for this kind of agreement owing to the relatively numerous large landholdings there – the share arrangement reflected that fact that land was still relatively abundant and labour stocks low, in other words, the landlord did not have an assured supply of labour. Accordingly, in order to entice sharecroppers to take up land, the proportion of the harvest the sharecropper made over to the landlord was small, and the range and size of landlord inputs in terms of such items as seed, cattle, labour costs for items like transplanting, access to transport facilities and credit proportionately greater. The landlord provided an interest-free ration of (relatively high priced) rice in instalments during the period of field preparation, to be repaid from the tenant's share of the crop and by performing various unpaid odd jobs for the landlord such as fencing or gardening. In this situation of relative balance, the landlord sought to increase his influence and to chain the tenant to his holding by putting him – and keeping him – in his debt. However, by the 1920s and 1930s, and even more markedly after World War II, the balance of power had swung decisively in favour of the landlord, and the division of inputs and outputs had moved correspondingly much more strongly to his benefit. Under a typical half-and-half rice-sharing agreement, the landlord furnished the land, managed the operation (including determining what was to be grown, but not the means to be used), and paid half the cost of seeds, the transplanting of seedlings, harvesting and threshing, and provided a houseplot. The tenant provided labour from his household, tools and other agricultural implements, an animal for field work, and constructed his own shelter. Landlord and tenant shared the costs of irrigation, fertiliser and any other costs.

As time went on, and the preponderance of power fell ever more to the favour of the landlord – a phenomenon evident not just in the Philippines but right across the region – conditions for tenants worsened. The increasing dependence of the sharecropper on the landlord was most obviously expressed in his dependence on the landlord for credit to carry through his productive cycle. Increasingly, however, the provision of credit became not so much a means of tying tenants down or expanding production, but rather of increasing the share of his harvest that the tenant was required to hand over. According to an inquiry made in central Luzon in the early 1950s, the returns for the tenant were so low in the 'demoralizing conditions' under which he lived that the landlord's own interests in maximising his own returns were being jeopardised; the result was 'an economy beset by cross-purposes'.[58] The inquiry found that 'almost 60 per cent of the palay produced by the average peasant cultivator was taken in settlement of farm rent, loans and advances, and interest on those loans'.[59]

Sharecropping may have been the dominant form of tenancy in Southeast Asia, practised in contexts as varied as the Philippines, the east coast of West Malaysia, the Minangkabau region and parts of northern Thailand, but there was, as well, a significant incidence of fixed-rent tenancy. In the

Rangsit region of the Central Plain of Thailand, fixed-cash rent was the most common tenancy arrangement. The major reason for its development was that, unlike the situation in the Philippines, most landlords were of the absentee variety who had invested in land as a means of profit rather than as a mode of life; they had little knowledge or experience of farming and, in any case, had employment elsewhere. Accordingly, they preferred fixed-rent contracts which assured them of an income and relieved them of managerial duties. Elsewhere on the Central Plain, too, money rent was generally more common than sharecropping, although the sudden fall in prices in the Depression brought tenants – successfully – to seek to convert to crop sharing to prevent them sinking into ruinous debt. In Lower Burma, too, most land came rented by full fixed share under the twin influences of greater competition for land among potential tenants and a greater proclivity for absenteeism among landlords; as competition increased in Upper Burma, fixed-share became more common. In the Tonkin delta region of Vietnam, cash rents seem to have been in force; the rapid decline in prices during the Depression forced landlords to cuts their rents severely – to as much as a quarter of the pre-slump price – but not, as far as I can judge, to convert to share forms of tenancy.

The cases of central Luzon, Rangsit and Lower Burma portray tenancy in bold relief because they were all sites of considerable large-landholding and landlessness. Tenancy, however, was evident elsewhere as well where the distinction and distance between rich and poor were not so obvious. In Malaya, for example, tenancy relations – controlled by a variety of different mechanisms ranging from fixed rent to conditional sale (jual janji) – were ubiquitous, but they were characteristically constructed around kinship ties which 'formed the basic feature of Malay land tenure systems'.[60] Notwithstanding the pressures of commercialisation, such kin-based tenancies (often between parents and children or older and younger relatives) remained 'flexible and relatively generous',[61] with the idea of 'renting them land as a way of starting them out on the ladder towards ownership'.[62] Similar forms of kin-structured tenancy were also to be found in parts of northern Thailand, in the Philippines (where ritual kinship was unusually important), and around Vientiane in Laos.

Such kin-based arrangements, however, did not always disguise the enhanced power exercised by the landlord, which was increasingly expressed in the growing requirement for cash rental rather than payment in rice and a tendency towards written rather than verbal contracts, while the 'increasingly common practice of registering tenancy agreements'[63] aggravated the tendency of landlords to insist that tenants fulfil their obligations exactly. In northern Thailand before World War II, tenants might grow risky and unpredictable dry season second crops of soybeans, tobacco or vegetables without having to provide a share of the fruits of these products to the landlord; 'by 1950 because of growing competition for rented riceland, even among relatives, landlords began to require some payment of cash rent or a small share of the crop as rent for dry season cultivation'.[64] Throughout the region, as the availability of land shrank even further, and as increasing numbers of poorer landed peasants were forced to sell their land, even the holding of a tenancy became a valuable thing in itself which could be bought and sold. Thus, tenants who required substantial income might sell off or pawn their tenancy to another – often an urban dweller – for cash. Increasing competition for tenanted land resulted not just in an increasing insecurity of tenancy – one mid 1950s study of Kelantan found that two-fifths of rice land under tenancy changed holder every year – but produced its own exquisite punishment, the notion of paying a premium for the right to be a tenant; this arrangement, indeed, was already in evidence in the Philippines before World War II. One form of this, *gadai*, was a kind of reverse pawning of land under which the tenant provided the landlord with a lump sum in advance, in return for which the tenant enjoyed cultivation rights to the land until the lump sum was repaid. *Puesto*, another variety of premium, was the 'compensation' provided by a new tenant to the tenant he was replacing. The fragmentation of tenanted holdings – that is, the decline in the size of the area held by a tenant – also became more evident. The payment of rent in the form of cash, or at least a fixed share of rent, before the cultivation process began, became normalised; more generally, cash rents and leases increasingly replaced crop shares as the usual mode of payment. Finally, landlords' greater power made tenure increasingly precarious, with short term tenure becoming common – even in the late 1930s in Lower Burma, around 50 per cent of tenants moved from one holding to another every year – and the notion of tenurial inheritance disappearing. Indeed, with the expansion of state-sponsored and supported commercial cropping and mechanisation, some landlords, in the Philippines, in the Muda region of West Malaysia, and elsewhere, contrived to rid themselves of their tenants and put their land wholly to mechanised large-scale cropping rather than rent it out.

As might be expected, the sharpening of landlord–tenant tensions was most evident where history and land scarcity pressed most heavily. Where circumstances were different and land relatively plentiful, the incidence of tenancy was less common and relations between landlord and tenant remained gentler. Notwithstanding the increasing concentration of holdings and consequent landlessness around Rangsit and more generally in the Central Plain, much of the farmland elsewhere in Thailand was owned by those who worked it. In 'Ban Ping' in northern Thailand in the early 1960s, only 5 per cent of farms were worked through tenancy; 'few Ban Ping households are entirely supported by rent; none think of themselves as landlords. Renting land is seen not as a way of life but as an expedient means of cooperation between a household with too few able-bodied members to work all the land it owns and a household with too many members for its land. Landlord and tenant are not distinct social classes but, rather, are best seen as transient stages through which anyone might pass during his career'.[65] In Thailand's northeast in 1973, only 8.7 per cent of rural households were renting land, and only just over 3 per cent of the cultivated area was under rent. In the Laotian province of Vientiane, the one-fifth of the population which owned no ricefields mostly rented land from more prosperous farmers for a share of the harvest ranging from 20 to 50 per cent, or worked other peasants' fields in return for a rice payment.

TENANCY AS A SOCIAL FORM

As tenancy came to be expressed in Southeast Asia, especially in regions of large-landholding and high levels of landlessness, it exercised – especially through the mechanism of credit dependency and the increasingly asymmetric relationship between landlord and tenant, not to mention low levels of taxation on land which 'failed to create a situation in which the landlords were encouraged to increase agricultural productivity'[66] – a strongly conservative influence on agriculture which served to bridle further economic and social development. McLennan remarked crisply of the Philippines that 'despite the growing scarcity of land and the increasing abundance of labor since about 1925 in the Central Plain, the social arrangements for the exploitation of land resources has prevented intensification of land use until now. The hacienda system in its mature stage has been neither labor intensive nor extensive in the usual sense of these words. A high density of laborers has occupied the land, but a high input of labor upon the land has not materialized'.[67] In Burma in the 1930s, again, an official report remarked that 'rents especially in the congested areas of Lower Burma are on a level which keeps the tenant's standard of living down to a subsistence level and maintains him in a state of permanent indebtedness from which there is no hope of escape'.[68] By 1930, 'only one out of four tenants who cultivated paddy was able in an average year to pay his rent and all his loans and could still put aside from his harvest sufficient paddy to feed himself and his family during the next cultivating season'.[69] To return to the Philippines, the well-travelled rate of indebtedness among tenants led to the refinement of categories of loans on a scale of ever more impossible conditions: '*Takalanan* designates the interest rate when advanced palay [unhusked rice] is returned at the rate of three cavans for every two cavans borrowed. *Terciohan* requires repayment of four cavans for three cavans advanced. *Talindua* signifies that for two cavans advanced three must be repaid. *Takipan* is the term employed when two cavans are paid back for every cavan advanced. These rates of interest, ranging up to 100 per cent, are for a six month period, doubling when accounted annually.'[70]

Such arrangements made of the landlord a narrow-minded rentier rather than an imaginative investor or entrepreneur; his interest was in extracting an ever greater proportion of the tenant's production and limiting ever more his own costs, in exploitation and extraction rather than creative development. In response, tenants had correspondingly little interest in improving their farm because the great bulk of increased production fell immediately into the hands of their landlords. In Rangsit, for example, the short term tenancies in vogue gave tenants no incentive to improve their land for fear that it might be tenanted out to another peasant in the following year. One scholar of Luzon, indeed, was led to argue that peasants sought to increase the earnings of their households by investing as little as possible of their family labour on their farms, and maximising their work investments as wage labourers on others' tenanted farms and in off-farm labour which provided them with the bulk of their income; 'to them, farmland was not so much a means of creating a profit from agricultural production as the means of having a dependable patron in the person of the proprietaryo [landlord]'.[71]

LAND REFORM

In the face of the tensions which often developed in relations over the ownership, control, rental and use of cultivated land, states attempted with varying degrees of conviction and enthusiasm to intervene in the realm of property relations in order to provide themselves and their subjects with greater measures of security and stability.

Their task was in some ways facilitated and in some ways made more difficult by other events. In the period of depression in the 1930s in Burma, for example, large numbers of peasants lost their land to creditors because of their inability to meet their commitments in the atmosphere of severely lowered prices. In Thailand, however, there was no comparable loss of holdings – although there were some cases where 'owners became renters and renters became hired laborers'[72] – partly because peasants were not so close to the margin as in Burma, and partly because of a reluctance to foreclose on land that had little value (in some cases just one-twelfth of its pre-crisis worth) under the circumstances, and which could not in any case be put to productive use. The collapse of European imperial power with the Japanese invasion worked against the trend of increasing land concentration. In Burma, for example, Burmese squatters took up the property left by fleeing multitudes of Indian non-agriculturalist landholders; large landholders in Upper Burma fled, too, before the Japanese advance, leaving their tenants free of their rent obligations. In similar circumstances of disorder and fear during the first Indochina war, many landlords in southern Vietnam took flight to the capital or to nearby towns and left their tenants to their own devices. Again, the flight of around one-tenth of Laos's population in the period after the regime change in 1975 helped to reduce pressure on land resources.

Incidents such as these, however, were minor interludes which had no substantial or structural role to play in curbing the powerful tendencies towards land concentration and tenantry. That task remained the work of government. As I have noted, the most serious and most systematic efforts at land reform occurred in those parts of Southeast Asia where Marxist-influenced regimes came to power. In the most important of these efforts, that undertaken in Vietnam, land reform was a revolutionary action. It was designed not just to rectify inequalities but to transform and even create anew the bases of rural power by stripping old forces of their property, their economic and political power, and their status; 'the goal of the land reform was not only to take away the land and other wealth of the landlords but to cut them off from the psychological and organizational bases of their power and to destroy their prestige, so that they would lose all influence over the peasants'.[73] It therefore required peasants to take an active role in the process of land reform; their participation would lead them logically to voluntary membership of cooperatives, envisaged as the longer range solution to poverty.

The first phase of land reform, as we have seen, involved a rent reduction campaign, essentially begun in 1949, and was brought to a crescendo by a series of mass mobilisation drives between 1953 and 1956. Land reform proper was initiated in 1953, again in a series of five waves lasting until 1956; its four-step process involved cadres proclaiming the policy and discerning the local situation, ascribing people to classes, confiscating and redistributing land and goods, and finally reviewing what had been achieved. In terms of a reallocation of land to poor and landless peasants, the reform was a significant success; it broke the back of landlord power and saw a wholesale redistribution of land among the peasantry. However, the overzealous and frantic efforts of many cadres in seeking out class enemies and purging allegedly corrupt and anti-revolutionary local party organisations brought numerous excesses, although tales of bloody atrocities committed against real or imagined landlords were later shown to be greatly exaggerated. Reportedly, by the end of the land reform period, 810 000 hectares – over one-third of north Vietnam's cultivable land – as well as tools, houses and cattle, had been expropriated and redistributed to 2 104 448 households (8.3 million peasants). Land reform was quickly succeeded by the stages of collectivisation: first, work-exchange schemes (1956–8), which aimed to pool the labour of farmers for common tasks, usually on a seasonal basis; then a rapid movement to low rank cooperatives (1958–60), involving the pooling of land and equipment as well as labour; and the more gradual movement to higher cooperatives (1960–72).

The weakness of the communist regime in Laos did not allow it to unleash the forces of social change to anything like the degree that occurred in Vietnam and Cambodia. There the movement into cooperatives was undertaken without a prior exercise in land reform; it may have been hoped that cooperativisation would gradually lead to a decline in larger private holdings. All it did, however, was to bring the problem of land into sharp relief and frighten landholders into sometimes violent antagonism against and non-cooperation with the cooperatives. Those who joined cooperatives retained their land and effectively leased it to the cooperative, but they retained the right to withdraw themselves and their land at any time. As we have seen the cooperatives soon wasted away because they offered landed peasants little; 'the history of collectivization . . . can be written as a story of the tug-of-war between collective institutions and household economies',[74] remarked one commentator. Household economies won.

The only other potentially revolutionary push for land reform was that promoted by the Indonesian Communist Party in 1963, in the wake of 1960 land legislation (among other things, setting minimum and maximum sizes for land holdings and seeking to protect the interests of sharecroppers) which was ideologically grounded, misconceived and in any case never intended for general implementation. The communist efforts at unilateral land reform, notably in east and central Java, were unsuccessful and contributed only to the rise in social tension which had its denouement in the failed 'coup attempt' of October 1965 and afterwards. Through the 1960s, something approximating one million hectares of land was redistributed, even though some of it was seized back after 1965. No attempt, however, was made to carry out the 1960 regulation which decreed that holdings less than two hectares could not be sold.

Socialist Burma legislated in 1963 to cap rents on land, and to protect peasant land and property from alienation through indebtedness, and in 1965 abolished tenancy outright, although the practice continued into the early 1970s, with tenants still comprising two-fifths of all farmers in 1970. By the late 1970s, however, there was evidence of a much more evenly distributed pattern landholding.

In non-socialist regimes, land reform was much more a passive process of gifting the wretched, both with the aim of hobbling the potential for agrarian unrest and on the assumption that tenancy was detrimental to enhancing production. For advice in achieving these aims, governments sometimes called on American experience and expertise which had been forged in other Asian contexts. In Thailand, a 1950 law restricted rents to one quarter of the produce, but no serious effort was made to enforce it. The 1974 Land Rent Act required that formal contracts be made between landlords and tenants, decreed that rent not exceed one-third of the produce, and set the term for contracts at six years rather than the single year that had gradually become the norm. In 1975 a land reform law sought to limit holdings to fifty rai [eight hectares], with all land surplus to that amount to be purchased by the state and allocated to landless farmers. Neither measure was ever seriously implemented, and rates of landlessness and tenancy grew with rising population.

In the Philippines, the Rice Share Tenancy Act of 1933 aimed to protect tenant interests by a more equal sharing of inputs and produce, an attack on usurious practices by landowners, and protection against arbitrary ejection of tenants, but the law was hobbled by its unworkable conditions of enforcement, requiring those whose very interests it would prejudice to petition for its local introduction; it was later amended, but without significant effect. The early Commonwealth period had also seen limited efforts by the government, apparently based on the turn of the century programme of the American colonial government to purchase friar lands for redistribution, to acquire large estate lands for resale to their peasant occupants. By the early 1950s there was 'a great inertia on the part of the government to give really serious consideration to agriculture's many besetting handicaps and long standing maladjustments'.[75] Thereafter, there were further flimsy efforts to combat the baleful effects of tenancy and to redistribute lands more broadly. In 1954, an act sought to provide the tenant as much as 70 per cent of the crop, and the following year a land reform act was passed which aimed to reduce large landholdings to a maximum of 150 hectares. A Land Tenure Administration was empowered to purchase and, if necessary, expropriate large holdings for subdivision and sale to landless tenants. In 1963, an Agricultural Land Reform Code sought to convert tenancies to leaseholds and redistribute land to cultivators. None of these measures bore much fruit in the face of landlord opposition, bound around as they were with defensive administrative provisions (notably the 'very high land retention ceilings'[76]) and unsuited to the realities of the poverty of the Filipino tenant. Only in 1971, under severe pressure from a mobilised peasantry, did there emerge an amended Code of Agrarian Reform which focused on the conversion of share tenancies into fixed-rent arrangements. In the following year, a presidential decree ordained that all rice and corn lands larger than seven hectares and worked by tenants were to be transferred into leaseholds and, after fifteen annual payments by the lessees, designed to approximate 25 per cent of average net yields, would become their property. Until such time as all payments were made and the title made over to the former tenant, he would hold a 'Certificate of Land Transfer'.

South Vietnam, similarly troubled by rural insurrection, similarly began upon the road of half-hearted efforts at land redistribution. Land reform decrees in 1951 and 1953 were not implemented. In 1955, Prime Minister Diem introduced measures aiming to reduce rents and enhance tenant security. In 1956, the government sought to limit riceland holdings to 100 hectares per owner (of which owners themselves could cultivate no more than 30 per cent) and sell the surplus to tenants. The need to appease landlord interests saw a watering down of the legislation; this, together with implementation foot-dragging, deprived the programme of potentially significant social effects, although by 1965 more than 400 000 hectares of land had been expropriated and around half that amount sold to tenants (landless peasants, as distinct from tenants, were excluded from the arrangements). In 1970, President Thieu introduced a new 'land-to-the-tiller campaign' which aimed to limit land cultivated by owners to fifteen hectares with surplus land to be redistributed to tenants. In Malaya, a 1955 ordinance restricted tenants' rent on rice land to a maximum of one-third of the produce; but 'in effect the provisions of the ordinance were ignored'.[77] A new act passed in 1967 aimed at setting maximum rent levels and improving tenants' security over their tenures; like its predecessor, however, it faced the insuperable problem of ratification by the state governments. In effect, 'no concrete legislation for land reform has ever been proposed in Malaysia'.[78] In Burma, a number of post World War II Land Nationalisation Acts and edicts dating from 1948 removed the right to mortgage, rent or sell land, and sought to reallocate land to farmers; by the late 1950s, more than half a million hectares of nationalised land had been allocated to cultivators.

Of these measures, only three enjoyed some (in one case stillborn) success. The Burmese programme, put into effect in 1951 alongside a two-year development plan, saw the virtual disappearance of large holdings by 1958 and, by 1961, the transfer of about 1.35 million hectares to cultivators. In the Philippines, Marcos's 'Operation Land Transfer' and 'Operation Leasehold' programmes, notwithstanding bureaucratic tardiness and confusion and landlord intransigence (often in the form of 'transferring' their large holdings to the names of relatives or changing its status, or even by ridding themselves of tenants and working the land themselves) enjoyed considerable success. They accelerated the process of the decline of the large classic haciendas; with inheritance division, the political difficulties of peasant complaint, and land reform, haciendas tended to degenerate into scattered holdings at sizes below those set down for division, and their land increasingly came to be farmed as mechanised units without tenants. By 1980, almost 600 000 hectares had been transferred from share tenancy to leaseholdings. Such progress, according to some recent observers, allowed these farmers to take advantage of the much higher returns to farming which came from the introduction of Green Revolution technologies in the 1970s; 'yields have nearly doubled in villages where MVs [new high yielding varieties] have been adopted, increasing the divergence between the rental value of the land and the fixed leasehold rents and amortization fees prescribed by law over time'.[79] The productivity gains effectively reduced tenant's real rent to around 10–15 per cent of the harvest. As for the old landlords, many 'end up in the growing and newly-emerging class of rural-based industrialists and businessmen. They find new roles for themselves in the new scheme of things as rural bankers, as tractor lenders, as handicraft entrepreneurs-exporters, as fertilizer dealers, as land speculators or developers . . .'[80] In south Vietnam, the success of Thieu's 'Land to the Tiller' programme (described by one writer as a 'frantic distribution of land titles toward the end when it was too late to stem the Communist tide'[81]) rested upon many years of growing antagonism to landlordism, as well as the military efforts of the Viet Minh which scared many large landholders out of the countryside and into the cities. Under the programme, ironically virtually completed just months before the fall of Saigon to communist forces in 1975, over 2 million hectares of land had been actually transferred or successfully applied for.

One major criticism of all these programmes, however, was that they sought to tackle only tenancy and not the growing problem of landlessness. In the Philippines, they 'left out of account those 3.3 million rice and corn workers without land at all'.[82] As one commentator remarked, 'the law is totally silent on what benefits the landless rural poor, who constitute over 50 per cent of the working population in rice and corn areas, will get from land reform'.[83] In Burma and south Vietnam as well, landless agricultural workers found no succour in the reforms. The problem with such criticisms, however, is that there could never be a land reform which provided land to all those rural landless who might have wished to take it up. Putting aside questions as to whether such a policy might be desirable economically, and even the dubious proposition that it might meaningfully alleviate poverty in the rural areas, there was no longer sufficient land to satisfy the huge numbers of people who might have wished to lay claim to it.

LAND RESETTLEMENT

With few exceptions, then, Southeast Asian states avoided the multifarious problems associated with redistributing already occupied lands to the landless and, where they attempted to reconstitute existing patterns of ownership, their efforts remained concentrated on tenancy reform. Most states, however, were much more enthusiastic about 'colonising' the more sparsely inhabited regions of their territories, partly to provide opportunities for economic growth, and partly to bring these places under greater central control. In the Philippines, for example, from early in the twentieth century a series of programmes was implemented, without notable success, to resettle people from crowded Luzon into colonies established in the south, especially Mindanao. In West Malaysia, a series of smaller colonisation schemes pre-dated the settlement schemes of FELDA, but FELDA far outstripped what had gone before. It sought to carve out economically viable farms of oil palm or rubber from the jungle, providing the colonising peasant households with (repayable) start-up and maintenance funds but expecting them to become self-sufficient once their crops started bearing. The idea was to move people out of rice growing and create a class of landowning Malay cash croppers; by the late 1980s, under FELDA's auspices, more than 800 000 hectares had been developed, most of it devoted to oil palm, by more than 100 000 resettler households, even if the achievement came at massive financial cost and its social goals appeared increasingly illusory as the children of settlers disappeared into urban areas. In Sarawak, efforts were made in the 1960s to settle swiddeners on lowland plots as commercial rubber growers, but proved unsuccessful; successor initiatives, often involving oil palm cultivation, were only marginally more successful.

Schemes in Indonesia, dating from 1905, sought to relieve the aching press of population in Java and exploit what was perceived as the bounteous emptiness of those parts of the archipelago (first Lampung in south Sumatra and more recently Irian Jaya) where population was small and development slow. Lampung, indeed, boasted (if that is the appropriate word) 174 000 Javanese settlers by the end of the colonial period. Even though post-independence and especially post-1965 efforts bore more fruit – the period of the third five-year plan saw the movement of more than half a million families from Java – they had only the slightest influence on the rate of growth of the population of Java. At the same time, the Indonesian government intensified its efforts to settle swiddeners and hunter-gatherers in sedentary communities. Similarly, land resettlement schemes in upland Thailand, developed under the umbrella of the National Tribal Welfare Committee established in 1959, and aiming to protect forest reservations, sought to transform swiddeners into settled agriculturalists; the effort failed to overcome the suspicion and antipathy of tribespeople who objected to being resettled. In northern Vietnam, the communist government created Special Economic Zones in upland areas from 1961 in which, over the following fifteen years, around a million people were settled; after the country was unified in 1975, a similar program was effected in the southern hill country to absorb people from the crowded north and the swollen cities of the south; ten years later they contained two million people, more than half of whom had moved in from northern Vietnam.

CONCLUSION

It was a considerable and significant irony that the combination of states, markets and population growth which had conspired to create and entrench the age of the peasantry in Southeast Asia also contained within the logic of their interconnectedness the means of its diminution. Even as the peasantry expanded its operations across the lowlands of the region, and as uplands and hinterland dwellers themselves endured a process of peasantisation, increasing numbers of petty cultivators found themselves denied access to the land which might sustain them. Some of them found their sustenance in labouring for their landed fellows as well as in other enterprises, others again were drawn into relations of tenanted subservience to large-holding landlords, while still others – especially from the early decades of the twentieth century as frontiers began to lose their indeterminateness – sought refuge in the cities. All these responses will be explored further in subsequent chapters.

What was extraordinary in all this, however, was the enduring tenacity of peasants in keeping even the smallest plots of land in their possession. Where, under other circumstances, the forces of change might have been expected to result in a simple concentration of holdings and a corresponding general landlessness, the pattern was rather one of large numbers of peasants hanging on to minuscule plots. The reasons for this phenomenon were complex. At one level it was perhaps explicable in terms of peasants' desire for security in the face of the uncertainties and instabilities of the broader economy; where other forms of income were precarious and uncertain, possession of even the smallest plot of land, perhaps no more than a house garden or orchard plot, provided a certainty of return which no other source of economic activity could promise. More convincing, however, were explanations that focused on patterns of entrepreneurial investment in rural areas and the development and enhancement of off-farm incomes. In some places in the recent past, the returns to rural entrepreneurs from landholding and rice farming were not competitive with other potential investments both within and outside the rural sector, so that 'the very forces that kept the small farmers poor also preserved their farms'.[84] At the same time, in a context of rapidly growing national economies, the opportunities provided to marginal landholders to enhance their incomes from non-farm employment – admittedly often of a low-return kind – allowed them to earn sufficient income for their household's sustenance 'without the distress sale of the "sublivelihood" plots'.[85]

Through a period of around 150 years, then, the importance of land in peasant life has taken a vaguely cyclical trajectory. From a stage of relative plenty and relative worthlessness in the early nineteenth century, land and its possession had advanced to a point of commercial pre-eminence by the early twentieth century – when it both signified and effected prosperity and status – a position it sustained into the 1950s. Thereafter, landholding's centrality subsided in the context of the development of more complex and modern economies and more diversified avenues of employment and livelihood; one scholar, indeed, suggested that in these circumstances some people were 'too busy to farm'.[86] It became no more than one of any number of methods of making capital and labour productive. Indeed, 'unlike the East Asian rice economies, where farm and non-farm incomes are inversely related, in Java it is the land rich households which obtain the greatest return from non-farm enterprises'.[87]

This was a gradual but nonetheless decisive transformation. It was part of a process which led, on the one hand, in the direction of the formation of a true class of consolidated modern farmers, specialists in agriculture, whose productive behaviour was shaped by the demands of the market, especially in its regional, national and international dimensions, and its ability to integrate its surpluses into these commercial circuits, rather than by the old prescriptions of village life, and on the other hand of a labour force which, transitionally, maintained its connection with the land in a fragile and tenuous way whilst it forged new productive relations – or embellished or elaborated upon older ones – with the larger world outside the village.

5 A Revolution in Labour

The distinguishing feature of the organisation of peasant labour around 1800 was its highly personal and informal cast. Within the village itself, many agricultural tasks and other work associated with agriculture were performed not by individual peasants alone, nor even by their households, but by larger horizontally-ordered groups formed within the village to carry out cooperative labour. In lowland rice agriculture, for example, the job of transplanting rice seedlings into a household holding or harvesting the mature crop had to be performed rapidly, and required the services of more workers than a single household itself could provide. Similarly, in swidden agriculture, planting was often done by larger work groups to ensure its rapid completion. Labour relations between village and supra-village authorities were mediated through vertical and personalised chains of leaders and followers; through them, the state laid obligations upon peasants to perform unpaid compulsory labour services, ranging from collecting forest produce to road and bridge building, as well as the construction and maintenance of water works. Outside the formal state sphere, the wealthy and influential enjoyed the services of their slaves and those bonded to them through debt.

Around the turn of the nineteenth century, then, wage labour existed in Southeast Asia in only localised and inconsequential forms. In Java, for example, there were groupings of porters who transported goods across the countryside in return for a wage, and there is also evidence of hired labour – either landless peasants or family members of landed households (sometimes, apparently, paid in money) – engaged for agricultural work on other peasants' fields or in processing plants. For the most part, however, wage labour was insignificant and exceptional. Over the course of the succeeding two centuries, there was a fundamental movement away from informal and personalised control of peasant labour and the widespread adoption of formalised wage labour. As before, the major agents in this process were the development of the state, the broader and deeper influence of markets, and the strengthening imperatives of demography.

THE 'DECLINE' OF COOPERATIVE AND RECIPROCAL LABOUR IN VILLAGE AGRICULTURE

Through the nineteenth and twentieth centuries, there are frequent references in the literature to the disappearance of reciprocal labour and its replacement by wage labour. 'The only significant change in the productive process between late nineteenth century Nueva Ecija and 1960', remarked one scholar of the Philippines, 'was the increasing substitution of hired labour for reciprocal labour'.[1] In a village of southern Vietnam in the late 1950s, noted another writer, 'to a surprising degree, money payments are made for labor services of all kinds, and to this extent work patterns reflect economic need rather than kinship obligations or considerations of mutual assistance'.[2] In the irrigated upland rice cultivation of the Lua' of northern Thailand, hired labourers were sometimes employed to assisting landholders with ploughing and harrowing.[3] As if to confirm the increasing prevalence of hired labour, observers occasionally noted peasants organising their production schedules to restrict the need to take on extra-family labour: thus, in one village in Thailand's Central Plain, 'by growing several varieties of different ripening dates, a farmer is able to spread out labor required in harvesting'.[4] In the same manner, the labour demanded by the tasks of uprooting and transplanting rice seedlings could be diluted by sowing seeds at different times.

The fading of supra-household reciprocal or cooperative labour has sometimes been the occasion of nostalgic sorrow, especially among urban-based nationalist politicians and Western romantics who grieved over the disappearance of what they took to be old indigenous values of social harmony, community solidarity, and selfless service for the group. Carter, for example, noted the neighbourly assistance offered to peasants at the time of planting and harvesting – 'the whole village turning out and working together on each owner's fields in turn'[5] – turning then to lament that 'in the lower plains . . . where the farmer is beginning to understand the profit to be derived from increase of production, this happy-go-lucky custom is falling into disuse, the merry amateurs being replaced by hard-working farm hands engaged at a wage for the season'.[6] Similarly, Moerman wrote that once 'huge work parties that ensured prompt transplanting were composed of everyone in Ban Ping and everyone in the next village'. But then things changed: 'with growing population, with an increasing number of farmers, and with smaller households, the old system disappeared to be replaced by a more carefully calculated exchange of labor among separate households, usually within the same village . . . . Exchange replaced fellowship; household organization replaced village organization; inexpensive food replaced elaborate hospitality; efficiency replaced fun; calculated reciprocity – and ultimately wages – came to dominate the work groups'.[7]

We need to be clear, however, about just what it was that had disappeared. For the most part, the cooperative labour celebrated by romantics was limited in its scope and was of a strictly reciprocal kind. It sprang from the insufficiency of the normal production unit, the household, for the specific task at hand – usually rice transplanting (requiring, according to one account, 165 000 plantings per hectare) or harvesting, but also things like fencing, the maintenance of irrigation channels, the construction and repair of religious buildings, forest slashing, felling and firing, or fishing through poisoning the water – which needed to be completed rapidly or which required large numbers of people working contemporaneously and in unison. Tasks which could be performed by the household unit of itself without outside assistance were not the subject of reciprocal labour. Rice cultivation, for example, was something predominantly performed by the household unit; as Leach remarked of his upland Burma swiddeners, 'each household cultivates its own individual plot (*yi*) and there is no communal ownership of produce'.[8] Accordingly, the drudgery of weeding the swiddens ('the most time consuming, most labor consuming, most uncomfortable, and most disliked portion of swidden agriculture'[9]) usually fell to the household. Moreover, because it did not have the immediacy of the tasks involved with rice farming, the work required for the second cropping of permanent fields, or for the cash cropping of produce like garlic, peanuts and soybeans, did not attract cooperative labour.

Supra-household cooperative labour groups were usually constructed between kin and friendship groups or local sub-groups rather than on a community wide basis. The work involved was reciprocal in the sense that assistance proffered to one household was expected to be returned in equal measure at an appropriate time, and the practice assumed a rough equivalence among participants in holding size and wealth and low levels of sales of surplus; 'since farmers could not expect to have much cash income to dispose of, they naturally had recourse to labour exchange'.[10] While no money changed hands, and while the landholder customarily provided free meals to the workers lending him aid, it was, then, in essence, a kind of non-monetised wage labour; labour itself was the wage. Its basis in hard- rather than softheadedness is made clear in the case of lowland rice harvesting, where reciprocal labour did not preclude the paying of a share of the quantity harvested, usually around one-fifth of the amount harvested, but sometimes only one-tenth or less. Amongst swiddeners, too, payments in rice or other goods were not unknown; they were made, for example, amongst the Lamet and the Hanunóo for work in such tasks as forest clearing, planting and harvesting, whilst the Iban allowed the opportunity for the performance of wage work in time of need, as when one's own crop failed to produce a proper harvest.

Where the practice of cooperative labour receded, its decline was not so much attributable to the intrusion of self-interested individualism – such individualists had always existed – but rather to its lack of consonance with changed conditions of production. In the first place, labour relations amongst the region's peasant producers changed decisively with the development of a large cohort of landless and near landless villagers as the strengthening state provided some guarantee of landed security, as it exchanged corvée for direct taxation, and as peasant societies became more tightly integrated into and influenced by a wider world economy. Up to a certain point, already existing landless labourers could be absorbed by the village community through their entering into relationships of dependence with wealthier peasants. Thus, in Java, the so-called *numpang* or dependent peasants, attached to the households of peasant landholders, provided their labour in exchange for sustenance. However, as levels of commercial exchange within and outside the village escalated, as hierarchies of power and inequalities of wealth developed, and as the number of landless increased, the competition for patrons grew so intense that the relationship of full dependency dissolved into a variety of formal and informal contracted arrangements. In other words, markets in labour had become institutionalised. Landed peasants had no longer to provide full sustenance in return for labour; they could now hire cheap labour as and when they wanted it, and dismiss it once the desired task was completed. In general, then, reciprocal labour was no longer so relevant in a situation where 'all households worked to the limits of their capacity for their own advancement. They exchanged labor grudgingly, when possible hiring labor to speed the extra tilling and to process a larger crop'.[11]

Siam's experience provides perhaps the best example of these processes at work. As we have seen, a major consequence of the dissolution of slavery and corvée, especially in the last decades of the nineteenth century, was to increase the supply of workers – wage labourers – available for the production of rice for the world market. While wage labour was not unknown in Siam – there were cases of its use in the 1860s – only in the 1890s did farmers begin to make use of it in a significant way, with the result that agricultural wages increased rapidly through this first and rather frantic period of agricultural development. Thereafter real wages declined, making wage labour even more attractive to rice producers. In Lower Burma, the relatively large holdings in evidence there were premised on a continuing supply of hired labourers, provided in the first instance by the immigration of poor peasants from Upper Burma (by the early 1880s, more than one person in ten in the delta region had been born in Upper Burma), then by the growing numbers unable to obtain or hold their own land, and later the immigration of farm labourers from India.

Under circumstances like these, with a poor and growing segment of the village population with limited or non-existent access to land and eager to obtain what they needed through the provision of their cheap labour to landed households or to other potential employers, there was no longer the need for landholding peasants to reciprocate their services amongst their landholding peers. Moreover, as larger holdings developed, their owners were unable themselves to service the labour obligations incumbent on their holdings and forced to rely on recruited workers. The trend towards hired labour was evident even on tenancies; 'especially where tenancy rates are high, transplanting is accomplished by the family concerned and help is hired especially for the purpose'.[12] And, as land size declined, landholders sometimes found it convenient to replace their tenants with less costly and troublesome wage workers.

Second, changing conditions of cropping no longer allowed – at least not nearly to the same extent – the successive application of large amounts of labour at discrete sites in the village through an extended period of time. This change was especially notable as cropping moved into a more intensive phase in the twentieth century. In particular, the growth of double (and triple) cropping meant a much more compressed and involved schedule of labour ('biological processes which formerly took six or eight months are now compressed into three',[13]) often governed by routinised water delivery timetables. Consequently, landholding peasant households were no longer in a position to proffer the kind of help to their fellows they had once made available, and peasant producers had perforce to take refuge in hired labour to accomplish what needed doing. In some places, indeed, tight schedules became even more hardened and inflexible because of irrigation schedules which had to be followed. Hired labour thus became indispensable in multiple-cropping regimes because of the tightly restricted time available to complete the various operations involved with cultivation, especially ploughing, transplanting and harvesting. In West Malaysia, for example, there was 'a growing tendency to employ a group of women for transplanting, since it [was] faster and fairly cheap'.[14] Even with the use of hand tractors and sickles, 'with the new varieties being planted and harvested three times a year on different fields at different times more constant labour inputs are needed'.[15] Moreover, some tasks, such as straight line planting, became more specialised and were therefore sometimes left to specifically skilled labour groups which performed their tasks for money or a share of the eventual product.

Third, the introduction of mechanisation in various forms frequently encouraged the development of specialised kinds of wage labour in the place of reciprocal labour. Hand pounding of rice by women gave way to large-scale localised machine milling, coordinated by a professional miller/broker. Again, the trend towards tractor ploughing 'completely changed the working system of ploughing from mutual aid among neighbours to wage work by tractor operator'.[16] Similarly, the introduction and adoption of combine harvesters owned and managed by contracted operators spelled the end of reciprocal harvesting arrangements.

It is noteworthy that hired labour was in the first instance a replacement for cooperative labour. Those tasks which, because of their nature, required the application of large amounts of labour at a specific time, were most likely to require the employment of hired labour. Thus, 'transplanting, harvesting, and threshing tasks are traditionally done by hired labour because they must be completed within a few days. Crop care, repair, and cleaning of dikes are traditionally performed by family members'.[17] In time, however, hired labour began gradually to replace tasks which had previously been the preserve of household members of the farming unit. In the recent past in north Thailand, for example, rice farming became increasingly dependent on the hired labour provided by landless workers, while farmers and their families – especially the wealthier ones – worked less and less on their own farms. A similar scenario was evident in lowland Java as well, with the great bulk of farm labour provided by hired labour (as much as 90 per cent); in such cases the farmer's household invested very little labour in growing rice, and none in harvesting it.

Like similar kinds of change, the movement away from cooperative labour towards wage labour took place gradually and unevenly across the region. Where populations were sparse and labour scarce and relatively expensive, or where peasantries were poor and commercialism not yet dominant, cooperative and household labor retained their pre-eminence. Among the Pwo Karen of Thailand, reciprocal labour in forest clearing and sowing was still in evidence in the 1960s. Among the Lua', cooperative labour exchanges, based first upon kinship, and upon friendship as well, remained important to a high degree; with the exception of the work required for clearing and levelling new irrigated fields, none of the agricultural work was performed for cash, and almost none against payment in kind. In West Malaysia, one scholar noted the difficulty some peasants had in finding paying farm work because of the persistence of cooperative labour and the small scale of farms.[18] In southern Vietnam in the 1950s, cooperative arrangements seem to have been most common among poorer villagers. In eastern Indonesia, harvesting teams were sometimes employed by wealthier peasants, but most harvesting was done by single farmers with the occasional help of family or friends.

Nonetheless, the undeniable trend almost everywhere was towards the wholesale adoption of hired labour for agricultural work. In the Minangkabau village studied by Kahn, 'a large proportion of families . . . hire wage workers for some or all agricultural work'.[19] In Hendry's study village in Vietnam, 'probably two-thirds to three-fourths of the adult villagers work as hired laborers at some time during a normal year'.[20] A key feature of this trend was the development of a constant and highly mobile stock of village wage labourers, who came to depend not just (if at all) upon the work opportunities in their own villages, but moved to where they could find work. In Vietnam, for example, 'there are seasonal migrations of workers, due to heavy demands for labor in one region coinciding with its availability in another. This availability is tied up with the fact that the tasks of agriculture are not simultaneous throughout the whole Delta . . . the inhabitants of the canton can hire themselves out for the harvests far from home, and return when the rice is ripe in their own paddy fields'.[21] And again: 'The cultivator is bound to employ paid labor at harvest-time, for the rice must be harvested when it is ripe, and cannot wait. The comfortably situated small proprietor must then hire several workers, whom he finds in his own village, or recruits in the neighbouring market-center from the coolies who have come from districts where the harvest falls later'.[22] In Java, 'literally thousands of landless families criss-cross the Javanese countryside, following the harvest from west to east, and then returning for the next season as the paddy starts to yellow on the fields again'.[23]

In the Philippines, similarly, 'hundreds of families' followed the rice harvest through Luzon, staring in the northern region of Ilocos and moving through to the central and southern part of the central plain, Pangasinan, Tarlac and Nueva Ecija, receiving one-fifth of what they harvested as their pay, and sometimes staying on as settlers. More recently, labourers helped to balance differences in regional resource bases and wealth by migrating in large numbers from less productive to more productive regions (in this context, those places where the new rice varieties were cultivated) in search of work. Many, again, left their provinces to work for long periods (as much as eight months) in the sugar industry of the island of Negros. In Palanan, sedentary peasant cultivators encroaching on the uplands sometimes hired the hunter-gatherer Agta people to perform agricultural labour; upland Mangyans were similarly employed as farm hands by 'invading' Christians. Many Malay peasants travelled from Kelantan to Kedah to seek work in the differently-timed rice harvest there. In the Thai uplands, landless households, unable to gain a livelihood from the resources of the village alone, were frequently forced – husbands, wives, single sons – to move further afield, often to the lowlands, to seek wage work; 'some Karen [spent] nearly all their time in wage labor, going from job to job and group to group, and thus spending almost no time in traditional activities'.[24]

Thailand's northeast, poor in resources, unable to provide for its inhabitants' welfare, and growing in population size at a rate of around 3 per cent per annum, became by the modern period a reservoir of seasonal labour for more prosperous rural areas on the Central Plain and especially for the booming city of Bangkok. In one village in 1980, for example, more than a third of all male and female villagers aged over 20 were found to be employed in extra income-earning activities stretching for months or even years in Bangkok or other towns or cities. The Central Plain itself was increasingly a source of labour for Bangkok; by the late 1960s, four-fifths of the region's recorded outmigration was directed towards the capital city. In Laos as well, wage labour developed strongly in the mid 1960s as migrant groups from Thailand's northeast thronged to the Vientiane plain. In many cases, mobile labour of this kind organised itself in labour gangs, under a foreman, who acted as broker between labourers and employers and sometimes even trained his workers in the skills they needed, such as straight row planting. Moreover, such gangs sometimes became specialised in the performance of certain kinds of work. In Lower Burma from the early twentieth century, gangs of Indian labourers worked their way from harvest to harvest; 'the harvesting near Rangoon is entirely done by men from Upper Burma, or even by Indian coolies. They work for very little, and it saves the farmer a good deal of time and dignity to get all the cutting done for him . . . [they] work away zealously with their queer sickles'.[25]

THE ABERRATION OF SOCIALIST COOPERATIVISATION

Emerging wage labour in something approaching a free market in labour was the pattern etched increasingly deeply across the region; its development met with but one major rebuff, the temporary dominance of socialist cooperativisation in parts of Southeast Asia after World War II, notably in communist Vietnam. At first, as we have seen, Vietnamese peasants joined together as work-exchange teams; landholders remained in possession of their land and their production equipment, and continued to work them, but were required to participate in collective seasonal and permanent work teams as well, performing such short term, seasonal tasks as harvesting as well as being permanently attached to a group with year-round duties. For the latter tasks, peasants were awarded work points, while also retaining a share of the output proportionate to their inputs of land, cattle and so on.

Thereafter, the emphasis of cadres remained on converting low-level to high-level cooperatives; by 1971, 96 per cent of families were in cooperatives, most of them of the high-level variety. As cooperatives moved to higher levels of organisation, land and other agricultural possessions became common property, and members' shares of the cooperative's production were based purely upon the works points (which themselves came quickly to measure only quantities of work and not its quality) they had attained by the end of the season. In the end, this project in cooperativisation, like its other manifestations in Laos and, much more starkly, Pol Pot's Kampuchea, was unable to stand against the general sweep of change.

TECHNOLOGY AND LABOUR

Until very recently, the cheapness and ready supply of poor and landless labourers in agriculture rendered inappropriate any attempt to improve levels of technology in peasant agriculture. However, from around the 1960s, government-sponsored programmes to raise agricultural production which, as we have seen, were essentially of a land-saving nature, brought a technological revolution to peasant production and further substantial changes to the nature of work and its organisation in the village setting.

The effects of new production technologies were most immediately obvious in the greater demands for labour in peasant cultivation. Some of this increase was attributable to the fact that greatly increased applications of fertiliser, together with the short stature of and lack of shade cast by the new rice varieties, gave rise to the need for significant extra inputs for field weeding. Before the introduction of the new varieties, many farmers in the Philippines did not bother to weed their rice fields. Thereafter, however, since the cost of failing to weed was correspondingly much higher than it had been before the changes of the mid 1960s, the incidence of the practice, usually in the shape of hand weeding, grew enormously. Because this extra weeding had to be performed quickly – within a few days – and was thus beyond the capacity of single households, 'much of it [was] done by hired labour'.[26] The same pattern of a greatly expanded practice of weeding as a result of the Green Revolution was evident elsewhere as well.

For the most part, however, it appears that the increase in the demand for labour came not from a greater concentration of labour inputs but rather from the much enhanced frequency of cropping which augmented both the seasonal and yearly demand for agricultural labour. Indeed, according to one calculation of the situation in Java, 'labour use per hectare per crop in wetland rice production . . . declined sharply between 1969 and 1980 and rose only slightly between 1980 and 1987'.[27] In Laguna in the Philippines, per land-unit labour use grew significantly from 1966 into the mid 1970s, thereafter falling below 1966 levels. Despite this decline in labour concentration, total labour requirements for village agriculture grew significantly; in Java by the mid 1970s, they were said to have increased by as much as 20 per cent. In West Malaysia, the Muda Irrigation Scheme, creating the conditions for a proliferation of double cropping, produced a 'massive intensification of labour'.[28] An important aspect of these new arrangements was a significant decline in seasonal unemployment.

Demand for labour and heightened returns from agriculture at the same time saw a growth in labour wages. In Java between 1969 and 1987, the real returns for rice production about doubled and, as a result, the returns to labour also increased through the first half of the 1980s. In east Java, the wages of poorer village inhabitants were found to have 'doubled in rice equivalents during the last decade'.[29] This development sometimes led to efforts by landholders to substitute household labour as far as possible for hired labour. In the Philippines, too, the fruits of the new technology were also a sharper demand for labour and at least a stabilisation of real wages.

LABOUR-SAVING TECHNOLOGY

Notwithstanding the benefits for wage workers in the form of increased demand for labour and higher wages, new technology brought with it other less favourable tendencies. The greater capital demands of the new technology sometimes meant that poorer farmers were strapped for cash to purchase seeds and fertiliser, and had to seek extra wage work to increase their income, thus swelling the numbers of those seeking work. More important than this, after an initial phase when Green Revolution technology appears to have created labour opportunities through increasing the amount of land available through improved irrigation, more rigorous cropping schedules and consequent higher yields, technology began to be harnessed for the task of saving labour as well as land, both in order to satisfy the demands its use had created and also to cope with greatly increased production. By the early 1970s, new tools had began to appear in abundance: herbicides to get rid of weeds, mechanical threshers, small rice mills, four-wheeled and hand tractors, and hand weeders. The rapidity of their introduction was startling. In Java, for example, almost the whole of the rice crop intended for domestic consumption had been hand-pounded in the 1950s. By 1979, only around 5 per cent was hand pounded and the rest milled mechanically; by the early 1980s the practise of hand pounding was hardly to be found within the villages of lowland Java. In the Philippines, where there had been just 73 mechanical rice mills in 1903, by 1967 the number had risen to 8607, and they were widely dispersed around the countryside. By around 1970, hand milling had virtually disappeared, with less than 5 per cent of rice hand pounded.

In Burma and Thailand, an increasing proportion of the rice produced had been machine milled from the late nineteenth century, and machine milling of rice intended for domestic use had spread and increased since the early twentieth century, and was ever more in evidence (in Thailand at least) from the 1950s. In the Philippines, there were already 14 000 (four wheeled) tractors in use by 1972; by the late 1970s, these had given way to hand tillers which were in common use by farmers by that time, often by way of hiring them (and their operators) in for the task of field preparation. In Thailand, owners of four-wheeled tractors similarly operated on a contract basis. In west Java, there were only 431 hand tractors in use in 1974, but 4675 by 1983, with much of the field preparation done by means of contract ploughing. In West Malaysia, as the pattern of double cropping spread, landholders took to using small hand tractors or tillers in order to be able to prepare their land quickly enough to accept two rice crops in a single year; in one village, 80 per cent of farmers were using power tillers even as early as 1968; some owners of ploughing machinery contracted out their services for land preparation. In central Luzon, the development of leaseholding in place of tenancy, together with the growth of double cropping, saw the rapid decline in the use of the large threshing machines (*tilyadora*) which had been commonly employed since the 1930s (as a means, it has been argued, for landlords to exercise a more controlled collection of crop shares), and their replacement with small and efficient portable threshers. Such machines found almost universal acceptance in other parts of the Philippines as well. In northern Thailand, threshing became increasingly mechanised, especially amongst the wealthy. Almost everywhere where harvesting remained a manual task, the sickle took over from the finger knife as the preferred tool. Although it had been in common use (in combination with threshing boxes) in places like Melaka and Krian for over half a century, and in Selangor from the 1950s, the sickle's use rapidly grew more popular, partly because the narrowing of varieties employed meant that fields matured at the same time, partly because of the need to harvest rapidly in order to begin preparing the field for the next crop, and partly, too, because of the peculiarities of the new varieties, notably their short stalks.

In some cases, increased mechanisation seems to have been a result of efforts by larger landholders to exercise greater control over the labour tasks in their fields. In the Muda Irrigation Area, for example, harvester/thresher machines began to proliferate in the 1970s and to dominate in the 1980s; the result was to deprive low-income women of harvesting work (and gleaning) and men of their task of threshing. To overcome the fact that no technology existed to mechanise transplanting and to capitalise on the combine harvester's indifference to straight line planting, there was a substantial movement back to broadcasting seed; 'the proportion of land that was broadcast rose from 20 per cent in 1982 to 65 per cent in the first season of 1986, although it has since fallen to 50 per cent'.[30] Overall, the combination of machine harvesting and broadcasting was thought to cut the demand for labour in Muda rice production by around 80 per cent.

Even though the spread of labour-saving technology was uneven across the region – in Java, for example, wheeled weeders and sickles were in common use by the early 1980s, but 'tractor use was still relatively rare, mechanised threshing still in its infancy, and mechanised harvesting virtually unknown'[31] – its overall impact was to remove labour opportunities, especially for hired labour, and also reduce the need for household labour from a large number of points in the production and processing cycles. The use of hand tractors, for example, drastically reduced labour inputs in land preparation; sickles, not to mention mechanical harvesters and threshers, made inroads in the work needed for reaping, as well as the labour which might otherwise have been invested in supervising this labour and even preparing food to sustain it through the day. The use of sickles reduced the number of harvesters required for reaping, as well as limiting the opportunities for gleaning, with fields being pressed into service again almost immediately following the harvest. Nonetheless, generally speaking, it seemed that the demand for labour remained greater than the available supply, partly because the extra work created by the new technology, as well as a greater availability of work outside the village, were greater than that lost to labour-saving machines. In some cases, indeed, the application of technology directly created new labour opportunities; the use of rotary weeders, for instance, had the effect of increasing the labour involved in transplanting because straight-row planting was more labour intensive than normal transplanting. According to one scholar of Java, 'rapid technological change in agriculture, especially as a consequence of the green revolution, has had diverse effects upon labor absorption. But the overall picture appears to have been one of increased employment associated with more intensive land use and substantial increases in output'.[32]

LABOUR RECRUITMENT AND CONTROL

The question of the recruitment and control of hired peasant labour has always been fundamentally a matter of supply and demand. Where labour was scarce, its control was always weaker; where it was more than sufficient for the available work, employers held the whip hand. In those places where labour was scarce and recruitment difficult, there developed a system of labour brokers/foremen. Such men acted as something akin to patrons for the workers they recruited, arranging their labour, managing their performance, disciplining them, often paying their wages and supplying their housing. As far as employers were concerned, such an arrangement had the advantage of providing a reliable and cheap source of disciplined labour; 'the function of the contractor is to distribute the available work evenly among the laborers attached to him, and provide farmers with an adequate supply of labor at the time it is needed'.[33] The dominant method of recruitment such brokers employed was the cash advance to prospective workers. This was a sum of money made over to the worker to entice him or her to work; the sum involved was deducted in instalments from the worker's pay during the period of employment. Generally, it was impossible to recruit labour without providing such advances, especially for piece work.

Somewhat paradoxically, the use of labour contractors and labour gangs persisted into the present, notwithstanding that, at times, the supply of labour often came to exceed the demand. In Java, for example, 'the general pattern seems to have been one of an accelerated emergence of collectivised female labour gangs during the 1970s'.[34] Under such circumstances, the function of brokers was not to recruit and manage scarce labourers but rather to provide to producers a restricted, disciplined and efficient gang of workers to perform specific tasks. The object of this kind of labour brokering was to have work performed as cheaply and efficiently as possible by means of excluding, not including, workers in the labour team. The practice expressed itself, for example, in the *gama* (*prendes/sagod*) system in the Philippines, where only those peasants who had performed weeding labour without pay were employed to assist in harvesting the crop, usually in return for one-sixth of the crop they had harvested; it was 'another way to reduce the [landholder's] wage rate'.[35] One writer described the Philippines version of the system in the following way:

> The emergence of the sagod arrangement has provided the 'petty capitalist' peasant production system with substantial economies that increase the amount of farm surplus appropriated by the tenant. It has

> minimised cash outlays in capital-starved areas, which otherwise would have been required to deal with severe problems of weeding arising from a 'defect' in the new rice technology package. Many rice farmers have since abandoned straight-row planting and reverted back to the 'broadcast' or direct seeding method. The result has been to obviate the need for transplanting and its related costs (but making weeding more difficult) and to hasten the turnover period to the next crop. Indeed, the gama system appears to be a more efficient management practice since it reduced risk and 'transaction costs' in the hiring of labour, and facilitates the substitution of hired labour in place of family labour . . . the net advantage has been decidedly in favour of the farm operator (who then has time for off-farm employment to earn cash that can support the peasant production system).[36]

In Java, a similar kind of system, already known in colonial times, came into widespread use. *Ceblokan* (or a variant known as *kedokan*) was an arrangement whereby (female) workers were paid nothing for their work in transplanting (and, with kedokan, weeding) but were given the right to assist in the harvest. The practice of performing work preparatory to the harvest as a means of gaining access to work on the harvest itself became commonplace early in the 1970s, partly in response to the fact that at that time, before the labour-creating effects of the Green Revolution began to bite, the supply of hired labourers far exceeded the demand and wealthier villagers – no longer under political pressure from communist peasant groupings – had no need to provide reciprocal services to poorer and dependent villagers and could exploit the situation as they wished.

In Java, too, around the same time, the old practice of *tebasan* harvesting became both more common and more widespread. The tebasan system involved the landholder selling his crop while it was still standing in the field to an entrepreneur who saw to its harvest and sale. The harvest was performed by employees of the entrepreneur. The system was attractive to the landholder because it provided him with money earlier than he might otherwise have obtained it, removed from him the costs and cares of overseeing the harvest, and dispelled the market risks in selling his crop. It gave the entrepreneur access to a crop at a much cheaper price than when it would normally be brought to sale, and his control over the crop allowed him to limit access to the harvest, reduce the number of harvesters, and thus depress harvesting costs.

These kinds of arrangements, however, retained their popularity only for as long as labour was plentiful. When things changed and labour shortages began to be reported – 'a largely competitive rural market in

Java, in which unskilled laborers move between the agricultural and non-agricultural sectors of the economy on a seasonal basis to find employment at comparable wages[37] – more inclusionary and non-discriminatory practices re-emerged. Seasonal labour shortages which began to be encountered in the 1980s saw the adaptation of labour control mechanisms to include pre-harvest payments and increased harvest income and the emergence of work groups who could negotiate piecework contracts with employers at higher wages; 'on Java, many of the labour institutions grew out of labor surplus conditions in rice production and are now being discarded as unskilled labor is pulled into off-farm employment activities'.[38]

OFF-FARM EMPLOYMENT

It is no exaggeration to say that the development of off-farm employment (meaning not just off-own-farm employment but also and especially non-agricultural employment) has been perhaps the most important single development in peasant society over the last century or so. I have already noted the growth of landlessness and the decline in the size of farms, a trend in evidence in most places in Southeast Asia's lowlands for at least a hundred years. This development meant that the increasing proportion of landless villagers – 'poor . . . occupying the lowest status in the village . . . the most unstable and socially disintegrated group'[39] – had to make ends meet by seeking work as hired farm labourers, assisting, for example, in harvesting and threshing the crops of wealthier households and, especially, in non-farm employment. In some localities of Java, where landlessness emerged earlier and was more widespread than in many other places, it meant that even at the turn of the twentieth century, at least one-third of the total labour force gained most of its income from non-farm employment. Its ability to do so indicates the expansion and diversification of the rural economy of the island which sprang, first, from the economic development engendered by the Cultivation System and, later, from the growth stimulated, directly and indirectly, by Western private investment in agriculture. Early in the twentieth century a Dutch report on Java commented that 'the number of those seeking wage work [*loontrekkenden*] has increased very significantly since 1919, so that gradually a greater proportion of the people has become increasingly dependent on government service and European employers'.[40]

Off-farm employment, however, was not the prerogative of the poor and landless, those seeking to eke out a livelihood by taking whatever unskilled, low-paying work they could find. The processes of land fragmentation, from whatever cause, meant that many landholders were unable to exist from their land alone and forced to seek extra income by working off their farms, sometimes seeking agricultural labour in other villages. Thus, remarked Gourou, 'the Tonkin peasants require supplementary means from secondary occupations: small industries, work in the towns, distant emigration'.[41] Most landholding peasants, then, engaged in some variety of off-farm employment as a means of supplementing their income from their own farm work, sometimes travelling considerable distances from their normal place of residence. Even with the enormous development in agriculture since the 1960s, this pattern of off-farm work remained strong and, indeed, intensified. In the Kemubu irrigation scheme in West Malaysia, for example, where double cropping was the rule, two-thirds of farming households obtained income from off-own-farm employment. Indeed, average off-farm income was greater than the income received from their own farms, notwithstanding the practice of double cropping. In other parts of West Malaysia, similarly, farmers spent considerable amounts of time engaged in off-farm labour. In some places, indeed, it took the greatest portion of time and returned the greatest amount of income; 'in the Bachang area, Melaka, where off-farm employment in town as trishaw riders, taxi drivers, in hawking, cottage industry, wood-cutting, and the like is available, rice-growing is little more that a part-time activity'.[42] Farmers unable to obtain enough income from just their own farming efforts often sought extra work in their local settlements; one investigation in a Malay kampung found 54 part-time farmers working at 28 different kinds of tasks.[43] In some places, villagers were restricted by their gender and the number of their dependents into only local forays into wage employment, and their rewards were often very low-paid jobs. Where they could, however, peasants were not averse to travelling far afield in search of off-farm income; indeed, inhabitants of rural West Malaysia often sought work outside their own districts, even moving as far afield as Singapore. In the Philippines and, indeed other places like Thailand and Indonesia, the phenomenon of workers going off to work overseas, notably in the Middle East, and sending remittances to their families at home, strengthened; indeed, such remittances 'became by the early 1980s the Philippines' largest single source of foreign exchange'.[44]

The landless, and also their landed fellows, increasingly turned to non-agricultural income for their sustenance. It was mute recognition that 'despite its potential for responding positively to increases in labour inputs, the intensification of rice monocultures is a far less efficacious way of absorbing labour and generating extra income than is economic diversification'.[45] The overall result of this continuing and intensifying press into non-agricultural activities was a rapidly increasing economic diversification at the village level, and a much more intensive incorporation into wider economies. Accordingly, agriculture's role in employing the rural labour force, especially since the early 1960s, declined rapidly. In the Philippines, for example, agriculture employed about 60 per cent of the work force around 1960; by the mid 1970s, this had fallen to less than 55 per cent, to less than 50 per cent in 1985, and to just over 45 per cent in 1989. In Malaysia, the proportion fell from 50.5 per cent in 1970 to 39.7 per cent in 1980, and to just 25 per cent in 1993. According to a report on one village in east Java, 'less than 50 per cent of the household heads . . . are actually farmers, with the remainder engaged in complex trade and labour exchange transactions both in [the village] and the city of Malang'.[46] In Java, according to one commentator, 'rice cultivation is no longer the dominant employment activity on a year round basis'.[47] Another remarked that 'while farming is the main occupation for 6 out of 10 rural households, half their income is derived from non-farm work',[48] while a third estimated that farming provided main income for only 30 per cent of households.[49] A survey from the late 1980s indicated, indeed, that on average more than half the income of rural households across Java came from sources other than agriculture; moreover, multiple sources of employment, and continual switching from one source of employment to another, became typical; 'each household survives on a basis of extreme "occupational multiplicity" and a highly flexible division of labour among household members . . . each household's income is derived from a great variety of sources which constantly change in response to available opportunities according to the season, the state of the market and even the time of day'.[50]

In Indonesia, more broadly, agriculture's contribution to the provision of employment shrank from 56.3 per cent in 1980 to 49.9 per cent in 1990, and the rural sector's share of total population declined from 83 per cent in 1971 to 74 per cent in 1985. In Thailand's northeast, 'casual wage labouring opportunities in the construction field have down-graded the importance of farming as the main source of income'.[51] In one village in Central Luzon in 1977, 'half of the total employed [household] heads reported their primary occupation either in construction work or in the service sector, and by 1984 this proportion had risen to almost two-thirds'.[52]

While peasants found work within and around the village in such areas as trade – for example, women making and selling snacks for passers-by, or acting as local collecting agents for traders – much non-agricultural labour was to be found in the cities, the nearby towns and also in rurally-based industries. In northern Vietnam in the French period, town-based weaving and match-making factories customarily recruited workers from delta villages; often, ties were created between a specific factory and a particular village so that 'it has become a tradition to work for a certain factory'.[53] As many as 40 000 villagers were also recruited to work as miners in the coal mines of Tonkin, especially at times of crop failure, where they could 'find the rice they cannot get at home'.[54] Then, 'as soon as the Tonkinese has a few piastres in his substitute for a purse he leaves the mines and returns to his rice fields',[55] a rapid turnover which 'surely delayed the formation of a distinct, self-conscious working class'.[56] By the late 1920s, a similar number of Tonkin peasants had been recruited on three-year contracts to work on the rubber plantations of Cochinchina; 'indebted landless villagers were virtually powerless to resist the enticements of itinerant labour recruiters'.[57] In Burma, the British sometimes used uplanders to work as porters and even on public works projects. Around the turn of the twentieth century, many people from Thailand's northeast gained employment on the rapidly expanding logging industry in the north or on railway construction; organised into labour gangs, they moved in thousands to take up new opportunities made available by Thailand's economic expansion. In Thailand's uplands, many people sought work in the lowlands, not just as farm labourers but also in fields like mining and construction; young unmarried men, for instance, supplemented their family's income by spending as much as a year in the mines near Chiang Mai. According to a report from a northern Thai village, large numbers of men left the village for two or three months to engage in the manufacture of charcoal from illegally felled timber.[58] One survey of a northern Thai village in 1963 found that more than 70 per cent of males aged between 20 and 40 and then resident in the village had performed wage work for at least a month in urban centres, and more than 60 per cent had worked in Bangkok.[59] The work they performed, often on a seasonal basis, was unskilled, such as labour on construction sites, or in the transport industry, such as driving pedicabs. During periods of crop shortage in hills, women, too, joined in the search for wage work. Much of this work was of a seasonal nature, especially in those places where the opportunity for second cropping was not available. In Laos, upland Khmu worked for wages during the dry season on construction sites and roadworks and as domestic servants in Luang Prabang, and also travelled to the logging camps of northern Thailand. In Java, it seems that a growing proportion of the sugar factories' fieldwork was performed by immigrant labourers rather than peasants resident in villages near the factories.

Throughout the region, then, villagers took up employment in a large array of concerns where their cheap and unskilled or semi-skilled labour could be employed, in processing or manufacturing industries such as cigarette making, sugar manufacture, furniture making, cloth manufacture, copra production, food preparation, tile making, and rice milling, in construction, in transport, and self-employed in a variety of manufacturing or trading pursuits like the manufacture of coconut sugar or furniture or in wood carving. Since towns and cities were often the prime sites or generators of this employment, the twentieth century saw a resumption of urban growth as cities began to take on something of the economic significance they had enjoyed in the sixteenth and seventeenth centuries, before the age of the peasantry temporarily subdued them.

Again, these processes worked unevenly and at different rates across the region. In Siam, for example, as rural industry went into decline under the pressure of foreign imports in the late nineteenth and early twentieth centuries, agriculture's share of employment rose from just over half in 1902 to 61 per cent in 1918 and 71 per cent in 1938. The areas of greatest decline were those normally associated with female labour, notably the weaving of cloth and the milling of rice; the response of female workers was to enter more fully into agricultural tasks. Only after World War II was this pattern turned around, and then only slowly, especially with the movement of people into urban areas to take up employment in the services sector. Even then, the total number of people engaged in agriculture continued to grow steadily, rising from 4.5 million in 1956 to 8.1 million in 1976. In south Sulawesi, where most people had access to land through either ownership or tenancy, labour continued to be focused on rice production. In the Philippines in the mid 1950s, the problem was somewhat different; farmers spent about five months working their farms, and another two in off-farm labour. But the lack of off-farm income-earning employment meant a huge amount of unemployment or underemployment for a considerable part of the year, with 'nearly half the potential workforce idle'.[60] Similarly, the lack of significant urban or industrial growth in Burma, both before and after 1962, resulted in difficulties for rural inhabitants who sought work outside the village. Accordingly, the proportion of Burma's labour force engaged in agriculture remained almost at the same level since the 1930s; in 1931 it stood at 66.4 per cent, in 1984–5 it was still 63.5 per cent.

These sites notwithstanding, the proportionately greater growth of non-agricultural, non-village employment for rural inhabitants indicated that the larger economy was developing quickly and in new directions. In Indonesia, for example, the enormous surpluses created by the oil boom of the 1970s and thereafter were directed to large scale infrastructural projects and general government expenditures in areas like education, creating employment in manufacturing and services, especially in urban areas. The push into export-oriented manufacturing, based on cheap and docile labour, by many of the region's economies in the late 1970s and 1980s led to greatly expanded employment opportunities off the farm. Agricultural surpluses themselves seemed not to have generated much employment in rural areas, but rather to have been directed towards higher levels of consumption and demands for consumer goods which invigorated production and trade in cities and towns rather than the rural areas themselves. Accordingly, 'it seems clear that the structure of population and employment has become far more urban during the 1970s'.[61]

Under these circumstances, it was not surprising that the movement of villagers to urban areas increased rapidly in the 1960s and thereafter and that employment in the non-agricultural sector, notably in industry, in petty trade, and in construction in urban areas, grew quickly. In the decades after 1970, urban growth rates in East Java approached 5.5 per cent per annum and, in the region as a whole, one person in four was an urbanite by the 1980s. The major improvements in transport services was a crucial component in this as well. One commentator on the development of Thailand's northeast wrote in 1978 that

> over the past ten years, extensive mileage of all-weather roads has been achieved to reach all the major concentrations of population, linking them to other areas outside the region. Journeys that used to take several days not too long ago can now be covered in a matter of hours. Village access roads bring almost every village within reach of the motor vehicle, at least in the dry season.[62]

The proportion of people from the countryside involved in urban employment swelled in the 1970s and 1980s on the back of these developments, becoming greater than at any time in the years since 1800. In turn, the income flows back into the village generated by this extra-village employment themselves stimulated non-agricultural employment growth within villages; 'broader based growth in rural incomes, which creates the demand for labor-intensive rural construction and services, and the expansion of employment opportunities in urban areas are more important in determining the level of demand and wages for unskilled labor in the rural economy'.[63] What developed was not a distinctive identification of urban-employed villagers with the cities so much as a more intimate association of the two sectors; previously distinct worlds, they became as it were, merged into one larger world, pulled together by the shrinking distances brought about by more efficient transport, by the provision in the rural areas of facilities like state schools and popular mass media which had previously been decidedly urban in reach, and the appearance everywhere of more diversified sources of employment. Thus it was that 'migration to large cities on an annual or monthly basis, and to nearby towns on a daily basis has become commonplace'.[64]

THE DIVISION OF LABOUR: GENDER AND AGE

Around 1800, the gender division of labour was notable for both its relative fixity and its regional diversity; in various parts of the region, men and women performed different tasks, but there was little evidence of local changes. Thus, as we have seen, a generalised division existed in lowland rice agriculture between land preparation, the uprooting of rice seedlings, and the threshing of harvested rice, performed by men, and transplanting, weeding, harvesting, and hulling, usually the task of women. Cutting and collection of firewood were mostly the work of women and children, while spinning and weaving of cloth were everywhere seen to be women's work. In swidden cultivation, men were left the work of forest clearing and felling virgin land, while women and young boys might assist in clearing areas of young regrowth. Nonetheless, these roles were not apportioned alike everywhere, nor were they always strictly adhered to. In the Philippines, according to an early twentieth-century observer,

> the division of labor has none of the hardened rigidity which most uncivilized peoples observe .... The Filipino takes turns with his wife tending the children and farming. If it is inconvenient for her to cook, he does so. He brings in the firewood. He does the heavier work of agriculture, while the more tedious occupations of transplanting and weeding rice generally fall to her. Often men and women go to their field labours together. Of course custom does considerably segregate the occupations of the sexes; but rarely to the point of enforcing the separation under penalty of stigma.[65]

In south Sulawesi, 'men, women and children all work together at harvest time, cutting the stalks of rice individually with a hand-held knife'.[66] Among the Iban, reported Freeman, weeding and harvesting were thought of as the domain of women, but men lent assistance in both these roles if such assistance was necessary. In West Malaysia, too, the sexual division of labour was not a hard and fast one; in rice cultivation it was 'based mainly on the strength required to carry out the various tasks',[67] while harvesting was regularly performed by both sexes. In southern Thailand, women harvested and threshed the rice crop, while men carried it to the village; elsewhere in Thailand, all those tasks were performed by both men and women. In Java around the turn of the twentieth century, although transplanting and weeding were usually done by women, men and children often shared in that labour, and in the work of reaping as well. Generally, the division of labour was often explained by reference to religious categories, and sometimes customary property relations; amongst the matrilineal Minangkabau, 'subsistence cultivation was, and is, predominantly women's work'.[68] More fundamentally, however, it seems to have reflected the physical and psychological qualities attributed to the respective sexes – the strength of men, the dexterity and patience of women – which different tasks demanded; 'in general, those tasks requiring great strength and energy fall to the men, while the women are responsible for work that is more onerous and time devouring but well within their physical capacities'.[69] But Southeast Asians always kept an eye focused on utilising available labour resources as fully as possible, acknowledging therein that necessity might require a crossing of roles.

With the economic, political and social transformations which enveloped the region during the course of the two centuries after 1800, the gender division of labour became both more complex and more flexible. Impositions from above of varying kinds brought change; thus, under the Cultivation System in Java, the work demanded of male households heads in the fields set aside for export production seems to have required women to devote themselves to tasks in domestic cultivation which were normally the preserve of men. In communist Vietnam, the cooperative regime 'contributed to the equalisation of male–female relations by transforming wives, unmarried daughters and daughters-in-law from "unpaid family labor" to co-operative members paid in workpoints. In other words, after co-operativisation, women's work in agriculture was remunerated by the same system as the men in their family, who no longer had a personalised control over the output of "their" land nor the field labour of "their" women'.[70] During the Emergency in Malaya, the absence of males on military duties saw women takes up the role of rubber tapping.

Economic necessity, as well, tended to dissipate the fixity of roles. Thus, peasants at the lower end of the economic scale tended to be much more flexible in their work roles because of the need to acquire as much income as possible from whatever source. In the practice of labour, the more tenuous the access to the means of subsistence, the less rigidly were gender roles maintained. By the turn of the twentieth century, women played a much enhanced role in fieldwork for the Java sugar industry.

More dramatic than this development, the disappearance of so many males in Cambodia during the 1970s left a disproportionate number of women as family heads, with the responsibility of supporting their dependents by taking up any kind of remunerative labour available.

Changes were also wrought by the introduction of new technologies. The proliferation of new high-yielding rice varieties and the barrage of new technology which accompanied and succeeded their appearance brought substantial change to the way in which work was apportioned according to gender. In general terms, the work customarily performed by men – notably land preparation – declined somewhat; the widespread use of tractors in West Malaysia, for example, saw the task of hoeing evaporate. By contrast, some tasks normally designated for women, such as transplanting and harvesting, grew more burdensome. Partly, it seems, as a result of this, there came something of a redistribution of tasks, with men sometimes performing 'women's work' and vice-versa, so as to fulfil the tasks that needed doing most efficiently and with the least need to take on hired labour; frequently, for example, men took up the job of rice harvesting with sickles. In many cases, however, the task of rice cultivation was increasingly left to women, while male workers used their new found freedom to seek non-farm work. Since women had customarily been proportionately more heavily involved in off-farm activities than men, this change was a significant reversal. Overall, however, it also appears that the amount of labour per land unit invested by women in rice cultivation and associated tasks declined, with the disappearance of hand pounding, the movement of men into harvesting, the much increased use of hired labour in planting ('monetization has led to a disintegration of this role'[71]), and the introduction of numerous kinds of mechanisation. Change of this kind may have contributed to the situation that 'the tempo of female temporary migration to large Indonesian cities has been increasing',[72] something evident in other parts of Southeast Asia as well.

With these changing conditions and circumstances, the flexibility and interchanging of roles became commonplace. Thus, in northern Thailand, 'when practical circumstances require it, women do uproot and men do plant'.[73] In one West Malaysia village, researchers reported that men now played a considerable role in transplanting.[74] In Java, while there were general patterns of labour division according to gender, along the lines already outlined, they were by no means inflexibly observed. In Laos, similarly, notwithstanding generalised understandings of appropriate gender roles, with men ploughing and irrigating and women transplanting and weeding, there existed 'no absolute barriers to sexual interchanges of work . . . one often sees men transplanting and weeding'.[75] In parts of southern Thailand, the evidence of change was more complete: 'when fully grown, a girl may plow while a boy uproots rice seedlings'.[76] In northern Thailand, apart from a generalised notion that hard physical work was for men, while tasks requiring greater dexterity belonged to women, 'both men and women take part in the harvest . . . . In fact, this division of labour is more ideal than real, and it is common to see women ploughing and men transplanting if there is a shortage of male or female labour in a particular household'.[77]

The role of children also varied, though perhaps not as markedly. Girls customarily performed more work than boys in almost all age groups, and that pattern continued to be evident. In Java, for example, girls aged between 12 and 14 contributed significantly in such areas as commerce, the manufacture of handicrafts and in wage labour; the corresponding duties of boys in the same age group were restricted to the care of animals. Throughout the region, both sexes in rural areas were trained in a large variety of farming tasks from an early age, such as firewood collection, hauling, and various kinds of cultivation work, so that by the time they reached the age of about sixteen they could participate in almost all those tasks of which adults were thought to be capable; 'children's work is less defined, but as the child gets older he more and more takes on the economic activities of that parent of the same sex'.[78] The major changes which children faced were those relating to the gradual but accelerating trend towards compulsory schooling – fuelled in Indonesia by the massive oil-funded expansion of rural primary schools in the 1970s and early 1980s – which took them away from the farming environment for long periods, often led them into careers outside farming, and in the longer term contributed – together with declining fertility rates – to an aging of the rural population engaged in agriculture and sometimes to local rural labour shortages. Local circumstances affected their role as well; in one village in West Java, for instance, children were not called upon for work because of the oversupply of adult female labour.

In general, then, the gathering complexity of social and economic life brought about the partial disintegration of traditionally allocated gender roles, as utility required. While these roles still endured in many places, they did so because the need to act differently had not yet made itself felt. In some villages in West Malaysia, for example, women were expected to prepare meals and perform all other jobs in the house, raise children, do most of the labour in rice nurseries, transplant the seedlings and harvest the paddy. Men's main tasks included 'daily shopping, ploughing and levelling the paddy fields, weeding, threshing, and attending the major religious events in the mosque and the meetings concerning important village affairs'.[79] The gender division of agricultural labour remained strong in swidden communities. Thus, in Sumbawa, swidden clearing was the work of men and their sons, especially those old enough to wield the long-handled scrub-cutting *batéq* knife, while 'the firing of the swiddens is entirely a man's job'.[80] While women family members sometime assisted in the clearing process, it was an ancillary and occasional participation. Planting was done by the whole family, rather than by wider cooperative groups, while weeding the swiddens was a female task. Among the Kalinga, weeding of swiddens was performed only by women. Among the Kachin, 'at a housebuilding, youths do the thatching, maidens fetch the thatch, married women prepare the beer, married men fetch the wood and bamboo, old men sit splitting bamboo to make tie cords (*pali*), while the old women carry on with their usual tasks of looking after the pigs and the geese and the chickens'.[81]

All this evidence point to the fact that men and women, and children too, for that matter, while subject to general guidelines on the division of labour governed by commonsense as much as by conceptions of appropriate behaviours, have always felt themselves free to do what needs doing, to change what needs changing, for the sake of the household. As the pace of change accelerated, peasants responded simply by changing their rate of adaptation so that essential goals remained within reach.

CONCLUSION

The transformations in the organisation of labour in Southeast Asia since 1800 had many aspects. There was the gradual diminution of cooperative labour arrangements and their replacement by wage labour, a result of the combination of economic and political changes, bringing peasants into closer contacts with markets and states, with demographic expansion. There was, too, the crucial expansion of off-farm employment with its characteristic 'occupational multiplicity',[82] which gave villagers without access to land the means to secure at least the elements of subsistence and which, as we saw in the previous chapter, was also important in allowing marginal landholders to retain minuscule holdings. There was, finally, the development of greater flexibility in the allocation of labour according to gender and age.

Looked at more broadly and in the longer term, all these developments seemed to point in the direction of fundamental, indeed revolutionary change. On the one hand, they presaged the creation, ultimately, of a group of farmers, increasingly specialised in their production, holding moderately sized landholdings which, through Green Revolution technology, would be capable of producing considerable surpluses. On the other, they signalled the development of something approaching a real proletariat, with few or no direct ties to the land and securing its livelihood through off-farm work – increasingly of a regular and productive kind rather than a low-return '"odd-job" regime'[83] – right across the rapidly fading demarcation line between rural and urban employment. In contexts where economic growth was more evident off the farm than on it, and where access to employment as such, rather than access to land, was the thing that mattered, the central importance of holding land was gradually dissolving. In such contexts, peasants – and peasant modes of life – faced only disappearance.

6 Commerce and Credit

The extraordinary growth in numbers of small-scale rural producers in Southeast Asia through the nineteenth century and their emergence as a new, expansive and dominant class of peasants was, to a substantial degree, a consequence of the transformative agency of markets. The greatly invigorated power and prominence of commerce in peasant life, exalted above and beyond its erstwhile role of simply supplying existing needs and disposing of limited and irregular surpluses, was crucial to the rise of peasantries and, as we shall see, to their eventual decline. It brought enormous changes to what peasants produced, the land upon which they produced it, the ways in which their labour was brought to bear in productive relationships, indeed, to virtually every aspect of their lives and livelihoods.

THE PENETRATION OF COMMERCE

Around the turn of the nineteenth century, as we have seen, notwithstanding the structural importance of commerce for Southeast Asian peasant livelihood, its reach and influence had remained severely restricted. The existence of a number of inhibitions to rural trade, including state monopolies and demands for corvée labour, undeveloped transport infrastructures, small and sparse populations, and rural banditry and general insecurity, left transaction costs high and commerce relatively marginalised in the world of peasant production. In short, the great bulk of what peasants grew, processed or manufactured remained in the village. The subsequent history of commerce in rural Southeast Asia can be depicted, in crude terms, as having passed through three distinct phases. The first, which might be said to have occupied much of the nineteenth century, was one in which the changes that took place were essentially ones of degree rather than of kind, a process of thickening of routines and a broadening of the local commercial networks that were already established in many places, rather than of outright transformation. It resulted from the increasing tempo of trade that came with the expansion and then consolidation of the region's links with world markets. It was conducted, for the most part, by existing channels of commerce, and sustained and lubricated by petty local credit, often originating from family, kin, neighbours or wealthier villagers.

The second phase, a decisively transformative one dating from around the later decades of the nineteenth century, was essentially connected with state formation and the panoply of effects, direct and indirect, which flowed from that – the development of sanctioned land tenure and land markets, the demise of corvée and its eventual replacement with new, intrusive and broader forms of monetised taxation, and the revolution in infrastructures. Its essential feature was an increasing specialisation of production and the organisation of commerce to meet needs which the village had, for the most part, itself previously met, and it was increasingly financed by an ever more concentrated thicket of local and supra-local production brokers.

The final phase, which began about the middle of the twentieth century, saw the construction of rural societies profoundly enmeshed in consumption and economic specialisation, and their activities increasingly reliant upon formal credit markets, notably those provided by the state; it was a phase that collapsed the spatial and social distinctions between town and country, and decisively signalled the end of the age of the peasantry in Southeast Asia. We should not, of course, think of these phases as sequentially exclusive, as though one replaced the preceding one completely and contemporaneously across the region. Everywhere, elements which had developed in one phase survived, and even thrived, in the succeeding one; as well, developments lagged in those places where exposure to capital and markets was less intrusive and compelling than elsewhere.

PHASE I: ENCLOSURE, AUGMENTATION, ELABORATION

The title of this section indicates its argument: that this first phase of commerce was one in which the reach of commerce expanded until it directly encompassed virtually all rural Southeast Asians, and in which the volume of trade was notably enhanced. The phase included the heightening of peasant production in hinterland Luzon and Java and the beginnings of the fabulous expansion of rice production on the mainland deltas. The effect, generally, was to bring larger numbers of people into more direct and frequent contact with commerce and commercial transactions, and to extend the spatial range of what had previously been essentially local transaction networks, but not always and necessarily to increase significantly the traded proportion of total production. On Siam's Central Plain, for example, rice production increased rapidly from around the mid nineteenth century, but that proportion of it which went for export to the world outside remained at levels comparable to those obtaining before the Bowring

Treaty. Elsewhere, there was a less dramatic but nonetheless considerable increase in the volume of forest products which were taken up into the international sphere, such as the gutta-percha and rattan harvested by Iban in the Bornean hinterland and passed on to Chinese traders for export to Singapore. In other words, international commerce was reaching more broadly, but not, it seems (with a few exceptions), more deeply into Southeast Asian peasant life. Thus, wrote one European observer of the Iban in the mid nineteenth century, 'most of them who did not know the value of a piece of money six years ago are now active traders'.[1] For the most part, in this early phase, the impediments to a more all-encompassing practice of commerce retained their durability, even if their influence was gradually less pronounced. There was a sense, too, that not only did commerce touch more directly a greater proportion of the peasantry, but it touched them more frequently and more regularly. Thus, in the city of Brunei, for example, 'every morning a market is held at various points, and hill people assemble and exchange agricultural produce for salt, fish, iron, and clothes'.[2] As they had long done, mountain dwellers in the Philippines indulged in the seasonal exchange of their products – wood carvings, weapons, woven fibres – for goods coming in from the Christian lowlands, notably salt and cloth, but now, seemingly, on a more regular and voluminous scale.

PHASE II: TRANSFORMATION

The fundamental trajectory of trade in the first period was elaborative. But by the last decades of the nineteenth century, the peasantisation of the region had been confirmed, with the extraordinary development in production and trade for the most part sustained by the labours of what were now vast arrays of small-scale rural producers. At the same time, new kinds of states were consolidating themselves through the region, increasingly able to control and order the multitudes of peasants that they now counted as subjects. The conjunction of these processes had important implications for the nature of commerce through the region.

First, it brought a new concentration in the direction of trade. In what was to become Thailand, for example, trade had up to this time been regionalised, polycentric and multi-directional; the northern part of the country was most heavily engrossed in trade with Burma and southern China, while the south focused on Singapore, Penang and the regions of southern Burma. As for the northeast, its extra-regional trade had never reached the scale of other regions and its primary orientation remained inward. Under the new regime of expanding global demand and augmented power for the nation-state, however, trade became more keenly (though never completely) focused upon just one, or just a few, nodal ports, the capital cities and key regional centres of the newly emerging nation-states. The new colonial-type cities, such as Rangoon, Manila, Saigon, Batavia, Surabaya, and even uncolonised Bangkok – many of them already on strong trajectories towards outlandish primacy – were both sign and effect of the potent marriage of state power and more intensive attachment to global markets.

Second, production itself, regimented more severely by market demand and capital infusion, became more specialised. The mainland deltas became, for the most part, tunnel-visioned panoramas of rice production; Java became renowned for its sugar; Malaya was the site par excellence for rubber. In those places where peasants grew products which the world wanted, they grew them more and more to the exclusion of other cultigens, and they correspondingly devoted a greater proportion of their time to their care.

Third, the new dispensation of international trade and its counterpart, vigorous rural production, called for improvements in product processing. Bangkok's first steam-powered mill, as I have already noted, was constructed in 1858; by the early 1890s, the city boasted 25 power mills, most of them operated by Chinese. In both Burma and Siam, the increasing need for processing facilities was met after the turn of the twentieth century by the development of smaller up-country milling centres, usually run by indigenous entrepreneurs. In the Java sugar industry, international competition and the corporatisation of enterprises led to the introduction of more efficient, and more heavily capitalised, processing technologies: First World factories sitting starkly in Third World fields.[3]

Fourth, all these developments called for improved transport infrastructures to provide more regular, more widespread and more varied commercial intercourse between villages, nearby towns and larger centres. In Burma by 1938 there existed over 10 000 kilometres of road traversable by motor vehicles all year, with another 10 000 kilometres of road offering dry season passage. The number of passengers on Burma's expanding railways grew from 8.4 million in 1896 to 27 million in 1928. Elsewhere, too, by the first decades of the twentieth century, good roads and cheap bus services enabled villagers to get into nearby towns for their special shopping, and also allowed local shops to bring produce daily, weekly or monthly from towns for sale to local inhabitants.

All these changes went hand in hand with the transformation of peasant economic life and its relationships with commercial forces outside the village. Among the more notable effects was the substantial growth in peasants' need for cash. This development came partly as a result of the rising levels of taxation visited upon them, and partly because of the expansion of their needs and of the availability of those things they desired. Money, throughout the region, had long been known and used, but it had not played a central role in commerce. Thus, in one village east of Bangkok, 'until the 1920s the cash economy had been a marginal affair. Most dealings . . . were in padi. Rents, temple offerings, even many trade obligations at the nearby stores . . . were paid in measured rice. If a farmer needed currency, he took a cash-paying job or asked his wife for some of her trading profits. When he paid his cash obligation he went back to padi dealings'.[4] But, through the 1920s, as 'cash dealings became increasingly important', peasants accordingly 'began to consider the heap of padi after harvest less as a glorious end in itself than as a symbol of the cash it might bring'.[5] Peasants felt the heavier press of money, too, in regions where cash had long been an intrinsic part of commerce and life in general. The people of early nineteenth-century Cagayan, for example, as the income from the sale of their tobacco rose, began to buy more of their food, increasingly taking to rice rather than the native corn which had been their staple. In Pahang in Malaya, by 1939, 'there were few Malay families . . . which did not receive a cash income of some kind';[6] more generally in the country, a British anthropologist expressed surprise that the household economy of Malays in 1942 'was to such a large degree a purely financial one'.[7]

A necessary result of the increasing leverage of commerce in peasant life was that an increasingly large proportion of peasant production was now carried off for sale. Before the turn of the twentieth century in the Philippines, 'the major portion of the palay crop was consumed largely on the farm. It seldom moved out of the confines of the barrio or municipality in which it was produced. By the 1920s roughly 20 percent of production was estimated to have entered the commercial trade channels'.[8] Things had developed much more strongly in Burma. A 1941 government report estimated that producer villages in Burma retained only 17 per cent of the rice they grew; the reminder went to the market, and around four-fifths of that was eventually exported.

Unlike the previous phase, such thoroughgoing transformations in peasant commerce required not just the embellishment and routinisation of existing commercial networks but the construction of a new commercial world for the vast and newly established populations of the region. Its central feature was the rapid development of a myriad of petty commercial brokers and their coupling with the direct agents of international trade. Petty part-time retailers, working with tiny supplies of capital and on even tinier margins, proliferated; professional retailing middlemen, usually Chinese, fanned out across the countryside; local shops, receiving peasant produce and supplying peasant needs of increasing voluminousness and variety, and providing the credit to finance those needs, grew in number; moneylenders multiplied to provide credit for productive expansion and for peasant consumption; pawnbrokers multiplied; the numbers of agents and sub-agents of rice-milling concerns or rubber processing plants which came to the village seeking rice for their mills or slabs for their smokehouses swelled; syndicates of wholesaling rice merchants developed. All the while the competition between all of these classes of operators hardened.

At the local level, commerce was normally in the hands of vast numbers of indigenous people, most of whom were but part-time, non-specialist, and sometimes only temporary traders working on the finest of margins and borrowing the capital they needed day by day; 'a woman vender will sometimes make only a few sous from a speculation which will sometimes have taken her a whole day's excursion'.[9] Commerce of this variety sometimes took the form of simple inter-village barter – in the hills of northern Burma, for example, the regular inter-village commerce in blankets, salt, beeswax, weapons – or more complex forms in the interchange of goods for cash or kind at village stalls, local rotating markets or more permanent town-based points of exchange where peasants, most of them women, might sell directly to middlemen or directly to consumers the items they had crafted or the snacks and confectioneries they had concocted, or where they might purchase items for carriage to and resale in – in broken-down form – their own or neighbouring villages at a fractional mark-up.

Most stalls at impermanent local retail outlets were themselves operated by indigenous traders, frequently women; there they purchased goods and products brought to them by other peasant women – craftwork, such as brooms, fishtraps and pots, vegetables, tobacco, cigars, pigs, chickens, rice, eggs, fish, maize, hand-loomed textiles – and sold them to others. Items grown in the village, like fruit and vegetables, might be sold in the village or taken to market and sold to stall-holders. Gourou described a small Vietnamese rural market in the 1930s as follows:

> Two or three hundred persons will squeeze into it during the times of greatest crowding. The sellers are almost as numerous as the buyers. Their flat-baskets are poorly furnished; a peasant women will sit a whole morning before a basket which holds only a few vegetables or a few sous worth of fish. Besides the peasant women who come to sell the produce of their fields, gardens or fishing, we only rarely find profes-

sionals that represent a more marked commercial specialization: one or two smiths who repair the tools that are brought to them and sell knives and choppers, nougat venders, pancake venders, soya cheese venders, or a women selling cloth.[10]

He described a larger market servicing two villages in the following terms:

There were four women vegetable venders whose flat-basket was not worth more than 0.20 piasters all together, seven salt traders who had brought along three hundred kilos of this product, three soya cheese merchants whose whole stock might be valued at three piasters. Four fish merchants had a spread of a total value not above four piasters, three female meat venders exhibited meat of a total worth of 12 piasters, eight women venders had about 100 kilos of betel nuts, four women venders had brought 50 kilos of tobacco, one male and ten female venders had a combined stock of rice and corn weighing all together 30 quintals, eight female fruit and cake venders had laid out an exhibit which might be valued at eight piasters; there were besides four female venders of roots for chewing and betel leaves, one female vender of chewing-lime, two female egg venders . . . . Besides venders of food items we found four barbers . . . a peddler of pottery goods, three pharmacists . . . two female venders of 'ma' or votive objects, an ironsmith, eight female mercers . . . . The most important persons of the market were the three female cloth merchants . . . . The venders are natives of twenty different villages.[11]

In addition to these general markets, which performed important bulking functions for agricultural produce, as well as providing employment opportunities for artisans, entertainers, porters/labourers and beggars, there were also specialised markets, particularly in places which concentrated on a particular industry such as copper working or silk making. Beyond this purely local setting, however, non-indigenous trading networks usually took over; in Java, for example, while natives themselves conducted a local trade in textiles, they required the assistance of Chinese middlemen to transmit them further afield. Exceptionally, indigenous networks penetrated beyond the purely local setting; in the early 1920s in Palembang, a network of native middlemen formed a guild to buy up local smallholder coffee and rubber and transmit it to the export market. However, local indigenous commerce on this scale was exceptional, partly because urban indigenous merchants were no match for the Chinese, and because few villagers could ever hope to acquire the capital necessary to sustain themselves from trading activities alone.

As the exchange economy developed, petty retailing middlemen, usually Chinese, came to play a major role in invigorating commerce; Kedah boasted 119 licensed Chinese rice dealers by 1911. The view expressed by an official post-World War II American report that 'the Philippines rural economy would collapse in most communities if the Chinese merchant were suddenly removed from the scene'[12] simply echoed a long established opinion. 'To the peasant', remarked a scholar of Thailand, 'the Chinese, whether peddler, miller, shopkeeper, or rice broker, is an essential link to the larger economic pattern of the country and a means of providing necessary and beneficial services'.[13] Perhaps the most important direct role of such middling middlemen was petty peddling, buying peasants' produce, affording them credit for land clearing, new tools, supplies of seed, hiring in labour, and even for personal purposes such as a family marriage or funeral or for other ritual requirements, to be paid back later in produce, selling them goods, both local and imported, they did not themselves produce. These small-scale and formally independent itinerant traders moved from place to place, shop to shop, market to market, exchanging goods like glassware, earthenware and textiles for peasant produce, buying and selling, and passing on the agricultural produce they obtained to processors or exporters: 'winding his way along major rivers and distant canals alike, the middleman gathered in his fleet of perhaps four or five rice boats the produce of numerous separate farmers. When his hulls were full, he floated them [or powered them, after the introduction of steam tugs in the 1890s] downstream to Bangkok, often purchasing goods to sell to isolated cultivators on his return trip'.[14] Similarly, the sampan traders of Tonkin were 'transportation entrepreneurs, but they are often also traders who carry merchandise for their own purpose . . . these are the ones that steer the great wood and bamboo rafts which go down the Red River, the Clear River, and the little rivers of the Thai Binh basin',[15] carrying forest products, fruit and animals down the delta and carrying up 'coal, nuoc mam, dried fish, mam tom, salt, stone and lime',[16] as well as engaging in the riverine transport and sale of rice, wood, pottery and similar goods.

Chinese enjoyed and exploited advantages that were not available to indigenous operators. In nineteenth century Siam, for example, they did not have the obligations of corvée labour that Thai peasants endured, nor were their movements restricted to particular areas; moreover, since most Thai rice was sold to China and Singapore, the Chinese enjoyed the inside running in commerce. In Java, the Chinese were effectively prohibited from owning land and effectively forced into the retailing sector where they remained an essential but politically impotent segment of society. Wherever they were, they enjoyed connections of both a local and broader kind – of kin, of language group – not available to would-be indigenous entrepreneurs.

Like petty middlemen, the local up-country shop, combining credit broking, petty marketing, and the local provision of consumables, played a key role in the commercial transformation; 'the village shopkeeper (almost always Chinese), lives in symbiosis with the peasant'.[17] This shop, often located in the village itself, provided peasants with the goods they needed: iron and copperware, tools, yarn, textiles, seeds, tinned food, soap and kerosene, and other goods not locally available. According to a later account,

> a typical general store . . . will carry a selection of goods such as these – metal kitchenware, chinaware, crude kitchen pottery, water jars, writing materials and school supplies, chop sticks, canned milk, tea, limited amounts of canned food, wines and brandies, beer, soft drinks, joss, votive paper, candles, lamps, kerosene, textiles, some ready-made clothing, mosquito netting, hats, haberdashery, drug items, flashlights, wooden clogs and rubber sandals, fish traps, mats, baskets, shoulder boards, sickles, knives, rope, glassware, patent medicines, tobacco and cigarettes, betel leaves and areca nut, lime, spices, sauces, small cakes, candies and limited amounts of fresh fruits and vegetables and dried fish. This is not intended to be an exhaustive list.[18]

The shop's importance, however, sprang not just from its ability to service local needs for consumables but also its role in extending credit. For example, a shop might make advances, usually in kind, say a measure of seed or some tools, to a peasant cultivator. At harvest, the peasant paid back with interest the debt incurred – or at least the greater part of it – with a portion of his produce. The shopkeeper himself was in a position to provide such services because he himself was reliant upon or served as the agent of a larger merchant who supplied him with his goods and provided him with a line of credit through which he could do business with the peasantry. Thus, in Kedah, shopkeepers who were themselves financed by Chinese rice millers frequently advanced rice to peasants when the fruits of their single rice crop were exhausted. Peasants repaid their debt in rice after the next harvest, to an amount calculated at the value of the rice when they had been advanced it, which in turn allowed rice millers to acquire large quantities of rice for their operations. In the Philippines, the multitude of rural stores (*sari-sari*) which developed across the landscape as the tendrils of commerce edged ever outwards from the centre were effectively controlled by Chinese entrepreneurs in Manila through their agents; the entrepreneur provided the goods often imported in bulk per medium of (usually British) importers for local retail sale, and received in return from the dependent shopkeeper the peasant produce exchanged for such goods. A Western visitor to Manila put it like this:

> Nearly the whole provincial trade in manufactured goods is in [Chinese] hands. Numerous traders of that nation have shops opened throughout the islands, their business being carried on by one of their own countrymen, generally the principal person of the concern, who remains resident at Manila, while his various agents in the country keep him advised of their wants, to meet which he makes large purchases from the merchants, and forwards the same to his country friends.[19]

In Burma, most small rural shops were managed by Burmese, but they were dependent upon Indian wholesalers for goods and credit. Where shops were run by Indian or Chinese shopkeepers themselves, they were often 'merely agents for Rangoon firms owned by their compatriots'.[20]

Sometimes commerce was a more directly focussed and specialised kind of activity, the work of agents of city merchants. Western commerce in Siam thrived on the Chinese compradore: 'every Western commercial house chose a Chinese merchant of some wealth, Western training, and standing in the Chinese community to serve as the firm's contact man . . . . From his familiarity with the local market he advised his employers as to the nature and quality of imports and personally guaranteed their sale by a security deposit with the Western firm. He established sales connections with local dealers and upcountry traders, disposed of the imports on arrival, and was responsible for collecting payment'.[21] Again, rice millers in Bangkok might despatch their agents to the countryside to buy up quantities of rice for delivery to the capital for milling and export.

Commercialisation on this scale was possible only with the parallel development of formal credit markets across the region. Generally speaking, as I have noted, in the early stages of commercial development, peasants received the credit they needed from their local communities. But as commerce grew in size and scope, as peasants moved away in large numbers from their natal villages to pioneer new stretches of land, and as the need for credit grew more encompassing and regular, credit needs surpassed what could be supplied by kin, and its provision became the task of those professionally involved in the business. By the 1880s in Lower Burma, for example, the greatest proportion of the money peasants needed for land preparation and clearing came from Chettiar firms which had expanded their operations from India into Burma, bringing into play their closely woven internal social connections, discipline and organisational and administrative skills, and their relationships with Western banks. The Chettiars provided credit at relatively cheap rates, around 2 per cent per month, but that relatively modest rate meant that loans were provided only to those deemed to be good risks and with adequate security in land, cattle, dwellings, crops, or ornaments. For the most part, they extended loans to peasants in the shape of crop loans, to be repaid at harvest time with a share of the crop. Those unable to obtain loans directly from Chettiars had to take recourse to Burmese lenders – many of them small-scale millers engaged in processing rice for local consumption – most of whom were themselves operating with capital in the form of Chettiar credits and thus required to set higher rates of interest. Chettiars also penetrated deeply into the credit markets of Malaya and Singapore and, from the turn of the twentieth century, Cochinchina. In much of the rest of Southeast Asia, notwithstanding the continuing function performed by landlords and kin, the role of credit provider, as we have seen, became largely the province of Chinese, a role they enhanced through their major business as retailing middlemen.

Trade within the uplands, and between uplands and lowlands, was more finely stranded than lowlands trade, but it, too, usually operated through ever more tightly meshed networks of intermediaries. In northern Laos, for example, the role of the immediate intermediary was played by the *lam*, himself a lowland Lao, who interposed himself 'between traders and occasionally the government on the one hand, and the tribal peoples – usually the Khmu and sometimes the Meo [Hmong] – on the other'.[22] Traditionally the Khmu came to their lam whenever they had some forest products to sell, or wanted to buy salt or clothing. He provided their food on these visits and would arrange the trade with a merchant. Sometimes the lam himself engaged in commerce directly with the tribal peoples. Sometimes, too, his intervention was broader than this. For instance, he might pay the head tax due to the French from the Khmu; in return Khmu might work his fields or provide him with forest products. Somewhat similarly, trade between the uplands and lowlands of Tonkin was conducted by petty peddlers from the delta who 'provide themselves with salt, nuoc mam, tea, and small manufactured articles, and sometimes with rice, and they return to the Delta with the most variegated products: dried mushrooms, cu nau, pharmaceutical products, woods, paper bark, latania leaves, citrons, fowl, bamboo shoots, etc.'[23] As well, there were also 'traders who set up a home establishment in the commercial centers of the mountainous regions and establish a regular system of exchange with the Delta'.[24] In contrast with these arrangements, the Hmong traded directly and without the intervention of a lam with the Yunnanese horse caravans which arrived in northern Laos; the Hmong provided opium in exchange for iron and copper pots, weapons, silk, cotton, woollens, tea, and horses. By the middle of the 1920s, however, as I have noted, the state-forming tendencies of the Bangkok rulers had seen the Thai capital become the fulcrum of trade, with a consequent decline of the caravan trade.

For the most part, it was the heavily populated lowlands that set the terms of trade with the uplands and interiors, providing the peoples of those places with items like salt, matches, kerosene, rice, enamel and ceramic pots and cups, blankets, cotton cloth and other clothing, rifles, ammunition, transistor radios and ornaments, and receiving in return the profitable products of the mountains. The commerce itself was often carried on by means of barter and, where cash was in evidence, it remained restricted to silver coins or pieces, since paper currency had neither legitimacy nor intrinsic value in those regions; 'but even silver must be initially purchased in the lowlands'.[25] Especially as the value of jungle products among lowlanders declined under increasing Westernisation, probably the only crop which the people of the uplands could manipulate to their own advantage was opium, because of the spiralling level of demand from lowlanders. One result was the practice employed by the opium-producing Yao acquiring children from the lowlands in satisfaction of the debts due to them.

On such wispy, slender, convoluted foundations, an intricate and multifaceted commercial operation was called into being. With the spread of commercialism, local stores and larger regional trading centres developed; thus in Siam, 'minor towns developed into commercial centers or market towns attracting more and more merchants and shopkeepers from Bangkok'.[26] Instead of there being, as had existed at the outset, relatively simple commercial connections between the export capital and the producing periphery, the middle ground of the region began to be filled in by a proliferation of agents, shopkeepers and, increasingly, rice millers themselves. To call once more upon the case of Siam, Thai peasants had previously brought their own rice to sale; as commerce became more commonplace, more central and more intricate, collecting and marketing became increasingly the terrain of middlemen. As one writer put it, 'as the economy expanded, so did the role of non-farming, full-time middlemen'.[27] The elaborating market created marketing niches where new middlemen increasingly proliferated; in Thailand, a peasant's rice might pass through the hands of a local collector, then to a transit merchant, a mill agent at the capital, and finally the mill itself, sold and resold at every turn. According to one observer of Malay society in the early 1940s, 'the most striking characteristic of Malay trade is the multiplicity of middlemen, together with a lack of clear distinction between retailer, wholesaler and producer, any of whom may at any time temporarily take over the functions of the others'.[28]

Detail and complexity dominated the scene. In Java, women earned income by borrowing capital and saleables from other traders and effectively working as their agents at markets; they found niches, too, by buying in towns and selling in villages, or collecting simple produce in village and hawking it in the town. Such local peddling of snacks, fruit, and vegetables was commonplace elsewhere as well. Increasingly, while producers themselves persisted in peddling their own produce, often through the agency of wives and daughters, brokering and fattened relations of credit replaced the independent peasant transmitting his own crop to the market and reaping his own rewards.

The strongly heightened commercialisation characteristic of this second phase was carried on the back of a proportional amplification of credit markets. It is difficult to emphasise too much the importance of the variety of produce brokers in providing the capital for the commercial development in Southeast Asia's hinterlands. They made money available for the reclamation of new lands, for the improvement of those already claimed, for new immigrants to set themselves up for production, for peasants to see out bad years and survive into the good. Their activities, however, were essentially premised upon persistent and chronic peasant indebtedness. The recurrent provision of credit, indeed, was the major tool for extracting produce from the peasantry and delivering it into the hands of the merchant. In Java, for example, even in the mid nineteenth century, the custom grew of moneylenders, mostly Chinese, advancing moneys to peasants as a means of gaining control of their produce. Often, this simply took the form of advancing capital for seeds, tools and cattle, to be repaid in kind from the subsequent harvest. In Thailand's Central Plain, advance payments – 'a kind of loan with as high a rate of interest as from 25 to 50 per cent per month'[29] – were common, with the result that peasants received only about 60 per cent of the normal value of their crop upon sale. In the Philippines, agents for rice mills toured the countryside, advancing money to peasants against the security of a future harvest; as we have seen, some also operated sari-sari stores in order to attracting farmers' produce. In Burma, moneylenders were equally ready to advance moneys to growers, sometimes even before the crop had been sown. In Malaya, the credit system known as *kunca* saw peasants extended credit which they paid back in quantities of rice (sometimes as much as three times the value of the sum originally received) at harvest time. In the Malayan smallholder rubber industry, too, the extension of credit to producers created continuing relations of debt which tied rubber producers to merchants.

Credit provision also took on more complex forms; in Java, some credit providers took to the practice, known as *ijon* (from the word *hijau*, green), of purchasing the peasant's crop still standing in the field and having it harvested themselves. By the early twentieth century, according to one source, ijon was 'very common'[30] in Java, reflecting the fact that peasants had little spare capital to manage their farms and service their immediate subsistence and other requirements. Japanese opposition to Chinese direct moneylending activities during the years of occupation resulted merely in the further development of Chinese credit provision through shops and traders. The practice of buying up the crop while it lay ripening in the field was also common in northern lowland Siam in the 1920s, with the same results: increased production for sale (to Chinese-controlled mills in Chiang Mai), a greater exposure of the peasant to modern commerce, and greater (and continuing) indebtedness. By the 1950s a pattern had emerged in which holders of tiny amounts of land especially were forced into continuing, exploitative debt, 'most commonly by selling their crop (despite insufficiency) in advance of the harvest to local traders and rich peasants, sometimes at less than one third of the eventual highest market price at the rice mill'.[31]

The interest charged for agricultural credit was usually very high, ranging from 50 to 200 per cent per annum; while it was normally repaid in produce, it could in some cases be redeemed in money or even in labour. But the combination of high interest rates, the inherent unpredictability of tropical agriculture, and the volatility of prices increasingly left peasants in a situation where they could never hope to pay back the debts they had incurred. For many peasants, however, this seems to have been of little consequence, provided that they always had a reliable line of credit open to them; reliance on credit became a normal and necessary part of life and livelihood. For others, however, it proved disastrously dangerous when, in time of crop failure or family need such as illness or obligatory ceremony, they found themselves so deeply in debt that they could not hope to secure credit for the next harvest. In such circumstances, the only route to follow – apart from catastrophic options like selling one's child into bondage – was that of disposing of or effectively pawning their lands and goods such as jewellery in the hope, often futile, of repaying their debt or at least allaying their debtors. This, as we have seen, was a consistent theme in rapidly expanding frontier areas such as the Burma delta, and the result was that many owner-cultivators found themselves consigned to the ranks of agricultural labourers.

This pattern, and its common replication across the region under the press of increasing commercialisation of production, brought angry words from observers of the scene. In Gourou's words, 'all in all usury leads . . . to the dispossession of the small landowners and to the bondage of the rent farmers, of the sharecroppers, and the proletarians. Besides, it has the unhappy effect of stripping agriculture, trade, and industry of its capital, since no agricultural improvement, no industrial enterprise, no trade could bring in profits equal to the profits of usury'.[32] For the most part, however, the system, such as it was, worked effectively up to the period of the 1930s Depression, when both the price of produce and of land fell so disastrously as to occasion a wholesale alienation of owner-cultivator land. As Owen puts, it, 'the network of brokerage, transportation, storage and credit that operated in mainland Southeast Asia was far from perfect, but it worked for over sixty years, and might have worked longer had not world prices crashed in the 1930s'.[33] Indeed, according to one scholar of Burma, 'the expanding structure of debt itself kept agricultural expansion going'.[34]

Efforts to escape the remorseless cycle of indebtedness usually proved futile. In the early twentieth century, for example, some Burmese paddy growers attempted to store their harvest until prices improved, but such speculation often over-extended their resources and plunged them into inescapable debt. Such efforts were not assisted by market manipulation, which reached its apogee with the Bullinger pool in Rangoon in the early 1920s, an arrangement designed to allow a ring of European traders to depress the rice price by selling cheap on the local market and make good by selling in much larger quantities for the European market. Saving was never a credible option for peasants. Apart from the difficulties most peasants experienced in accumulating any noteworthy capital that was not required for immediate use of some kind, whether productive or otherwise, there were, at least until the turn of the twentieth century, few local institutions of sufficient legitimacy or security with which to deposit moneys. Consequently, whatever capital was available from time to time tended to be diverted into land or into assets like precious metal jewellery, which provided not just relative security but also served as a prized marker of status. As one commentator noted in Java early in the twentieth century, 'a small part of the native population does save, but for their own purposes. In general, those goals do not include those which men in Western countries place uppermost; securing the future of individual or family, expanding and improving production. The great mass does not save, but lives on credit'.[35]

By around 1900, most peasants were inescapably caught up in commercial relations of this kind, and credit dependency had become an integral part of their lives. As I have noted, the credit that fuelled the extraordinary expansion of export crop production had come for the most part from alien moneylenders and merchants. Until the turn of the century, governments saw little if any role for themselves in credit provision, and Western-style banks kept themselves aloof from direct involvement in the small-scale and scrabbling world of peasant credit. In 1883, the government of British Burma passed the Land Improvements Loans Act, and in 1884 the Agricultural Loans Act, but lending to peasants was poorly managed and loans little used. Through the first decades of the twentieth century, however, as an ethos of paternalistic management ate away at old-style liberalism, Southeast Asian states began to offer facilities designed to save small cultivators from what they saw as the crippling depredations of small-scale alien credit. In 1904 in the Indies, the government instituted a popular credit system (*Volkscredietwezen*) which established local rural banking and credit facilities; in the same year in Java, the government established a state-run monopoly in pawnbroking to replace the old system of farmed-out pawnshops. In Burma, the government in 1904 proclaimed an Indian Co-operative Societies Act to promote state-sponsored credit societies, fed by a cooperative bank. The movement enjoyed some statistical success, with 1250 credit societies formed by 1915, 3319 by 1920 and 4057 by 1925, but the movement collapsed in a flood of debt at the end of that decade. Such societies either never reached the bulk of the population – participation was usually restricted to wealthy peasants who knew a good thing when they spied it, or at least those who could pledge land as security – or encountered a mood of incredulity, bewilderment and distrust when they did.

In Thailand, progress in providing state-sponsored credit devices was even slower and weaker; the first credit cooperatives were established in 1916, and 16 years later the number of cooperatives was only about 150, although (under more encouragement from the civilian leaders after the overthrow of the absolute monarchy) it reached nearly 3000 by 1941. Capital, however, was channelled not to those in greatest need but to landholders, so that 'the government's long-range steps to alter the patterns of rural trade and credit had little effect on the role of the Chinese prior to World War II'.[36] In the Philippines, cooperatives appeared in

1915, but made little progress in the face of peasant apathy and poor management. In Vietnam, the government created the Crédit Populaire Agricole in 1927 to provide peasants with cheap loans so as to prevent them from seriously damaging their livelihoods striving to meet payments on usurious private loans. But 'the enterprise met with complete failure: it was not the small peasant who borrowed, but only the middlingly wealthy and wealthy landowners, who had no need for money; the funds of the People's Trust have been used for ends other than agricultural: the borrowers have gambled, paid for their electoral campaigns, organized automobile transportation services; the more prudent among them have gone in for usury'.[37] Similar failure resulted from the attempt in 1927 to establish rice marketing cooperatives in the Philippines; the major problem appears to have been that of providing income or credit to peasants in the interval between the harvest and the sale of the crop.

Over many decades, especially from the turn of the twentieth century, the pattern of agricultural commercialisation in Southeast Asia continued and intensified, reaching – at different paces in different places – ever further, more widely and more deeply into peasant societies. Thus, in one Kelantan village, 'before the war, there was only one shop, that of the Chinese rubber dealer, who also bought coconuts and areca nuts, and sold sundries, coffee and other refreshments. By 1958 there were thirteen other shops in the village',[38] most of them small, but selling a great variety of items ranging from snacks to nails to haircuts. Similarly, as late as 1957, one observer of a peripheral area of northern Thailand noted the establishment in the village of 'a local "green" or "horizontal" market for locally produced goods, and in 1960 the first permanent ("Chinese-run") store selling manufactured goods'.[39] Equally, a place of simple commercial interchange might develop beyond its role as a simple rural market and become 'a real commercial market with settled merchants established in permanent shops'.[40]

The continuing proliferation of markets and middlemen through this phase in commercial development had two important – even if only laggingly felt – effects. The first was a tendency for enhanced specialisation of production and dependence upon purchase as many peasants became accustomed to selling the bulk of what they produced in exchange for money. In Sumatra, for example, rubber smallholders frequently sold their rubber to the village shopkeeper/middleman; indeed, 'in some areas a farmer must tap his trees and sell the latex to the middleman before he can buy food for breakfast'.[41] Similarly, it became quite common for peasants to dispose of all their harvested rice and to purchase milled rice as their short-term needs dictated. Again, speed to market enhanced the possibility and profitability of specialised cash cropping, notably of fresh quickly-perishable vegetables, for urban consumption. While no village had been self-sufficient in the past, under the changing circumstances the need for local provisioning waned substantially as the dynamics of this second phase exerted their influence more deeply. Even if some villages continued to produce most of what they consumed, they required 'scores of items'[42] of daily consumption which could be obtained only outside the village. In the last three decades of the nineteenth century, consumer goods imported into Burma grew at an average annual rate of around 4.5 per cent; in Siam, the rate was close to 6 per cent per annum through the same period. Second, as transport facilities developed rapidly, especially after World War II, and middlemen proliferated because of the ease of entry, competition within groups of trading intermediaries intensified. This meant, in effect, that the potential for monopsonistic behaviour by traders was for the most part restricted, except in those places where transportation was expensive and surpluses so small as to restrict the viability of commerce to just a small number of operators.

The signs and effects of the commercial transformation were more muted, of course, in those places which had not been so directly exposed to global demand and where continuity with the first phase was more in evidence. 'Among the Tonkin peasants', remarked Gourou, 'commercial life is full of activity; the total turnover is rather small, the transactions are insignificant, but the villagers make frequent transactions'.[43] Of course, where market forces did not achieve the required aim, commerce could be imposed by force; in Indochina, according to one Western traveller, 'the government forced [opium] upon the people for the benefit of the treasury'.[44] Moreover, there were still serious impediments in many places to regular and sustained commerce. Notwithstanding the relative improvements made in rural infrastructures, for example, much remained to be done. In the Philippines in the early twentieth century, rice could be marketed only in the dry season, since 'in a land with few roads, land transportation is completely closed during the rainy season. When dry weather sets in, the water is drained off or evaporates and communication between towns and to outlying barrios is again established'.[45] In Malaya, even up to the 1940s, the great majority of padi was milled within the village rather than by large commercial steam-powered mills, and the transport infrastructure remained relatively rudimentary. Circumstances like these led some observers to denigrate the role of trade in peasant life and to breathe new life into the old concept of the closed peasant economy. According to Gourou, for example, 'the 6 500 000 peasants of the Tonkin Delta live in a closed economy; they buy and sell little; a family subsists by consuming its own products, and reduces as it can the needs it cannot satisfy without expense or money. And so, the delta, generally considered, engages in very paltry exchange with the region which surround it. Its role in world trade, moreover, is practically nil. This closed-economy existence is striking.'[46] Such a view is at odds with the evidence that shows the importance and increasing indispensability of commerce for peasant livelihood across the region.

PHASE III: ENMESHMENT AND CONSUMERISM

The third phase of commercial development, the last fifty years or so of the twentieth century (a period I have earlier labelled the 'statist phase'), delivered Southeast Asia's peasantry wholly into the world of commodities. It was an age when the state moved into the central directing position in agricultural development. We have already noted what this meant in terms of the development of agricultural land, the introduction of new technologies for rice production, and the development of infrastructures. But it also extended to other areas of production, notably those of credit and marketing. All these developments combined in a context of ever expanding commercialism to enmesh the peasant in relations of exchange.

Accordingly, this period was one in which the proportion of peasant production marketed rose to hitherto unknown levels. In Indonesia by the late 1970s, 'the average annual paddy marketing ranges between 30 and 40 percent of the total harvest. This is almost double the percentage of 17½ percent estimated in the late 1950s'.[47] In the Philippines, the impact of commercialisation was felt even more strongly; 'in the mid-1950s the marketed surplus [of rice] grew to about 40 per cent. By 1969–70, it rose to 60 per cent, which meant that rice production had by then been irreversibly set along the course of maximum production of surplus for the market'.[48] In Kedah, where the marketable surplus of rice had been estimated at around 50 per cent in the mid 1950s, the proportion had reached 90 per cent in some places by 1980. In other words, as government became more intensely involved in stimulating production and distribution, and to a lesser extent in marketing, the amount of rice sold increased both absolutely and as a proportion of all rice produced. In addition, as the proportion of marketed rice increased, there was a corresponding rise in the amount being offered for commercial milling; in the Philippines, the percentage rose from a mere 11 per cent in 1918 to 50 per cent in 1948. Thus, according to one writer, 'the peasant is no longer integrated into the market economy via his consumption needs but rather by a direct integration of the circuit of production into that of marketing'.[49]

The more deep-seated involvement of peasants with trade sprang from various causes, amongst them greatly improved yields, the disproportionate speed of urbanisation, and the availability of an ever more-enticing range of consumer goods. The radical improvement in transport infrastructures, especially in roads and vehicles, which took place in the decades after World War II, and especially since the 1970s, was of extraordinary significance. Highways spread throughout the Southeast Asian countryside, equalling and then far surpassing the importance of canals; they consolidated and provided a further incentive for smaller secondary roads and tracks. They in turn brought trucks, buses, speedy passenger vans such as the ubiquitous Colts of Java, cars, motorcycles and bicycles into common usage – by contrast, there were less than 20 000 registered motor vehicles in Burma on the eve of World War II, most of them operating in and around urban areas, while in 1952 there were 45 trucks and 48 cars in all of Laos – evaporating distances and regularising relationships between cities, towns and villages that had previously been inconstant and episodic. Increasing mobility itself served to accelerate change; 'in 1981, unlike a decade ago, many now travel to town and city on a regular basis and bring new ideas and techniques back to the village'.[50] More important, in one respect, than the movement of people was the much improved potential for the rapid transit of goods, creating new markets for the produce of the rural areas and bringing in manufactured commodities in great profusion.

But an integral component of the drive for greater production and commercialisation was the development of credit mechanisms to support more intensive agricultural activity. This was particularly important during the first decade or so of the Green Revolution from the mid 1960s, with the high capital requirements of the new bundled technologies needing to be serviced if peasants were to be induced to take part in the campaigns for enhanced production, and with well-founded fears that existing private credit providers would be neither sufficient nor appropriate to handle heightened demand. Thus, in Indonesia, the Bimas programme included subsidised credits to rice growers, initially repayable in kind and later in cash, to encourage them to adopt new technologies; the programme was responsible for introducing small scale banking units widely into villages, under the auspices of the Bank Rakyat Indonesia.[51] In central Java about the same, the provincial government instituted the Badan Kredit Kecamatan scheme to provide credit to rural enterprises. In the late 1970s, smallholder cash-croppers also began to enjoy the provision of state-sponsored credit. In Malaysia, the government established an Agricultural Bank in 1969 'to strengthen and to co-ordinate public sector credit programmes for agriculture'.[52] In Thailand, the Bank for Agriculture and Agricultural Cooperatives (BAAC), established in 1966, provided a pool of government credit for agriculture, lending both to growers and to cooperatives. In Burma, the government tripled the amount of official agricultural credit in the decade after 1962.

To transmit and monitor these credit programmes at the local level, governments also sought to create – or revitalise – rural administrative machinery, typically in the form of peasant cooperatives or associations in the village. Notwithstanding the chequered career of these organisations in the early part of the century, in the statist phase they gathered a much more obdurate degree of institutional permanency, if not a proportionate efficiency. They served both as the mechanism for channelling state credit to peasants and also as the means of diffusing the new technologies of the Green Revolution.

In the immediate post-World War II period, efforts to establish such bodies had been as unsuccessful as in pre-war days. In southern Vietnam, for example, cooperatives established with the aim of saving peasants from having to sell off their rice while still in the field proved to be failures. A similar scheme in the Philippines, FACOMAs (Farmers' Cooperative Marketing Associations), begun in 1952, spread rapidly but by the end of the decade was suffering grievously from varieties of corruption. In Thailand, cooperatives after World War II included less than 10 per cent of peasant landholders, while in 1950 there existed just a handful of marketing societies.

Things began to change somewhat as the state pressed more closely on the village from around the mid 1960s onwards. In Malaysia, a Farmers' Association was established in 1967 which came to act as a conduit for the supply of fertiliser and other production inputs and to coordinate the granting of loans raised from the Agricultural Bank to peasant producers. In the Philippines, credit programmes expanded significantly, notably in association with the Masagana 99 campaign and the move from tenancy to leasehold which saw the role of landlords in dispensing credit (and marketing tenants' produce) decline and a corresponding rise in credit provision 'by cooperatives, the Agricultural Credit Association, or the rural bank'.[53] In Indonesia, the government in the late 1970s established KUDs (village level cooperatives, though in fact mostly established at sub-district level) 'to help in the implementation of the government's rice programs, especially the channelling of credit to the villagers adopting the new high-yielding varieties and the marketing of their rice'.[54] These organisations attracted their critics, not only because of an alleged insufficiency of available funds but also because it was a narrow band of wealthier peasants, with ties to local officialdom, who gained greatest access to the benefits they provided.

Things were organised somewhat similarly in Thailand; even as late as 1976, only one-fifth of rural households belonged to cooperatives in Thailand, in large part a result of the fact that membership was restricted to landowners. Moreover, richer peasants were more likely to gain access to cheap loans than their poorer colleagues, who often had to seek expensive loans in the private credit market. Nonetheless, formal credit began to play an increasingly important role in financing agriculture, at least in part because of the relative ease with which it could be obtained – and defaulted on. Whereas in 1962–3 in Thailand it was responsible for only 5 per cent of agricultural credit, by 1975–6 it accounted for more than half, and by 1981 was said to provide 64 per cent of farm credit. Around 1980, it was thought to comprise around 25 per cent of all rural credit in the Philippines and Malaysia. In those places, as elsewhere, cooperatives tended to institutionalise an existing group of prosperous peasants who acted in tandem with local officials to carry through ideas of development. Their significance was that they provided a harder and more efficient edge to government intervention in the affairs of the village; elite villagers naturally found that 'their position as agents of the State in the village is often further enhanced by their rural development roles'.[55]

Marketing, too, increasingly fell under the sway of government. In Malaysia, a National Padi and Rice Authority was formed to control marketing, license dealers and set minimum and maximum prices by manipulating the local and imported stocks under its control. It also involved itself directly in the market by establishing its own large rice mills and selling the processed product. To service such enterprises, the government called upon the local Farmers' Association to act as collecting agents. In Indonesia, the government attempted to stabilise prices by setting floor prices for rice sold to KUDs. Wealthier peasants (sometimes leaders in local KUDs), however, were often able to circumvent such efforts through controlling such mechanisms as tebasan and ijon to their own advantage. Moreover, many peasants living considerable distances from their KUD preferred to sell their harvest to local private traders. The result was that the vast majority of rice continued to be handled by private rather than government means, with prices reflecting that fact.

Heightened government intervention reached its purest forms in the socialist economies of Southeast Asia, although their aim was to protect peasants from commerce rather than forcing them to embrace it. In north Vietnam, for example, once the cooperative movement was in place by around 1960, inputs required for agriculture were retailed from a State Trading Corporation to the cooperatives. However, attempts to construct a similar system in the south after 1976 were less successful as a result of the halting and indecisive progress towards cooperatives, and private traders came to provide the bulk of the necessary inputs to peasant producers. Similarly, with the progressive collapse of cooperative agriculture throughout the country through the 1980s, and the concomitant re-emergence of notions of individual ownership of productive equipment, difficulties in financing their purchase became more pronounced in the absence of a state-sponsored structure of credit provision. In Laos, the initial efforts of the communist government after 1975 to control commerce brought a serious downturn and, as I have noted, the flight of many people who had served to sustain the country's commerce; 'by 1978 the commercial centres of the Mekong towns were but dead shells of barred and shuttered shops'.[56]

In the non-socialist economies, government also sponsored and encouraged private rural credit institutions as an ancillary to state credit. In the Philippines, for example, the government legislated for private rural banks in 1952, 'ostensibly to break the pernicious role of usurers in rural communities'.[57] Government encouragement saw their numbers leap from 18 to 369 between 1953 and 1967, their capitalisation grow by a factor of 60 to P121 million and, with government guarantees against losses and cheap loans from the Central Bank, their rural lending role to growers eventually outstrip that of government rural loan bodies.

Notwithstanding the enormous elaboration of credit provision by supra-village official agencies and its central importance in engendering the penetration of commercial relationships across the region, local sources of credit retained a measure of popularity, with peasants often more comfortable, even in socialist economies, seeking easily organised and informal loans from their neighbours or wealthier peers rather than running the gauntlet of the daunting bureaucracy above and the restrictiveness of its prolific supplies of red tape.

There was, as well, the common mechanism of the rotating credit association, providing lumps of capital periodically to its members. Nonetheless, the general trend seemed to be moving inexorably away from private credit. It was increasingly the case in many places that the proliferation of state-sponsored credit had substantially relieved the peasants' oft-felt need to dispose of their crops to private moneylender/brokers in order to obtain cash. Moreover, as money channels became more extensive and well-lubricated, private credit providers sought the best returns available, and they were not always to be found in village production. Thus, in southern Vietnam in the 1950s, 'most large landowners prefer not to lend to villagers, whether tenants or not, but instead will channel loanable funds into the larger towns for the use of the merchants, rice mill operators, and similar types of borrowers there'.[58] At least as far as the hefty lumps of production credit were concerned, government-sponsored credit became increasingly important for the peasant.

Nonetheless, the escalating scale, the broader reach, the pervasive probing of the commercialisation of peasant production stimulated a complex and many-layered structure of private commercial and credit enterprise which far exceeded what had gone before. It serviced those people unable or unwilling to partake of government-sponsored credit, and also those, like many upland peoples, still beyond the effective reach of such government services. Its membership provided employment for huge numbers of people and included the humble and the high: landless or near-landless villagers, for example, whose role extended no further than collecting produce from growers in their own settlements as well as outlying hamlets and wholesaling it further up the marketing chain; harvesting agents who procured access to crops through advances; rural credit providers who were rewarded with a share of the harvest for the cash, seeds, and fertiliser they had earlier advanced producers; landlords who gathered their share of the harvest and the interest in kind they had extended from their tenant producers, often, as in the Philippines, by managing and monitoring the process of mechanical threshing; small scale paddy traders who accumulated and dispensed goods as they journeyed from village to village; smallvillage rice-mill owners; larger commercial mills with their bevies of contracted agents and suppliers; and, on the distribution side, a panoply of warehousers, wholesalers and a myriad of retailers ranging from merchant-truckers and shopkeepers to petty peddlers who finally brought the product to the consumer.

In some places, many of these roles of credit provision, collecting, purchasing, milling, storage and retailing were concentrated in a single hand, often that of a big landholder or rural entrepreneur. In other places, as in northern Thailand, coalitions of Chinese rice millers were able to impose a 'virtual monopoly' on milling and sale. In others again, wealthier landholders turned from agricultural production to commerce, focussing their efforts on the collection and wholesaling of produce and having their land worked either by wage labourers and renters. But, we are reminded by one writer, 'in general local marketing and processing of foods in developing countries are carried out mainly by unincorporated informal agents who do business on a small-scale with few permanent employees. These agents are linked to each other through informal contracts and tacit understandings to form an intricate marketing network'.[59] Credit, always needed by nearly everyone on a regular basis – 'the villager needs a *small amount* of cash *every day* in order to be able to purchase the necessaries of life'[60] – was the major bond between the various layers; 'typically, a hamlet collector is tied to a village or an inter-village collector, from whom he receives an advance payment to finance the purchase of produce from farmers, and to whom he then delivers his collection'.[61] The great majority of these operators depended heavily on a quick turnover of the goods they handled in order to service the credit relations that were so vital to the sustenance of their various enterprises.

There has been considerable debate about the implications of expanded production and credit. On some accounts, 'the expansion of institutional credit has increased the overall level of debt rather than replaced exploitative non-institutional debt';[62] moreover, elaborated production and its social consequences have simply increased the level of indebtedness and dependence, and placed creditors in a more powerful position. According to one scholar, however, advances in production and income have helped to lessen the debt load of growers; 'the accumulation of debts leading to long-term indebtedness, pledging of land and loss of land ownership have substantially disappeared. Also purchases on credit are now cleared every season'.[63] Given the intense competition between entrepreneurs, however, as well as the vast sums of credit now readily available, it appears most likely that the cost of credit, and therefore its potential for exerting pernicious effects upon peasants, generally declined.

By the last part of the twentieth century commercial relationships stretched more broadly and effectively than they had ever done before as previously localised or peripheral communities became increasingly pressed to supply what they needed from their own thinning resources and more thoroughly enmeshed in the political and economic systems emanating from the lowlands. Among the Karen, for example, village women consigned goods for sale to a village collector/seller who carried them to a Thai marketplace for sale. More adventurous traders went further afield, dealing 'almost entirely in nonlocal goods and travel[ling] great distances'.[64] Armed with money borrowed from a Thai moneylender, they might go to Burma to buy cattle, sell them on their return to Thailand, repay their debt and retain what remained. Thus, 'these external economic relations became more important for sustaining the society. As time went on, more goods necessary for survival had to be obtained from the outside; or, more luxury goods were acquired and more efficient tools of production were necessary, thus changing the subsistence pattern and making the Karen more dependent'.[65] As relations developed, they also became more fluid, unrestricted and, for those who were essentially subservient to them, unpredictable. Thus, a road link forged between the Indochina coast and Luang Prabang allowed lowland Lao merchants to buy rice more cheaply from Vietnam than from the Lamet people; similarly, the availability of motor boats meant they could also buy cheap rice from neighbouring districts of Thailand.

More generally, these processes brought peripheral peoples in more regular and intimate contact with lowland commercial and political centres. This closer engagement involved in the first instance a broadening of the range of commerce. 'In the last fifteen years', remarked one observer in the 1950s, 'and particularly within the last five years, a whole range of new consumer items has become more easily available to the Lao villager. Bicycles, manufactured cloth, kerosene lamps, flashlights, vacuum flasks, tinned condensed milk and suitcases for storing cloth.'[66] The Karen found themselves pressed to expand their relations with the lowlands beyond the meagre necessities of salt and iron partly to fulfil their growing need for food, partly to fuel their desire for a broader range of manufactured goods; to earn the extra income to service this trade, many were forced to undertake wage labour in the lowlands.

Greater proximity and regularity also saw the extension of more weighty credit relations, with lowland rice traders extending credits to hill farmers for the delivery of crops which were not yet harvested. In other words, the kinds of credit and commercial relationships which had characterised the lowlands for around a hundred years were spreading inexorably to the old periphery. This meant not just a development in the regularity, variety and liveliness of trade, and the relations which sustained it, but also an increasing dominance and direction from lowland commercial centres. 'Most hill village households have to sell some of their rice', remarked Kunstadter, 'even though they may not have enough for home consumption, in order to buy a few manufactured necessities, such as hoe blades or salt, and perhaps a few luxuries, such as matches, tobacco and flashlight batteries'.[67] The social and cultural, not to mention geographical, distance that had characterised trade between centre and periphery had evaporated; with it went such special institutions as the lam system of mediation. Now, 'almost every Lao village of any size, located along the Mekong or one of its major tributaries, is a centre of trade with tribal peoples',[68] while the Lao themselves, especially in the dry season, became an army of petty traders, distributing the products of urban civilisation – soap, guns, currency, cloth, tools – through the hills. Increasing economic dominance, of course, ran side by side with growing cultural dominance and the loss of cultural autonomy. At the same time, it opened new options for employment livelihood amongst uplanders themselves which had never existed in more limiting times, in shopkeeping and general commerce, in transport, in a variety of wage labour opportunities.

The reach and power of commerce finally ushered out the last few traces of barter as an important means of supra-local exchange and replaced it with transactions in cash. While barter persisted quite strongly into the 1950s – paddy was then still commonly and widely used as a means of exchange within some villages in Thailand – it could not survive under circumstances where a vast range of food and goods were readily and rapidly obtainable from any number of sources and where states demanded the satisfaction of taxation demands in money.[69] Barter, such as it was, was left to the realm of local interchange of a simple and restricted kind between friends and neighbours.

There were signs, too, that towards the end of the twentieth century commerce itself was entering a new phase of development and sophistication that might both herald and promote further significant structural changes. The greater efficiency and speed of communications, for example, allied with more developed, larger and more centralised forms of private and government-sponsored business activity and manufacture, with more sophisticated targeting and marketing of product, were threatening the composite layerings of intermediaries which had supported and themselves fed off commerce; 'in contradiction to classical theory, there is today in Minahasa hardly any step-wise up-and-downward movement of commodities through a "chain of markets"'.[70] One associated effect of this process was already evident in some places with a reduction in the number of localised and small-scale markets and perhaps, too, the beginnings of a decline in the importance of the small town as a commercial centre as trade became more centralised and concentrated in larger centres.

CONCLUSION

Commerce, then, was continually transforming both the nature of peasant production and the manner in which peasants related to other parts of the wider society. On one account, 'there are now no "subsistence" villages in Java. All villages are engaged in complex trade and labour exchange transactions and, in many villages, no more than half the household heads are actually farmers. The remainder engage in a wide variety of agricultural and commercial support operations so that land-holdings alone do not necessarily determine family wealth'.[71] The general result was the integration of local systems of production and exchange into broader national and international orders, bringing with it enhanced demand, greater production, increased local specialisation, greater mobility, and increased dependence and interdependence. The broader social impact of such changes was to blur and then diminish the category of 'peasant' in Southeast Asia. The ever heightened intensity and inescapable reach of commerce, in the long term, served to make farmers out of those peasants who still had the wherewithal to produce from the soil. Perhaps more important, for those rural residents whose access to agricultural work and its fruits was increasingly insufficient, segmented, episodic and tenuous, it created – directly and indirectly – the niches of opportunity within the complex ordering of commercial life, to make them into paid workers. For them, the notion of subsistence production, and even of through involvement in the agricultural cycles of the village, had long since disappeared into the remote past. By the 1980s, it was reported of one northern Thai village that 'most families purchase[d] the bulk of their food requirements, including rice'.[72] This was a sign – and, notably, one from the periphery – of the emergence of a new age of commerce in Southeast Asia, and the effective end of the pre-eminence of peasant production – and of the peasantry itself.

7 Power and Prosperity

The outline of village social structure sketched in the opening chapter characterised it in terms of personal ties with both a horizontal orientation – kin and kin, neighbour and neighbour – and a vertical one, attachment to beaded series of patrons within and especially outside the village. In many places, it was the component hamlets of villages – *dusun* in Java, *thon* in Vietnam, for example – rather than the village as such which were the local, historically and socially forged cores of fellowship and community. The village was, in essence, institutionally fragile and often impermanent, ceaselessly subject to the tensions inherent in personalised politics. In the course of the development of stronger states in the last decades of the nineteenth century, the basis of village politics and its relation to the state were transformed, fundamentally and forever, as the village was created as a permanent administrative component of state power. This chapter analyses this process, and how it both built upon and shaped relationships of power within the village and between the village and the state, and considers how such relationships affected the distribution of prosperity amongst villagers.

FROM COMPOSITE TO COMMUNITY

This pattern of development into some kind of more strongly institutionalised community had already occurred in those places where states were stronger or at least able to make continuing, effective and relatively heavy demands of their peasantries. The most notable example of this process was in the Tonkin delta of Vietnam. There, remarked Gourou,

> man exists only as a member of the village, and he cannot be envisioned living in isolation, surrounded only by his family. Moreover this was the official point of view of the Annamite government, which knew neither individual nor families and did not penetrate the village: the obligations which weighed on the land, such as taxes, corvees, military service, the government fixed by village and was not in the least concerned about the manner of distribution.[1]

Consequently, he went on, 'these villages [in Tonkin] are highly coherent social groups, autonomous political organisms',[2] spatially distinguished 'by a hedge of bamboos, whose close and thorny stems form an efficient barrier against thieves', which was also 'the mark of its individuality and of its independence'.[3]

Something resembling this picture of organic solidarity, of a collectivity of common interests and obligations and subject in its unity to the wishes and demands of the state, was also to be found, although perhaps not in so impressively regimented a form, in Java and parts of Luzon from the early part of the nineteenth century, owing to the imposition of forced labour upon the peasantries of those two islands by, respectively, Dutch and Spanish colonialism. In Cagayan, for instance, the region most heavily affected by the tobacco monopoly in the Philippines, 'the meticulous record keeping required by the monopoly deprived the Indio of the protection that obscurity had provided. The domestication of the peasantry was achieved as much by the pen as by the sword'.[4] The administrative and political scrutiny to which the Cagayan peasantry was subjected was probably exceeded by the Dutch efforts on Java in the decades after 1830. There, with as much as 60 and 70 per cent of peasant households in the regions under direct Dutch control called up for regular and intense forced cultivation work on export crops, not to mention a heavy regime of other compulsory services, the Dutch needed to create new kinds of administrative discipline, efficiency and purpose within villages which had previously been little more than vaguely demarcated territorial peasant settlements. One result of this imperative was the collapsing of multitudes of smaller and disparate settlements into a much smaller number of larger 'administrative villages' and, as we shall see, the consolidation and formalisation of local authority in the hands of a village chief.

In west Sumatra, where Dutch authority made itself more forcefully felt from the 1830s onwards, the situation was analogous to (and to a considerable extent guided by) the experience of Java. There, as in Java, the Dutch found it most useful to deal with specific administrative entities and with a specific individual who was the core of power in the village and who could be employed as a local agent of Dutch policy. Apparently unable to fathom the complexity of the Minangkabau nagari, and unable to deal with its plethora of penghulu and the dispersal of authority along lines of lineage, the Dutch decided to remake the village institution as the local unit of government administration, and to construct an indigenous officialdom appropriate to their purpose. The result was that numerous nagari were subdivided into sizes that the Dutch thought more appropriate for their administrative purposes, while other smaller nagari were brought together to form new single administrative units; indigenous officials of precarious and dependent legitimacy – 'pseudotraditional' is the description given them by one scholar[5] – were called into being. With the passage of time, the same general process of administrative construction – although rarely with the confusing complications of the Minangkabau arrangements – was applied to other political entities brought under the expanding umbrella of the Netherlands Indies. In Bali in the early twentieth century, for instance, the colonial impress resulted in the creation of villages for administrative purposes, the boundaries of which often bore little relation to those of local communities long mapped by custom.

Further north, the Bangkok regime, busy with the task of accumulating and consolidating what was to become Thailand, insinuated a somewhat similar process of administrative definition in the rural areas. A turn-of-the-century European observer described things like this:

> The district is again divided into villages under a village headman, and the villages are subdivided into hamlets under an elder. A hamlet is a collection of about ten houses or one hundred people, who elect their own elder under the presidency of the district officer . . . . The duties of the elder are to report any case of crime to the headman and to preserve a register of people in his hamlet, to summon the people in cases of flood or fire, and to assist in arresting criminals. All the inhabitants are bound under penalties to assist their elders in the execution of the law when called upon . . . . A village consists of ten hamlets. The headman is elected by the council of elders and receives confirmation from the governor of the province. His duties are to supervise the elders and to inform them of any new government regulation, to provide transport and assistance for persons travelling on government business, which must, however, be paid by such persons, the headman having no power to requisition either goods or labor without proper pay.[6]

This administrative structure was differently labelled by different observers, but its essential form – district (controlled by a district officer), commune or collection of settlements (*tambon*), headed by a kamnan, selected from the hamlet chiefs, and hamlet (*muban*), under the supervision of a hamlet chief (*pu yai bun*), elected by his fellows – endured thereafter. While the kamnan and hamlet chief were not, strictly speaking, government officials, they came to act as such; indeed, by 1938 these figures were granted government stipends to add to their existing list of special official privileges such as commissions on the taxation they collected. Perhaps more than was the case with Java, these arrangements sometimes cut across existing patterns of settlement, so that it sometimes occurred that the boundaries of tambon cut through the heart of existing communities and that not all existing individual settlements were accorded the status of muban. Similar processes took place elsewhere right across the region, the lines drawn for to demarcate administrative villages often cutting across – and sometimes severing – existing social ties: marketing networks, irrigation societies, temple associations, neighbourhoods.

THE POWER OF THE VILLAGE CHIEF

This recasting of village administration was made in the name of more pervasive and effective state management; the key to its proper functioning was the installation of a single figure of authority in the village to act as the conduit of the state's wishes and demands and, indeed, to be its representative. Accordingly, right across the region, the position of the village chief became more clearly and sharply identified as a focus of village authority. The major responsibilities of the village chief were to communicate orders from above and ensure their implementation, to police the maintenance of order and security, and to report to his superiors those aspects of the village and village life of bearing to their exercise of authority.

As I have mentioned, this was a process already well under way in those parts of the region already subject to systematic intrusion by colonial governments. In Java from the 1830s, for example, the enhanced importance placed upon the village chief as agent of the state and especially as provider and organiser of labour for the system of forced cultivations and ancillary activities saw a corresponding decline in the influence of the old council of elders which had previously acted as a counterweight to his influence. More and more, the Javanese village chief became an independent power in village affairs, no longer so reliant upon the support of his villagers now that he basked in state-reinforced authority, and now more firmly tied to the spheres of supra-village power. In west Sumatra, similarly, the Dutch created the new single post of nagari head in order to mobilise and monitor the labour needed for the operation of the forced coffee cultivation system. Those lineage penghulu who did not receive appointment to this new position – and they were numerous despite the divisions visited upon the existing nagari – were left confused and languishing. Those appointed as heads of nagari became dependent upon the Dutch for the influence they enjoyed and exercised; in time, 'the imposition of a new power and authority system by the Dutch colonial administration was an important factor contributing to the disintegration of the traditional socio-political units and the growing individualization'.[7]

Elsewhere, in regions where colonial governments were installed only in the last decades of the nineteenth century, the twin processes of consolidating the village as an administrative unit and enhancing the authority of its chief were set in train. In Cochinchina, for example, 'the French administrators . . . elevated the mayor in the village commune to a position of authority unknown in precolonial Indochina';[8] he was required to inform villagers of the government's wishes, see to the implementation of government policies, assist in the collection of taxation and the administration of government tax monopolies, report miscreants, and generally ensure a secure and peaceful environment. In 1904, the French made further efforts to regularise village affairs and institutions with the establishment of an eleven member village council (later expanded to twelve), equipped with a duty roster of secular business which included budgeting, police and justice administration, responsibility for health, land records maintenance and tax collection. In Cambodia, the head of the rural commune was appointed by higher authority rather than by villagers, and his role became that of administering according to orders from on high rather than representing the people in his settlement. In the Tonkin region, despite the continuing formal importance of the council of notables, 'very fortunately, in reality, things are simplified, and very often the authority rests in the hands of a man who owes his influence to his prestige as a mandarin or scholar, to his cleverness, or to his genius for intrigue'.[9]

In Burma, by 1879 the chief of a circle of villages in Lower Burma (*taikthugyi*) was required to pass a formal examination in things like revenue collection and land surveying; such men became the tax-collecting agents for administrative circles, servile towards an increasingly centralised state. The position of village chief – previously blurred, but generally carried on by the *goung*, a policing official responsible to the district police superintendent – was formalised in the person of the *kyedangyi*, the chief village taxpayer; the goung became a circle police officer, and 'people began to look upon them as government officials who looked essentially after the peace and order of the circle in the interest of the State'.[10] The formal position of village chief was not thereby enhanced; 'whatever was wanted in the village had to be done by the kyedangyi unless he could induce the villagers to do it for him; and except for a single instance he had absolutely no power to enforce any order which he gave to the villagers. With harassment from above and below, and little by way of emolument, holders of the post tended to be unsuitable'.[11] Thereafter, the intermediate position of taikthugyi was slowly dispensed with, and people of some influence and importance were to be appointed and thereafter elected, marking the demise of the kyedangyi. The new village head, called *thugyi*, possessed revenue collection, policing and magistracy powers. With the annexation of Upper Burma in 1886, the British began a purposeful consolidation of rural areas, based upon the village as the central unit of administration; according to Furnivall, 'the village system in Burma is a modern invention of the British devised in 1886, partly under the influence of Indian traditions, but chiefly for administrative convenience, to make the country easier to rule'.[12] Sir Charles Crosthwaite's self-satisfaction with his work is clear: 'the policy of dealing with the people by villages and not by individuals has been a very powerful instrument for suppressing disorder and establishing our authority . . . the village system must be maintained in vigour'.[13] With the framing of the so-called Village Regulation of 1887, the British sought to destroy the old system of circles and myothugyis in Upper Burma and put in their stead smaller units with their own appointed headmen who 'were no longer representatives of the people; they were the lowest in the official hierarchy and could be suspended, fined or dismissed'.[14]

Notwithstanding their weakness, the early colonial states in these places, together with the emerging Thai state, set about administering their domains with results for lowland villages similar to those already described for the Philippines and the Netherlands Indies. Villages which had been vaguely defined and spatially diffuse clusters of peasants, without fixed boundaries, were now considered as fixed territorial entities with a concurrent administrative identification. Similarly, the bureaucratisation of the role of village chief meant that these figures now leant much more on coercion than on conciliation and service as a means of ensuring their (and their superiors') will.

These processes, set in motion in the course of the nineteenth century, were further consolidated and reinforced as states grew in strength and reach through the twentieth century. In general, this meant that administrative convenience, rather than any existing pattern of settlement or cultural affiliation, became the defining characteristic of the village. In Java, for example, as the Dutch reformed and refined their land rent system in 1907, 'villages were split or combined in order to attain a suitable size, village borders were sharply drawn, enclaves were terminated, all taxable land was surveyed and classified, [lands allocated to officials in place of salary] were identified and registered, individual plot holders were aware of their tax obligations and tax assessments were no longer bargained'.[15] In general, the pattern was one of consolidation into larger units rather than the reverse. In Burma in 1926, for example, the notion that villages might be combined for the sake of more efficient administration was unambiguously set forth.

This pattern of state disposal over the village was underlined during the period of Japanese occupation, although with rather different outcomes in mind than the peace and order so beloved of the colonial mind. In Java, for example, Japanese readiness to appoint and dismiss village chiefs and regularise their functions and terms of office served often to break down long established oligarchies of village authority and provide new avenues to power for ambitious but less prestigious candidates. That attitude, however, simply confirmed the importance of the position and the state's desire to command the rural sector. Moreover, the Japanese desire to mobilise the peasantry both spiritually and materially for the sake of their war effort saw the occupation government intrude more deeply than any Dutch authority had previously done. This was especially evident in the creation of new village social organisations like *tonarigumi* (neighbourhood associations) and cooperatives which were intended to improve the production and collection of goods and their distribution. For the most part, these new institutions, in a context of greater mobilisation and heavy Japanese patronage, served further to enhance the controlling power of the village chief.

The immediate postwar period was one of great fluidity and instability in many parts of the region. For a short time, the structures of village power and privilege which many decades of strengthening state intervention had constructed were placed under severe strain as central authority endured crises of legitimacy and control. In Java, for example, in the early months of the independence struggle, 'a period of administrative breakdown, competing and divided loyalties, and an uncertain future, there was a considerable increase in the amount of disruptive rural crime';[16] this juncture saw the downfall of many village chiefs who had prospered under Japanese patronage and their replacement by leaders from outside the traditional circles who enjoyed the support of newly emerging social groups. According to one scholar's survey, 'in 32 out of 50 sample villages there were 33 replacements of the chief during immediate post-war days (1945–46) . . . most of the 33 replacements during 1945–6 were caused by pressure from the villagers, which the people called kedaulatan rakyat (people's sovereignty)'.[17] In west Sumatra, village elections in 1946 brought a surge of support for the Islamic Masyumi party which swept many traditional leaders from office; 'the change in village leadership was paralleled by a return to a pattern of authority in the region that more closely approximated its traditional, precolonial organization. The nagari was revived as the key unit of government, and the hierarchical system, engineered by the Dutch and maintained by the Japanese, was virtually abolished throughout the period of crisis'.[18] In Burma, too, the temporary feebleness of the mechanisms of state control, in the context of the economic and social deprivation resulting from the period of war, gave ordinary peasants the momentary opportunity to assert themselves over those, like landlords, who had previously controlled their lives. In revolutionary Vietnam, as we have seen, the process of land reform brought to power in the village many of those who had previously been cast down at the lower end of the social and economic scale within the village.

Developments of this kind, however, were for the most part exceptional throughout the region and, in retrospect, temporary aberrations in the pattern of development of village politics. Elsewhere, things remained much as they always had in the recent past. In Thailand, for example, leadership remained in the hands of those already dominant in the village sphere through other means, and who usually controlled larger holdings of land and other village resources. Much the same could be said of village politics and leadership in the lowland Philippines.

MORE GRADUAL INCORPORATION

As with other developments, this process of village consolidation and the sharpening of the focus of village authority worked unevenly and with varying degrees of success across the whole region. Generally, one can assert that in those places where the state's intervention was less frequent and weighty, the pattern of administrative establishment in villages was less thorough. In the periphery, distant from the lowland centres of power, villages and village politics remained essentially unchanged, except that local heads were often saddled with new and strange tasks by the state. In upland Burma, Leach reported,

> the British Administration had always taken it for granted that a Kachin chief *ought* to be an autocrat. He was expected to execute without question all instructions received from the British District Officer ('Assistant Superintendent') by way of the Government Native Officer (*taungok*); furthermore he was made responsible for the collection of house tax and he was entitled to a commission of his collection; he was also responsible for the law and order of his community and for adjudicating upon matters of native law and custom. Nearly all these functions are quite alien to the traditional role of a duwa [chief], and most chiefs under the British found themselves in an awkwardly ambiguous position.[19]

In Mindanao, Subanu leaders found themselves acquiring new titles from the state, such as barrio lieutenant, but also discovered that these titles were accompanied by taxation and policing impositions upon their people as well as other interference in their land and livelihoods. In Borneo, the Brookes raised the authority of the Iban orang kaya by converting them into penghulu, without significantly enhancing their real power. This position was finally consolidated into that of a *tuai rumah*, effectively the connecting point between government and longhouse, but not a hereditary position and with no special privileges, save the existing prestige of the holder, who exerted authority only through 'a subtle mixture of persuasion and admonition, for he knows that his position is dependent on the continued goodwill and approval of . . . the other members of the house'.[20] His legitimating function was to preserve, interpret and administer *adat.*

A similar process of partial consolidation was at work in both uplands and lowlands of northern Thailand. In some places there was no one recognisably exercising a role as village chief, nor any functionally specific higher-level administrators; 'there were only "the elders", male householders aged roughly 40–60, whose previous experience as monks (and to a lesser extent as novices only) and subsequent successful use of various rituals and specialist knowledge, and other personal characteristics, had especially qualified them for the respect of their fellow villagers. They formed a fairly readily discernible if not discrete set of community leaders'.[21] The role of village chief under such circumstances had in a real sense to be created as an administrative position rather than simply built upon; those who came into the office were 'likely to belong to the "rich peasant" class',[22] served no more than part-time and received only small remuneration from the state, 'approximately one quarter of the lowest official wage'.[23] The administrative heavy-handedness that accompanied the process was exemplified in one northern Thailand site, where ten existing hamlets were arranged into four 'legal' hamlets, each with its own chief, and one of them in the role of chief of the commune. In another site again, muban were sometimes constructed 'of a mixture of both Thai and Karen villages, and it may not coincide with the village-cluster of Karen social organization'.[24] Nonetheless, by the 1960s in lowland northern Thailand, there could be no doubt that the state had largely succeeded in creating the villages it wanted: 'Chiengmai village is a corporate group in that it has an independent social identity and owns common property, and its people have organized themselves to make decisions for the village community as a whole'.[25] In the Thai uplands, by contrast, remarked one observer in the mid 1960s, 'until about ten years ago . . . with few exceptions, there was no taxation, no conscription, no education, and no legal registration of hill tribesmen. The population census did not include them. Their legal position as residents or citizens of the country was never clearly defined, and virtually no governmental administration was extended into the remote mountain areas'.[26]

In Malaya, where British official and unofficial interests focused most heavily on the tin and plantation rubber industries in which the local peasantry were not heavily involved, the administrative regularity of villages was not a prime concern of the colonial authorities. Accordingly, Malay villages continued to display those characteristics which the British interpreted as administrative and spatial raggedness; in Winstedt's eyes, for example, the kampung of Malaya were 'unconfined and straggling'.[27] Even much later, the Malay village was said to show 'little or no unity arising out of the interlocking of social relations among villagers',[28] which mostly turned on smaller clusters of villagers, notably the household, so that 'relations within the village are more incidental than structured'.[29] As a result, 'the village is a unit only in certain designated spheres, mostly imposed from outside, either by the administration or as a religious unit'.[30] According to Dobby, writing around 1950, 'villages are almost formless; houses are scattered'.[31]

The administrative vagueness that characterised the shaping of the village in Malaya under British colonialism is instructive, especially when contrasted to the firmer hand evident in such places as Java and Vietnam. The British authorities, like other ambitious states of the period, sought to make firm contact with compliant indigenous rural leaders in order to establish and confirm their control of the countryside. In the case of Malaya, the person upon whom they alighted was the penghulu. What the British sought were leaders 'who were loyal and efficient government servants and at the same time men accepted at the local level as leaders and representatives of the villages'.[32] Penghulus were in charge of a *mukim*, the area of settlement surrounding a mosque; only when populations grew and the social and political distance between penghulu and people was stretched did the need for lower levels of headship become evident, evolving through various functional roles and eventually and informally taking shape as the headship of a local settlement, the *ketua kampung* (kampung head). Official recognition and designation of the post of village chief apparently occurred unevenly; in some places village chiefs were proclaimed in the 1920s, in others the process had to await the period of Japanese occupation. Even then (and thereafter), the village remained relatively shapeless; the mukim remained the major administrative unit of rural areas, not the kampung, and many villagers were unaware either where their village ended and another began or to which village they belonged. In one region, villages were said 'to comprise a series of overlapping neighbourhood circles',[33] while in the Muda region, 'nearly all the existing mukim and district boundaries are simply lines drawn on cadastral maps by land office personnel'.[34]

The village chief, despite his undergoing a formal process of approval by the state government and his enjoying some privileges provided him by the state in the way of allowances and tax concessions, was not formally a state official and relied on his existing prestige to perform his functions. In some cases, indeed, there might be two village headmen in a single settlement, or even one kampung head in authority over more than one kampung. While these changes did not bring an immediate transformation of village life, they signified that the power of the state was moving things in altogether new directions and creating new kinds of power within the village which were to be both responsible to and dependent upon the state and which were armed with the means to enforce its will throughout the countryside; 'village headmen came to personify the machinery of modern government, and to symbolize both the declining fortunes of clan spokesmen and the devaluation and ever-narrowing range of adat owing to the state's progressive consolidation of power'.[35]

THE MODERN CONSOLIDATION OF VILLAGE POWER

Throughout Southeast Asia, the statist period saw a further buttressing of this administrative consolidation. In the Philippines, for example, the 1960 Barrio Charter confirmed the administrative status of the village in the state order by requiring the election of a barrio captain (who enjoyed a range of state-provided perquisites as recompense for his duties) and barrio councillors, and giving the barrio authority to tax villagers, to plan developments and to disperse funds, and administratively transforming all settlements into barrios. In Burma from 1962, Village Security and Administrative Committees were appointed from above to plan, direct and monitor social and economic life in the villages. In Indonesia, a Village Government Law of 1979 made formal the de facto centralisation of power within the village and its direct subordination to the chain of supra-village government officials. Increasingly through the region, the village administration became a channel for the proclamation and implementation within rural areas of the policies decreed by the state, and for informing the state of the behaviour of its rural subjects. Orders, regulations, policies, grants, pronouncements and even competitions originating from the centre of state power were transmitted down through the various levels of the administrative machinery that had been created, through provinces, districts, sub-districts, the village head and to the villagers themselves. Equally, information flowed upwards from the village chief to those above; thus, in a village in southern Vietnam, 'during the first three months of 1958 the Village Council received from fifty to seventy requests from higher authorities for information on agricultural activities'.[36] Moreover, the village chief, increasingly the man-in-between, had to mediate the concerns both of state and villagers to each other, to represent his villagers in their dealings with authorities outside, whom they commonly feared and avoided, and to convince them, in turn, that the state was working with their best interests at heart.

Right through the whole period, then, the trend was for the position and power of the village chief to wax. This meant not only that much more was demanded of the village chief in terms of both administrative and political skills, but also that the village chief's power to dispose over resources within the village was correspondingly enhanced. In Java, for example, the tone expressed itself in the village's chief's ability to control larger amounts of land than other villagers, to avail himself of the benefits of the village labour pool, and to siphon off a share of moneys collected in the name of higher authority. Similarly in Thailand, the kamnan might use his influence to persuade other villagers to assist him in the work on his own land, such as planting, weeding and reaping. As state-sponsored rural development programmes proliferated from the mid 1960s on, this tendency became even more pronounced. Village chiefs became, in an important sense, the personification of the drive for development; their power of disposal over the torrent of resources which flowed into villages – such as the annual cash grant made available to every village in Indonesia for the development of local infrastructure – put them even more in a position of securing and tending 'substantial material interests'.[37]

Increasingly, organisations established by the state to channel inputs like fertiliser and credit and act as supervisors and agents in processing and marketing, like BUUDs and their successor organisation, KUDs, in Indonesia, became the means for village elites to enhance their power and corner a disproportionate share of the resources which development programmes made available and stimulated. Moreover, the roles of village chiefs (especially in a context where the state was wary in the extreme about rural unrest or expressions of dissatisfaction and what they might portend) insulated them even more from the concerns of their villagers, and decreased the influence of villagers over the general course of events within their settlements; 'local elites have managed, to a great degree, to free themselves from the diffuse and costly obligations of the traditional distribution system, and they appear to be maintaining this freedom by relying upon existing sources of economic, political and administrative support'.[38] There was, of course, nothing particularly new about this situation; much the same could have been said (and was) about village chiefs during the course of the Cultivation System in Java in the nineteenth century. The novelty was that the more direct and intrusive attitude of the state had provided their local agents with the political and financial wherewithal to carry through this project much further than ever before. This was reflected, indeed, in Indonesia's 1979 village legislation which – finally – formally transformed village chiefs into salaried government officials.

The power wielded by village chiefs was partly a result of the formal importance of the position they held, but it was mainly rooted in the relationships that successful village chiefs were able to forge with those controlling from above. This strategy often meant that, notwithstanding disturbances such as those of the immediate post-World War II period and even administrative changes to the role of the village chief, village headship tended to remain within a narrow and usually kin-based band of economically powerful villagers who had enduring contacts and common interests with their extra-village superiors and patrons.

FROM COMMUNITY TO CITIZENRY

Paradoxically, it was just when the village had reached the apogee of its usefulness as a tool of management, and the village chief the height of his power, that the village began to fray at its administrative edges. The emphasis on the local community as the mode of administrative coherence began to break down, or at least to lose its immediacy, under a phalanx of social, political and economic changes. Partly this diminution came about as a result of the success of the state's encouragement of nationalism. Thus, one writer asserted of a village in northern Thailand in the mid 1970s, 'commune Baw citizens are much more conscious of being part of the whole Thai nation than they were twenty years ago',[39] perhaps in response to the resources that the Thai government had funnelled to the village to dispose as it wished. Partly, too, it resulted from a variety of social and economic changes that tended to transform the village's sense of identity, such as the growth of absentee landlordism (including the practice of holding plots in villages other than one's own), the much enhanced mobility of people which saw many workers leave villages and many outsiders find employment there, and the increasing tendency of extra-village marriage. The growth of commercialism in productive relations also played its part, as the escalating cost of land saw the breakup of many kin-oriented centres within villages so that 'the former hamlet or neighbourhood cluster of siblings and their children became the exception',[40] and as settlements in many places began to take on a more dispersed and atomised spatial pattern of occupation in place of the clumped settlements of the past. There was, too, the fact that just as heightened state intrusion had confirmed the power of the village chief, it had also introduced mechanisms to ensure that that power was not exercised with unresponsive arbitrariness.[41] In addition, the development of more diversified patterns of cropping, often in locations other than the wet-rice sites upon which village chiefs had customarily based their ability to control their peoples, tended to weaken village authority. There was, finally, the revolution of culture and communications, with schools, magazines, radio and television, not to mention rapid road transport, breaking down for ever the sense of distance and isolation which had always been a dominant motif of village life.

In general, the pattern was one of increasing individualisation, a decline in the immediacy of broader intra-village social networks, and a greater readiness to identify with the world outside the village in all its diversity. 'Villagers often remark that they do not know fellow villagers from other hamlets . . . there are no real focal centers to attract sizable segments of the village population'.[42] In other words, the village was in the process of becoming just a place to live rather than a rural settlement where interests enjoyed some general degree of broad acceptance. Villagers, in other words, were becoming citizens of a much wider community than their own settlements, and many of their connections with that world were of greater importance than those they had in common with their neighbours close by. It needs to be emphasised that this trend was only emergent, and not yet dominant, but it clearly pointed the way to the future.

PATTERNS OF SOCIAL AND ECONOMIC DIFFERENTIATION

The gathering strength and effectiveness of state intrusion into the village through the late nineteenth and the twentieth centuries tended to concretise already existing differences in status, power and wealth, and, indeed, to amplify them. Right across the region, the predominant pattern of village society became one of increasing economic differentiation and, indeed, in some places, polarisation. As we have seen, this was partly a result of changing economic contexts, notably the rapid growth of commercialised agriculture, largely unstructured and unmonitored, which took root in the late nineteenth century across the region. Owen has argued, with some justification, that 'when the expansion is allowed to go unregulated and unrestrained, and the demand is shown to be finite, the lands to be limited, then all the specialization, diversity, and increased population could prove to be handicaps rather than blessings. The rice industry of mainland Southeast Asia, 1850–1914, planted the seeds for the agrarian crisis of mainland Southeast Asia, 1914–??'.[43]

But increasing and enduring social stratification and differentiation also flowed directly from the injection of greater coercive power into village leadership. Many scholars have noted the widening gap in access to resources and power between rich and poor in villages, and its relation to greater involvement with markets, heavier population pressure, and ever more regular and purposeful state intervention in village life. Such stratification – by which I mean the furtherance and institutional consolidation of inequality – was evident even in places which had earlier been peripheral to the exercise of state power but which had gradually found themselves drawn under its sway. Among the Kalinga, for example, 'the poorest households in Pasil have one to three small rice fields; the richest, 30 to 40 large rice fields. The difference in rice production is about one to 100. The poor households may have one swidden; the rich, four or five large swiddens. The difference in production of vegetables is about one to twenty. The poorest have no carabaos, pigs or chickens; the richest may have ten carabaos and numerous pigs and chickens. The difference in meat consumption may be as high as one to 500'.[44] Amongst the Iban, efforts to adjust agricultural practices to cope with increasing population pressure, especially by employing perennial tree crops on swiddens, increased competition for land, promoted the tendency for its tenure to be expressed in individual rather than communal terms, and allowed some villagers to advance economically at the cost of others who adapted more slowly.

SOCIAL AND SPATIAL MOBILITY

Through all these processes, social mobility amongst peasant groups was not a feature of enduring significance in Southeast Asia. While it is true that social mobility was much enhanced in times of rapid change and economic expansion, such as the great age of rapid development in Lower Burma when landless and impoverished immigrants could make rapid ascents to the status of prosperous landholders, or the revolutionary context of post-World War II Vietnam, when political and bureaucratic astuteness and devotion to the prevailing cause, rather than landholding, became the key to success, such phases were generally short-lived and socially inconsequential. After periods of intensive shuffling, the successful participants in political agitation and economic booms sought nothing more than to replicate in new sites the prevailing hierarchies of power which were structured to stultify rather than lubricate the forces of change, and which were continually reinforced by ever enhanced state power which itself placed a high priority on security and control in the rural areas. Unfortunately, the generational aspects of social mobility have received virtually no sustained scholarly attention. I have already noted the impact of the custom of equal inheritance, which made it 'almost impossible for the ordinary farmers [that is, those dependent upon land] to accumulate wealth over several generations',[45] but we know little, in terms of a longer historical dimension, of the effects of intergenerational flows of wealth through marriage and reproduction. In general, then, while it might be the case that 'everyone has seen the rise of a poor family and the fall of a rich one',[46] it seems likely that those born into well-to-do families or very poor families generally remained where they began; the prospects of social improvement, episodic exceptions to one side, remained elusive and impractical.

Given the inefficacy of social mobility as a means of redressing the deepening problem of social stratification, many Southeast Asians took refuge in geographical movement of various kinds to defend what they had or to improve their lot. Movement had always been a favoured option of Southeast Asian peasants in times of stress or opportunity, and this pattern intensified as the transformations since 1800 magnified the incidence of both. There was, for example a great shift of population – perhaps 30 000 people – from Kedah consequent upon the Siamese invasion of 1821. Notwithstanding enduring myths about the settled fixity of Java's peasants ('The Javanese was not an enthusiastic emigrant . . . . The social ties of the village, of which attachment to the soil was but one factor, militated against leaving'[47]), they have proved to be, in fact, obstinate journeyers, moving from what they saw as intolerable oppression, fleeing in vast numbers from the threat of disease and famine, and always looking further afield to improve their livelihoods. The 1930 census reflected – albeit not as fully as it might have done because of its inability to capture intra-district movement – their tendency to move, revealing that almost 12 per cent of the indigenous residents of East Java were living outside the district in which they had been born, while West Java's share of Java's total population grew from 24.2 per cent to 27.3 per cent between 1905 and 1930. The Javanese moved not just to unreclaimed and promising lands in Java but also took up indentures to labour in (or elected to migrate of their own volition to) places like Sumatra, Malaya, the Pacific islands, and even distant Surinam. As well, they moved to Java's cities in ever-increasing numbers; Batavia's annual rate of population growth averaged 5.5 per cent between 1905 and 1930, much higher than rural growth rates.

In West Malaysia, urban population as a percentage of the total population grew from 10.7 in 1911 to 14.0 in 1921, 15.1 in 1931, 15.9 in 1947, 26.5 in 1957 and 28.7 in 1970, indicating increasingly greater rates of movement from countryside to city. Much the same liberal attitude to movement can be attributed to the rural Burmese; I have already discussed the descent upon the delta of great numbers of peasants from Upper Burma in the last part of the nineteenth century. One aspect of such movement was that by 1931 only one-third of the population of Rangoon was a native of that city. The Vietnamese, like the Javanese, were often said to be characteristically immobile because of the spiritual connection they held with their villages; 'a [Far Eastern] peasant', remarked Gourou in one place, 'leaves his village with regret and will willingly return to it if he has been obliged to emigrate',[48] while in another he asserted that 'the Annamese is extremely attached to his native soil, where his ancestors have dwelt, to the village to which all his memories cling, where he has all his family and friends'.[49] But Hendry, acknowledging that 'there appears to be resistance to mobility on the part of a majority of villagers', reported that 'even so, there is a substantial number of household heads who seem willing to move, and another substantial number of villagers who have already moved'.[50] Hickey, similarly, noted that 'despite the fact that the Vietnamese villager traditionally has had strong attachments to his village, particularly to his farmstead and the tombs of his ancestors, emigration has been an outstanding feature of Vietnamese history'.[51] In West Malaysia, vast new areas were opened up for settlement by immigrants. Krian, for example, had it frontier pushed back by immigrants from Kedah, Pattani and Indonesia; by far the most important and most numerous of them were Banjarese from the swamplands of southeastern Borneo. Indeed, the continual pattern of movement amongst the Malays was reflected in place names; 'in Perak there are places called Kampung Trengganu and Kampung Selangor; in Selangor there is a Kampung Kedah and way down in Johore, there is a Kampung Patani'.[52]

In Luzon, notably after the Americans proclaimed their homesteading policy, the flow of people into the sparsely inhabited Luzon plain around the Nueva Ecija region, previously dominated by the great Ilocano permanent and circular migrations of the nineteenth century, was enhanced by growing numbers of Tagalog-speakers from the south; as the Ilocano migrations spent themselves about 1920, settlement came almost solely from the south. Ilocanos also moved in great numbers into Cagayan, so that by 1903, 'nearly one-third of the Christian population in the [Cagayan] valley were Ilocanos'.[53] Moreover, as formerly peripheral areas were 'pacified' and tribal warfare diminished, those on the erstwhile periphery who had previously found themselves tied to their villages for the sake of security were now able to move with greater freedom in response to economic enticement. Responding to the opportunities of closer involvement with the market, young Iban males, both married and unmarried, moved out of their communities for extended periods of time; 'throughout the year, about 20% of the adult male population of an Iban community is absent on some kind of journey or enterprise'.[54]

The post-war era saw an even greater tendency for population mobility. In some cases it expressed itself in terms of movement from less prosperous to more prosperous rural areas where employment prospects were greater. Thus, in the Philippines, the 'differential adoption of modern rice technology induced permanent migration from unfavorable to favorable production environments so as to equalize the wage rates in different areas'.[55] Much of this movement seems to have been of a permanent character; whereas the census figures indicated only a 'modest redistribution' of people amongst different regions before World War II, interregional movement accelerated rapidly thereafter, with Mindoro and southern Mindanao experiencing (apart from Manila itself) the most rapid rise in population. In Thailand's Central Plain, mobility was also common; in Bang Chan, nearly 10 per cent of the population had moved away in the period 1949–53, which 'suggests a rather large, restless, and mobile segment of the population',[56] with those at the lower end of the social stratum, 'always . . . shifting and changing their residences or their means of livelihood or both',[57] to be replaced by newcomers who often sought to rent in land. The transmigration programme of the Indonesian government moved increasing numbers of people from crowded Java to more sparsely-populated regions in the archipelago; while the number of transmigrants in the period 1952–68 was only 416 471, the period of the first REPELITA saw another 182 414 resettled, and under the third five-year plan a rate of resettlement of around 150 000 people a year was achieved. There was at the same time a significant counter-flow of people from the Outer islands to the cities of Java, notably Jakarta; in Jakarta itself in 1971, four out of every ten residents was a migrant. Within Java itself, people appear to have become more mobile. According to one observer, large-scale migration of both a permanent and a circular kind from the poor upland region of Gunungkidul in central Java began only in the 1960s, and stood in stark contrast to the population immobility which had previously characterised the region.[58]

There was also a spectacular surge in the rate of movement from countryside to urban setting, from low-income employment to the centres of industrial expansion. In such cases, it was often not the poorest inhabitants of the village who moved but rather those occupying the 'middle level of the village community',[59] those with above-average education and landholdings and, disproportionately, the young. Partly, the move to the city was motivated by economic considerations, whether springing from a desire for greater wealth or from a defensive and desperate need to find new or extra income in a context where village land was increasingly unavailable or fragmented. But movement was certainly encouraged by a shrinking of the social and economic distance between town and countryside: 'Bang Chan moved cityward; whereas in 1948 many had never visited the capital, by 1955 four-fifths of all household heads had visited Bangkok once or more during the past twelve months'.[60] Sometimes such movement was of a purely temporary or circular kind, and sometimes it was permanent. Whatever the case, movement to the city from the rural areas was nearly always mediated through family, kin or acquaintanceship relationships with former village inhabitants who had made a new life in the city. The alacrity of peasants to move in the recent past was a further indication of the fact that isolation and apartness were no longer features of life for Southeast Asian peasants. Their lives could no longer be conceived purely in terms of settled rural categories. For most people who did not enjoy large fixed assets in the countryside, movement became the key to earning greater wealth; 'households receiving remittances from short-term circular migration tend, on average, to have raised household income and living standards quite rapidly compared with those of 10 years ago'.[61]

PROSPERITY AND ITS DISTRIBUTION

The evidence of restless searching by peasants for a better future through both vertical and (more successfully) horizontal mobility leads us inevitably to a discussion of prosperity. There are two fundamental and interrelated questions which require an answer. The first is whether the prosperity of Southeast Asians has improved over the last two centuries. The second, and more important, is to decide how such prosperity as was obtained has been distributed, and with what effect. Debate about these questions has been lively and sustained, and can in a crude sense be seen as a struggle between two camps. On the one hand there are those who, in general, argue that the processes of commercialisation, state formation and demographic growth around which the subject-matter of this book has been organised brought nothing but ever-increasing impoverishment for the great majority of Southeast Asians. On the other hand are those who claim, notwithstanding the evidence for increasing social stratification within peasant society and between the peasant sector and other sectors, that economic growth, a major feature of the period and perhaps most notable in the recent past, has brought hitherto unavailable prosperity to the mass of peasants.

THE IMPOVERISHMENT CRITIQUE

In this view, the long period of colonial and semi-colonial domination, and all it entailed, structured Southeast Asian rural societies in ways that necessarily, if not immediately, brought impoverishment to the region's peasantry. The problems to which this domination gave rise simply exacerbated, and were in turn exacerbated by, the rapid and sustained growth in the region's rural population. Thus, argued Tichelman, 'the changes which western penetration wrought in the condition of stagnation were not of such type as to lead to the rise of a strong, indigenous propertied class able to bring about a capitalist breakthrough. Instead, they led to a population explosion, to marginal modernization, to an expansion of parasitic administrative apparatuses and to the beginning of capitalistic class differentiation without indigenous capital accumulation of any significance'.[62] In the period of independence, there was no movement of any significance – with the exception of the revolutionary successes in Indochina, themselves prey in the end to bureaucratic corruption – to change these structures which privileged elites at the expense of everyone else. The ameliorating effects of land reform, such as it was, were viewed with sceptical eyes: 'the socio-economic consequences of agrarian reform in the Philippines have been ambivalent at best, and oftentimes self-contradictory – i.e., beneficial to those who were to be expropriated, and prejudicial to those who were to be the beneficiaries'.[63]

Champions of this view pointed to the enduring and deepening character of rural poverty throughout the region; 'it is certain that undernourishment [in the Tonkin delta] is very widespread',[64] remarked Gourou. He underlined his point by stating that

> if the Tonkin Delta were inhabited with French people, it would sustain a rural population which would not reach the figure of one hundred inhabitants to the square kilometer. It is not that the French peasant has so much greater an appetite than the Tonkin peasant does, but, for his upkeep and dress, to meet the expenses corresponding to his standard

> of living, he must sell large quantities of produce, whereas the Tonkin peasant, living in a closed economy, sells and buys very little.[65]

In the early 1960s, over 60 per cent of Java's rural inhabitants were living below a poverty line established at a level equivalent to an income of 240 kilograms of rice per year; even by 1984, 46 per cent could still be classed as 'poor'. This state of affairs was reflected in widespread nutritional deficiency disorders and a high level of infant mortality. In Thailand, notwithstanding general rural poverty, there were significant differences in income levels between various parts of the country, notably between the region around Bangkok and the traditionally impoverished northeastern sector of the country on the Korat plateau, measured at 3 to 1 in the period between 1960 and 1979.[66] Vickery, analysing the refugee situation in Thailand in the aftermath of the Cambodian tragedy, remarked grimly that 'one of the spin-offs of the refugee operations . . . has been the revelation that much of the rural Thai population normally lives in conditions approximating those the Cambodian refugees wished to escape'.[67]

Scholars sought to link this evident and general poverty with features of structural change which had emerged over the last two centuries. The adoption of technological innovation, for example, was often claimed to have advantaged the rich systematically at the expense of the poor. To cite one case, through the nineteenth century the destruction of the indigenous weaving and textile industry wiped out the income stream of women – usually at the lower end of the social scale – who had woven cloth for sale for ancillary household income. In more recent times, the employment of new agricultural technology was accused of much the same thing. In the 1930s, Gourou argued that the introduction of agricultural machinery in the Tonkin delta 'would reduce the sum of work available to the peasant and would do away with the salaries of workers who would then have only the resources of dying unobtrusively'.[68] By the 1970s, his prediction was apparently being fulfilled. According to Collier and his colleagues, the spread of rice hullers in Java from about that time and their replacement of hand pounding had 'probably worsened the distribution of income in a substantial way'.[69] While hullers provided – at around one-third of the cost of hand pounding – a milled product of higher quality and higher selling price, thus advantaging the wealthier peasants with rice surpluses for sale, their introduction came at the expense of poor female peasants who had relied for employment and income (in the form of milled rice) on hand milling the rice crop bought up by rice merchants. Collier estimated in 1974 that the introduction of mechanical hullers had cost 1.2 million full-time jobs in Java and $50 million in wages.[70] In similar mould, Palmer argued that 'the new rice technology in Java seems to have had the net effect of reducing employment, which together with increasing population means an accelerated increase in poverty'.[71] In the Muda region of West Malaysia, the use of tractors and mechanised harvesting led to a situation in which 'large farmers and contractors are now the recipients of payments from poorer farmers in return for ploughing and combine harvesting'.[72] Moreover, the argument went, the loss of traditional income had not been replaced by an enhanced availability of alternative employment.

The agricultural revolution of the 1960s and after was credited also with broader impoverishing effects. Because of the high and often 'lumpy' costs associated with the new technologies – for rice strains, fertiliser, pesticides, farming machinery and so on – critics argued that wealthier peasants, with larger amounts of land, greater capital resources, favoured by disproportionate access to state-sponsored pools of credit, and able to sustain themselves through the periods of erratic yields which often characterised cultivation of high yielding varieties, were in a position to benefit disproportionately from the higher yields which the new technology produced, and to capitalise on that advantage by devouring more of the resources of poorer peasants, notably their land and their cheap labour. The poor, accordingly, were increasingly forced into the market to buy their rice, the price of which was artificially high because of state rice support schemes. Overall, then, critics argued that the Green Revolution had done little more than to confirm and seriously exacerbate the existing situation; even if they enjoyed some access to the new technology, 'a majority of the farmer-innovators continue to live in absolute poverty while a minority is prospering'.[73]

Such impoverishment was often linked with the self-interested policies adopted by colonial rulers. In the Depression of the 1930s, for example, there was evidence that government economic strategies were aimed at sustaining the Western sector of the economy rather than the welfare of the society as a whole. Thus, the rubber restriction scheme of the 1930s had the effect of privileging Western rubber estates over indigenous smallholdings; in one state of Malaya, only two-fifths of the smallholdings were still being tapped a year after the scheme came in operation. Sometimes, paradoxically, such policies actually assisted some peasants. In Tonkin, for example, rice prices fell so much that it became uneconomic to export the grain, with the result that 'the peasant was better fed during the depression than he was during the period of so-called prosperity'.[74] Generally, however, peasants suffered badly in the unprotected and ravaging economic climate they encountered. Rice consumption declined in Java through the 1930s and, according to one estimate, was thought to have dropped by one-quarter in Burma through the same period as producers offered greater proportions of their harvests for sale (which saw the country's net rice exports increase) in an effort to protect their incomes, and compensated either by consuming less food overall or changing their consumption to cheaper foods. In the Philippines, too, peasants' food intake was thought to have been affected by the exigencies of the Depression.

Finally, there was the fear that the environment could not long endure the punishment meted out to it by the activities flowing from the structures ordering peasant society. By the late 1980s, environmentalists in Thailand pointed out what they saw as a trend towards decline in productivity in both artificially irrigated areas and those reliant upon rainfall.[75] There was, as well, the related problem of how to cope with the growing numbers of uplanders whose environment could no longer sustain them: 'given their present state of poverty, and the amount of investment in cash or labour for terracing, and in cash for draft animals and their demands for cash for other purposes, it is not reasonable to expect these upland peoples to become subsistence wet rice farmers on the model of the typical lowland Thai peasant'.[76] In the meantime, such communities languished, caught in a situation where their old methods could no longer support their bulging numbers, yet at the same time powerless to prevent the states which now controlled them from removing their most worthwhile resources, such as timber, and distributing the benefits to lowland and international entrepreneurs.

THE ALTERNATIVE VIEW

It is extraordinary, to say the least, that virtually every point in the array of the impoverishment critique was turned on its head by those who saw things in a more positive light. For the most part, those arguing that the welfare of Southeast Asian peasants has been enhanced by the experience of the last two centuries have impugned the significance of structural inequalities as a source of enduring poverty and emphasised the dramatic productive increases which have taken place through these decades.

Where the critics saw poverty, the protagonists of the alternative view stressed heightened rural living standards. Even in such crude ventures to raise agricultural production as the forced cultivation system in Java in the nineteenth century, some scholars saw that peasants in general profited from enhanced incomes, despite having to work much harder and more regularly than had previously been the case. The smallholder rubber boom of the early twentieth century clearly brought vastly increased incomes to peasants who took to its cultivation, without the need for the input of much capital or risk. In south Kalimantan, for example, 'the prosperity due to high rubber prices in the 1920s took more manifest forms and affected more people. In Hulu Sungai the few roads were crowded by imported cars and bicycles. Thousands went down to Banjarmasin to embark on the long journey to Mecca and the "Queen Wilhelmina" cinema in Kandangan doubled its performances'.[77] According to Johnston, 'because it was fuelled largely by indigenous factors of production, the Thai rice economy became not a source of dislocation but rather the relatively solid foundation upon which the country's post-war economic development has been based'.[78] With growing prosperity in the Central Plain, houses of sawn teak began to be raised in place of the old dwellings constructed of bamboo.

Generally, in post-World War II Southeast Asia, material life in the village took on a more varied and sophisticated style than ever before, often with heavy overtones of consumerism. Houses improved in quality, sometimes equipped with flush toilets and tiled floors, and were increasingly filled with furniture and labour-saving items like sewing machines, electric irons, gas stoves and refrigerators and the communications paraphernalia of modernity: radios, television sets, and stereos, not to mention more mundane consumer items such as soap, shoes, plastics, curtains, clocks and cushions. Their occupiers wore a wider array of clothing: underpants, brassieres, T-shirts. Sanitation and hygiene improved, as did the quantity and quality of food. One observer noted in Indonesia a 13 per cent increase in the per capita consumption of rice in the decade after 1964[79] – a trend that continued through the 1980s – while Naylor, speaking of Java, asserted that 'high rates of growth in per capita income since the mid 1970s, and particularly in the early 1980s, have allowed an increasing share of the population to consume rice'.[80] More generally, scholars pointed to a declining incidence of poverty measured according to food availability, as well as other indicators of improvement in living standards such as enhanced participation in education and declining rates of infant mortality.

As far as structural changes in the allocation of resources were concerned, notably in the area of agrarian reform, the alternative view either denigrated the usefulness of such strategies, questioned the possibility of their introduction, or applauded the usefulness of what little was achieved. The tenure reforms in the Philippines in the 1970s, for example, were thought to have allowed previously tenanted farmers to reap higher returns from the yield advances which accrued in the wake of the introduction of new production technologies in the 1970s.

In the vexed area of the social and economic effects of the introduction of new agricultural technology, the alternative view argued that the rate of adoption between wealthy and less wealthy peasants had been only marginally and insignificantly different; indeed, on one account, 'on the average, small farmers were even faster to adopt [high-yielding varieties] than large farmers'.[81] The new technology, moreover, had provided two gains of fundamental significance. The first was the enormous increase in yields and thus of output, in the main a result of a vastly improved cropping ratio, which led to a heightened standard of living among producers. The second was in the area of employment, both in farm and non-farm tasks, and both directly and indirectly attributable to the productive and procedural consequences of the adoption of new technology. Thus, new technology brought new demands for hired farm labour which could not properly be met in many places and which therefore resulted in stable wages in a context of cheaper food or even wage increases; moreover, as economies expanded, wage labour opportunities for unskilled workers developed in non-farm sectors such as trade and construction in both local and urban settings.

Insofar as there were displacement effects from the introduction of mechanisation in land preparation, harvesting, weeding, threshing and milling – and such effects were not evident everywhere – they were more than amply compensated for by the employment creation effects of the new technologies. The result, according to one observer, was that 'rice farm laborers and groups who purchase their rice consumption needs probably gained as a result of the changes over the period'.[82] Put in its simplest terms, 'the way to escape the Ricardian trap resulting from population pressure on land is to concentrate on developing land-saving and labor-using technologies that increase demand for labor faster than the supply of labor is increasing, and food supply more rapidly than demand for it is increasing'.[83] In Hayami's view, 'persistent rural poverty and inequality in developing Asia have resulted not from the green revolution, but from insufficient efforts to develop and diffuse the new agricultural technologies'.[84] One commentator on Java remarked that, as a result of the Green Revolution, 'rich landowners or village officials . . . had prospered and were much better-off than before, but poor landless farmers had also benefited and were less destitute than in the past. The gap between rich and poor had increased, but both had progressed in the same direction. Social differentiation had taken place, but it was relative and bore no relation to the kind of absolute polarization I had been expecting from theories of agricultural modernization'.[85]

CONCLUSION

There can be no question that the processes of social and economic change that Southeast Asia's peasants have experienced over the last two centuries have seen the development of broad patterns of differentiation between different peasant groups. While some live in villages in urban-like splendour with full stomachs, others scrape together a livelihood constructed around long hours of low-return drudgery and which involves strategies like consuming poor-quality food substitutes in place of rice. While some live comfortably from their considerable lands, others are forced to partake in whatever multiplicity of tasks might be available to provide them and their families with survival income. Such divisions have partly been the result of political choices resulting from attempts by the strengthening state to impose its will more directly and regularly upon its subjects and which saw, for example, village leaders acquire disproportionate access to rural resources at the expense of other villagers. Partly, too, they have come from some peasants seizing and capitalising upon opportunities which other have missed or missed taking.

Nonetheless, it seems possible to argue that, in a general sense, the material standard of living of most Southeast Asian peasants, notwithstanding occasional vicissitudes such as the periods of depression and occupation, has risen in the course of the last two centuries. What has allowed this to happen is a fundamental change in their world which has seen them move from the isolation and limitations of their fundamentally rural orientation into a thoroughgoing participation in a wider, richer, vastly more powerful and infinitely more variegated economy.

Commentators on contemporary Southeast Asia rarely use the term 'peasant' to describe the inhabitants of rural areas. Their practice is not just a manifestation of political correctness but rather stems from a realisation, for the most part unconscious because the phenomenon has not been properly analysed, that the peasantry is in the process of passing away. The changes which have been visited upon Southeast Asia's rural societies over the last 200 years have transformed the lives of their members fundamentally. There is no longer a 'rural sector' which can be considered in splendid isolation, nor are there significant groups of people which can possibly be viewed as being contained in a mode of rural existence. The experience of Bang Chan village is instructive: 'Bang Chan was changing from gaining nourishment to gaining a profit, from accumulating implements to accumulating goods, from sustaining life to sustaining income, from a way of living to earning a living'.[86] Expanding national and international economies, ever more intrusive states and contracting spatial distances have gradually transmogrified the category of peasant into that of farmer and worker and, now, citizen.

Conclusion

Time passes quickly. Its rapid passage brings changes which our minds, fervently seeking constancy and tranquillity, are slow to recognise and sometimes reluctant to admit. It is this cerebral stubbornness that renders shocking the idea that the age of the peasantry in Southeast Asia has come to an end. It is true, of course, that Southeast Asia's populations are still overwhelmingly rural in residence and that the majority of the region's workforces find employment in spheres closely associated with rural production. It is also true that many rural Southeast Asians still construct their sense of self and community in ways not wildly dissimilar to that of their forebears a century ago. But simply to proclaim these things in the name of enduring continuity is to ignore the longer trajectory of the region's history, and the manner in which multiple, varying and ever-changing contexts have shaped the structures of society at different times.

There was, I have argued, a time in which peasants and their activities were not the dominant motif of Southeast Asian social and economic life. Reid's 'age of commerce', for example, was characterised by spices, silver, ships, and cities. By the early nineteenth century, however, the Southeast Asian peasantry was on the first steps of its rise to prominence. It was then that peasant numbers began to swell and spread across the Southeast Asian landscape, then that states moved to modes of economic activity which prized the large-scale production of simple export produce. Its march to ascendancy may be dated roughly from the mid nineteenth century and its florescence at the turn of the twentieth, by which time a combination of population growth and the political and economic policies and practices of Western colonial powers had conspired to raise peasants' numbers dramatically and to make their productive activities the centrepoint of the region's economic life.

The age of the Southeast Asian peasantry endured for some decades thereafter. But we can now see that, even by the 1910s, there were clear signs that the very forces which had made for the construction of an age of peasantry were combining to dislodge peasants from their central role in the region's social and economic history. The mutually reinforcing dynamisms of commercialism and demography worked, it must be said, slowly: there was no sudden realisation that peasantness was passing. But the elements of its ending were already solidly planted in the structure of the region's history. Increasing numbers of rural residents were making their livelihoods not from toiling on their own lands but in working the lands of others or, more important, finding wage employment outside the sphere of rural production. Upland and hinterland swiddeners, many of whom had, indeed, themselves become peasants only in the recent past, found themselves at the limits of that mode of production almost as soon as they had begun it, and retreated to the lowlands, and to lowland cities and towns.

Those that stayed where they were changed, and had their lives changed for them, in fundamentally transformative ways. In Sarawak in 1990, 'even the most physically isolated longhouse several days' boat ride from the urban-port complex of Bintulu is connected with the District and Divisional administration, the international commodity markets, the regional and the national market for labour and the Japanese demand for tropical timber'.[1] The vast multitudes of lowland small-scale producers, the people whose lives and labour had provided the region with most of its enduring images of rurality and hard-working simplicity, remained in the countryside. Many of them grimly hung to the dwarfed pockets of land which had come down to them, even as the importance and value of such holdings evaporated, and as the trajectory of change saw them reallocating their labour and their social lives to more diverse and remunerative tasks and pursuits than agricultural production. By the last decade of the twentieth century, those peoples who might in the past have been called peasants were thoroughly enmeshed in larger national, regional and global economies. They earned money from activities only distantly connected with rural production, sold a larger proportion of their crop than they retained, changed what they grew in response to changing market demands, and organised the labour of their families to secure income from a diversity of sources rather than focussing substantially on increasing rural production. Devices such as these allowed rural dwellers to continue, even if in attenuated forms, the lifestyles and even something of the livelihood of the age of the peasantry, but it was increasingly a performance rather than the substance of their lives. The trajectory of this development is one that suggests a general (though by no means unqualified) historical pattern of movement from dependence on subsistence production towards proportionately (and ever) greater reliance on cash production, and, increasingly, on off-farm income.

It may seem to some strange to say that the end of the peasantry has come in Southeast Asia. Such people may, to rebut such an assertion, point to the enduring existence of rural production and of the social and economic circuits of life and livelihood which accompany it. The point, however, is that the rural producers of today are productive and enduring only insofar as they have moved from being peasants into new and different worlds of production and, consequently, of social and economic life. There can be no mistaking the romanticised shadow for the substance, which is that the peasantry, gradually from the early twentieth century, and from the mid-century on at an accelerating rate, has been radically reconstituted, through its own agency and that of broader forces of change, into a series of more modern categories of social formation. The world of Southeast Asia is no longer a world dominated by peasants and peasant modes of life.

Notes and References

Preface

1. Benjamin White, 'Political aspects of poverty, income distribution and their measurement: some examples from rural Java', *DC* 10, (1979), p. 92.
2. C.A. Bayly, 'State and economy in India over seven hundred years', *EHR* 38 (1985), p. 583.
3. Morton H. Fried, 'On the concepts of "tribe" and "tribal society"', in June Helm (ed.), *Essays on the problem of tribe: proceedings of the 1967 annual spring meeting of the American Ethnological Society* (Seattle: American Ethnological Society, 1968), p. 5.
4. For key discussions of the concept, see George Dalton, 'Peasantries in anthropology and history', *CA* 13, 3–4 (1972), pp. 385–407; Sidney W. Mintz, 'A note on the definition of peasantries', *JPS* 1, 1 (1973), pp. 91–106; Eric Wolf, *Peasants* (Englewood Cliffs, N.J.: Prentice Hall, 1966). An important contribution cast in a Marxist framework is David Goodman and Michael Redclift, *From peasant to proletarian: capitalist development and agrarian transitions* (Oxford: Basil Blackwell, 1981).
5. Raymond Firth, 'Capital, savings and credit in peasant societies: a viewpoint from economic anthropology', in Raymond Firth and B.S. Yamey (eds), *Capital, savings and credit in peasant societies: Studies from Asia, Oceania, the Caribbean and middle America* (London: George Allen and Unwin, 1964), p. 17.
6. Ibid.
7. M. Moerman, *Agricultural change and peasant choice in a Thai village* (Berkeley: University of California Press, 1968), p. 19.
8. C. Geertz, 'Form and variation in Balinese village structure', *AA* 61 (1959), pp. 1008–9.
9. Teodor Shanin, 'Introduction', in Teodor Shanin (ed.), *Peasants and peasant societies: selected readings* (Harmondsworth: Penguin, 1971), p. 16.

1 An Embryonic Peasantry

1. R.G. Cant, *An historical geography of Pahang* (Singapore: MBRAS Monograph No. 4, 1973), p. 29.
2. Horace St. John, *The Indian archipelago: its history and present state* (London: Longman, Brown, Green, and Longmans, 1853), vol. 1, p. 12.
3. James Low, *The British settlement of Penang* (repr. Singapore: Oxford University Press, 1972) [1836], p. 101.
4. Victor B. Lieberman, *Burmese administrative cycles: anarchy and conquest c. 1580–1760* (Princeton: Princeton University Press, 1984), pp. 20–1.
5. Although, as we shall see, the term 'village' is not necessarily coterminous with the concept of settlement.
6. Walter Knaags, 'A visit to Perak', *Journal of Eastern Asia* 1, 1 (1875), p. 28.

7. Howard Malcolm, *Travels in south-eastern Asia* (London: Charles Tilt, 1839), vol. 1, p. 195.
8. Dominique Lefevre, 'Details respecting Cochin China', *JIAEA* 1 (1847), p. 63. Cochinchina refers at this time to the former southern kingdom of Vietnam; only with the onset of French colonialism does the term come to mean the southernmost region of the country.
9. Munshi Abdullah, cited in R.O. Winstedt, *Papers on Malay subjects. Life and customs. Part II. The circumstances of Malay life. The kampung, the house, furniture, dress, food* (Kuala Lumpur: The Government Printer, 1909), p. 2.
10. J.H. Moor, *Notices of the Indian archipelago, and adjacent countries* (repr. London: Frank Cass, 1968) [1837], p. 238.
11. John Crawfurd, *Journal of an embassy from the Governor-General of India to the court of Ava* (London: R. Bentley, 1834), vol. 1, p. 47; Crawfurd, *History of the Indian archipelago, containing an account of the manners, arts, languages, religions, institutions, and commerce of its inhabitants* (repr. London: Frank Cass, 1967) [1820], vol. 1, pp. 40–1.
12. George Finlayson, *The mission to Siam and Hue, the capital of Indo-China in the years 1821–1822* (London: John Murray, 1826), p. 215.
13. William Marsden, *The history of Sumatra* (repr. Kuala Lumpur: Oxford University Press, 1966) [1811], p. 59.
14. C.J.F.S. Forbes, *British Burma and its people: being sketches of native manners, customs, and religion* (London: John Murray, 1878), p. 76.
15. Hugh Low, *Sarawak: its inhabitants and productions* (repr. London: Frank Cass, 1968) [1848], p. 233.
16. Low, *The British settlement*, p. 177.
17. John Crawfurd, *Journal of an embassy from the Governor-General of India to the courts of Siam and Cochin China; exhibiting a view of the actual state of those kingdoms* (repr. London: Oxford University Press, 1967) [1828], p. 279.
18. Forbes, *British Burma*, p. 109.
19. Malcolm, *Travels*, vol. 1, p. 218.
20. William J. Koenig, *The Burmese polity, 1752–1819: politics, administration, and social organization in the early Kon-baung period* (Ann Arbor: Michigan Papers on South and Southeast Asia No. 34, Center for South and Southeast Asian Studies, University of Michigan, 1990), pp. 57–8.
21. Crawfurd, *History*, vol. 1, pp. 346–7.
22. Peter Hinton, 'Introduction', in Peter Hinton (ed.), *Tribesmen and peasants in north Thailand: proceedings of the first symposium of the Tribal Research Centre, Chiang Mai, Thailand, 1967* (Chiangmai: Tribal Research Centre, 1967), p. 5.
23. E.R. Leach, *Political systems of highland Burma: a study of Kachin social structure* (Cambridge, Mass.: Harvard University Press, 1954), p. 114.
24. Karl Gustav Izikowitz, *Lamet: hill peasants in French Indochina* (repr. New York: AMS Press, 1979) [1951], p. 82.
25. Michael R. Dove, 'The agroecological mythology of the Javanese and the political economy of Indonesia', *Indonesia* 39 (1985), p. 9.
26. Mary Backus (ed.), *Siam and Laos as seen by our American missionaries* (Philadelphia: Presbyterian Board of Publication, 1884), p. 27.

27. Georges Condominas, 'Aspects of economics among the Mnong Gar of Vietnam: multiple money and the middleman', *Ethnology* 2, 3 (1972), p. 203.
28. Anon., 'Remarks on the Phillippine islands and on their capital Manila, 1819 to 1822', in E.H. Blair and J.A. Robertson, *The Philippine islands 1493–1898* (Cleveland: A.H. Clark, 1903–09), vol. 51, p. 81.
29. Edward P. Dozier,*Mountain arbiters: the changing life of a Philippine hill people* (Tucson: University of Arizona Press, 1966), p. 151.
30. Bertram S. Carey and H.N. Tuck, *The Chin hills: A history of the people, British dealings with them, their customs and manners and a gazeteer of their country* (repr. Delhi: Cultural Publishing House, 1983) [1896], vol. 1, p. 211.
31. Derek Freeman, *Report on the Iban* (London: Athlone Press, 1970), p. 163.
32. Low, *The British settlement*, p. 102.
33. Forbes, *British Burma*, p. 75.
34. Paul P. de la Gironiere,*Twenty years in the Philippines* (New York: Harper and Brothers, 1854), p. 309.
35. Crawfurd, *History*, vol. 1, p. 354. But Crawfurd did notice in his travels in Cochinchina that 'the poverty of the soil was attempted to be remedied by manuring it with a species of alga, or sea-weed, fished up from the bottom of the creek' (*Journal of an embassy . . . to the courts of Siam and Cochin China*, p. 291).
36. Albert S. Bickmore, *Travels in the East Indian archipelago* (repr. Singapore: Oxford University Press, 1991) [1869], p. 37.
37. Low, *The British settlement*, p. 95.
38. John Crawfurd, 'Notes on the population of Java', *JIAEA* 3 (1849), p. 42.
39. Crawfurd, *History*, vol. 1, p. 355.
40. Ibid., vol. 1, pp. 346–7.
41. Crawfurd, *Journal of an embassy . . . to the court of Ava*, vol. 1, p. 144.
42. Ibid.
43. John Barrow, *A voyage to Cochin China in the years 1792 and 1793* (repr. Kuala Lumpur: Oxford University Press, 1975) [1806], p. 315.
44. Crawfurd, *Journal of an embassy . . . to the court of Ava*, vol. 1, p. 145.
45. De la Gironiere, *Twenty years*, p. 310.
46. Lefevre, 'Details respecting Cochin China', p. 64.
47. Finlayson, *The mission to Siam*, p. 386.
48. Crawfurd, *Journal of an embassy . . . to the courts of Siam and Cochin China*, p. 522.
49. Carl Bock, *Temples and elephants: the narrative of a journey of exploration through upper Siam and Lao* (London: Sampson Low, Marston, Searle and Rivington, 1884), p. 317.
50. Cant, *Pahang*, p. 56.
51. V. Sangermano, *A description of the Burmese empire compiled chiefly from Burmese documents* (repr. London: Susil Gupta, 1966) [1833], p. 185.
52. Backus (ed.), *Siam and Laos*, p. 442.
53. Pierre Gourou, *The peasants of the Tonkin delta* (New Haven: HRAF, 1955) [1936], pp. 486, 487.

54. Backus (ed.), *Siam and Laos*, p. 26.
55. George Windsor Earl, *The eastern seas, or voyages and adventures in the Indian archipelago in 1832–33–34* (London: Wm. H. Allen, 1837), p. 262.
56. Carey and Tuck, *The Chin hills*, vol. 1, p. 215.
57. Moor, *Notices*, p. 92.
58. Sangermano, *A description*, p. 185.
59. John Joseph Stockdale, *Sketches, civil and military of the island of Java and its immediate dependencies* (London: S. Gosnell, 1812), p. 41.
60. Earl, *The eastern seas*, p. 65.
61. Hiram Cox, *Journal of a residence in the Burmhan empire, and more particularly at the court of Amarapoorah* (repr. London: Gregg International Publishers, 1971) [1821], p. 23.
62. Malcolm, *Travels*, vol. 1, p. 245.
63. John Anderson, *Acheen, and the ports on the north and east coasts of Sumatra* (repr. Kuala Lumpur: Oxford University Press, 1971) [1840], p. 25.
64. Crawfurd, *Journal of an embassy . . . to the court of Ava*, vol. 2, p. 99.
65. Backus (ed.), *Siam and Laos*, p. 440.
66. William Henry Scott, *The discovery of the Igorots: Spanish contact with the pagans of northern Luzon* (Quezon City: New Day Publishers, 1974), p. 177.
67. Low, *Sarawak*, p. 55.
68. Tomas de Comyn, *State of the Philippine islands in 1810, being an historical, statistical and descriptive account of the interesting portion of the Indian archipelago* (repr. Manila: Filipiniana Book Guild, 1969) [1820], p. 32.
69. Crawfurd, *History*, vol. 1, p. 280.
70. Robert MacMicking, *Recollections of Manilla and the Philippines during 1848, 1849 and 1850* (repr. Manila: Filipiniana Book Guild, 1967) [1852], p. 197.
71. Izikowitz, *Lamet*, p. 315.
72. Sangermano, *A description*, pp. 216–17.
73. Anon., 'Remarks on the Phillippine islands', p. 82.
74. P.J. Begbie, *The Malayan peninsula* (repr. Kuala Lumpur: Oxford University Press, 1967) [1834], pp. 8–9.
75. Forbes, *British Burma*, pp. 111–12.
76. Low, *Sarawak*, p. 226.
77. De Comyn, *State of the Philippines in 1810*, p. 33.
78. John Leroy Christian, *Modern Burma: a study of political and economic development* (Berkeley: University of California Press, 1942), p. 127.
79. Sangermano, *A description*, p. 217.
80. Victor B. Lieberman, 'Secular trends in Burmese economic history, c. 1350–1830, and their implications for state formation', *MAS* 25, 1 (1990), p. 15.
81. Holt S. Hallett, *A thousand miles on an elephant in the Shan states* (Edinburgh: William Blackwood and Sons, 1890), p. 280.
82. Pornpun Futrakul, 'The environmental history of pre-modern provincial towns in Siam to 1910', PhD dissertation, Cornell University, 1989, p. 115.

83. Crawfurd, *Journal of an embassy . . . to the court of Ava*, vol. 2, p. 189.
84. Pornpun, 'The environmental history', p. 121.
85. Charles Wilkes, 'Narrative of the U.S. exploring expedition', in Anon., *Travels accounts of the islands* (Manila: Filipiniana Book Guild, 1974), p. 27.
86. E.R. Leach, 'The frontiers of "Burma"', *CSSH* 3, 1 (1960–1), p. 50.
87. May Ebihara, 'Societal organization in sixteenth and seventeenth century Cambodia', *JSEAS* 15, 2 (1984), p. 282.
88. Hong Lysa, *Thailand in the nineteenth century: evolution of the economy and society* (Singapore: ISEAS, 1984), p. 9.
89. Lieberman, *Burmese administrative cycles*, p. 10.
90. Robert H. Taylor, *The state in Burma* (Honolulu: University of Hawaii Press, 1987), p. 45.
91. T.S. Raffles, *Substance of a minute recorded by the honourable Thomas Stamford Raffles, lieutenant-governor of Java and its dependencies, on the 11th February 1814* (London: Black, Parry, 1814), p. 81.
92. Crawfurd, *History*, vol. 3, pp. 53–4.
93. Crawfurd, *Journal of an embassy . . . to the court of Ava*, vol. 2, p. 166.
94. Raffles, *Substance of a minute*, p. 99.
95. Crawfurd, cited in Raffles, *Substance of a minute*, p. 88.
96. Ibid., p. 82.
97. Margaret Lindley Koch, 'Malay society in Temerloh, Pahang, under British colonial rule 1889–1948', PhD dissertation, Columbia University, 1982, pp. 7–8.
98. Gerald C. Hickey, 'Some aspects of hill tribe life in Vietnam', in Peter Kunstadter (ed.), *Southeast Asian tribes, minorities and nations*, vol. 2 (Princeton: Princeton University Press, 1967), p. 755.
99. Izikowitz, *Lamet*, p. 112.
100. Crawfurd, *Journal of an embassy . . . to the court of Ava*, vol. 2, p. 161.
101. C. Dobbin, *Islamic revivalism in a changing peasant economy: central Sumatra, 1784–1847* (London: Curzon Press, 1983), p. 17.
102. Crawfurd, cited in Raffles, *Substance of a minute*, p. 85.
103. Lieberman, *Burmese administrative cycles*, p. 167.
104. Ma Mya Sein, *Administration of Burma. Sir Charles Crosthwaite and the consolidation of Burma* (repr. Kuala Lumpur: Oxford University Press, 1973) [1938], p. 67.
105. Charles Crosthwaite, *The pacification of Burma* (repr. London: Frank Cass, 1968) [1912], p. 5.
106. Lauriston Sharp and Lucien M. Hanks, *Bang Chan: social history of a rural community in Thailand* (Ithaca: Cornell University Press, 1978), p. 74.

2 The Context of Change: Politics, Economics and Demography

1. The pioneering analytical and synthetic work of Anthony Reid, presented most engagingly and persuasively in his two-volume *Southeast Asia in the age of commerce, 1450–1680* (New Haven: Yale University Press, 1988–93), is the major point of departure.
2. 'Reducción' was the name the Spanish gave to the process of incorporating

and settling down the scattered communities they encountered in much of Luzon.

3. Ed. C. de Jesus, *The tobacco monopoly in the Philippines: bureaucratic enterprise and social change, 1766–1880* (Quezon City: Ateneo de Manila University Press, 1980), p. 68.
4. John S. Ambler, 'Historical perspectives on sawah cultivation and the political and economic context for irrigation in west Sumatra', *Indonesia* 46 (1988), p. 52.
5. De Jesus, *The tobacco monopoly*, p. 199.
6. Ibid.
7. Wong Lin Ken, 'Singapore: its growth as an entrepot port, 1819–1941', *JSEAS* 9, 1 (1978), p. 59.
8. Hong, *Thailand*, p. 61.
9. G. William Skinner, *Chinese society in Thailand: an analytical history* (Ithaca: Cornell University Press, 1957), p. 32.
10. Finlayson, *The mission to Siam*, p. 167.
11. Crawfurd, *Journal of an embassy . . . to the courts of Siam and Cochin China*, p. 322.
12. Hong, *Thailand*, p. 84.
13. Hong Lysa, 'The tax farming system in the early Bangkok period', *JSEAS* 14, 2 (1983), p. 383.
14. John Bowring, *The kingdom and people of Siam* (repr. Kuala Lumpur: Oxford University Press, 1969) [1857], p. 200.
15. David Bruce Johnston, 'Rural society and the rice economy in Thailand, 1880–1930', PhD dissertation, Yale University, 1975, p. 33.
16. Takeshi Motooka, 'Rice exports and the expansion of cultivation', in Yonei Ishii (ed.), *Thailand: a rice growing society* (Honolulu: University Press of Hawaii, 1978), p. 283.
17. Bowring, *The kingdom and people of Siam*, vol. 1, p. 123.
18. Johnston, 'Rural society and the rice economy', p. 41.
19. Hong, *Thailand*, p. 127.
20. Ibid., p. 150.
21. Michael Adas, *The Burma delta: economic development and social change on an Asian rice frontier 1852–1941* (Madison: University of Wisconsin Press, 1974), p. 223.
22. Charles Lee Keeton, *King Theebaw and the ecological rape of Burma: the political and commercial struggle between British India and French Indo-China in Burma, 1878–1886* (Delhi: Manohar, 1974), pp. 143–4, 342.
23. Martin J. Murray, *The development of capitalism in colonial Indochina (1870–1940)* (Berkeley: University of California Press, 1980), p. 58. Growth in the rice area expanded even more rapidly thereafter; according to one scholar of the colonial period, about two-thirds of Cochinchina's rice land was brought into cultivation after 1880 (Guy Gran, 'Vietnam and the capitalist road to modernity: village Cochinchina 1880–1940', PhD dissertation, University of Wisconsin, 1975, p. 61).
24. MacMicking, *Recollections of Manilla*, p. 16.
25. John A. Larkin, 'Philippine history reconsidered: a socioeconomic perspective', *AHR* 87, 3 (1982), p. 613.
26. De Jesus, *The tobacco monopoly*, p. 135.

27. Onghokham, 'The residency of Madiun. Pryayi and peasant in the nineteenth century', PhD dissertation, Yale University, 1975), p. 200.
28. Gerald Cannon Hickey, *Sons of the mountains: ethnohistory of the Vietnamese central highlands to 1954* (New Haven: Yale University Press, 1982), p. 321.
29. Grant Evans, *Lao peasants under socialism* (New Haven: Yale University Press, 1990), p. 32.
30. John Park Finley and William Churchill, *The Subanu: studies of a sub-Visayan mountain folk of Mindanao* (Washington, DC: Publication No. 184, Carnegie Institution, 1913), p. 18.
31. Cited in Johnston, 'Rural society and the rice economy', p. 276.
32. Zaharah Mahmud, 'The population of Kedah in the nineteenth century', *JSEAS* 3, 2 (1972), pp. 205–6.
33. Taylor, *The state in Burma*, p. 71.
34. Arturo Garcia Corpuz, 'Railroads and regional development in the Philippines: views from the colonial iron horse, 1875–1935', PhD dissertation, Cornell University, 1989, p. 62.
35. Anthony Reid, *The blood of the people: revolution and the end of traditional rule in northern Sumatra* (Kuala Lumpur: Oxford University Press, 1979), p. 3.
36. Sharom Ahmat, 'The structure of the economy of Kedah: 1879–1905', *JMBRAS* 43, 2 (1970), p. 5.
37. Akimi Fujimoto, *Income sharing among Malay peasants: a study of land tenure and rice production* (Singapore: Singapore University Press, 1983), p. 23.
38. Charles Robequain, *The economic development of French Indo-China* (London: Oxford University Press, 1944), p. 111.
39. Glenn Anthony May, *Social engineering in the Philippines: the aims, execution and impact of American colonial policy, 1900–1913* (Westport: Greenwood Press, 1980), p. 140.
40. Chattip Nartsupha, Suthy Prasartset, and Montri Chenvidyakarn, 'Introduction', in Chattip Nartsupha, Suthy Prasartset, and Montri Chenvidyakarn (eds), *The political economy of Siam, 1910–1932* (Bangkok: Social Science Association of Thailand, 1978), p. 11.
41. Lim Teck Ghee, *Peasants and their agricultural economy in colonial Malaya, 1874–1941* (Kuala Lumpur: Oxford University Press, 1977), p. 87.
42. Evans, *Lao peasants*, p. 28.
43. William Joseph O'Malley, 'Indonesia in the Great Depression: a study of East Sumatra and Jogjakarta in the 1930s', PhD dissertation, Cornell University, 1977, p. 365.
44. John O. Sutter, *Indonesianisasi: politics in a changing economy, 1940–1955* (Ithaca: Data Paper No. 38, Southeast Asia Program, Cornell University, 1959), vol. 1, p. 190.
45. J.C. Jackson, 'Rice cultivation in West Malaysia: relationships between culture, history, customary practices, and recent developments', *JMBRAS* 45, 2 (1972), p. 82.
46. Norman G. Owen, 'Economic and social change', in Nicholas Tarling (ed.), *The Cambridge history of Southeast Asia*, vol. 2 (Cambridge: Cambridge University Press, 1992), p. 467.

47. Leon A. Mears, Meliza H. Agabin, Teresa L. Anden and Rosalinda C. Marquez, *Rice economy of the Philippines* (Quezon City: University of the Philippines Press, 1974), p. 17.
48. Kamol Odd Janlekha, 'A study of the economy of a rice growing village in central Thailand', PhD dissertation, Cornell University, 1955.
49. Philippine Assistant on Community Development, 'The barrio in 1957', in Socorro C. Espiritu and Chester L. Hunt (eds), *Social foundations of community development* (Manila: R.M. Garcia, 1964), p. 28.
50. Cited in Sharp and Hanks, *Bang Chan*, p. 151.
51. Lance Castles, 'Socialism and private business: the latest phase', *BIES* no. 1 (1965), p. 19.
52. Wolf Donner, *The five faces of Thailand: an economic geography* (London: C. Hurst, 1978), p. 176.
53. Philip Hirsch, *Development dilemmas in rural Thailand* (Singapore: Oxford University Press, 1990), p. 12.
54. Ibid., p. 81.
55. Gerald Cannon Hickey, *Free in the forest: ethnohistory of the Vietnamese central highlands 1954–1976* (New Haven: Yale University Press, 1982), p. 290.
56. Ken Kampe, 'Northern highlands: development, bureaucracy and life on the margins', *PV* 33, 2 (1992), p. 160.
57. Adam Fforde, *The agrarian question in North Vietnam, 1974–1979: a study of cooperator resistance to state policy* (Armonk: M.E. Sharpe, 1989), p. xi.
58. Ibid., p. 185.
59. Evans, *Lao peasants*, p. 122.
60. David P. Chandler, 'A revolution in full spate: Communist Party policy in Democratic Kampuchea, December 1976', in David A. Ablin and Marlowe Hood (eds), *The Cambodian agony* (Armonk: M.E. Sharpe, 1987), p. 167.
61. Gourou, *Peasants of the Tonkin delta*, p. 116.
62. Robequain, *The economic development*, p. 55.
63. Owen, 'Economic and social change', p. 484.

3 The Changing Varieties of Peasant Production

1. Ambler, 'Historical perspectives', p. 56.
2. Norman G. Owen, 'The rice industry of mainland Southeast Asia, 1850–1914', *JSS* 59, 2 (1971), p. 141.
3. Christian, *Modern Burma*, p. 110.
4. Zaharah, 'The population of Kedah', p. 206.
5. John Bowring, *The Philippine islands* (London: Smith, Elder, 1859), pp. 251–2.
6. Evans, *Lao peasants*, p. 39.
7. E.H.G. Dobby, *Southeast Asia* (9th ed. London: University of London Press, 1966), p. 173.
8. J.D.G. Campbell, *Siam in the twentieth century: being the experiences and impressions of a British official* (London: Edward Arnold, 1902), p. 25.
9. Johnston, 'Rural society and the rice economy', p. 210.
10. Ibid., p. 213.
11. Donner, *The five faces of Thailand*, p. 601.

12. Ambler, 'Historical perspectives', p. 56.
13. Robert Huke (ed.), *Shadows on the land: an economic geography of the Philippines* (Manila: Bookmark, 1963), p. 123.
14. Percy A. Hill and Kilmer A. Moe, 'The cultivation of rice', *JEAS* 9, 4 (1960), p. 102 (extracted from their *A handbook of Philippine rice production* [1917]).
15. Cited from a Philippine Bureau of Agriculture bulletin in Hill and Moe, 'The cultivation of rice', p. 100.
16. V.D. Wickizer and M.K. Bennett, *The rice economy of monsoon Asia* (Stanford: Institute of Pacific Relations, Food Research Institute, Stanford University, 1941), p. 248.
17. Arsenio M. Balisacan, 'Agricultural growth, landlessness, off-farm employment, and rural poverty in the Philippines', *EDCC* 41, 3 (1993), p. 536.
18. F.G.B. Keen, 'Land use', in John McKinnon and Wanat Bhruksasri (eds), *Highlanders of Thailand* (Kuala Lumpur: Oxford University Press, 1983), p. 302.
19. E.C. Chapman, 'Shifting cultivation and economic development in the lowlands of northern Thailand', in Peter Kunstadter, E.C. Chapman, and Sanga Sabhasri (eds), *Farmers in the forest: economic development and marginal agriculture in northern Thailand* (Honolulu: University Press of Hawaii, 1978), p. 222.
20. Edward van Roy, *Economic systems of northern Thailand: structure and change* (Ithaca: Cornell University Press, 1971), p. 106.
21. James F. Eder, 'Hunter-gatherer/farmer exchange in the Philippines: some implications for ethnic identity and adaptive well-being', in A. Terry Rambo, Kathleen Gillogly, and Karl L. Hutterer (eds), *Ethnic diversity and the control of natural resources in Southeast Asia* (Ann Arbor: Michigan Papers on South and Southeast Asia No. 32, Center for South and Southeast Asian Studies, University of Michigan, 1988), p. 46.
22. Cheng Siok Hwa, 'The rice industry of Malaya: a historical survey', *JMBRAS* 42, 2 (1969), p. 138.
23. Thomas Stamford Raffles, *A history of Java* (repr. Kuala Lumpur: Oxford University Press, 1978) [1817], vol. 1, p. 108.
24. Gourou, *Peasants of the Tonkin delta*, p. 405.
25. Ibid., p. 412.
26. Ibid., p. 427.
27. Ibid., pp. 435–6.
28. Generoso F. Rivera and Robert T. McMillan, *An economic and social survey of rural households in central Luzon* (Manila: Philippine Council for United States Aid/United States of America Operations Mission to the Philippines, 1954), p. 13.
29. Pierre Gourou, *Land utilization in French Indochina* (Washington: Institute of Pacific Affairs, 1945), p. 334.
30. James B. Hendry, *The small world of Khanh Hau* (Chicago: Aldine Publishing Company, 1964), p. 52.
31. Jackson, 'Rice cultivation in West Malaysia', pp. 83–4.
32. Ambler, 'Historical perspectives', p. 66.
33. Alfian Lains, 'West Sumatra: the road to Parasamya Purnakarya Nugraha', in Hal Hill (ed.), *Unity in diversity: regional economic development in*

Indonesia since 1970 (Singapore: Oxford University Press, 1989), pp. 441–2.

34. Anan Ganjanapan, 'The partial commercialization of rice production in northern Thailand (1900–1981)', PhD dissertation, Cornell University, 1984, p. 416.
35. David Feeny, 'Agricultural expansion and forest depletion in Thailand, 1900–1975', in John F. Richards and Richard P. Tucker (eds), *World deforestation in the twentieth century* (Durham: Duke University Press, 1988), p. 116.
36. Robert Lawless, 'Societal ecology in northern Luzon: Kalinga agriculture, organization, population, and change', *Papers in Anthropology* 18, 1 (1977), p. 107.
37. Prabhu L. Pingali and Vo-Tong Xuan, 'Vietnam: decollectivisation and rice productivity growth', *EDCC* 40 (1992), p. 703.
38. Hill and Moe, 'The cultivation of rice', p. 112.
39. Cheng, 'The rice industry of Malaya', p. 141.
40. Moerman, *Agricultural change*, p. 186.
41. Hendry, *The small world*, p. 89.
42. Rene E. Ofreneo, *Capitalism in Philippines agriculture* (Quezon City: Foundation for Nationalist Studies, 1980), p. 76.
43. John V. Dennis, Jr, 'Kampuchea's ecology and resource base: natural limitations on food production strategies', in David Ablin and Marlowe Hood (eds), *The Cambodian agony* (Armonk: M.E. Sharpe, 1987), p. 216.
44. Huke (ed.), *Shadows on the land*, p. 347.
45. A. Cecil Carter (ed.), *The kingdom of Siam* (repr. Bangkok: The Siam Society, 1988) [1904], p. 24.
46. W.A. Graham, *Siam* (3rd ed. London: Alexander Moring, 1924), vol. 1, p. 31.
47. R.D. Hill, 'The history of rice cultivation in Melaka', in Kernial Singh Sandhu and Paul Wheatley (eds), *Melaka: the transformation of a Malay capital c. 1400–1980* (Kuala Lumpur: Oxford University Press, 1983), p. 558.
48. J. Thomas Lindblad, 'Economic change in southeast Kalimantan 1880–1940', *BIES* 21 (1985), p. 77.
49. Cited in Michael Gates Peletz, *A share of the harvest: kinship, property, and social history among the Malays of Rembau* (Berkeley: University of California Press, 1988), p. 151.
50. Peletz, *A share of the harvest*, p. 151.
51. H.V. Richter and C.T. Edwards, 'Recent economic developments in Thailand', in Robert Ho and E.C. Chapman (eds), *Studies of contemporary Thailand* (Canberra: Department of Human Geography, Research School of Pacific Studies, Australian National University, 1973), p. 26.
52. Hirsch, *Development dilemmas in rural Thailand*, p. 46.
53. A.M.P.A. Scheltema, 'De voeding van de inlandsche bevolking van Nederlandsch-Indië', *Koloniale Studiën* 14, 2 (1930), p. 384.
54. James A. Le Roy, *Philippine life in town and country* (New York: Putnam's Sons, 1905), p. 91.
55. Gourou, *Peasants of the Tonkin delta*, p. 465.
56. Janlekha, 'A study of the economy of a rice growing village', p. 50.

57. Gourou, *Peasants of the Tonkin delta*, p. 470.
58. Janlekha, 'A study of the economy of a rice growing village', pp. 50–1.
59. John E. deYoung, *Village life in modern Thailand* (Berkeley: University of California Press, 1955), p. 100.
60. Dove, 'The agroecological mythology', p. 15.
61. Dobby, *Southeast Asia*, pp. 349, 181–2, 270, 210.
62. Evans, *Lao peasants*, p. 39.
63. Boediono, 'An economic survey of North Sulawesi', *BIES* 8, 3 (1972), p. 67.
64. James Rush, *The last tree: reclaiming the environment in tropical Asia* (New York: The Asia Society, 1991), p. 40.
65. Keen, 'Land use', p. 301.
66. Ibid., p. 302.
67. Aram A. Yengoyan, 'Hierarchy and social order: Mandaya ethnic relations in southeast Mindanao, Philippines', in A. Terry Rambo, Kathleen Gillogly, and Karl L. Hutterer (eds), *Ethnic diversity and the control of natural resources in Southeast Asia* (Ann Arbor: Michigan Papers on South and Southeast Asia No. 32, Center for South and Southeast Asian Studies, University of Michigan, 1988), p. 180.
68. Dozier, *Mountain arbiters*, p. 127.
69. Lawless, 'Societal ecology', p. 80.
70. Ibid., p. 48.
71. Violeta Lopez-Gonzaga, *Peasants in the hills: a study of the dynamics of social change among the Buhid swidden cultivators in the Philippines* (Quezon City: University of the Philippines Press, 1983), pp. 10–12.
72. Dozier, *Mountain arbiters*, p. 24.
73. Ronald E. Seavoy, 'The origin of tropical grasslands in Kalimantan, Indonesia', *JTG* 40 (1975), p. 48.
74. Lawless, 'Societal ecology', p. 67.
75. Michael R. Dove, 'Man, land and game in Sumbawa: some observations on agrarian ecology and development policy in eastern Indonesia', *SJTG* 5, 2 (1984), p. 120.
76. E.R. Leach, 'Some aspects of dry rice cultivation in north Burma and British Borneo', *Advancement of Science* 6 (1949), p. 27.
77. James W. Hamilton, *Pwo Karen: at the edge of mountain and plain* (St Paul: West Publishing Co., 1976), p. 83.
78. J. Peter Brosius, *After Duwagan: deforestation, succession and adaptation in upland Luzon, Philippines* (Ann Arbor: Michigan Studies of South and Southeast Asia Number 2, Center for South and Southeast Asian Studies, University of Michigan, 1990), p. 19.
79. Ibid., p. 23.
80. Dove, 'The agroecological mythology', p. 8.
81. Laurence C. Judd, *Chao rai Thai: dry rice farmers in northern Thailand* (Bangkok: Suryaban Publishers, 1977), p. 85.
82. Ibid., p. 416.
83. R.D. Hill, *Agriculture in the Malaysian region* (Budapest: Akademiai Kiado, 1982), p. 74.
84. Dusit Banijbatana, 'Forest policy in northern Thailand', in Peter Kunstadter, E.C. Chapman, and Sanga Sabhasri (eds), *Farmers in the forest: economic*

development and marginal agriculture in northern Thailand (Honolulu: University Press of Hawaii, 1978), p. 54.

85. Freeman, *Report on the Iban*, p. 305.
86. R.A. Cramb, 'Shifting cultivation and resource degradation in Sarawak: perceptions and policies', *RIMA* 22, 1 (1988), pp. 127–32.
87. Alfredo Barrera, 'Soils and natural vegetation', in Robert Huke (ed.), *Shadows on the land: an economic geography of the Philippines* (Manila: Bookmark, 1963), p. 64.
88. F.L. Wernstedt and J.E. Spencer, *The Philippine island world: a physical, cultural and regional geography* (Berkeley: University of California Press, 1967), p. 99.
89. Jerome Rousseau, *Central Borneo: ethnic identity and social life in a stratified society* (Oxford: Clarendon Press, 1990), p. 130.
90. Joel M. Halpern, *The rural and urban economies* (Los Angeles: Laos Project Papers No. 8, Department of Anthropology, University of California, 1961), p. 49.
91. Moor, *Notices*, p. 230.
92. Cited in Chattip Nartsupha and Suthy Prasartset, 'Introduction', in Chattip Nartsupha and Suthy Prasartset (eds), *The political economy of Siam 1851–1910* (Bangkok: Social Science Association of Thailand, 1981), p. 4.
93. Charles Stuart Leckie, 'The commerce of Siam in relation to the trade of the British empire', in Chattip Nartsupha and Suthy Prasartset (eds), *The political economy of Siam 1851–1910* (Bangkok: Social Science Association of Thailand, 1981), p. 135.
94. Carter (ed.), *The kingdom of Siam*, p. 253.
95. J. Homan van der Heide, 'The economical development of Siam during the last half century', in Chattip and Suthy, *Political economy*, p. 88.
96. Cited in Akira Oki, 'Social change in the west Sumatran village: 1908–1945', PhD dissertation, Australian National University, 1977, p. 29.
97. Khoo Kay Jin, 'Revenue farming and state centralisation in nineteenth-century Kedah', in John Butcher and Howard Dick (eds), *The rise and fall of revenue farming: business elites and the emergence of the modern state in Southeast Asia* (Houndmills: Macmillan, 1993), p. 133.
98. Andrus, *Burmese economic life*, p. 335.
99. Le Roy, *Philippine life*, p. 82.
100. Evans, *Lao peasants*, p. 86.
101. James M. Andrews, *Siam: 2nd rural economic survey. 1934–1935* (Bangkok: Bangkok Times Press, 1935), p. 123.
102. Halpern, *The rural and urban economies*, pp. 18, 56.
103. deYoung, *Village life in modern Thailand*, p. 103.
104. Ibid.
105. Hickey, *Free in the forest*, p. 27.
106. deYoung, *Village life in modern Thailand*, p. 103.
107. Evans, *Lao peasants*, p. 84.
108. Gourou, *Peasants of the Tonkin delta*, p. 511.
109. Stephen A. Resnick, 'The decline of rural industry under export expansion: a comparison among Burma, Philippines, and Thailand, 1870–1938', *JEH* 30, 1 (1970), p. 64.
110. Homan van der Heide, 'The economical development', p. 92.

111. Hendry, *The small world*, p. 158.
112. O.H.K. Spate, 'The Burmese village', *GR* 35 (1945), p. 523.
113. Hill and Moe, 'The cultivation of rice', p. 105.

4 Land and Landholding

1. Gourou, *Peasants of the Tonkin delta*, p. 386.
2. Gourou, *Land utilization*, p. 283. Communal lands were also held for cult and religious purposes, but the amount involved was usually very small and was leased out to cover expenses (Gourou, *Peasants of the Tonkin delta*, p. 391).
3. Gourou, *Peasants of the Tonkin delta*, pp. 384–5.
4. Ibid., p. 389.
5. Ibid.
6. Ibid., pp. 389–90.
7. Graham, *Siam*, vol. 2, p. 3.
8. Johnston, 'Rural society and the rice economy', p. 224.
9. Marshall Seaton McLennan, 'Peasant and hacendero in Nueva Ecija: the socio-economic origins of a Philippine commercial rice-growing region', PhD dissertation, University of California at Berkeley, 1973, p. 352.
10. Ofreneo, *Capitalism in Philippines agriculture*, p. 26. See also McLennan, 'Peasant and hacendero', p. 356.
11. Gourou, *Peasants of the Tonkin delta*, p. 394.
12. Ibid., pp. 394–5.
13. Ofreneo, *Capitalism in Philippines agriculture*, p. 26.
14. Anat Arbhabhirama et al., *Thailand natural resources profile* (Singapore: Oxford University Press, 1988), p. 5.
15. Gourou, *Land utilization*, p. 455.
16. *Bilek* refers to the individuated family living rooms/areas in the longhouse.
17. Freeman, *Report on the Iban*, p. 105.
18. Sophon Ratanakhon, 'Legal aspects of land occupation and development', in Peter Kunstadter, E.C. Chapman, and Sanga Sabhasri (eds), *Farmers in the forest: economic development and marginal agriculture in northern Thailand* (Honolulu: University Press of Hawaii, 1978), pp. 48–9.
19. Freeman, *Report on the Iban*, p. 101.
20. Peter Kunstadter, 'Alternatives for the development of upland areas', in Peter Kunstadter, E.C. Chapman, and Sanga Sabhasri (eds), *Farmers in the forest: economic development and marginal agriculture in northern Thailand* (Honolulu: University Press of Hawaii, 1978), p. 304.
21. McLennan, 'Peasant and hacendero', p. 357.
22. Murray, *The development of capitalism*, p. 64.
23. Koch, 'Malay society in Temerloh', p. 146.
24. Murray, *The development of capitalism*, p. 66.
25. Gourou, *Peasants of the Tonkin delta*, p. 381.
26. Gehan Wijeyewardene, 'Hydraulic society in contemporary Thailand?', in Robert Ho and E.C. Chapman (eds), *Studies of contemporary Thailand* (Canberra: Department of Human Geography, Research School of Pacific Studies, Australian National University, 1973), p. 101.

27. Diana Wong, *Peasants in the making: Malaysia's Green Revolution* (Singapore: ISEAS, 1987), p. 37.
28. Gourou, *Peasants of the Tonkin delta*, pp. 381–2.
29. William L. Collier, 'Institutional constraints on food security programmes for the poor: case study of Java', *KEM* 18, 1–2 (1981), p. 79.
30. Wade C. Edmundson and Stella A. Edmundson, 'A decade of village development in East Java', *BIES* 19, 2 (1983), p. 47.
31. Brian Fegan, 'Rural Philippines: central Luzon', in R.J. May and Francisco Nemenzo (eds), *The Philippines after Marcos* (New York: St. Martin's Press, 1985), p. 166.
32. Masao Kikuchi and Yujiro Hayami, 'Technological and institutional response and income shares under demographic pressure: a comparison of Indonesian and Philippine villages', in Geoffrey B. Hainsworth (ed.), *Village-level modernization in Southeast Asia: the political economy of rice and water* (Vancouver: University of British Columbia Press, 1982), pp. 175–6.
33. R.E. Downs, 'A Kelantanese village in Malaya', in Julian H. Steward (ed.), *Contemporary change in traditional societies. Volume II. Asian rural societies* (Urbana: University of Illinois Press, 1967), p. 153.
34. T.B. Wilson, *The economics of padi production in north Malaya. Part I. Land tenure, rents, land use and fragmentation* (Kuala Lumpur: Department of Agriculture, 1958), p. 63.
35. Anan, 'The partial commercialization', p. 323.
36. Moerman, *Agricultural change*, p. 105.
37. H. Demaine and C.J. Dixon, 'Land tenure patterns and agricultural development in N.E. Thailand: a case study of the Lam Pao irrigation area in changwat Kalasin', *JSS* 60, 2 (1972), p. 58.
38. F. Landa Jocano, *The Ilocanos: an ethnography of family and community life in the Ilocos region* (Quezon City: Asian Center, University of the Philippines, 1982), p. 27.
39. Evans, *Lao peasants*, p. 152.
40. Paul H. Kratoska, '"Ends that we cannot foresee": Malay reservations in British Malaya', *JSEAS* 14, 1 (1983), p. 167.
41. Gourou, *Peasants of the Tonkin delta*, p. 371.
42. Ibid., p. 372.
43. Gourou, *Land utilization*, p. 277.
44. Evans, *Lao peasants*, p. 122.
45. Kenzo Horii, *Rice economy and land tenure in West Malaysia: a comparative study of eight villages* (Tokyo: IDE Occasional Paper No. 18, Institute of Developing Economies, 1981), p. 90. See also Masuo Kuchiba, Yoshihiro Tsubouchi, and Narifumi Maeda (eds), *Three Malay villages: a sociology of paddy growers in West Malaysia* (Honolulu: University of Hawaii Press, 1979), p. 54.
46. Andrew Turton, 'Northern Thai peasant society: twentieth-century transformations in political and jural structures', *JPS* 3, 3 (1976), p. 275.
47. Leon A. Mears, *The new rice economy of Indonesia* (Yogyakarta: Gadjah Mada University Press, 1981), pp. 46–7.
48. Under the rubric 'tenancy' I include such arrangements as land rental and land leasing.
49. Gourou, *Peasants of the Tonkin delta*, p. 398.

50. Paul H. Kratoska, 'The peripatetic peasant and land tenure in British Malaya', *JSEAS* 16, 1 (1985), p. 43.
51. Dobby, *Southeast Asia*, pp. 276–7.
52. McLennan, 'Peasant and hacendero', p. 375.
53. Ibid., p. 375.
54. Anan, 'The partial commercialization', p. 201.
55. Andrus, *Burmese economic life*, p. 70.
56. Gillian Hart, *Power, labor, and livelihood: processes of change in rural Java* (Berkeley: University of California Press, 1986), p. 102.
57. Hirsch, *Development dilemmas in rural Thailand*, p. 143.
58. Rivera and McMillan, *An economic and social survey*, p. 9.
59. McLennan, 'Peasant and hacendero', pp. 365–6.
60. Horii, *Rice economy*, p. 161. See also Fujimoto, *Income sharing*, p. 153. Luong, writing of Vietnam, makes the sensible point that 'Given the inherent socioeconomic differentiation over time within any large kin group and the exceedingly high rate of village endogamy, most tenants would have been related, either consanguinally or affinally, to some degree to most landlords within the same village' (Hy Van Luong, 'Agrarian unrest from an anthropological perspective: the case of Vietnam', *Comparative Politics* 17, 2 (1985), pp. 163–4).
61. Francesca Bray, *The rice economies: technology and development in Asian societies* (Oxford: Basil Blackwell, 1986), p. 179.
62. Ibid.
63. Hill, *Agriculture in the Malaysian region*, p. 115.
64. Anan, 'The partial commercialization', p. 205.
65. Moerman, *Agricultural change*, p. 113.
66. Harry Luton, 'American internal revenue policy in the Philippines to 1916', in Norman G. Owen (ed.), *Compadre colonialism: studies on the Philippines under American rule* (Ann Arbor: Michigan Papers on South and Southeast Asia No. 3, Center for South and Southeast Asian Studies, University of Michigan, 1971), p. 144.
67. McLennan, 'Peasant and hacendero', p. 440.
68. Report of the Land and Agriculture Committee, 1938, cited in Cheng, *The rice industry of Burma*, p. 166.
69. Cheng, *The rice industry of Burma*, p. 165, summarising the 1930 Report of the Provincial Banking Enquiry Committee.
70. Harlan P. Crippen, 'Philippine agrarian unrest', *Science and Society* 10, 4 (1946), p. 340.
71. Akira Takahashi, 'The peasantization of kasama tenants', *PSR* 20 (1972), p. 131.
72. Sharp and Hanks, *Bang Chan*, p. 147.
73. Edwin E. Moise, *Land reform in China and North Vietnam: consolidating the revolution at the village level* (Chapel Hill: University of North Carolina Press, 1983), p. 4.
74. Evans, *Lao peasants*, p. 219.
75. Daniel W. Bell et al., *U.S. Economic Survey Mission's report* (Manila: Philippine Book Company, 1950), p. 63.
76. Ofreneo, *Capitalism in Philippines agriculture*, p. 37.

77. David Lim, *Economic growth and development in West Malaysia, 1947–1970* (Kuala Lumpur: Oxford University Pres, 1973), p. 195.
78. Bray, *The rice economies*, p. 191.
79. Keijiro Otsuka, Violeta Cordova and Cristina C. David, 'Green Revolution, land reform, and household income distribution in the Philippines', *EDCC* 40 (1992), pp. 722–3.
80. Ofreneo, *Capitalism in Philippines agriculture*, p. 89.
81. Antonio Ledesma, 'Land reform in East and Southeast Asia: a comparative approach', *PS* 28 (1980), p. 320.
82. Eduardo C. Tadem, *Grains and radicalism: the political economy of the rice industry in the Philippines: 1965–1985* (Quezon City: Third World Studies Center, University of the Philippines, 1986), p. 29.
83. Ofreneo, *Capitalism in Philippines agriculture*, p. 63.
84. Brian Fegan, 'The Philippines: agrarian stagnation under a decaying regime', in Gillian Hart, Andrew Turton and Benjamin White with Brian Fegan and Lim Teck Ghee (eds), *Agrarian transformations: local processes and the state in Southeast Asia* (Berkeley: University of California Press, 1989), p. 141.
85. Benjamin White and Gunawan Wiradi, 'Agrarian and nonagrarian bases of inequality in nine Javanese villages', in Gillian Hart, Andrew Turton and Benjamin White with Brian Fegan and Lim Teck Ghee (eds), *Agrarian transformations: local processes and the state in Southeast Asia* (Berkeley: University of California Press, 1989), p. 299.
86. David A. Preston, 'Too busy to farm: under-utilisation of farm land in central Java', *JDS* 26, 1 (1989), pp. 43–57.
87. Paul Alexander, P. Boomgaard and B. White, 'Introduction', in Paul Alexander, P. Boomgaard and B. White (eds),*In the shadow of agriculture: non-farm activities in the Javanese economy, past and present* (Amsterdam: Royal Tropical Institute, 1991), p. 5.

5 A Revolution in Labour

1. McLennan, 'Peasant and hacendero', p. 415.
2. Hendry, *The small world*, p. 265.
3. Peter Kunstadter, 'The Lua? and Skaw Karen of Maehongson province, northwestern Thailand', in Peter Kunstadter (ed.), *Southeast Asian tribes, minorities and nations*, vol. 2 (Princeton: Princeton University Press, 1967), p. 659.
4. Janlekha, 'A study of the economy of a rice growing village', p. 253.
5. Carter (ed.), *The kingdom of Siam*, p. 159.
6. Ibid., p. 160.
7. Moerman, *Agricultural change*, pp. 136–7.
8. Leach, *Political systems of highland Burma*, p. 116.
9. Peter Kunstadter, 'Subsistence agricultural economies of Lua' and Karen hill farmers, Mae Sariang district, northwestern Thailand', in Peter Kunstadter, E.C. Chapman, and Sanga Sabhasri (eds), *Farmers in the forest: economic development and marginal agriculture in northern Thailand* (Honolulu: University Press of Hawaii, 1978), p. 90.
10. Tsutomu Ouchi, Naomi Saeki, Akira Takahashi, Kenzo Horii and Manabu

Tanaka, *Farmers and villagers in West Malaysia* (Tokyo: Faculty of Economics, University of Tokyo, 1977), p. 72.

11. Sharp and Hanks, *Bang Chan*, p. 137.
12. Huke (ed.), *Shadows on the land*, p. 232.
13. Grace E. Goodell, 'Untying the HYV package: a Filipino farmer grapples with the new technology', *JPS* 11, 4 (1984), p. 240.
14. Kuchiba, Tsibouchi and Maedo, *Three Malay villages*, p. 73.
15. Edmundson and Edmundson, 'A decade of village development', p. 49.
16. Minoru Fukuda, 'Transition in the traditional rice harvesting system in a Javanese village', in A. Fujimoto and T. Matsuda (eds), *An economic study of rice farming in west Java* (Tokyo: Nodai Research Institute, University of Agriculture, 1986), p. 139.
17. Violeta G. Cordova, 'New rice technology and its effects on labour use and shares in rice production in Laguna, Philippines, 1966–78', in Geoffrey B. Hainsworth (ed.), *Village-level modernization in Southeast Asia: the political economy of rice and water* (Vancouver: University of British Columbia Press, 1982), p. 199.
18. Horii, *Rice economy*, p. 165.
19. Joel S. Kahn, *Minangkabau social formations: Indonesian peasants and the world-economy* (Cambridge: Cambridge University Press, 1980), p. 67.
20. Hendry, *The small world*, p. 133.
21. Gourou, *Land utilization*, p. 185.
22. Ibid., p. 284.
23. Richard William Franke, 'The Green Revolution in a Javanese village', PhD dissertation, Harvard University, 1972, p. 181.
24. Hamilton, *Pwo Karen*, p. 136. See also Kunstadter, 'Subsistence agricultural economies of Lua' and Karen hill farmers', p. 75.
25. J.G. Scott [Shway Yoe], *The Burman: his life and notions* (repr. New York: W.W. Norton, 1963) [1909], p. 245.
26. Randolph Barker, 'Recent trends in labour utilization and productivity in Philippine agriculture (with comparisons to other Asian experiences)', in Geoffrey B. Hainsworth (ed.), *Village-level modernization in Southeast Asia: the political economy of rice and water* (Vancouver: University of British Columbia Press, 1982), p. 156.
27. Rosamund Lee Naylor, 'Rice and the rural labor market in Indonesia', PhD dissertation, Stanford University, 1989, p. 176.
28. Gillian Hart, 'Engendering everyday resistance: gender, patronage and production politics in rural Malaysia', *JPS* 19, 1 (1991), p. 101.
29. Edmundson and Edmundson, 'A decade of village development', p. 52.
30. Hart, 'Engendering everyday resistance', p. 102.
31. Chris Manning, 'Rural employment creation in Java: lessons from the Green Revolution and the oil boom', *Population and Development Review* 14, 1 (1988), p. 55.
32. Ibid., pp. 47–8.
33. Hendry, *The small world*, p. 134.
34. Hart, 'Engendering everyday resistance', p. 106.
35. Yujiro Hayami and Masao Kikuchi, *Asian village economy at the crossroads: an economic approach to institutional change* (Tokyo: University of Tokyo Press, 1981), p. 92.

36. Filomeno V. Aguilar, Jr, 'The Philippine peasant as capitalist: beyond the categories of ideal-typical capitalism', *JPS* 17, 1 (1989), p. 56.
37. Naylor, 'Rice and the rural labor market', p. 71.
38. Ibid., p. 115.
39. Janlekha, 'A study of the economy of a rice growing village', p. 100.
40. Anon., *Verslag van den economischen toestand der inlandsche bevolking*. 1924, vol. 1 (J. Gravenhage: Martinus Nijhoff, 1926) p. 229.
41. Gourou, *Peasants of the Tonkin delta*, p. 369.
42. Hill, *Agriculture in the Malaysian region*, pp. 122–3.
43. Ouchi et al., *Farmers and villages in West Malaysia*, p. 167.
44. Owen, 'Economic and social change', p. 506.
45. Bray, *The rice economies*, p. 125.
46. Edmundson and Edmundson, 'A decade of village development', p. 47.
47. Naylor, 'Rice and the rural labor market', p. 71.
48. Alexander, Boomgaard and White, 'Introduction', p. 5.
49. Jennifer Alexander, *Trade, traders and trading in rural Java* (Singapore: Oxford University Press, 1987), p. 29.
50. Benjamin White, 'Population, involution and employment in rural Java', *DC* 7 (1976), p. 280.
51. Ronald Ng, 'Man and land in northeast Thailand', in P.A. Stott (ed.), *Nature and man in Southeast Asia* (London: School of Oriental and African Studies, 1978), p. 46.
52. Cynthia Banzon-Bautista, 'The Saudi connection: agrarian change in a Pampangan village, 1977–1984', in Gillian Hart, Andrew Turton and Benjamin White with Brian Fegan and Lim Teck Ghee (eds), *Agrarian transformations: local processes and the state in Southeast Asia* (Berkeley: University of California Press, 1989), p. 149.
53. Gourou, *Peasants of the Tonkin delta*, p. 257.
54. Harry A. Franck, *East of Siam: ramblings in the five divisions of French Indo-China* (New York: Grosset and Dunlap, 1926), p. 229.
55. Ibid., p. 228.
56. Robequain, *The economic development*, p. 82.
57. Martin J. Murray, '"White gold" or "white blood"? The rubber plantations of colonial Indochina, 1910–40', in E. Valentine Daniel, Henry Bernstein and Tom Brass (eds), *Plantations, proletarians and peasants in colonial Asia* (London: Frank Cass, 1992), p. 51.
58. E.C. Chapman, 'Villagers as clients: a study of land development in northern Thailand', in Robert Ho and E.C. Chapman (eds), *Studies of contemporary Thailand* (Canberra: Department of Human Geography, Research School of Pacific Studies, Australian National University, 1973), pp. 190–1.
59. Charles F. Keyes, 'In search of land: village formation in the central Chi river valley, northeastern Thailand', *CAS* 9 (1976), p. 59.
60. Horst and Judith Oppenfeld et al., 'Labor force and utilization', in Socorro C. Espiritu and Chester L. Hunt (eds), *Social foundations of community development* (Manila: R.M. Garcia, 1964), p. 50.
61. Manning, 'Rural employment creation', p. 61.
62. Ng, 'Man and land', p. 36.
63. Naylor, 'Rice and the rural labor market', p. 73.

64. W. Collier et al., 'Acceleration of rural development of Java', *BIES* 18, 3 (1982), p. 87.
65. A.L. Kroeber, *Peoples of the Philippines* (repr. Westport: Greenwood Press, 1973) [1928], pp. 152–3.
66. Jacqueline Lineton, 'Pasompe' ugi': Bugis migrants and wanderers', *Archipel* 10 (1975), p. 187.
67. Downs, 'A Kelantanese village in Malaya', p. 159.
68. Ken Young, *Islamic peasants and the state: the 1908 anti-tax rebellion in west Sumatra* (New Haven: Monograph 40, Yale Southeast Asia Studies, Yale University, 1994), p. 160.
69. Freeman, *Report on the Iban*, p. 227.
70. Christine Pelzer White, 'State, culture and gender: continuity and change in women's position in rural Vietnam', in Halef Afshar (ed.), *Women, state and ideology: studies from Africa and Asia* (Albany: State University of New York Press, 1987), p. 229.
71. L.J. Fredericks, 'Some socio-economic characteristics of rural labour with special reference to a rice double-cropping area in Selangor, West Malaysia', in S. Hirashima (ed.), *Hired labor in rural Asia* (Tokyo: Institute of Developing Economies, 1977), p. 183.
72. Graeme J. Hugo, 'Migrant women in developing countries', in United Nations, *Internal migration of women in developing countries: proceedings of the United Nations expert meeting on the feminization of internal migration, Aguascalientes, Mexico, 22–25 October 1991* (New York: United Nations, 1993), p. 55.
73. Moerman, *Agricultural change*, p. 55.
74. Kuchiba, Tsibouchi and Maedo, *Three Malay villages*, p. 183.
75. Evans, *Lao peasants*, p. 145.
76. Sharp and Hanks, *Bang Chan*, p. 47.
77. Hirsch, *Development dilemmas in rural Thailand*, pp. 154–5.
78. Hamilton, *Pwo Karen*, p. 130.
79. Kuchiba, Tsibouchi and Maedo, *Three Malay villages*, p. 28.
80. Peter R. Goethals, 'Rarak: the annual swidden cycle', *Indonesia* 20 (1975), p. 123.
81. Leach, *Political systems of highland Burma*, pp. 134–5.
82. Achmad T. Birowo and Gary Hansen, 'Agricultural and rural development: an overview', in Gary Hansen (ed.), *Agricultural and rural development in Indonesia* (Boulder: Westview, 1981), p. 6.
83. R.T. Shand et al., 'Conclusions' in R.T. Shand (ed.), *Off-farm employment in the development of rural Asia* (Canberra: National Centre for Development Studies, Australian National University; 1986), p. 239.

6 Commerce and Credit

1. Spenser St. John, *Life in the forests of the Far East* (repr. Kuala Lumpur: Oxford University Press, 1974) [1862], vol. 1, p. 71.
2. Ibid., p. 86.
3. The evocative turn of phrase is Roger Knight's.
4. Sharp and Hanks, *Bang Chan*, pp. 160–1.

5. Ibid., p. 161.
6. Cant, *Pahang*, p. 135.
7. Rosemary Firth, *Housekeeping among Malay peasants* (2nd ed. London: University of London/ The Athlone Press, 1966), p. 73.
8. Mears et al., *Rice economy of the Philippines*, p. 78
9. Gourou, *Peasants of the Tonkin delta*, p. 620.
10. Ibid., p. 613.
11. Ibid., pp. 613–16.
12. Bell et al., *U.S. Economic Survey Mission's Report*, p. 65.
13. deYoung, *Village life in modern Thailand*, pp. 106–7.
14. Johnston, 'Rural society and the rice economy', p. 257.
15. Gourou, *Peasants of the Tonkin delta*, p. 622.
16. Ibid., p. 623.
17. Delvert, *Le paysan cambodgien*, p. 511.
18. Hendry, *The small world*, p. 140.
19. MacMicking, *Recollections of Manilla*, p. 18.
20. Christian, *Modern Burma*, p. 128.
21. Skinner, *Chinese society*, p. 102.
22. Halpern, *The rural and urban economies*, p. 26.
23. Gourou, *Peasants of the Tonkin delta*, p. 628.
24. Ibid.
25. Van Roy, *Economic systems of northern Thailand*, p. 55.
26. Pornpun, 'The environmental history', p. 139.
27. Johnston, 'Rural society and the rice economy', p. 256.
28. Firth, *Housekeeping among Malay peasants*, p. 139.
29. Janlekha, 'A study of the economy of a rice growing village', p. 314.
30. Anon., *Verslag van den economischen toestand*, vol. 1, p. 312.
31. Turton, 'Northern Thai peasant society', p. 275.
32. Gourou, *Peasants of the Tonkin delta*, p. 403.
33. Owen, 'The rice industry', p. 118.
34. John F. Cady, *A history of modern Burma* (Ithaca: Cornell University Press, 1958), p. 158.
35. Anon., *Verslag van den economischen toestand*, vol. 1, p. 349.
36. Skinner, *Chinese society*, p. 224.
37. Gourou, *Peasants of the Tonkin delta*, p. 403.
38. Downs, 'A Kelantanese village in Malaya', p. 174.
39. Turton, 'Northern Thai peasant society', p. 275.
40. Gourou, *Peasants of the Tonkin delta*, p. 612.
41. William Collier and Suhud Tjakra Werdaja, 'Smallholder rubber production and marketing', *BIES* 8, 2 (1972), p. 78.
42. Janlekha, 'A study of the economy of a rice growing village', p. 296.
43. Gourou, *Peasants of the Tonkin delta*, p. 610.
44. Franck, *East of Siam*, p. 26.
45. Hill and Moe, 'The cultivation of rice', p. 112.
46. Gourou, *Peasants of the Tonkin delta*, p. 639.
47. Mears, *The new rice economy of Indonesia*, p. 100.
48. Ofreneo, *Capitalism in Philippines agriculture*, p. 41.
49. Wong, *Peasants in the making*, p. 155.
50. Edmundson and Edmundson, 'A decade of village development', p. 57.

51. Inmas, instituted in 1973, did not offer credit facilities as part of its package.
52. Lim, *Economic growth*, p. 197.
53. Brian Fegan, 'Between the lord and the law: tenants' dilemmas', *PSR* 20, 1–2 (1972), p. 114.
54. J.A.C. Mackie and W.J. O'Malley, 'Productivity decline in the Java sugar industry from an Olsonian perspective', *CSSH* 30, 4 (1988), p. 735 n.
55. Hirsch, *Development dilemmas in rural Thailand*, p. 16.
56. Martin Stuart-Fox, *Laos: politics, economics and society* (London: Frances Pinter, 1986), p. 54.
57. Ofreneo, *Capitalism in Philippines agriculture*, p. 43.
58. Hendry, *The small world*, p. 218.
59. Yujiro Hayami et al., *Agricultural marketing and processing in upland Java: a perspective from a Sunda village* (Bogor: CGPRT Centre, 1987), p. 19.
60. E. de Vries and H. Cohen, 'On village shopkeeping in Java and Madura', *Bulletin of the Colonial Institute of Amsterdam* 1, 4 (1937–8), p. 265.
61. Hayami et al., *Agricultural marketing*, p. 20.
62. Hirsch, *Development dilemmas in rural Thailand*, p. 105.
63. Ouchi et al., *Farmers and villagers in West Malaysia*, p. 87.
64. Hamilton, *Pwo Karen*, p. 186.
65. Ibid., p. 225.
66. Joel M. Halpern, 'Capital, savings and credit among Lao peasants', in Raymond Firth and B.S. Yamey (eds), *Capital, saving and credit in peasant societies: studies from Asia, Oceania, the Caribbean and middle America* (London: George Allen and Unwin, 1964), p. 98.
67. Kunstadter, 'Subsistence agricultural economies of Lua' and Karen hill farmers', pp. 119–20.
68. Halpern, 'Capital, savings and credit among Lao peasants', p. 92.
69. H.N.C. Stevenson, *The economics of the central Chin tribes* (Bombay: The Times of India Press, 1943), pp. 103–4.
70. Ulrich Mai, 'Small-town markets and the urban economy in kabupaten Minahasa', *Indonesia* 37 (1984), p. 56.
71. Edmundson and Edmundson, 'A decade of village development', pp. 57–8.
72. Hirsch, *Development dilemmas in rural Thailand*, p. 110.

7 Power and Prosperity

1. Gourou, *Peasants of the Tonkin delta*, p. 272.
2. Gourou, *Land utilization*, p. 100.
3. Gourou, *Peasants of the Tonkin delta*, p. 292.
4. De Jesus, *The tobacco monopoly*, p. 156.
5. Ken Young, *Islamic peasants and the state*, p. 14.
6. Carter (ed.), *The kingdom of Siam*, pp. 13–14.
7. Franz von Benda-Beckmann, *Property in social continuity: continuity and change in the maintenance of property relationships through time in Minangkabau, west Sumatra* (The Hague: Martinus Nijhoff, 1979), p. 364.
8. Murray, *The development of capitalism*, p. 71.
9. Gourou, *Peasants of the Tonkin delta*, p. 309.

10. Ma Mya Sein, *Administration of Burma*, pp. 105–6.
11. Ibid., p. 108.
12. J.S. Furnivall, *An introduction to the political economy of Burma* (3rd ed. Rangoon: Burmese Advertising Press, 1957) [1931], p. 30.
13. Crosthwaite, *Pacification*, p. 23.
14. Daw Mya Sein, 'The historical background of the new constitution', in Josef Silverstein (ed.), *The future of Burma in perspective: a symposium* (Athens, Ohio: Center for International Studies, Papers in International Studies, Southeast Asia Series No. 35, 1974), p. 2.
15. W.R. Hugenholtz, 'The land rent question and its solution 1850–1920', in Robert Cribb (ed.), *The late colonial state in Indonesia: political and economic foundations of the Netherlands Indies 1880–1942* (Leiden: KITLV Press, 1994), p. 171.
16. Soejatno, 'Revolution and social tensions in Surakarta 1945–1950', *Indonesia* 17, 1974, p. 107.
17. Aiko Kurasawa, 'Japanese occupation and leadership changes in Javanese villages', in J. van Goor (ed.), *The Indonesian revolution* (Utrecht: Utrechtse Historische Cahiers, 1986), p. 65.
18. Audrey Kahin, 'The impact of the Indonesian independence struggle on Minangkabau society', in Lyn L. Thomas and Franz von Benda-Beckmann (eds), *Change and continuity in Minangkabau: local, regional and historical perspectives on west Sumatra* (Athens, Ohio: Ohio University Press, 1985), p. 319.
19. Leach, *Political systems of highland Burma*, p. 183.
20. Freeman, *Report on the Iban*, pp. 113. For a discussion along similar lines, describing the assigning of authority by the state to a longhouse head, designated *kepala kampung*, see Michael R. Dove, 'The myth of the "communal" longhouse in rural development: the Kantu' of Kalimantan', in Colin MacAndrews and Chia Lin Sien (eds), *Too rapid rural development: perceptions and perspectives from Southeast Asia* (Athens, Ohio: Ohio University Press, 1982), p. 33.
21. Turton, 'Northern Thai peasant society', p. 282.
22. Ibid, p. 283.
23. Ibid.
24. Hamilton, *Pwo Karen*, p. 146.
25. Jack Potter, *Thai peasant social structure* (Chicago: University of Chicago Press, 1976), p. 35.
26. Hans Mannsdorf, 'The hill tribe program of the Public Welfare Department, Ministry of Interior, Thailand: research and socio-economic development', in Peter Kunstadter (ed.), *Southeast Asian tribes, minorities and nations*, vol. 2 (Princeton: Princeton University Press, 1967), p. 529.
27. Winstedt, *The circumstances of Malay life*, p. 1.
28. Peter Wilson, *A Malay village and Malaysia: social values and rural development* (New Haven: HRAF, 1967), p. vii.
29. Ibid., p. 145.
30. Ibid.
31. E.H.G. Dobby, 'The Kelantan delta', *GR* 41 (1951), p. 243.
32. Paul H. Kratoska, 'Penghulus in Perak and Selangor: the rationalization and decline of a traditional Malay office', *JMBRAS* 57, 2 (1984), p. 33. See also

R.D. Hill, *Rice in Malaya: a study in historical geography* (Kuala Lumpur: Oxford University Press, 1977), p. 44.
33. Kuchiba, Tsibouchi and Maedo, *Three Malay villages*, p. 206.
34. Afifuddin bin Haji Omar, 'Peasants, institutions, and development in Malaysia: the political economy of development in the Muda region', PhD dissentation, Cornell University, 1978, pp. 265–6.
35. Peletz, *A share of the harvest*, p. 104.
36. Gerald Cannon Hickey, *Village in Vietnam* (New Haven: Yale University Press, 1964), p. 187.
37. Hirsch, *Development dilemmas in rural Thailand*, p. 79.
38. Timothy Mahoney, 'Local political and economic structures', in Gary Hansen (ed.), *Agricultural and rural development in Indonesia* (Boulder: Westview, 1981), p. 195.
39. Judd, *Chao rai Thai*, p. 398.
40. Sharp and Hanks, *Bang Chan*, p. 223.
41. Hickey, *Village*, p. 282.
42. Ibid., p. 278.
43. Owen, 'The rice industry', p. 141.
44. Lawless, 'Societal ecology', p. 33.
45. Kuchiba, Tsibouchi and Maedo, *Three Malay villages*, p. 202.
46. Manning Nash, *The golden road to modernity: village life in contemporary Burma* (Chicago: University of Chicago Press, 1965), p. 43.
47. Craig A. Lockard, 'The Javanese as emigrant: observations on the development of Javanese settlements overseas', *Indonesia* 11 (1971), pp. 44–5.
48. Pierre Gourou, *Man and land in the Far East* (trans. S.H. Beaver) (London: Longman, 1975), p. 206.
49. Gourou, *Peasants of the Tonkin delta*, p. 6.
50. Hendry, *The small world*, p. 29.
51. Hickey, *Village*, p. 48.
52. Khoo Kay Kim, 'Malay society, 1874–1920s', *JSEAS* 5, 2 (1974), pp. 183–4.
53. De Jesus, *The tobacco monopoly*, p. 200.
54. Freeman, *Report on the Iban*, p. 225. See also pp. 232–4.
55. Otsuka, Cordova and David, 'Green revolution', p. 725. See also Barker, 'Recent trends', p. 159.
56. Sharp and Hanks, *Bang Chan*, p. 24.
57. Ibid., p. 26.
58. Jan Willem Nibbering, 'Crisis and resilience in upland land use in Java', in Joan Hardjono (ed.), *Indonesia: resources, ecology and environment* (Singapore: Oxford University Press, 1991), p. 123.
59. Koentjaraningrat, 'Population mobility in villages around Jakarta', *BIES* 11, 2 (1975), p. 114.
60. Sharp and Hanks, *Bang Chan*, p. 225.
61. Carol B. Hetler, 'The impact of circular migration on a village economy', *BIES* 25, 1 (1989), p. 72.
62. F. Tichelman, *The social evolution of Indonesia: the Asiatic mode of production and its legacy* (The Hague: Martinus Nijhoff, 1980), p. 92.
63. Ledesma, 'Land reform in East and Southeast Asia', p. 328.
64. Gourou, *Peasants of the Tonkin delta*, p. 659.

65. Ibid., p. 661.
66. Hirsch, *Development dilemmas in rural Thailand*, p. 10.
67. Michael Vickery, 'Refugee politics: the Khmer camp system in Thailand', in David Ablin and Marlowe Hood (eds), *The Cambodian agony* (Armonk: M.E. Sharpe, 1987), p. 294.
68. Gourou, *Peasants of the Tonkin delta*, p. 658.
69. William A. Collier, Jusuf Colter, Sinarhadi and Robert d'A. Shaw, 'Choice of technique in rice milling on Java', *BIES* 10, 1 (1974), p. 107.
70. Ibid., pp. 116, 120.
71. Ingrid Palmer, 'Technology and peasant production: a comment', *DC* 8, 3 (1977), p. 369.
72. Sukor Kasim and Mustafa Najimudin, 'Evolution of sources of income in the Muda Irrigation Scheme, Malaysia, 1972/73 to 1981/82', in R.T. Shand (ed.), *Off-farm employment in the development of rural Asia* (Canberra: National Centre for Development Studies, Australian National University, 1986), p. 39.
73. David S. Gibbons, Rodolphe de Koninck, and Ibrahim Hasan, *Agricultural modernization, poverty and inequality: the distributional impact of the Green Revolution in regions of Malaysia and Indonesia* (Westmead: Gower, 1980), p. 21.
74. Gourou, *Peasants of the Tonkin delta*, p. 658.
75. Anat et al., *Thailand*, p. 35.
76. Peter Kunstadter, 'Hill and valley populations in northwestern Thailand', in Peter Hinton (ed.), *Tribesmen and peasants in north Thailand: proceedings of the first symposium of the Tribal Research Centre, Chiang Mai, Thailand, 1967* (Chiang Mai: Tribal Research Centre, 1967), p. 82.
77. Lindblad, 'Economic change', p. 93.
78. Johnston, 'Rural society and the rice economy', p. 424.
79. Anon., 'Survey of recent developments', *BIES* 11, 3 (1975), p. 12.
80. Naylor, 'Rice and the rural labor market', p. 5.
81. Hayami and Kikuchi, *Asian village economy*, p. 54.
82. Robert W. Herdt, 'A retrospective view of technological and other changes in Philippine rice farming, 1965–1982', *EDCC* 35, 2 (1987), p. 343.
83. Yujiro Hayami, 'Asian development: a view from the paddy fields', *Asian Development Review* 6, 1 (1988), p. 59.
84. Ibid.
85. Jean-Luc Maurer, 'Beyond the sawah: economic diversification in four Bantul villages, 1972–1987', in Paul Alexander, P. Boomgaard and B. White (eds), *In the shadow of agriculture: non-farm activities in the Javanese economy, past and present* (Amsterdam: Royal Tropical Institute, 1991), p. 97.
86. Sharp and Hanks, *Bang Chan*, p. 196.

Conclusion

1. Philip S. Morrison, 'Transitions in rural Sarawak: off-farm employment in the Kemena Basin', *PV* 34, 1 (1993), p. 50.

Bibliography

Aass, Svein, 'The relevance of Chayanov's macro theory to the case of Java', in E.J. Hobsbawm et al. (eds), *Peasants in history: essays in honour of Daniel Thorner* (Calcutta: Oxford University Press, 1980).

Adam, L., *De autonomie van het Indonesisch dorp* (Amersfoort: S.W. Melchior, 1924).

Adams, John, and Nancy Hancock, 'Land and economy in traditional Vietnam', *JSEAS* 1, 2 (1970), pp. 90–8.

Adas, Michael, 'Imperialist rhetoric and modern historiography. The case of lower Burma before and after conquest', *JSEAS* 3, 2 (1972), pp. 175–92.

Adas, Michael, *The Burma delta: economic development and social change on an Asian rice frontier, 1852–1941* (Madison: University of Wisconsin Press, 1974).

Adas, Michael, 'Immigrant Asians and the economic impact of European imperialism: the role of the south Indian Chettiars in British Burma', *JAS* 33, 3 (1974), pp. 385–401.

Adas, Michael, '"Moral economy" or "contest state"? Elite demands and the origins of peasant protest in Southeast Asia', *Journal of Social History* 13 (1980), pp. 521–46.

Adas, Michael, 'From avoidance to confrontation: peasant protest in precolonial and colonial Southeast Asia', *CSSH* 23 (1981), pp. 217–47.

Afifuddin bin Haji Omar, 'Peasants, institutions, and development in Malaysia: the political economy of development in the Muda region', PhD dissertation, Cornell University, 1978.

Afifuddin Haji Omar, 'The role of Kedah rice peasantry in economic and political development of Malaysia', in Asmah Haji Omar (ed.), *Darulaman: essays on linguistic, cultural and socio-economic aspects of the Malaysian state of Kedah* (Kuala Lumpur: University of Malaya Press, 1979).

Aguilar, Filomena V., 'The agrarian proletariat in the rice-growing areas of the Philippines', *PhS* 31 (1983), pp. 338–66.

Aguilar, Filomeno V., Jr, 'The Philippine peasant as capitalist: beyond the categories of ideal-typical capitalism', *JPS* 17, 1 (1989), pp. 41–67.

Akin Rabibhadana, 'Clientship and class structure in the early Bangkok period', in G. William Skinner and A. Thomas Kirsch (eds), *Change and persistence in Thai society: essays in honor of Lauriston Sharp* (Ithaca: Cornell University Press, 1975).

Akin Rabibhadana, 'Self-help organizations in Thai villages: the question of appropriate policy inputs', in Colin MacAndrews and Chia Lin Sien (eds), *Too rapid rural development: perceptions and perspectives from Southeast Asia* (Athens, Ohio: Ohio University Press, 1982).

Alexander, Jennifer, *Trade, traders and trading in rural Java* (Singapore: Oxford University Press, 1987).

Alexander, Jennifer, and Anne Booth, 'The service sector', in Anne Booth (ed.), *The oil boom and after: Indonesian economic performance in the Soeharto era* (Singapore: Oxford University Press, 1992).

Alexander, Jennifer, and Paul Alexander, 'Sugar, rice and irrigation in colonial Java', *Ethnohistory* 25, 3 (1978), pp. 207–23.

Alexander, Jennifer, and Paul Alexander, 'Labour demands and the "involution" of Javanese agriculture', *Social Analysis* 3 (1979), pp. 22–44.

Alexander, Jennifer, and Paul Alexander, 'Shared poverty as ideology: agrarian relationships in colonial Java', *Man* (new series) 17, 4 (1982), pp. 597–619.

Alexander, Jennifer, and Paul Alexander, 'Protecting peasants from capitalism: the subordination of Javanese traders by the colonial state', *CSSH* 33 (1991), pp. 370–94.

Alexander, Jennifer, and Paul Alexander, 'Trade and petty commodity production in early twentieth century Kebumen', in Paul Alexander, P. Boomgaard and B. White (eds), *In the shadow of agriculture: non-farm activities in the Javanese economy, past and present* (Amsterdam: Royal Tropical Institute, 1991).

Alexander, Paul, 'Women, labour and fertility: population growth in nineteenth century Java', *Mankind* 14, 5 (1984), pp. 361–71.

Alexander, Paul, 'Colonial capitalism in Java', *Mankind* 16, 1 (1986), pp. 49–54.

Alexander, Paul, 'Labour expropriation and fertility: population growth in nineteenth century Java', in W. Penn Handwerker (ed.), *Culture and reproduction: An anthropological critique of demographic transition theory* (Boulder: Westview, 1986).

Alexander, Paul, P. Boomgaard and B. White, 'Introduction', in Paul Alexander, P. Boomgaard and B. White (eds), *In the shadow of agriculture: non-farm activities in the Javanese economy, past and present* (Amsterdam: Royal Tropical Institute, 1991).

Ali, S. Husin, 'Land concentration and poverty among the rural Malays', *Nusantara* 1 (1972), pp. 100–13.

Allen, G.C., and A.G. Donnithorne, *Western enterprise in Indonesia and Malaya* (London: George Allen and Unwin, 1954).

Allen, James S., 'Agrarian tendencies in the Philippines', *PA* 11 (1938), pp. 52–65.

Alting von Geusau, Leo, 'The Akha: ten years later', *PV* 33, 2 (1992), pp. 178–84.

Ambler, John S., 'Historical perspectives on sawah cultivation and the political and economic context for irrigation in west Sumatra', *Indonesia* 46 (1988), pp. 39–77.

Ammar Siamwalla, *Land, labour and capital in three rice-growing deltas of Southeast Asia 1800–1940* (New Haven: Discussion Paper No. 150, Economic Growth Center, Yale University, 1972).

Ammar Siamwalla, 'A history of rice policies in Thailand', *FRIS* 14, 3 (1975), pp. 233–49.

Ammar Siamwalla, Suthad Setboonsarng and Direk Patamasiriwat, 'Agriculture', in Peter G. Warr (ed.), *The Thai economy in transition* (Cambridge: Cambridge University Press, 1993).

Anan Ganjanapan, 'The partial commercialization of rice production in northern Thailand (1900–1981)', PhD dissertation, Cornell University, 1984.

Anan Ganjanapan, 'Conflicts over the deployment and control of labor in a northern Thai village', in Gillian Hart, Andrew Turton and Benjamin White with Brian Fegan and Lim Teck Ghee (eds), *Agrarian transformations: local processes and the state in Southeast Asia* (Berkeley: University of California Press, 1989).

Anat Arbhabhirama, Dhira Phantumvanit, John Elkington and Phaitoon Ingkasuwan, *Thailand natural resources profile* (Singapore: Oxford University Press, 1988).

Anderson, A. Grant, 'The rural market in west Java', *EDCC* 28, 4 (1980), pp. 753–78.

Anderson, A. Grant, 'Rural and smalltown markets in Java: continuity or change?', *PV* 29, 1 (1988), pp. 45–73.

Anderson, D., and M.W. Leiserson, 'Rural non-farm employment in developing countries', *EDCC* 28, 2 (1980), pp. 227–48.

Anderson, James N., 'Land and society in a Pangasinan community', in Socorro C. Espiritu and Chester L. Hunt (eds), *Social foundations of community development* (Manila: R.M. Garcia, 1964).

Anderson, James N., 'Rapid rural "development": performance and consequences in the Philippines', in Colin MacAndrews and Chia Lin Sien (eds), *Too rapid rural development: perceptions and perspectives from Southeast Asia* (Athens, Ohio: Ohio University Press, 1982).

Anderson, John, *Political and commercial considerations relative to the Malayan Peninsula and the British settlements in the Straits of Malacca* (repr. Singapore: MBRAS, 1965) [1824].

Anderson, John, *Mission to the east coast of Sumatra in 1823* (Edinburgh: William Blackwood, 1826).

Anderson, John, *Acheen, and the ports on the north and east coasts of Sumatra* (repr. Kuala Lumpur: Oxford University Press, 1971) [1840].

Andrews, James M., *Siam: 2nd rural economic survey. 1934–1935* (Bangkok: Bangkok Times Press, 1935).

Andrus, J. Russell, *Burmese economic life* (Stanford: Stanford University Press, 1948).

Angeles-Reyes, Edna, 'Nonfarm work in the Philippine rural economy: an omen of change or a change of omens?', in Bruce Koppel, John Hawkins, William James (eds), *Development or deterioration? Work in rural Asia* (Boulder: Lynne Rienner, 1994).

Anon., *Report of the Philippines Commission to the President, 1900* (Washington: Government Printing Office, 1901).

Anon., *Nota over de conversie van communaal in erfelijk individueel grondbezit op Java en Madoera* (Batavia: Landsdrukkerij, 1902).

Anon., 'Remarks on the Phillippine islands and on their capital Manila, 1819 to 1822', in E.H. Blair and J.A. Robertson, *The Philippine islands 1493–1898* (Cleveland: A.H. Clark, 1903–9), vol. 51.

Anon., *Verslag van den economischen toestand der inlandsche bevolking. 1924* ('s Gravenhage: Martinus Nijhoff, 1926).

Anon., 'Survey of recent developments', *BIES* 11, 3 (1975), pp. 1–24.

Anon., *Poverty and landlessness in rural Asia* (Geneva: International Labor Office, 1977).

Anon., *Gazeteer of Burma, compiled by authority* (repr. Delhi: Gian Publishing House, 1987), [?].

Antlöv, Hans, and Thommy Svensson, 'From rural home weavers to factory labour: the industrialization of textile manufacturing in Majalaya', in Paul Alexander, P. Boomgaard and B. White (eds), *In the shadow of agriculture: non-farm activities in the Javanese economy, past and present* (Amsterdam: Royal Tropical Institute, 1991).

Antolin, Francisco, 'Notices of the pagan Igorots in 1789', *Asian Folklore Studies* 30 (1971), pp. 27–132.

Anuman Rajadhon, Phya, *Life and ritual in old Siam: three studies of Thai life and customs*, trans. and ed. William J. Gedney (repr. Westport: Greenwood Press, 1979) [1961].

Arief, Burhan, 'Social and administrative system of the two villages in west Java', in A. Fujimoto and T. Matsuda (eds), *An economic study of rice farming in west Java* (Tokyo: Nodai Research Institute, University of Agriculture, 1986).

Arndt, H.W., 'Survey of recent developments', *BIES* 5, 3 (1969), pp. 1–28.

Arndt, H.W., 'Survey of recent developments', *BIES* 13, 3 (1977), pp. 1–33.

Arndt, H.W., 'Survey of recent developments', *BIES* 14, 1 (1978), pp. 1–28.

Arndt, H.W., 'Survey of recent developments', *BIES* 14, 3 (1978), pp. 1–23.

Arndt, H.W., 'Development and equality: themes in economic thought about Indonesia', *JSEAS* 12, 2 (1981), pp. 464–75.

Arndt, H.W., 'Survey of recent developments', *BIES* 17, 3 (1981), pp. 1–24.

Asad, Talal, 'Are there histories of people without Europe? A review article', *CSSH* 29 (1987), pp. 594–607.

Asian Development Bank, *Rural Asia: challenge and opportunity* (Singapore: Federal Publications, 1977).

Aung-Thwin, Michael, 'The British "pacification" of Burma: order without meaning', *JSEAS* 16, 2 (1985), pp. 245–61.

Aung-Thwin, Michael, *Irrigation in the heartland of Burma: foundations of the pre-colonial Burmese state* (DeKalb: Occasional Paper No. 15, Center for Southeast Asian Studies, Northern Illinois University, 1990).

Aye Hlaing, 'Trends of economic growth and income distribution in Burma', *JBRS* 47 (1964), pp. 80–148.

Aziz, Ungku, 'Land disintegration and land policy in Malaya', *MER* 3 (1958), pp. 22–9.

Aziz, Ungku, 'Poverty and rural development in Malaysia', *KEM* 1 (1964), pp. 70–105.

Ba Maw, *Breakthrough in Burma: memoirs of a revolution* (New Haven: Yale University Press, 1968).

Bacdayan, Albert S., 'From isolation to articulation: the Barrio Charter and social change in northern Philippines', in Mario D. Zamora, Vinson H. Sutlive, and Nathan Altshuler (eds), *Culture change in the Philippines* (Williamsburg: Studies in Third World Societies No. 1, Department of Anthropology, College of William and Mary, 1976).

Bach, Robert L., 'Historical patterns of capitalist penetration in Malaysia', *JCA* 6, 4 (1976), 458–76.

Backus, Mary (ed.), *Siam and Laos as seen by our American missionaries* (Philadelphia: Presbyterian Board of Publication, 1884).

Bacon, George B., *Siam, the land of the white elephant, as it was and is* (New York: Scribner, Armstrong, and Co., 1873).

Bailey, Connor, *Broker, mediator, patron and kinsman: an historical analysis of key leadership roles in a rural Malaysian district* (Athens, Ohio: Center for International Studies, Ohio University, 1976).

Bailey, Connor, *The sociology of production in rural Malay society* (Kuala Lumpur: Oxford University Press, 1983).

Baker, Christopher, 'Economic reorganization and the slump in South and Southeast Asia', *CSSH* 23, 3 (1981), pp. 325–49.

Bakker, Johannes I., 'Bureaucratization of patrimonialism: colonial taxation and land tenure in Java, 1830–1850', in G.P. Means (ed.), *The past in Southeast Asia's present* (Ottawa: Canadian Council for Southeast Asian Studies, 1978).

Balisacan, Arsenio M., 'Agricultural growth, landlessness, off-farm employment, and rural poverty in the Philippines', *EDCC* 41, 3 (1993), pp. 533–62.

Banzon-Bautista, Cynthia, 'The Saudi connection: agrarian change in a Pampangan village, 1977–1984', in Gillian Hart, Andrew Turton and Benjamin White with Brian Fegan and Lim Teck Ghee (eds), *Agrarian transformations: local processes and the state in Southeast Asia* (Berkeley: University of California Press, 1989).

Barker, Randolph, 'Recent trends in labour utilization and productivity in Philippine agriculture (with comparisons to other Asian experiences)', in Geoffrey B. Hainsworth (ed.), *Village-level modernization in Southeast Asia: the political economy of rice and water* (Vancouver: University of British Columbia Press, 1982).

Barker, Randolph, William H. Meyers, Cristina M. Cristostimo, and Bart Duff, 'Employment and technological change in Philippine agriculture', *International Labour Review* 106, 2–3 (1972), pp. 111–39.

Barker, Randolph, Robert W. Herdt, with Beth Rose, *The rice economy of Asia* (Washington, DC: Resources for the Future, 1985).

Barlow, Colin, 'Indonesian and Malayan agricultural development, 1870–1940', *BIES* 21, 1 (1975), pp. 81–112.

Barlow, Colin, 'A comparison of factors influencing agricultural development in Malaya and Indonesia, 1870–1940', in A. Maddison and G. Prince (eds), *Economic growth in Indonesia, 1870–1940* (Leiden: Koninklijk Instituut voor Taal-, Land- en Volkenkunde, 1987).

Barlow, Colin, 'Changes in the economic position of workers on rubber estates and smallholdings in peninsular Malaysia, 1910–1985', in Peter J. Rimmer and Lisa M. Allen (eds), *The underside of Malaysian history: pullers, prostitutes, plantation workers . . .* (Singapore: Singapore University Press, 1990).

Barlow, Colin, 'Developments in plantation agriculture and smallholder cash-crop production', in Joan Hardjono (ed.), *Indonesia: resources, ecology and environment* (Singapore: Oxford University Press, 1991).

Barlow, Colin, and Corinne Condie, 'Changing economic relationships in Southeast Asian agriculture, and their implications for small farmers', *Outlook on Agriculture* 15, 4 (1986), pp. 167–78.

Barlow, Colin, and John Drabble, 'Government and the emerging rubber industries in Indonesia and Malaya, 1900–1940', in Anne Booth, W.J. O'Malley, and Anna Weidemann (eds), *Indonesian economic history in the Dutch colonial era* (New Haven: Monograph Series No. 35, Yale University Southeast Asia Studies, 1990).

Barlow, Colin, and Muharminto, 'The rubber smallholder economy', *BIES* 18, 2 (1982), pp. 86–119.

Barlow, Colin, and S.K. Jayasurija, 'Stages of development in smallholder tree crop agriculture', *DC* 17 (1986), pp. 635–58.

Barlow, Colin, and Thee Kian Wie, 'North Sumatra: growth with unbalanced performance', in Hal Hill (ed.), *Unity in diversity: regional economic development in Indonesia since 1970* (Singapore: Oxford University Press, 1989).

Barlow, Colin, and Thomas Tomich, 'Indonesian agricultural development: the awkward case of smallholder tree crops', *BIES* 27, 3 (1991), pp. 29–53.

Barnard R., 'The role of capital and credit in a Malay rice-producing village', *PV* 14, 2 (1973), pp. 113–36.

Barnett, Anthony, 'Democratic Kampuchea: a highly centralized dictatorship', in David P. Chandler and Ben Kiernan (eds), *Revolution and its aftermath in Kampuchea: eight essays* (New Haven: Monograph Series No. 5, Southeast Asia Studies, Yale University, 1983).

Barrera, Alfredo, 'Soils and natural vegetation', in Robert Huke (ed.), *Shadows on the land: an economic geography of the Philippines* (Manila: Bookmark, 1963).

Barrow, John, *A voyage to Cochin China in the years 1792 and 1793* (repr. Kuala Lumpur: Oxford University Press, 1975) [1806].

Bastin, John, 'Crawfurd and Baud on free and forced labour in Java', *JMBRAS* 29, 1 (1956), pp. 195–9.

Bauer, P.T., 'Some aspects of the Malayan rubber slump 1929–33', in T.H. Silcock (ed.), *Readings in Malayan economics* (Singapore: Eastern Universities Press, 1961).

Bauer, P.T., *The rubber industry: a study in competition and monopoly* (London: Longmans, Green, 1948).

Bautista, Germelino, 'Socio-economic conditions of the landless rice workers in the Philippines: the landless of barrio Sta. Lucia as a case in point', in S. Harashima (ed.), *Hired labor in rural Asia* (Tokyo: Institute of Developing Economies, 1977).

Bayly, C.A., 'State and economy in India over seven hundred years', *EHR* 38 (1985), pp. 583–96.

Becka, Jan, *The national liberation movement in Burma during the Japanese occupation period (1941–1945)* (Prague: Oriental Institute, Dissertationes Orientales, vol. 42, 1983).

Becker, Elizabeth, *When the war was over: the voices of Cambodia's revolution and its people* (New York: Simon and Schuster, 1986).

Beckett, J., 'The defiant and the compliant: the datus of Magindanao under colonial rule', in Alfred W. McCoy and Ed. C. de Jesus (eds), *Philippine social history: global trade and local transformations* (Sydney: Allen and Unwin, 1981).

Begbie, P.J., *The Malayan peninsula* (repr. Kuala Lumpur: Oxford University Press, 1967) [1834].

Bell, Daniel W., et al., *U.S. Economic Survey Mission's report* (Manila: Philippine Book Company, 1950).

Bell, Peter F., *The historical determinants of underdevelopment in Thailand* (New Haven: Discussion Paper No. 84, Economic Growth Center, Yale University, 1970).

Bennett, Christopher P.A., and Ricardo A. Godoy, 'The quality of smallholder coffee in South Sumatra: the production of low-quality coffee as a response to world demand', *BIES* 28, 1 (1992), pp. 85–100.

Bennett, Don C., 'Three measurements of population pressure in eastern Java', *EKI* 14 (1961), pp. 97–106.

Beresford, Melanie, *Vietnam. Politics, economy and society* (London: Pinter Publishers, 1988).

Bergsma, W.B., *Eindresume van het bij gouvernements besluit dd. 10 Juni 1867 no. 2 bevolen onderzoek naar de rechten van den inlander op den grond op Java en Madoera* (Batavia: Ernst, 1876–96).

Bernatzik, Hugo Adolf, with collaboration of Emmy Bernatzik, *The spirits of the yellow leaves* (London: Robert Hale, 1958).

Bickmore, Albert S., *Travels in the East Indian archipelago* (repr. Singapore: Oxford University Press, 1991) [1869].

Binns, B.O., *Agricultural economy of Burma* (Rangoon: Government Printing and Stationery, 1948).

Bird, Isabella L., *The golden Chersonese and the way thither* (repr. Kuala Lumpur: Oxford University Press, 1967) [1883].

Birowo, Achmad T., and Gary Hansen, 'Agricultural and rural development: an overview', in Gary Hansen (ed.), *Agricultural and rural development in Indonesia* (Boulder: Westview, 1981).

Black, Ian, 'Interethnic relations and culture change under colonial rule: a study of Sabah', in G.N. Appell (ed.), *Studies in Borneo societies: social process and anthropological explanation* (De Kalb: Special Report No. 12, Center for Southeast Asian Studies, Northern Illinois University, 1976).

Black, Ian, 'The "lastposten": eastern Kalimantan and the Dutch in the nineteenth and early twentieth centuries', *JSEAS* 16, 2 (1985), pp. 281–91.

Bock, Carl, *Temples and elephants: the narrative of a journey of exploration through upper Siam and Lao* (London: Sampson Low, Marston, Searle and Rivington, 1884).

Boediono, 'An economic survey of North Sulawesi', *BIES* 8, 3 (1972), pp. 66–92.

Boediono, and Ibrahim Hasan, 'An economic survey of D.I. Aceh', *BIES* 10, 2 (1974), pp. 35–55.

Boeke, J.H., 'Inlandsche budgetten', *Koloniale Studiën* 10, 2 (1926), pp. 229–335.

Bogaars, George, 'The effect of opening of the Suez canal on the trade and development of Singapore', *JMBRAS* 42, 1 (1969), pp. 208–51.

Bolnick, Bruce R., 'Financial liberalization with imperfect markets: Indonesia during the 1970s', *EDCC* 35, 3 (1987), pp. 581–99.

Boomgaard, P., 'Bevolkingsgroei en welvaart op Java (1800–1942)', in R.N.J. Kamerling (ed.), *Indonesië toen en nu* (Amsterdam: Intermediar Bibliotheek, 1980).

Boomgaard, P., 'The Javanese rice economy 800–1800', in Akira Hayami and Yoshihiro Tsubouchi (eds), *Economic and demographic development in rice producing societies: some aspects of East Asian economic history, 1500–1900* (Tokyo: n.p., 1989).

Boomgaard, P., 'The non-agricultural side of an agricultural economy: Java, 1500–1900', in Paul Alexander, P. Boomgaard and B. White (eds), *In the shadow of agriculture: non-farm activities in the Javanese economy, past and present* (Amsterdam: Royal Tropical Institute, 1991).

Boomgaard, P., and A.J. Gooszen (eds), *Changing economy in Indonesia. A selection of statistical source material from the early 19th century up to 1940. Volume 11. Population trends 1795–1942* (Amsterdam: Royal Tropical Institute, 1991).

Boomgaard, P., and J.L. van Zanden (eds), *Changing economy in Indonesia. A selection of statistical source material from the early 19th century up to 1940. Volume 10. Food crops and arable lands, Java 1815–1942* (Amsterdam: Royal Tropical Institute, 1990).

Boomgaard, Peter, 'Female labour and population growth on nineteenth century Java', *RIMA* 15, 2 (1981), pp. 1–30.
Boomgaard, Peter, 'Buitenzorg in 1805: the role of money and credit in a colonial frontier society', *MAS* 20, 1 (1986), pp. 33–58.
Boomgaard, Peter, 'The welfare services in Indonesia, 1900–1942', *Itinerario* 10, 1 (1986), pp. 57–81.
Boomgaard, Peter, 'Morbidity and mortality in Java, 1820–1880: changing patterns of disease and death', in Norman G. Owen (ed.), *Death and disease in Southeast Asia: explorations in social, medical and demographic history* (Singapore: Oxford University Press, 1987).
Boomgaard, Peter, 'Forests and forestry in colonial Java: 1677–1942', in John Dargavel et al. (eds), *Changing tropical forests: historical perspectives on today's challenges in Asia, Australasia and Oceania* (Canberra: Centre for Resource and Environmental Studies, Australian National University, 1988).
Boomgaard, Peter, *Between sovereign domain and servile tenure: the development of rights to land in Java, 1780–1870* (Amsterdam: Free University Press, 1989).
Boomgaard, Peter, *Children of the colonial state: population growth and economic development in Java 1795–1880* (Amsterdam: Free University Press, 1989).
Boomgaard, Peter, 'The Javanese village as a Cheshire cat: the Java debate against a European and Latin American background', *JPS* 18, 2 (1991), pp. 289–304.
Boon Chuey Srisavadi, *The hill tribes of Siam* (Bangkok: Khun Aroon, 1962?).
Booth, Anne, 'Ipeda – Indonesia's land tax', *BIES* 10, 1 (1974), pp. 55–81.
Booth, Anne, 'Land ownership in Klaten', *BIES* 10, 3 (1974), pp. 135–40.
Booth, Anne, 'Irrigation in Indonesia Part I', *BIES* 13, 1 (1977), pp. 33–75.
Booth, Anne, 'Irrigation in Indonesia Part II', *BIES* 13, 2 (1977), pp. 49–77.
Booth, Anne, 'The agricultural surveys, 1970–75', *BIES* 15 (1979), pp. 45–68.
Booth, Anne, 'The burden of taxation in colonial Indonesia in the twentieth century', *JSEAS* 11, 1 (1980), pp. 91–109.
Booth, Anne, 'The role of agricultural taxation', in Gary Hansen (ed.), *Agricultural and rural development in Indonesia* (Boulder: Westview, 1981).
Booth, Anne, 'Accommodating a growing population in Javanese agriculture', *BIES* 21 (1985), pp. 115–45.
Booth, Anne, 'The development of commercial agriculture in Indonesia: 1830–1980', *MI* 14, 3 (1987), pp. 223–68.
Booth, Anne, *Agricultural development in Indonesia* (Sydney: Allen and Unwin, 1988).
Booth, Anne, 'Living standards and the distribution of income in colonial Indonesia: a review of the evidence', *JSEAS* 29, 2 (1988), pp. 310–34.
Booth, Anne, 'Foreign trade and domestic development in the colonial economy', in Anne Booth, W.J. O'Malley, and Anna Weidemann (eds), *Indonesian economic history in the Dutch colonial era* (New Haven: Monograph Series No. 35, Yale University Southeast Asia Studies, 1990).
Booth, Anne, 'The evolution of fiscal policy and the role of government in the colonial economy', in Anne Booth, W.J. O'Malley, and Anna Weidemann (eds), *Indonesian economic history in the Dutch colonial era* (New Haven: Monograph Series No. 35, Yale University Southeast Asia Studies, 1990).
Booth, Anne, 'Regional aspects of Indonesian agricultural growth', in Joan Hardjono (ed.), *Indonesia: resources, ecology and environment* (Singapore: Oxford University Press, 1991).

Booth, Anne, 'Growth and structural transformation in the New Order', in Anne Booth (ed.), *The oil boom and after: Indonesian economic performance in the Soeharto era* (Singapore: Oxford University Press, 1992).

Booth, Anne, 'Income distribution and poverty', in Anne Booth (ed.), *The oil boom and after: Indonesian economic performance in the Soeharto era* (Singapore: Oxford University Press, 1992).

Booth, Anne, and Bruce Glassburner, 'Survey of recent developments', *BIES* 11, 1 (1975), pp. 1–40.

Booth, Anne, and Sundrum, 'The 1973 agricultural census', *BIES* 12 (1976), pp. 90–105.

Booth, Anne, and Amina Tyabji, 'Survey of recent developments', *BIES* 15, 2 (1979), pp. 1–44.

Booth, Anne, and Konta Damanik, 'Central Java and Yogyakarta: Malthus overcome?', in Hal Hill (ed.), *Unity in diversity: regional economic development in Indonesia since 1970* (Singapore: Oxford University Press, 1989).

Bose, Swadesh R., 'Has economic growth immiserized the rural poor in Indonesia? A review of conflicting evidence', in Geoffrey B. Hainsworth (ed.), *Village-level modernization in Southeast Asia: the political economy of rice and water* (Vancouver: University of British Columbia Press, 1982).

Boserup, Ester, *The conditions of agricultural growth: the economics of agrarian change under population pressure* (Chicago: Aldine, 1965).

Boua, Chantou, 'Observations of the Heng Samrin government, 1980–1982', in David P. Chandler and Ben Kiernan (eds), *Revolution and its aftermath in Kampuchea: eight essays* (New Haven: Monograph Series No. 5, Southeast Asia Studies, Yale University, 1983).

Bowen, John R., 'On the political construction of tradition: *gotong royong* in Indonesia', *JAS* 45 (1986), pp. 454–61.

Bowen, John R., 'The transformation of an Indonesian property system: adat, Islam, and social change in the Gayo highlands', *AE* 15, 2 (1988), pp. 274–93.

Bowen, John R., *Sumatran politics and poetics: Gayo history, 1900–1989* (New Haven: Yale University Press, 1991).

Bowie, Katherine A., 'Unraveling the myth of the subsistence economy: textile production in nineteenth-century northern Thailand', *JAS* 51, 4 (1992), pp. 797–823.

Bowring, John, *The kingdom and people of Siam* (repr. Kuala Lumpur: Oxford University Press, 1969) [1857].

Bowring, John, *The Philippine islands* (London: Smith, Elder, 1859).

Branfman, Fred, 'Presidential war in Laos, 1964–1970', in Nina S. Adams and Alfred W. McCoy (eds), *Laos: war and revolution* (New York: Harper Colophon, 1970).

Brass, Tom, and Henry Berstein, 'Introduction: proletarianisation and deproletarianisation on the colonial plantation', in E. Valentine Daniel, Henry Bernstein and Tom Brass (eds), *Plantations, proletarians and peasants in colonial Asia* (London: Frank Cass, 1992).

Bray, Francesca, *The rice economies: technology and development in Asian societies* (Oxford: Basil Blackwell, 1986).

Breman, Jan, 'The village on Java and the early-colonial state', *JPS* 9, 4 (1982), pp. 189–240.

Breman, Jan, *Control of land and labour in colonial Java: a case study of agrarian crisis and reform in the region of Cirebon in the first decades of the twentieth century* (Dordrecht: Foris, 1983).

Breman, Jan, *The shattered image: construction and deconstruction of the village in colonial Asia* (Amsterdam: Comparative Asian Studies-2, Centre for Asian Studies, 1987).

Breman, Jan, 'Work and life of the rural proletariat in Java's coastal plain', *MAS* 29, 1 (1995), pp. 1–44.

Breman, Jan, and E. Valentine Daniel, 'Conclusion: the making of a coolie', in E. Valentine Daniel, Henry Bernstein and Tom Brass (eds), *Plantations, proletarians and peasants in colonial Asia* (London: Frank Cass, 1992).

Brocheux, Pierre, 'Moral economy or political economy? The peasants are always rational', *JAS* 42, 4 (1983), pp. 791–803.

Brosius, J. Peter, *After Duwagan: deforestation, succession and adaptation in upland Luzon, Philippines* (Ann Arbor: Michigan Studies of South and Southeast Asia Number 2, Center for South and Southeast Asian Studies, University of Michigan, 1990).

Brown, C.P., 'Rice price stabilization and support in Malaysia', in David Lim (ed.), *Readings on Malaysian economic development* (Kuala Lumpur: Oxford University Press, 1975).

Brown, Colin, 'The intensified smallholder cane programme: the first five years', *BIES* 18, 1 (1982), pp. 19–60.

Brown, Ian, 'Rural distress in Southeast Asia during the world depression of the early 1930s: a preliminary reexamination', *JAS* 45, 5 (1986), pp. 995–1025.

Brown, Ian, *The élite and the economy in Siam c. 1890–1920* (Singapore: Oxford University Press, 1988).

Brown, Ian, 'Imperialism, trade and investment in the late nineteenth and early twentieth centuries', in John Butcher and Howard Dick (eds), *The rise and fall of revenue farming: business elites and the emergence of the modern state in Southeast Asia* (Houndmills: Macmillan, 1993).

Bryant, Raymond L., 'Shifting the cultivator: the politics of teak regeneration in colonial Burma', *MAS* 28, 2 (1994), pp. 225–50.

Buck, David D., 'Forum on universalism and relativism in Asian studies: editor's introduction', *JAS* 50, 1 (1991), pp. 29–34.

Burger, D.H., *Structural changes in Javanese society: the village sphere* (Ithaca: Modern Indonesia Project, Cornell University, 1957).

Burhamzah, 'An economic survey of Maluku', *BIES* 6, 2 (1970), pp. 31–45.

Burns, P.L., 'Capitalism in the Malay states', in Hamza Alavi et al., *Capitalism and colonial production* (London: Croom Helm, 1982).

Butcher, John G., 'The demise of the revenue farm system in the Federated Malay States', *MAS* 17, 3 (1983), pp. 387–412.

Butcher, John G., 'Revenue farming and the changing state in Southeast Asia', in John Butcher and Howard Dick (eds), *The rise and fall of revenue farming: business elites and the emergence of the modern state in Southeast Asia* (Houndmills: Macmillan, 1993).

Buttinger, Joseph, *Vietnam: a dragon embattled* (London: Pall Mall, 1967).

Cadelena, Rowe V., 'A comparison of Batak and Ata subsistence styles in two different social and physical environments', in A. Terry Rambo, Kathleen Gillogly, and Karl L. Hutterer (eds), *Ethnic diversity and the control of natural resources in Southeast Asia* (Ann Arbor: Michigan Papers on South and

Southeast Asia No. 32, Center for South and Southeast Asian Studies, University of Michigan, 1988).

Cady, John F., *A history of modern Burma* (Ithaca: Cornell University Press, 1958).

Cady, John F., *The United States and Burma* (Cambridge, Mass.: Harvard University Press, 1976).

Calavan, Michael M., *Decisions against nature: an anthropological study of agriculture in northern Thailand* (DeKalb: Special Report No. 15, Center for Southeast Asian Studies, Northern Illinois University, 1977).

Callison, Charles Stuart, *Land-to-the-tiller in the Mekong delta: economic, social and political effects of land reform in four villages of South Vietnam* (Berkeley: Centre for South and Southeast Asian Studies, University of California, 1983).

Camagay, Maria Luisa T., 'A look into the working Filipina during the 19th century: the cigarreras of Manila', *Archipel* 31 (1986), pp. 177–84.

Cameron, John, *Our tropical possessions in Malayan India* (repr. Kuala Lumpur: Oxford University Press, 1965) [1865].

Campbell, J.G., *Siam in the twentieth century: being the experiences and impressions of a British official* (London: Edward Arnold, 1902).

Cant, R.G., 'Historical reasons for the retarded development of Pahang state, eastern Malaya', *New Zealand Geographer* 21 (1965), pp. 26–37.

Cant, R.G., *An historical geography of Pahang* (Singapore: MBRAS Monograph No. 4, 1973).

Capistrano, Ana Doris, and Gerald G. Marten, 'Agriculture in Southeast Asia', in Gerald G. Marten (ed.), *Traditional agriculture in Southeast Asia: a human ecology perspective* (Boulder: Westview, 1986).

Carey, Bertram S., and H.N. Tuck, *The Chin hills: A history of the people, British dealings with them, their customs and manners, and a gazeteer of their country* (repr. Delhi: Cultural Publishing House, 1983) [1896].

Carey, P.B.R., 'The origins of the Java war (1825–30)', *English Historical Review* 91 (1976), pp. 52–78.

Carey, P.B.R., *Babad Dipanagara: an account of the outbreak of the Java War (1825–30)* (Kuala Lumpur: MBRAS Monographs No. 9, 1981).

Carey, P.B.R., 'Waiting for the "just king": the agrarian world of south-central Java from Giyanti (1755) to the Java war (1825)', *MAS* 20, 1 (1986), pp. 59–137.

Carey, Peter, 'Changing Javanese perceptions of the Chinese communities in central Java', *Indonesia* 37 (1984), pp. 1–47.

Carter, A. Cecil (ed.), *The kingdom of Siam* (repr. Bangkok: The Siam Society, 1988) [1904].

Castillo, G.T., 'Diversity in unity: the social component of changes in rice farming in Asian villages', in Anon., *Changes in rice farming in selected areas of Asia* (Los Baños: International Rice Research Institute, 1975).

Castles, Lance, 'Socialism and private business: the latest phase', *BIES* no. 1 (1965), pp. 13–45.

Chandler, David P., 'A revolution in full spate: Communist Party policy in Democratic Kampuchea, December 1976', in David A. Ablin and Marlowe Hood (eds), *The Cambodian agony* (Armonk: M.E. Sharpe, 1987).

Chandler, David P., *The tragedy of Cambodian history: politics, war and revolution since 1945* (New Haven: Yale University Press, 1991).

Chandler, G., *Market trade in rural Java* (Clayton: Papers on Southeast Asia No. 11, Centre of Southeast Asian Studies, Monash University, 1984).

Chapman, E.C., 'Shifting cultivation and economic development in the lowlands of northern Thailand', in Peter Kunstadter, E.C. Chapman, and Sanga Sabhasri (eds), *Farmers in the forest: economic development and marginal agriculture in northern Thailand* (Honolulu: University Press of Hawaii, 1978).

Chapman, E.C., 'Villagers as clients: a study of land development in northern Thailand', in Robert Ho and E.C. Chapman (eds), *Studies of contemporary Thailand* (Canberra: Department of Human Geography, Research School of Pacific Studies, Australian National University, 1973).

Charny, Joel R., 'Appropriate development aid for Kampuchea', in David Ablin and Marlowe Hood (eds), *The Cambodian agony* (Armonk: M.E. Sharpe, 1987).

Chattip Nartsupha and Suthy Prasartset, 'The rise of dependent commodity production in Siam, 1855–1910', in Vichitvong na Pombhejara (ed.), *Readings in Thailand's political economy* (Bangkok: Bangkok Printing Enterprise, 1978).

Chattip Nartsupha, Suthy Prasartset, and Montri Chenvidyakarn (eds), *The political economy of Siam, 1910–1932* (Bangkok: Social Science Association of Thailand, 1978).

Chattip Nartsupha and Suthy Prasartset (eds), *The political economy of Siam, 1851–1910* (Bangkok: Social Science Association of Thailand, 1981).

Cheng Siok-Hwa, *The rice industry of Burma: 1852–1940* (Kuala Lumpur: University of Malaya Press, 1968).

Cheng Siok Hwa, 'The rice industry of Malaya: a historical survey', *JMBRAS* 42, 2 (1969), pp. 130–44.

Cheong, W.E., 'The decline of Manila as the Spanish entrepot in the Far East, 1785–1826: its impact on the pattern of Southeast Asian trade', *JSEAS* 2, 2 (1971), pp. 142–58.

Chinben See, 'Chinese clanship in the Philippine setting', *JSEAS* 12, 1 (1981), pp. 224–47.

Chovanes, Andrew B., 'On Vietnamese and other peasants', *JSEAS* 17, 2 (1986), pp. 203–35.

Christian, John Leroy, *Modern Burma: a study of political and economic development* (Berkeley: University of California Press, 1942).

Clauss, Wolfgang, *Economic and social change among the Simalungun Batak of North Sumatra* (Saarbrücken: Breitenbach, 1982).

Cochlanis, Peter A., 'Distant thunder: the creation of a world market in rice and the transformation it wrought', *AHR* 98, 4 (1993), pp. 1050–78.

Cochlanis, Peter A., 'Southeast Asia's incorporation into the world rice market: a revisionist view', *JSEAS* 24, 2 (1993), pp. 251–67.

Cohen, Paul T., 'Opium and the Karen: a study in indebtedness in northern Thailand', *JSEAS* 15, 1 (1984), pp. 150–65.

Collier, W.L., Jusuf Colter, Sinarhadi, and R. d'A. Shaw, 'Choice of technique in rice milling on Java', *BIES* 10, 1 (1974), pp. 106–20.

Collier, W.L., 'Agricultural evolution in Java: the decline of shared poverty and involution', in Gary Hansen (ed.), *Agricultural development in Indonesia* (Ithaca: Cornell University Press, 1978).

Collier, William, 'Technology and peasant production: a comment', *DC* 8, 3 (1977), pp. 351–62.

Collier, William L., 'Declining labor absorption (1878–1980) in Javanese rice production', *KEM* 16 (1979), pp. 102–36.

Collier, William L., 'Institutional constraints on food security programmes for the poor: case study of Java', *KEM* 18, 1–2 (1981), pp. 79–98.

Collier, William L., and Sayogyo, 'Employment opportunities created by the high yielding rice varieties in several areas of Java', *EKI* 20, 2 (1972), pp. 52–8.

Collier, William L., Gunawan Wiradi, and Soentoro, 'Recent changes in rice harvesting methods', *BIES* 9 (1973), pp. 36–45.

Collier, William L., Gunawan Wiradi, Soentoro, and Makali, 'Agricultural technology and institutional change in Java', *FRIS* 13, 2 (1974), pp. 169–94.

Collier, William L., Soentoro, Gunawan Wiradi, Effendi Pasandaran, Kabul Santoso, and Joseph F. Stepanek, 'Acceleration of rural development in Java', *BIES* 18, 3 (1982), pp. 84–101.

Collier, William, and Suhud Tjakra Werdaja, 'Smallholder rubber production and marketing', *BIES* 8, 2 (1972), pp. 67–92.

Condominas, Georges, *We have eaten the forest: the story of a Montagnard village in the central highlands of Vietnam* (repr. New York: Hill and Wang, 1977) [1957].

Condominas, Georges, 'The Lao', in Nina S. Adams and Alfred W. McCoy (eds), *Laos: war and revolution* (New York: Harper Colophon, 1970).

Condominas, Georges, 'Aspects of economics among the Mnong Gar of Vietnam: multiple money and the middleman', *Ethnology* 2, 3 (1972), pp. 202–19.

Conklin, H.C., *Hanunóo agriculture: a report on an integral system of shifting cultivation in the Philippines* (repr. Northford: Elliot's Books, 1975) [1957].

Cordova, Violeta G., 'New rice technology and its effects on labour use and shares in rice production in Laguna, Philippines, 1966–78', in Geoffrey B. Hainsworth (ed.), *Village-level modernization in Southeast Asia: the political economy of rice and water* (Vancouver: University of British Columbia Press, 1982).

Corner, Lorraine, 'The prospects for off-farm employment as an anti-poverty strategy among Malaysian paddy farm households: macro and micro views', in R.T. Shand (ed.), *Off-farm employment in the development of rural Asia* (Canberra: National Centre for Development Studies, Australian National University, 1986).

Corpuz, Arturo Garcia, 'Railroads and regional development in the Philippines: views from the colonial iron horse, 1875–1935', PhD dissertation, Cornell University, 1989.

Coward, E. Walter, 'Local organization and bureaucracy in a Lao irrigation project', in E. Walter Coward, Jr (ed.), *Irrigation and agricultural development in Asia* (Ithaca: Cornell University Press, 1980).

Cox, Hiram, *Journal of a residence in the Burmhan empire, and more particularly at the court of Amarapoorah* (repr. London: Gregg International Publishers, 1971) [1821].

Cramb, R.A., 'Shifting cultivation and resource degradation in Sarawak: perceptions and policies', *RIMA* 22, 1 (1988), pp. 115–49.

Cramb, R.A., 'The commercialization of Iban agriculture', in R.A. Cramb and H.W.C. Reece (eds), *Development in Sarawak* (Clayton: Monash Papers on Southeast Asia No. 17, Centre of Southeast Asian Studies, Monash University, 1988).

Cramb, R.A., and I.R. Wills, 'The role of traditional institutions in rural development: community-based land tenure and government land policy in Sarawak, Malaysia', *WD* 18, 3 (1990), pp. 347–60.

Crawfurd, John, *A descriptive dictionary of the Indian archipelago and adjacent countries* (repr. London: Frank Cass, 1967) [1820].

Crawfurd, John, *History of the Indian archipelago, containing an account of the manners, arts, languages, religions, institutions, and commerce of its inhabitants* (repr. London: Frank Cass, 1967) [1820].

Crawfurd, John, *Journal of an embassy from the Governor-General of India to the courts of Siam and Cochin China; exhibiting a view of the actual state of those kingdoms* (repr. London: Oxford University Press, 1967) [1828].

Crawfurd, John, *Journal of an embassy from the Governor-General of India to the court of Ava* (London: R. Bentley, 1834).

Crawfurd, John, 'Notes on the population of Java', *JIAEA* 3 (1849), pp. 42–9.

Creutzberg, P., *Het ekonomisch beleid in Nederlandsch-Indië* (Groningen: Wolters-Noordhof/H.D. Tjeenk Willink, 1972–5).

Crippen, Harlan P., 'Philippine agrarian unrest', *Science and Society* 10, 4 (1946), pp. 337–60.

Crisostomo, Cristina, and Randolph Barker, 'Growth rates of Philippine agriculture, 1948–1969', *PEJ* 11 (1972), pp. 102–12.

Crosthwaite, Charles, *The pacification of Burma* (repr. London: Frank Cass, 1968) [1912].

Cruikshank, Bruce, 'Continuity and change in the economic and administrative history of 19th century Samar', in Alfred W. McCoy and Ed.C. de Jesus (eds), *Philippine social history: global trade and local transformations* (Sydney: Allen and Unwin, 1981).

Cullinane, Michael, 'Implementing the "new order"; the structure and supervision of local government during the Taft era', in Norman G. Owen (ed.), *Compadre colonialism: studies on the Philippines under American rule* (Ann Arbor: Michigan Papers on South and Southeast Asia No. 3, Center for South and Southeast Asian Studies, University of Michigan, 1971).

Cushman, J.W., 'Siamese state trade and the Chinese go-between, 1767–1855', *JSEAS* 12, 1 (1981), pp. 47–61.

Dalisay, Amando, 'Types of tenancy contracts on rice farms in Nueva Ecija', *Philippine Agriculturalist* 26 (1937–38), pp. 159–98.

Dalisay, Amando, *Agricultural and rural development in the Philippines (post-war period)* (Manila: Herald Printing Services, 1974).

Dalton, George, 'Peasantries in anthropology and history', *CA* 13, 3–4 (1972), pp. 385–407.

Daroesman, Ruth, 'Survey of recent developments', *BIES* 17, 2 (1981), pp. 1–41.

David, Christina C., and Keijiro Otsuka, 'The modern seed-fertiliser technology and adoption of labour-saving technologies: the Philippine case', *Australian Journal of Agricultural Economics* 34, 2 (1990), pp. 132–46.

Davide, Jorge G., 'Agrotechnology transfer in the Philippines: corporate versus individual approach', in B.G. Cagauan, G.Y. Tsuji, and L.W. Peterson (eds), *Agrotechnology transfer in Indonesia and the Philippines* (Honolulu: College of Tropical Agriculture and Human Resources, University of Hawaii, 1983).

Daw Mya Sein, 'The historical background of the new constitution', in Josef

Silverstein (ed.), *The future of Burma in perspective: a symposium* (Athens, Ohio: Center for International Studies, Papers in International Studies, Southeast Asia Series No. 35, 1974).

De Bie, H.C.H., *De landbouw der inlandsche bevolking op Java* (Batavia: G. Kolff and Co., 1901–2).

de Comyn, Tomas, *State of the Philippine islands in 1810, being an historical, statistical and descriptive account of the interesting portion of the Indian archipelago* (repr. Manila: Filipiniana Book Guild, 1969) [1820].

de Jesus, Ed. C., *The tobacco monopoly in the Philippines: bureaucratic enterprise and social change, 1766–1880* (Quezon City: Ateneo de Manila University Press, 1980).

De Jong, Wouter, and Frank van Steenbergen, *Town and hinterland in central Java: the Banjarnegara production structure in regional perspective* (Yogyakarta: Gadjah Mada University Press, 1987).

De Koninck, Rodolphe, 'Getting them to work profitably: how the small peasants help the large ones, the state and capital', *BCAS* 15, 2 (1983), pp. 32–41.

De Koninck, Rodolphe, 'The integration of the peasantry: examples from Malaysia and Indonesia', *PA* 52 (1979), pp. 265–93.

De Koninck, Rodolphe, and Lise Audet, 'Fertilizers for rice; who wins, who loses? A contribution to the analysis of dependency in Malaysia and Indonesia', in Geoffrey B. Hainsworth (ed.), *Village-level modernization in Southeast Asia: the political economy of rice and water* (Vancouver: University of British Columbia Press, 1982).

De Koninck, Rodolphe, *Malay peasants coping with the world: breaking the community cycle?* (Singapore: ISEAS, 1992).

de la Gironiere, Paul P., *Twenty years in the Philippines* (New York: Harper and Brothers, 1854).

de los Reyes, Basilio N., 'Can land reform succeed?', *PSR* 20, 1–2 (1972), pp. 79–92.

De Vries, E., and H. Cohen, 'On village shopkeeping in Java and Madura', *Bulletin of the Colonial Institute of Amsterdam* 1, 4 (1937–38), pp. 263–73.

Delvert, Jean, *Le paysan cambodgien* (Paris: Mouton, 1961).

Demaine, H., and C.J. Dixon, 'Land tenure patterns and agricultural development in N.E. Thailand: a case study of the Lam Pao irrigation area in changwat Kalasin', *JSS* 60, 2 (1972), pp. 45–60.

Dennis, John V. Jr, 'Kampuchea's ecology and resource base: natural limitations on food production strategies', in David Ablin and Marlowe Hood (eds), *The Cambodian agony* (Armonk: M.E. Sharpe, 1987).

Deuster, Paul, 'The Green Revolution in a village of West Sumatra', *BIES* 18, 1 (1982), pp. 86–95.

Dewey, Alice G., *Peasant marketing in rural Java* (Glencoe: Free Press, 1962).

Dewey, A.G., 'Trade and social control in Java', *Journal of the Royal Anthropological Institution of Great Britain and Ireland* 92 (1962), pp. 177–90.

Dewey, Alice, 'Capital, credit and saving in Javanese marketing', in Raymond Firth and B.S. Yamey (eds), *Capital, saving and credit in peasant societies: studies from Asia, Oceania, the Caribbean and middle America* (London: George Allen and Unwin, 1964).

deYoung, John E., *Village life in modern Thailand* (Berkeley: University of California Press, 1955).

Dick, H.W., 'Inter-island trade, economic integration, and the emergence of the national economy', in Anne Booth, W.J. O'Malley, and Anna Weidemann (eds), *Indonesian economic history in the Dutch colonial era* (New Haven: Monograph Series No. 35, Yale University Southeast Asia Studies, 1990).

Dick, Howard, 'Survey of recent developments', *BIES* 15, 1 (1979), pp. 1–44.

Dick, Howard, 'Survey of recent developments', *BIES* 18, 1 (1982), pp. 1–38.

Dick, Howard, and Dean Forbes, 'Transport and communications: a quiet revolution', in Anne Booth (ed.), *The oil boom and after: Indonesian economic performance in the Soeharto era* (Singapore: Oxford University Press, 1992).

Dick, Howard, 'A fresh approach to Southeast Asian history', in John Butcher and Howard Dick (eds), *The rise and fall of revenue farming: business elites and the emergence of the modern state in Southeast Asia* (Houndmills: Macmillan, 1993).

Diehl, F.W., 'Revenue farming and colonial finances in the Netherlands East Indies, 1816–1925', in John Butcher and Howard Dick (eds), *The rise and fall of revenue farming: business elites and the emergence of the modern state in Southeast Asia* (Houndmills: Macmillan, 1993).

Dixon, Chris, *South East Asia in the world-economy: a regional geography* (Cambridge: Cambridge University Press, 1991).

Dixon, Gale, 'Social adjustments in a planned village in Malaysia', *JTG* 47 (1978), pp. 31–9.

Dixon, John, 'Production and consumption of cassava in Indonesia', *BIES* 15, 3 (1979), pp. 83–106.

Djoko Suryo, 'Social and economic life in rural Semarang under colonial rule in the later 19th century', PhD dissertation, Monash University, 1982.

Dobbin, C., *Islamic revivalism in a changing peasant economy: central Sumatra, 1784–1847* (London: Curzon Press, 1983).

Dobby, E.H.G., 'The Kelantan delta', *GR* 41 (1951), pp. 226–55.

Dobby, E.H.G., 'The north Kedah plain: a study in the environment of pioneering for rice cultivation', *EG* 27 (1951), pp. 287–315.

Dobby, E.H.G., *Southeast Asia* (9th ed. London: University of London Press, 1966).

Dodge, Nicholas N., 'Population estimates for the Malay peninsula in the nineteenth century, with special reference to the east coast states', *Population Studies* 34, 3 (1980), pp. 437–75.

Doeppers, Daniel F., 'The development of Philippine cities before 1900', *JAS* 31 (1972), pp. 769–92.

Doeppers, Daniel F., 'Destination, selection and turnover among Chinese migrants to Philippine cities in the nineteenth century', *Journal of Historical Demography* 12, 4 (1986), pp. 381–401.

Doering, Otto Charles, 'Malaysian rice policy and the Muda river irrigation project', PhD dissertation, Cornell University, 1973.

Donner, Wolf, *The five faces of Thailand: an economic geography* (London: C. Hurst, 1978).

Doshi, Tilak, 'Peasants, the state and policy constraints: the political economy of rural development in peninsular Malaysia 1957–69', *JPS* 15, 4 (1988), pp. 475–99.

Douglas, Donald E., 'An historical survey of the land tenure situation in the Philippines', *Solidarity* 7 (1970), pp. 65–70.

Douglass, Mike, *Regional integration on the capitalist periphery: the central plains of Thailand* (The Hague: Institute of Social Studies, 1984).

Dove, Michael R., 'Household composition and intensity of labour: a case study of the Kantu' of West Kalimantan', *BIES* 17, 3 (1981), pp. 86–93.

Dove, Michael R., 'The myth of the "communal" longhouse in rural development: the Kantu' of Kalimantan', in Colin MacAndrews and Chia Lin Sien (eds), *Too rapid rural development: perceptions and perspectives from Southeast Asia* (Athens, Ohio: Ohio University Press, 1982).

Dove, Michael R., 'Theories of swidden agriculture, and the political economy of ignorance', *Agroforestry Systems* 1 (1983), pp. 85–99.

Dove, Michael R., 'The Chayanov slope in a swidden society', in E. Paul Durrenberger (ed.), *Chayanov, peasants and economic anthropology* (New York: Academic Press, 1984).

Dove, Michael R., 'Man, land and game in Sumbawa: some observations on agrarian ecology and development policy in eastern Indonesia', *SJTG* 5, 2 (1984), pp. 112–24.

Dove, Michael R., 'The agroecological mythology of the Javanese and the political economy of Indonesia', *Indonesia* 39 (1985), pp. 1–36.

Dove, Michael R., 'Peasant versus government perception and use of the environment: a case-study of Banjarese ecology and river basin development in south Kalimantan', *JSEAS* 17, 1 (1986), pp. 113–36.

Dove, Michael R., 'Review article: social-political aspects of home gardens in Java', *JSEAS* 21, 1 (1990), pp. 155–63.

Downs, R.E., 'A Kelantanese village in Malaya', in Julian H. Steward (ed.), *Contemporary change in traditional societies. Volume II. Asian rural societies* (Urbana: University of Illinois Press, 1967).

Dozier, Edward P., *Mountain arbiters: the changing life of a Philippine hill people* (Tucson: University of Arizona Press, 1966).

Drabble, J.H., 'Investment in the rubber industry in Malaya, 1900–22', *JSEAS* 3, 2 (1972), pp. 247–61.

Drabble, J.H., 'Peasant smallholders in the Malayan economy', in James C. Jackson and Martin Rudner (eds), *Issues in Malaysian development* (Singapore: Heinemann, 1979).

Drabble, J.H., and P.J. Drake, 'The British agency houses in Malaysia: survival in a changing world', *JSEAS* 12, 2 (1981), pp. 297–328.

Drabble, John, 'Politics of survival: European reactions in Malaya to rubber smallholding in the inter-war years', in Peter J. Rimmer and Lisa M. Allen (eds), *The underside of Malaysian history: pullers, prostitutes, plantation workers . . .* (Singapore: Singapore University Press, 1990).

Drabble, John H., *Malayan rubber: the interwar years* (Houndmills: Macmillan, 1991).

Drake, P.J., 'The economic development of British Malaya to 1914: an essay in historiography with some questions for historians', *JSEAS* 10, 2 (1979), pp. 262–90.

Dros, Nico, 'Javanese labour relations in a changing rural economy, 1830–1870', *Economic and Social History in the Netherlands* 3 (1991), pp. 133–53.

Dudung Abdul Adjid, 'Vertical transfer of agrotechnology in Indonesia: the case of the Bimas program', in B.G. Cagauan, G.Y. Tsuji, and L.W. Peterson (eds), *Agrotechnology transfer in Indonesia and the Philippines* (Honolulu:

College of Tropical Agriculture and Human Resources, University of Hawaii, 1983).
Dumont, Jean-Paul, *Visayan vignettes: ethnographic traces of a Philippine island* (Chicago: University of Chicago Press, 1992).
Dusit Banijbatana, 'Forest policy in northern Thailand', in Peter Kunstadter, E.C. Chapman, and Sanga Sabhasri (eds), *Farmers in the forest: economic development and marginal agriculture in northern Thailand* (Honolulu: University Press of Hawaii, 1978).
Ea, Meng-Try, 'Recent population trends in Kampuchea', in David A. Ablin and Marlowe Hood (eds), *The Cambodian agony* (Armonk: M.E. Sharpe, 1987).
Earl, George Windsor, *The eastern seas, or voyages and adventures in the Indian archipelago in 1832–33–34* (London: Wm. H. Allen, 1837).
East Asia Analytical Unit, Department of Foreign Affairs and Trade, Australia, *Subsistence to supermarket: food and agricultural transformation in South-East Asia* (Canberra: Australian Government Publishing Service, 1994).
Ebihara, May, 'Societal organization in sixteenth and seventeenth century Cambodia', *JSEAS* 15, 2 (1984), pp. 280–95.
Ebihara, May, 'Revolution and reformulation in Kampuchean village culture', in David Ablin and Marlowe Hood (eds), *The Cambodian agony* (Armonk: M.E. Sharpe, 1987).
Eden, Joseph Anfield, 'Female labor and regional economic development in Malaysia', PhD dissertation, University of North Carolina at Chapel Hill, 1989.
Eden, Joseph Anfield, 'Mobilisation and employment of female labour in Malaysia', *PV* 32, 1 (1991), pp. 66–77.
Eder, James F., 'Agricultural intensification and the returns to labour in the Philippine swidden system', *PV* 18, 1 (1977), pp. 1–21.
Eder, James F., *Who shall succeed? Agricultural development and social inequality on a Philippine frontier* (Cambridge: Cambridge University Press, 1982).
Eder, James F., 'Hunter-gatherer/farmer exchange in the Philippines: some implications for ethnic identity and adaptive well-being', in A. Terry Rambo, Kathleen Gillogly, and Karl L. Hutterer (eds), *Ethnic diversity and the control of natural resources in Southeast Asia* (Ann Arbor: Michigan Papers on South and Southeast Asia No. 32, Center for South and Southeast Asian Studies, University of Michigan, 1988).
Edmundson, Wade, 'Land, food and work in three Javanese villages', PhD dissertation, University of Hawaii, 1972.
Edmundson, Wade C., 'Two villages in contrast', *BIES* 13, 1 (1977), pp. 95–110.
Edmundson, Wade C., and Stella A. Edmundson, 'A decade of village development in East Java', *BIES* 19, 2 (1983), pp. 46–59.
Edmundson, Wade C., and Stella Anderson, 'Geographic variation and changing economic status in two Javanese villages', *SJTG* 7, 1 (1986), pp. 28–39.
Effendi, Tadjuddin N., and Chris Manning, 'Rural development and nonfarm employment in rural Java', in Bruce Koppel, John Hawkins, William James (eds), *Development or deterioration? Work in rural Asia* (Boulder: Lynne Rienner, 1994).
Elliott, Charles Burke, *The Philippines to the end of the Commission Government: a study in tropical democracy* (repr. New York: Greenwood Press, 1968) [1917].
Elliott, David W.P., 'Political integration in North Vietnam: the cooperativization

period', in Joseph J. Zasloff and MacAlister Brown (eds), *Communism in Indochina: new perspectives* (Lexington: D.C. Heath, 1975).

Ellis, F., *Peasant economics: farm households and agrarian development* (Cambridge: Cambridge University Press, 1988).

Elson, R.E., *Javanese peasants and the colonial sugar industry: impact and change in an east Java residency, 1830–1940* (Singapore: Oxford University Press, 1984).

Elson, R.E., 'The famine in Demak and Grobogan in 1849–50: its causes and circumstances', *RIMA* 19, 1 (1985), pp. 39–85.

Elson, R.E., 'International commerce, the state and society: economic and social change', in Nicholas Tarling (ed.), *The Cambridge history of Southeast Asia*, vol. 2 (Cambridge: Cambridge University Press, 1992).

Elson, R.E., *Village Java under the Cultivation System, 1830–1870* (Sydney: Allen and Unwin, 1994).

Elwert, G., and D. Wong, 'Subsistence production and commodity production in the Third World', *Review* 3, 3 (1980), pp. 501–22.

Ennis, Thomas E., *French policy and developments in Indochina* (repr. New York: Russell and Russell, 1973) [1936].

Erskine, Bruce, 'Thailand's food processing industry: a model of success for other developing countries', *Journal of Southeast Asian Business* 7, 2 (1991), pp. 1–14.

Evans, David B., and Nirimansjah Hasibuan, 'South Sumatra: dualism and export orientation', in Hal Hill (ed.), *Unity in diversity: regional economic development in Indonesia since 1970* (Singapore: Oxford University Press, 1989).

Evans, Grant, 'The accursed problem: communists and peasants', *PS* 15, 2 (1988), pp. 73–102.

Evans, Grant, *Lao peasants under socialism* (New Haven: Yale University Press, 1990).

Evers, Hans-Dieter, 'Trade and state formation: Siam in the early Bangkok period', *MAS* 21, 4 (1987), pp. 751–71.

Evers, Hans-Dieter, 'Javanese petty trade', in Hans-Dieter Evers and Heiko Schrader (eds), *The moral economy of trade: ethnicity and developing markets* (London: Routledge, 1994).

Fabella, Raul V., 'Rural non-farm employment in the Philippines: composition, growth and seasonality', in R.T. Shand (ed.), *Off-farm employment in the development of rural Asia* (Canberra: National Centre for Development Studies, Australian National University, 1986).

Fasseur, C., 'The cultivation system and its impact on the Dutch colonial economy and the indigenous society in nineteenth-century Java', in C.A. Bayly and D.H.A. Kolff (eds), *Two colonial empires: comparative essays on the history of India and Indonesia in the nineteenth century* (Dordrecht: Martinus Nijhoff, 1986).

Fasseur, C., and D.H.A. Kolff, 'Some remarks on the development of colonial bureaucracies in India and Indonesia', *Itinerario* 10, 1 (1986), pp. 31–55.

Fatimah Halim, 'Differentiation of the peasantry: a study of the rural communities of West Malaysia', *JCA* 10 (1980), pp. 400–22.

Fatimah Halim, 'The major mode of surplus labour appropriation in the west Malaysian countryside: the sharecropping system', *JPS* 10, 2–3 (1983), pp. 256–78.

Favre, P., 'A journey in the Menangkabau states of the Malay peninsula', *JIAEA* 3, 3 (1849), pp. 153–61.

Feeny, David, 'Induced technical and institutional change: a Thai case study', in Gordon P. Means (ed.), *The past in Southeast Asia's present* (Ottawa: Canadian Council for Southeast Asian Studies, 1978).

Feeny, David, 'Competing hypotheses of underdevelopment: a Thai case study', *JEH* 19, 1 (1979), pp. 113–27.

Feeny, David, 'Paddy, princes and productivity: irrigation and Thai agricultural development, 1900–1940', *EEH* 16, 2 (1979), pp. 132–50.

Feeny, David, 'Infrastructure linkages and trade performance: Thailand, 1900–1940', *EEH* 19 (1982), pp. 1–27.

Feeny, David, *The political economy of productivity: Thai agricultural development, 1880–1975* (Vancouver: University of British Columbia Press, 1982).

Feeny, David, 'Extensive versus intensive agricultural development: induced public investment in Southeast Asia 1900–1940', *JEH* 43, 3 (1983), pp. 687–704.

Feeny, David, 'The moral or the rational peasant? Competing hypotheses of collective action', *JAS* 42, 4 (1983), pp. 769–89.

Feeny, David, 'Agricultural expansion and forest depletion in Thailand, 1900–1975', in John F. Richards and Richard P. Tucker (eds), *World deforestation in the twentieth century* (Durham, NC: Duke University Press, 1988).

Feeny, David, 'The decline of property rights in man in Thailand, 1800–1913', *JEH* 49, 2 (1989), pp. 285–96.

Fegan, Brian, 'Between the lord and the law: tenants' dilemmas', *PSR* 20, 1–2 (1972), pp. 113–28.

Fegan, Brian, 'Jobs and farms: the lessee's alternative and peasantization', *PSR* 20 (1972), pp. 134–42.

Fegan, Brian, 'The social history of a Central Luzon barrio', in Alfred W. McCoy and Ed. C. de Jesus (eds), *Philippine social history: global trade and local transformations* (Sydney: Allen and Unwin, 1981).

Fegan, Brian, 'Establishment fund, population increase and changing class structure in central Luzon', *PSR* 31 (1983), pp. 31–43.

Fegan, Brian, 'Land reform and technical change in central Luzon: the rice industry under martial law', *PSR* 31, 1–2 (1983), pp. 67–86.

Fegan, Brian, 'Rural Philippines: central Luzon', in R.J. May and Francisco Nemenzo (eds), *The Philippines after Marcos* (New York: St. Martin's Press, 1985.

Fegan, Brian, 'Accumulation on the basis of an unprofitable crop', in Gillian Hart, Andrew Turton and Benjamin White with Brian Fegan and Lim Teck Ghee (eds), *Agrarian transformations: local processes and the state in Southeast Asia* (Berkeley: University of California Press, 1989).

Fegan, Brian, 'The Philippines: agrarian stagnation under a decaying regime', in Gillian Hart, Andrew Turton and Benjamin White with Brian Fegan and Lim Teck Ghee (eds), *Agrarian transformations: local processes and the state in Southeast Asia* (Berkeley: University of California Press, 1989).

Feingold, David, 'Opium and politics in Laos', in Nina S. Adams and Alfred W. McCoy (eds), *Laos: war and revolution* (New York: Harper Colophon, 1970).

Fernando, M.R., 'Growth of non-agricultural indigenous economic activities in Java, 1820–1880', in J. Thomas Lindblad (ed.), *New challenges in the modern economic history of Indonesia: proceedings of the first conference on Indonesia's modern economic history* (Leiden: Programme of Indonesian Studies, 1993).

Fernando, Radin, 'Rice cultivation in Cirebon residency, west Java, 1830–1940', *RIMA* 22, 1 (1988), pp. 1–68.

Fernando, Radin, and William J. O'Malley, 'Peasants and coffee cultivation in Cirebon Residency, 1800–1900', in Anne Booth, W.J. O'Malley, and Anna Weidemann (eds), *Indonesian economic history in the Dutch colonial era* (New Haven: Monograph Series No. 35, Yale University Southeast Asia Studies, 1990).

Fforde, Adam, *The agrarian question in North Vietnam, 1974–1979: a study of cooperator resistance to state policy* (Armonk: M.E. Sharpe, 1989).

Finlayson, George, *The mission to Siam and Hue, the capital of Indo-China in the years 1821–1822* (London: John Murray, 1826).

Finley, John Park, and William Churchill, *The Subanu: studies of a sub-Visayan mountain folk of Mindanao* (Washington DC: Publication No. 184, Carnegie Institution, 1913).

Firth, Raymond, 'Capital, savings and credit in peasant societies: a viewpoint from economic anthropology', in Raymond Firth and B.S. Yamey (eds), *Capital, savings and credit in peasant societies: studies from Asia, Oceania, the Caribbean and middle America* (London: George Allen and Unwin, 1964).

Firth, Rosemary, *Housekeeping among Malay peasants* (2nd ed. London: University of London/The Athlone Press, 1966).

Forbes, C.J.F.S., *British Burma and its people: being sketches of native manners, customs, and religion* (London: John Murray, 1878).

Forbes, Henry O., *A naturalist's wanderings in the eastern archipelago* (repr. Singapore: Oxford University Press, 1989) [1885].

Foreman, John, *The Philippine islands* (2nd ed. New York: Charles Scribner's Sons, 1899).

Foster, George M., 'Introduction: what is a peasant?', in Jack M. Potter, May N. Diaz and George M. Foster (eds), *Peasant society: a reader* (Boston: Little, Brown and Co., 1967).

Fox, James J., 'Managing the ecology of rice production in Indonesia', in Joan Hardjono (ed.), *Indonesia: resources, ecology and environment* (Singapore: Oxford University Press, 1991).

Fox, James J., 'The rice baskets of East Java: the ecology and social context of *sawah* production', in Howard Dick, James J. Fox, and Jamie Mackie. (eds), *Balanced development: East Java in the New Order* (Singapore: Oxford University Press, 1993).

Frake, Charles O., 'The eastern Subanu of Mindanao', in George Peter Murdock (ed.), *Social structure in Southeast Asia* (Chicago: Quadrangle Press, 1960).

Franck, Harry A., *East of Siam: ramblings in the five divisions of French Indo-China* (New York: Grosset and Dunlap, 1926).

Franke, Richard William, 'The Green Revolution in a Javanese village', PhD dissertation, Harvard University, 1972.

Fredericks, L.J., 'Some socio-economic characteristics of rural labour with special reference to a rice double-cropping area in Selangor, West Malaysia', in S. Hirashima (ed.), *Hired labor in rural Asia* (Tokyo: Institute of Developing Economies, 1977).

Fredericks, L.J., and R.J.G. Wells, 'Some aspects of tenancy reform measures in Southeast Asia', *AS* 18, 6 (1978), pp. 644–58.

Freeman, Derek, *Report on the Iban* (London: Athlone Press, 1970).
Freeman, J.D., 'The Iban of western Borneo', in G.P. Murdock (ed.), *Social structure in Southeast Asia* (Chicago: Quadrangle Books, 1960).
Freer, William B., *The Philippine experiences of an American teacher, a narrative of work and travel in the Philippine islands* (New York: Charles Scribner's Sons, 1906).
Fried, Morton H., 'On the concept of "tribe" and "tribal society", in June Helm (ed.), *Essays on the problem of tribe: proceedings of the 1967 annual spring meeting of the American Ethnological Society* (Seattle: American Ethnological Society, 1968).
Fry, Howard T., *A history of the Mountain Province* (Quezon City: New Day Publishers, 1983).
Fuhs, Friedrich W., *Labour utilization and farm income in rural Thailand: results of case studies in rural villages (1969/1970)* (Wiesbaden: Franz Steinder Verlag, 1979).
Fujimoto, Akimi, 'The effects of farming techniques on rice yields: a case study in Kelantan, Malaysia', *KEM* 14, 1 (1977), pp. 51–8.
Fujimoto, Akimi, *Income sharing among Malay peasants: a study of land tenure and rice production* (Singapore: Singapore University Press, 1983).
Fujimoto, Akimi, 'Share tenancy and rice production: lessons from two village studies in west Java', in A. Fujimoto and T. Matsuda (eds), *An economic study of rice farming in west Java* (Tokyo: Nodai Research Institute, University of Agriculture, 1986).
Fukuda, Minoru, 'Transition in the traditional rice harvesting system in a Javanese village', in A. Fujimoto and T. Matsuda (eds), *An economic study of rice farming in west Java* (Tokyo: Nodai Research Institute, University of Agriculture, 1986).
Fukui, Hayao, 'Paddy production technology, present and future', in Yoneo Ishii (ed.), *Thailand: a rice growing society* (Honolulu: University Press of Hawaii, 1978).
Furnivall, J.S., *An introduction to the political economy of Burma* (3rd ed. Rangoon: Burmese Advertising Press, 1957). [1931].
Furnivall, J.S., 'Safety first: a study in the economic history of Burma', *JBRS* 40, 1 (1957), pp. 24–38.
Furukawa, Hisao, 'Environment and agriculture in the Batang Hari river basin of Jambi, Sumatra', in Tsuyoshi Kato, Muchtar Lutfi, and Narifumi Maeda (eds), *Environment, agriculture and society in the Malay world* (Kyoto: Center for Southeast Asian Studies, Kyoto University, 1986).
Fytche, H., *Burma, past and present* (London: C. Kegan Paul, 1878).
Geddes, William R., 'The Tribal Research Centre, Thailand: an account of plans and activities', in Peter Kunstadter (ed.), *Southeast Asian tribes, minorities and nations*, vol. 2 (Princeton: Princeton University Press, 1967).
Geddes, William Robert, *Migrants of the mountains: the cultural ecology of the Blue Miao (Hmong Njua) of Thailand* (Oxford: Clarendon Press, 1976).
Geertz, C., 'Form and variation in Balinese village structure', *American Anthropologist* 61 (1959), pp. 991–1012.
Geertz, C., *Agricultural involution; the processes of ecological change in Indonesia* (Berkeley: University of California Press, 1963).
Geertz, C., 'Culture and social change: the Indonesian case', *Man* (new series) 19, 4 (1984), pp. 511–32.

Gesick, Lorraine, 'Traditional societal organization in Thailand and Burma: comments', *JSEAS* 15, 2 (1884), pp. 266–70.

Gibbons, David S., Rodolphe de Koninck, and Ibrahim Hasan, *Agricultural modernization, poverty and inequality: the distributional impact of the Green Revolution in regions of Malaysia and Indonesia* (Westmead: Gower, 1980).

Gibson, Joyce, 'Rice production and imports', *BIES* no. 1 (1965), pp. 46–67.

Gillogly, Kathleen, et al. (eds), *Two upland agroecosystems in Luang Prabang Province, Lao PDR: a preliminary analysis* (Khon Kaen: Farm Systems Research Project, Khon Kaen University, 1990).

Glassburner, Bruce, 'Survey of recent developments', *BIES* 14, 2 (1978), pp. 1–33.

Glassburner, Bruce, 'Survey of recent developments', *BIES* 22, 1 (1986), pp. 1–33.

Goethals, Peter R., 'Rarak: the annual swidden cycle', *Indonesia* 20 (1975), pp. 113–54.

Goh, Taro, 'Review of the nineteenth and early twentieth century debate on the origin of communal landownership with special reference to Java', *MI* 3, 3 (1986), pp. 243–76.

Golay, Frank H., *The Philippines: public policy and national economic development* (Ithaca: Cornell University Press, 1968).

Golay, Frank H., 'The search for revenues', in Peter W. Stanley (ed.), *Reappraising an empire: new perspectives on Philippine-American history* (Cambridge, Mass.: Harvard University Press, 1984).

Goldman, Richard H., 'Staple food self-sufficiency and the distributive impact of Malaysian rice policy', *FRIS* 14, 3 (1975), pp. 251–93.

Golomb, Louis, 'The origin, spread and persistence of glutinous rice as a staple crop in mainland Southeast Asia', *JSEAS* 7, 1 (1976), pp. 1–15.

Goodell, Grace E., 'Untying the HYV package: a Filipino farmer grapples with the new technology', *JPS* 11, 4 (1984), pp. 238–66.

Goodell, Grace E., 'Bugs, bunds, banks, and bottlenecks: organizational contradictions in the new rice technology', *EDCC* 33, 1 (1984), pp. 23–42.

Goodman, David, and Michael Redclift, *From peasant to proletarian: capitalist development and agrarian transitions* (Oxford: Basil Blackwell, 1981).

Gosling, L.A. Peter, 'Chinese crop dealers in Malaysia and Thailand: the myth of the merciless monopsonistic middleman', in Linda Y.C. Lim and L.A. Peter Gosling (eds), *The Chinese in Southeast Asia*, vol. 1 (Singapore: Maruzen Asia, 1983).

Gourou, Pierre, *The peasants of the Tonkin delta* (New Haven: HRAF, 1955) [1936].

Gourou, Pierre, *Land utilization in French Indochina* (Washington: Institute of Pacific Affairs, 1945).

Gourou, Pierre, *Man and land in the Far East* (trans. S.H. Beaver) (London: Longman, 1975).

Gourou, Pierre, *The tropical world* (4th ed. London: Longman, 1975).

Graham, W.A., *Kelantan, a state in the Malay peninsula: a handbook of information* (Glasgow: James Maclehose and Sons, 1908).

Graham, W.A., *Siam* (3rd ed. London: Alexander Moring, 1924).

Gran, Guy, 'Vietnam and the capitalist road to modernity: village Cochinchina 1880–1940', PhD dissertation, University of Wisconsin, 1975.

Grandstaff, Terry B., 'Northeast: the human environment: variation and uncertainty', *PV* 33, 2 (1992), pp. 135–44.

Graves, Elizabeth E., *The Minangkabau response to Dutch colonial rule in the nineteenth century* (Ithaca: Monograph Series No. 60, Cornell Modern Indonesia Project, 1981).

Gregory, James R., 'Image of limited good, or expectation of reciprocity?' *CA* 16, 1 (1975), pp. 73–92.

Grenville, S.A., 'Survey of recent developments', *BIES* 13, 1 (1977), pp. 1–32.

Grijpstra, B.B.G., *Common efforts in the development of rural Sarawak, Malaysia* (Assen: Van Gorcum, 1976).

Grist, D.H., *Rice* (5th ed. London: Longman, 1975).

Guermonprez, Jean-François, 'On the elusive Balinese village: hierarchy and values versus political models', *RIMA* 24 (1990), pp. 55–89.

Guest, Philip, *Labor allocation and rural development: migration in four Javanese villages* (Boulder: Westview, 1989).

Guinness, Patrick, and Imron Husin, 'Industrial expansion into a rural subdistrict: Pandaan, East Java', in Howard Dick, James J. Fox, and Jamie Mackie (eds), *Balanced development: East Java in the New Order* (Singapore: Oxford University Press, 1993).

Gullick, J.M., *Indigenous political systems of western Malaya* (London: University of London/Athlone Press, 1958).

Gullick, J.M., 'The entrepreneur in late 19th century Malay peasant society', *JMBRAS* 58, 1 (1985), pp. 59–70.

Gullick, J.M., *Malay society in the late nineteenth century: the beginnings of change* (Singapore: Oxford University Press, 1987).

Gullick, John, *Malaysia: economic expansion and national unity* (London: Ernest Benn, 1981).

Gutzlaff, Charles, *Journal of three voyages along the coast of China in 1831, 1832, and 1833, with notices of Siam, Corea, and the Loo-Choo islands* (London: Thomas Ward and Co., 1840).

Hainsworth, Geoffrey B., 'Beyond dualism? Village-level modernization and the process of integration into national economies in Southeast Asia', in Geoffrey B. Hainsworth (ed.), *Village-level modernization in Southeast Asia: the political economy of rice and water* (Vancouver: University of British Columbia Press, 1982).

Halib, Mohammed bin, 'The state, rice and irrigation: historical development and contemporary cases of small-scale irrigation systems in peninsular Malaysia', PhD dissertation, Cornell University, 1985.

Hall, D.G.E., *Burma* (London: Hutchison House, 1950).

Hall, D.G.E. (ed.), *Michael Symes: journal of his second embassy to the court of Ava in 1802* (London: George Allen and Unwin, 1955).

Hallett, Holt S., *A thousand miles on an elephant in the Shan states* (Edinburgh: William Blackwood and Sons, 1890).

Halpern, Joel M., *The rural and urban economies* (Los Angeles: Laos Project Papers No. 8, Department of Anthropology, University of California, 1961).

Halpern, Joel M., 'Capital, savings and credit among Lao peasants', in Raymond Firth and B.S. Yamey (eds), *Capital, saving and credit in peasant societies: studies from Asia, Oceania, the Caribbean and middle America* (London: George Allen and Unwin, 1964).

Halpern, Joel M., *Economy and society in Laos: a brief survey* (New Haven: Monograph Series No. 5, Southeast Asia Studies, Yale University, 1964).

Hamilton, James W., *Pwo Karen: at the edge of mountain and plain* (St Paul: West Publishing Co., 1976).

Hanks, Lucien M., 'Symposium on societal organization in mainland Southeast Asia prior to the eighteenth century: foreword', *JSEAS* 15, 2 (1984), pp. 219–23.

Hansen, Gary, 'Episodes in rural modernization: problems with the Bimas program', *Indonesia* 11 (1971), pp. 63–81.

Hansen, Gary, *The politics and administration of rural development in Indonesia* (Berkeley: Center for South and Southeast Asian Studies, University of California, 1973).

Hardjono, J.M., 'Rural development in Indonesia: the "top-down" approach', in D.A.M. Lea and D.P. Chaudhri (eds), *Rural development and the state: contradictions and dilemmas in developing countries* (London: Methuen, 1983).

Hardjono, Joan, *Land, labour and livelihood in a west Java village* (Yogyakarta: Gadjah Mada University Press, 1987).

Hardjono, Joan, 'The dimensions of Indonesia's environmental problems', in Joan Hardjono (ed.), *Indonesia: resources, ecology and environment* (Singapore: Oxford University Press, 1991).

Hardjono, Joan, and Hal Hill, 'West Java: population pressure and regional diversity', in Hal Hill (ed.), *Unity in diversity: regional economic development in Indonesia since 1970* (Singapore: Oxford University Press, 1989).

Harrison, Robert, 'Hamlet organization and its relationship to productivity in the swidden-rice communities of Ranau, Sabah, Malaysia', in George N. Appell (ed.), *The societies of Borneo: explorations in the theory of cognatic social structure* (Washington, DC: American Anthropological Association, 1976).

Hart, Mrs Ernest, *Picturesque Burma, past & present* (London: J.M. Dent and Co., 1897).

Hart, Gillian, 'Patterns of household labour allocation in a Javanese village', in Hans Binswanger et al. (eds), *Rural household studies in Asia* (Singapore: Singapore University Press, 1981).

Hart, Gillian, 'Productivity, poverty and population pressure: female labor deployment in rice production in Java and Bangladesh', *AJAE* 66 (1983), pp. 1037–42.

Hart, Gillian, 'Exclusionary labour arrangements: interpreting evidence on employment trends in rural Java', *JDS* 22, 4 (1986), pp. 681–96.

Hart, Gillian, 'Interlocking transactions: obstacles, precursors or instruments of agrarian capitalism?', *Journal of Development Economics* 23 (1986), pp. 177–203.

Hart, Gillian, *Power, labor, and livelihood: processes of change in rural Java* (Berkeley: University of California Press, 1986).

Hart, Gillian, 'Agrarian structure and the state in Java and Bangladesh', *JAS* 47, 2 (1988), pp. 249–67.

Hart, Gillian, 'Agrarian change in the context of state patronage', in Gillian Hart, Andrew Turton and Benjamin White with Brian Fegan and Lim Teck Ghee (eds), *Agrarian transformations: local processes and the state in Southeast Asia* (Berkeley: University of California Press, 1989).

Hart, Gillian, 'Engendering everyday resistance: gender, patronage and production politics in rural Malaysia', *JPS* 19, 1 (1991), pp. 93–121.

Hart, Gillian, 'Household production reconsidered: gender, labor conflict, and technological change in Malaysia's Muda region', *WD* 20, 6 (1992), pp. 809–23.

Hart, Gillian, 'The dynamics of diversification in an Asian rice region', in Bruce Koppel, John Hawkins, William James (eds), *Development or deterioration? Work in rural Asia* (Boulder: Lynne Rienner, 1994).

Harvey, G.E., *British rule in Burma 1824–1942* (London: Faber and Faber, 1946).

Hasan, Ibrahim, 'Rice marketing in Aceh', *BIES* 12, 3 (1976), pp. 77–94.

Hayami, Yujiro, *Anatomy of a peasant economy: a rice village in the Philippines* (Los Baños: International Rice Research Institute, 1978).

Hayami, Yujiro, 'Asian development: a view from the paddy fields', *Asian Development Review* 6, 1 (1988), pp. 49–63.

Hayami, Yujiro, and Anwar Hafid, 'Rice harvesting and welfare in rural Java', *BIES* 15 (1979), pp. 94–112.

Hayami, Yujiro, and Masao Kikuchi, *Asian village economy at the crossroads: an economic approach to institutional change* (Tokyo: University of Tokyo Press, 1981).

Hayami, Yujiro, and Toshihiko Kawagoe, *The agrarian origins of commerce and industry: a study of peasant marketing in Indonesia* (London: Macmillan, 1993)

Hayami, Yujiro, et al., *Agricultural marketing and processing in upland Java: a perspective from a Sunda village* (Bogor: CGPRT Centre, 1987).

Heersink, Christiaan A., 'Selayar and the green gold: the development of the coconut trade on an Indonesian island (1820–1950)', *JSEAS* 25, 1 (1994), pp. 47–69.

Heesterman, J.C., 'State and adat', in C.A. Bayly and D.H.A. Kolff (eds), *Two colonial empires: comparative essays on the history of India and Indonesia in the nineteenth century* (Dordrecht: Martinus Nijhoff, 1986).

Hefner, Robert W., *The political economy of mountain Java: an interpretive history* (Berkeley: University of California Press, 1990).

Hendry, James B., *The small world of Khanh Hau* (Chicago: Aldine Publishing Company, 1964).

Herdt, Robert W., 'A retrospective view of technological and other changes in Philippine rice farming, 1965–1982', *EDCC* 35, 2 (1987), pp. 329–49.

Hetler, Carol B., 'The impact of circular migration on a village economy', *BIES* 25, 1 (1989), pp. 53–75.

Hewison, Kevin J., 'The state and capitalist development in Thailand', in R. Higgott and R. Robison (eds), *Southeast Asia: essays in the political economy of structural change* (London: Routledge and Kegan Paul, 1985).

Heytens, Paul, 'Policy alternatives for future rice production growth', in Scott Pearson, Walter Falcon, Paul Heytens, Eric Monke and Rosamund Naylor, *Rice policy in Indonesia* (Ithaca: Cornell University Press, 1991).

Heytens, Paul, 'Rice production systems', in Scott Pearson, Walter Falcon, Paul Heytens, Eric Monke and Rosamund Naylor, *Rice policy in Indonesia* (Ithaca: Cornell University Press, 1991).

Heytens, Paul, 'Technical change in wetland rice agriculture', in Scott Pearson, Walter Falcon, Paul Heytens, Eric Monke and Rosamund Naylor, *Rice policy in Indonesia* (Ithaca: Cornell University Press, 1991).

Hickey, Gerald Cannon, *Village in Vietnam* (New Haven: Yale University Press, 1964).

Hickey, Gerald C., 'Some aspects of hill tribe life in Vietnam', in Peter Kunstadter (ed.), *Southeast Asian tribes, minorities and nations*, vol. 2 (Princeton: Princeton University Press, 1967).

Hickey, Gerald Cannon, *Free in the forest: ethnohistory of the Vietnamese central highlands 1954–1976* (New Haven: Yale University Press, 1982).

Hickey, Gerald Cannon, *Sons of the mountains: ethnohistory of the Vietnamese central highlands to 1954* (New Haven: Yale University Press, 1982).

Higgins, B., 'Survey of recent developments', *BIES* 8, 1 (1972), pp. 1–31.

Higgott, R., et al., 'Theories of development and underdevelopment: implications for the study of Southeast Asia', in R. Higgott and R. Robison (eds), *Southeast Asia: essays in the political economy of structural change* (London: Routledge and Kegan Paul, 1985).

Hill, Hal, 'Manufacturing industry', in Anne Booth (ed.), *The oil boom and after: Indonesian economic performance in the Soeharto era* (Singapore: Oxford University Press, 1992).

Hill, Hal, and Anna Weidemann, 'Regional differences in Indonesia: patterns and issues', in Hal Hill (ed.), *Unity in diversity: regional economic development in Indonesia since 1970* (Singapore: Oxford University Press, 1989).

Hill, Percy A., and Kilmer O. Moe, 'The cultivation of rice', *JEAS* 9, 4 (1960), pp. 90–134.

Hill, Polly, *Development economics on trial: the anthropological case for a prosecution* (Cambridge: Cambridge University Press, 1986).

Hill, R.D., 'Agricultural land tenure in West Malaysia', *MER* 12, 1 (1967), pp. 99–116.

Hill, Roland D., 'Peasant rice cultivation systems with some Malaysian examples', *Geographica Polonica* 19 (1970), pp. 91–8.

Hill, R.D., *Rice in Malaya: a study in historical geography* (Kuala Lumpur: Oxford University Press, 1977).

Hill, R.D., *Agriculture in the Malaysian region* (Budapest: Akademiai Kiado, 1982).

Hill, R.D., 'The history of rice cultivation in Melaka', in Kernial Singh Sandhu and Paul Wheatley (eds), *Melaka: the transformation of a Malay capital c. 1400–1980* (Kuala Lumpur: Oxford University Press, 1983).

Hill, Ron, '"Primitives" to "peasants"? The "sedentarisation of the nomads" in Vietnam', *PV* 26, 1 (1985), pp. 448–57.

Hinton, Peter, 'Introduction', in Peter Hinton (ed.), *Tribesmen and peasants in north Thailand: proceedings of the first symposium of the Tribal Research Centre, Chiang Mai, Thailand, 1967* (Chiang Mai: Tribal Research Centre, 1967).

Hinton, Peter, 'Declining production among swidden cultivators: the case of the Pwo Karen', in Peter Kunstadter, E.C. Chapman, and Sanga Sabhasri (eds), *Farmers in the forest: economic development and marginal agriculture in northern Thailand* (Honolulu: University Press of Hawaii, 1978).

Hipsley, E.H., 'Hunger in Indonesia: comments', *BIES* 9 (1968), pp. 71–2.

Hirsch, Philip, *Development dilemmas in rural Thailand* (Singapore: Oxford University Press, 1990).

Hirschman, Charles, 'Population and society in twentieth-century Southeast Asia', *JSEAS* 25, 2 (1994), pp. 381–416.

Ho, R., *Farmers of central Malaya* (Canberra: Australian National University, 1967).

Ho, Robert, 'Land ownership and economic prospects of Malayan peasants', *MAS* 4, 1 (1970), pp. 83–92.

Hobsbawm, E.J., 'Peasants and politics', *JPS* 1, 1 (1973), pp. 3–21.

Homan van der Heide, J., 'The economic development of Siam during the last half century', in Chattip Nartsupha and Suthy Prasartset (eds), *The political economy of Siam 1851–1910* (Bangkok: The Social Science Association of Thailand, 1981).

Hong Lysa, 'The tax farming system in the early Bangkok period', *JSEAS* 14, 2 (1983), pp. 379–99.

Hong Lysa, *Thailand in the nineteenth century: evolution of the economy and society* (Singapore: ISEAS, 1984).

Hooley, Richard W., 'Long-term economic growth of the Philippine economy, 1902–61', *PEJ* 7, 1 (1968), pp. 1–24.

Horii, Kenzo, 'Farming technique and rural labor of Krian rice producing area, Malaysia – cases of kampong Sungei Megat Aris and kampong Parit Lebai Akir', in S. Hirashima (ed.), *Hired labor in rural Asia* (Tokyo: Institute of Developing Economies, 1977).

Horii, Kenzo, *Rice economy and land tenure in West Malaysia: a comparative study of eight villages* (Tokyo: IDE Occasional Paper No. 18, Institute of Developing Economies, 1981).

Hose, C., *Natural man: a record from Borneo* (repr. Singapore: Oxford University Press, 1988). [1926].

Houtart, Francois, and Genevieve Lemercinier, *Hai Van: life in a Vietnamese commune* (London: Zed Press, 1984).

Huang, Yukon, 'Tenancy patterns, productivity, and rentals in Malaysia', *EDCC* 23, 4 (1975), pp. 703–18.

Huang, Yukon, 'Some reflections on padi double cropping in West Malaysia', in David Lim (ed.), *Readings on Malaysian economic development* (Kuala Lumpur: Oxford University Press, 1975).

Hudson, Alfred B., 'The Padju Epat Ma'anjan Dajak in historical perspective', *Indonesia* 4 (1967), pp. 8–42.

Huff, W.G., 'Bookkeeping, barter, money, credit, and Singapore's international rice trade, 1870–1939', *EEH* 26 (1989), pp. 161–89.

Huff, W.G., 'Sharecroppers, risk, management, and Chinese estate rubber development in interwar British Malaya', *EDCC* 40, 4 (1992), pp. 743–73.

Hugenholtz, W.R., 'Famine and food supply in Java 1830–1914', in C.A. Bayly and D.H.A. Kolff (eds), *Two colonial empires: comparative essays on the history of India and Indonesia in the nineteenth century* (Dordrecht: Martinus Nijhoff, 1986).

Hugenholtz, W.R., 'Taxes and society: regional differences in central Java around 1830', in Sartono Kartodirdjo (ed.), *Papers of the fourth Indonesian–Dutch history conference*, vol. 1 (Yogyakarta: Gadjah Mada University Press, 1986).

Hugenholtz, W.R., 'The land rent question and its solution 1850–1920', in Robert Cribb (ed.), *The late colonial state in Indonesia: political and economic foundations of the Netherlands Indies 1880–1942* (Leiden: KITLV Press, 1994).

Hugo, Graeme J., 'Population movements in Indonesia during the colonial period', in James J. Fox et al. (eds), *Indonesia: Australian perspectives* (Canberra: Research School of Pacific Studies, Australian National University, 1980).

Hugo, Graeme J., 'Migrant women in developing countries', in United Nations, *Internal migration of women in developing countries: proceedings of the United Nations expert meeting on the feminization of internal migration, Aguascalientes, Mexico, 22–25 October 1991* (New York: United Nations, 1993).

Hugo, Graeme J., et al. (eds), *The demographic dimension in Indonesian development* (Singapore: Oxford University Press, 1987).

Huke, Robert (ed.), *Shadows on the land: an economic geography of the Philippines* (Manila: Bookmark, 1963).

Hull, Terence H., *The influence of social class on the need and effective demand for children in a Javanese village* (Yogyakarta: Working Paper series No. 7, Population Institute, Gadjah Mada University, 1976).

Hull, Terence H., 'East Java's family planning revolution, 1961–1987', in Howard Dick, James J. Fox, and Jamie Mackie (eds), *Balanced development: East Java in the New Order* (Singapore: Oxford University Press, 1993).

Hull, Terence H., and Ida Bagus Mantra, 'Indonesia's changing population', in Anne Booth and Peter McCawley (eds), *The Indonesian economy during the Soeharto era* (Kuala Lumpur: Oxford University Press, 1981).

Hull, Valerie J., 'Fertility, women's work, and economic class: a case study from Southeast Asia', in Stanley Kupinsky (ed.), *The fertility of working women: a synthesis of international research* (New York: Praeger, 1977).

Hung, G. Nguyen Tien, *Economic development of socialist Vietnam, 1955–1980* (New York: Praeger, 1977).

Hurst, Philip, 'Forest destruction in South East Asia', *The Ecologist* 17, 4–5 (1987), pp. 170–4.

Hurst, Philip, *Rainforest politics: ecological destruction in South-East Asia* (London: Zed Books, 1990).

Husin Ali, S., *Social stratification in Kampong Bagan: a study of class, status, conflict and mobility in a rural Malay community* (Singapore: MBRAS, 1964).

Husin Ali, S., 'Land concentration and poverty among the rural Malays', *Nusantara* 1 (1972), pp. 100–13.

Hüsken, Frans, 'Landlords, sharecroppers and agricultural labourers: changing labour relations in rural Java', *JCA* 9 (1979), pp. 140–51.

Hüsken, Frans, 'Cycles of commercialization and accumulation in a central Javanese village', in Gillian Hart, Andrew Turton and Benjamin White with Brian Fegan and Lim Teck Ghee (eds), *Agrarian transformations: local processes and the state in Southeast Asia* (Berkeley: University of California Press, 1989).

Hüsken, Frans, and Benjamin White, 'Java: social differentiation, food production, and agrarian control', in Gillian Hart, Andrew Turton and Benjamin White with Brian Fegan and Lim Teck Ghee (eds), *Agrarian transformations: local processes and the state in Southeast Asia* (Berkeley: University of California Press, 1989).

Ikmal Said, Muhammad, 'Large-farmer strategies in an undiversified economy', in Gillian Hart, Andrew Turton and Benjamin White with Brian Fegan and Lim Teck Ghee (eds), *Agrarian transformations: local processes and the state in Southeast Asia* (Berkeley: University of California Press, 1989).

Inamoto, Shiro, 'New phase of labour-saving technology in rice farming in west

Java: an analysis of characteristics and implications of tractorization in two villages', in A. Fujimoto and T. Matsuda (eds), *An economic study of rice farming in west Java: a farm household survey of two villages in Bandung and Subang* (Tokyo: Nodai Research Institute, University of Agriculture, 1986).

Ingleson, John, 'Life and work in colonial cities: harbour workers in Java in the 1910s and 1920s' *MAS* 17, 3 (1983), pp. 455–76.

Ingram, James C., 'Thailand's rice trade and the allocation of resources', in C.D. Cowan (ed.), *The economic development of South-East Asia* (London: George Allen and Unwin, 1964).

Ingram, James C., *Economic change in Thailand 1850–1970* (Stanford: Stanford University Press, 1971).

Innes, Emily, *The Chersonese with the gilding off* (repr. Kuala Lumpur: Oxford University Press, 1974) [1885].

Ireson, W. Randall, and Carol J. Ireson, 'Laos: Marxism in a subsistence rural economy', *BCAS* 21, 2–4 (1989), pp. 59–75.

Ishikawa, S., *Economic development in Asian perspective* (Tokyo: Kinokuniya Bookstore, 1968).

Ishikawa, Shigeru, *Essays on technology, employment and institutions in economic development: comparative Asian experience* (Tokyo: Kinokuniya Bookstore, 1981).

Islam, Rizwanul, 'Non-farm employment in rural Asia: dynamic growth or proletarianisation?', *JCA* 14, 3 (1984), pp. 306–24.

Izikowitz, Karl Gustav, *Lamet: hill peasants in French Indochina* (repr. New York: AMS Press, 1979) [1951].

Jackson, James C., 'Smallholding rubber cultivation in Malaya, 1952–1962', *OG* 9 (1965), pp. 33–40.

Jackson, James C., *Planters and speculators: Chinese and European agricultural enterprise in Malaya, 1786–1921* (Kuala Lumpur: University of Malaya Press, 1968).

Jackson, J.C., 'Rice cultivation in West Malaysia: relationships between culture, history, customary practices, and recent developments', *JMBRAS* 45, 2 (1972), pp. 76–96.

Jacobs, Norman, *Modernization with development: Thailand as an Asian case study* (New York: Praeger, 1971).

Jagor, Feodor, *Travels in the Philippines* (repr. Manila: Filipiniana Book Guild, 1965) [1875].

Jamieson, Neil L., 'Towards a paradigm for paradox: observations on the study of social organization in Southeast Asia', *JSEAS* 15, 2 (1984), pp. 321–9.

Janlekha, Kamol Odd, 'A study of the economy of a rice growing village in central Thailand', PhD dissertation, Cornell University, 1955.

Jay, Robert R., *Religion and politics in rural central Java* (New Haven: Cultural Reports Series No. 12, Southeast Asia Studies, Yale University, 1963).

Jayasuriya, S.K., and R.T. Shand, 'Technical change and labor absorption in Asian agriculture: some emerging trends', *WD* 14, 3 (1986), pp. 415–28.

Jocano, F. Landa, *Sulod society: a study in the kinship system and social organization of a mountain people of central Panay* (Quezon City: University of the Philippines, 1968).

Jocano, F. L., *Growing up in a Philippine barrio* (New York: Holt, Rinehart and Winston, 1969).

Jocano, F. Landa, *The Ilocanos: an ethnography of family and community life in the Ilocos region* (Quezon City: Asian Center, University of the Philippines, 1982).

John, David W., and James C. Jackson, 'The tobacco industry of north Borneo; a distinctive form of plantation agriculture', *JSEAS* 4, 1 (1973), pp. 88–106.

Johnston, David Bruce, 'Rural society and the rice economy in Thailand, 1880–1930', PhD dissertation, Yale University, 1975.

Johnston, David B., 'Opening a frontier: the expansion of rice cultivation in central Thailand in the 1890s', *CAS* 9 (1976), pp. 27–44.

Johnston, David B., 'Bandit, *nakleng*, and peasant in rural Thai society', *CAS* 15 (1980), pp. 90–101.

Johnston, David B., 'Rice cultivation in Thailand: the development of an export economy by indigenous capital and labor', *MAS* 15, 1 (1981), pp. 107–26.

Johnstone, Michael, 'The evolution of squatter settlements in peninsular Malaysian cities', *JSEAS* 12, 2 (1981), pp. 364–80.

Jomo Kwane Sundaram, *A question of class: capital, the state and uneven development in Malaya* (Singapore: Oxford University Press, 1986).

Jones, Christine, 'The mobilization of women's labor for cash crop production', *AJAE* 65, 5 (1983), pp. 1049–54.

Jones, Gavin W., 'Urbanization trends in Southeast Asia: some issues for policy', *JSEAS* 19, 1 (1988), pp. 137–54.

Jones, Gavin W., 'East Java: educational change and changing employment structure', in Howard Dick, James J. Fox, and Jamie Mackie (eds), *Balanced development: East Java in the New Order* (Singapore: Oxford University Press, 1993).

Jones, Gavin W., and Chris Manning, 'Labour force and employment during the 1980s', in Anne Booth (ed.), *The oil boom and after: Indonesian economic performance in the Soeharto era* (Singapore: Oxford University Press, 1992).

Judd, Laurence C., *Chao rai Thai: dry rice farmers in northern Thailand* (Bangkok: Suryaban Publishers, 1977).

Kahin, Audrey, 'The impact of the Indonesian independence struggle on Minangkabau society', in Lyn L. Thomas and Franz von Benda-Beckmann (eds), *Change and continuity in Minangkabau: local, regional and historical perspectives on west Sumatra* (Athens, Ohio: Ohio University Press, 1985).

Kahn, J., 'Economic scale and the cycle of petty commodity production in west Sumatra', in Maurice Bloch (ed.), *Marxist analyses and social anthropology* (London: Malaby Press, 1975).

Kahn, Joel S., *Minangkabau social formations: Indonesian peasants and the world-economy* (Cambridge: Cambridge University Press, 1980).

Kahn, Joel S., 'From peasant to petty commodity production in Southeast Asia', *BCAS* 14, 1 (1982), pp. 3–15.

Kahn, Joel, 'Commercialization and change in Minangkabau: a re-examination of the historical watershed', in Lyn L. Thomas and Franz von Benda-Beckmann (eds), *Change and continuity in Minangkabau: local, regional and historical perspectives on west Sumatra* (Athens, Ohio: Ohio University Press, 1985).

Kahn, Joel S., 'Indonesia after the demise of involution: critique of a debate', *CrA* 5, 1 (1985), pp. 69–76.

Kahn, Joel S., *Constituting the Minangkabau: peasants, culture and modernity in colonial Indonesia* (Oxford: Berg, 1993).

Kaida, Yoshihiro, 'Irrigation and drainage present to future', in Yoneo Ishii (ed.), *Thailand: a rice growing society* (Honolulu: University Press of Hawaii, 1978).

Kampe, Ken, 'Northern highlands: development, bureaucracy and life on the margins', *PV* 33, 2 (1992), pp. 159–64.

Kanahele, George Sanford, 'The Japanese occupation of Indonesia: prelude to independence', PhD dissertation, Cornell University, 1967.

Kano, Hiroyoshi, *Land tenure system and the desa community in nineteenth-century Java* (Tokyo: Special Paper No. 5, Institute of Developing Economies, 1977).

Kano, Hiroyoshi, 'Continuity and change in geographical size, population and land tenure of Javanese villages: the case of Ungaran', in Akira Hayami and Yoshihiro Tsubouchi (eds), *Economic and demographic development in rice producing societies: some aspects of East Asian economic history, 1500–1900* (Tokyo: n.p., 1989).

Kasryno, Faisal, 'Technological progress and its effect on income distribution and employment in rural areas: a case study of three villages in west Java', *KEM* 18 (1981), pp. 113–38.

Kato, Tsuyoshi, 'Social change in a centrifugal society: the Minangkabau of west Sumatra', PhD dissertation, Cornell University, 1977.

Kato, Tsuyoshi, 'Change and continuity in the Minangkabau matrilineal system', *Indonesia* 25 (1978), pp. 1–16.

Kato, Tsuyoshi, 'Different fields, similar locusts: adat communities and the village law of 1979 in Indonesia', *Indonesia* 47 (1989), pp. 89–114.

Kaufman, Howard Keva, *Bangkhuad: a community study in Thailand* (2nd ed. Rutland: Charles E. Tuttle, 1976) [1960].

Kaur, Amarjit, 'The impact of railroads on the Malayan economy, 1874–1941', *JAS* 39, 4 (1980), pp. 693–710.

Kaur, Amarjit, '"Hantu" and highway: transport in Sabah 1881–1963', *MAS* 28, 1 (1994), pp. 1–49.

Kaur, Amarjit, 'The babbling Brookes: economic change in Sarawak 1841–1941', *MAS* 29, 1 (1995), pp. 65–109.

Kawagoe, Toshihiko, and Yujiro Hayami, 'Farmers and middlemen in a transmigration area in Indonesia', *BIES* 25, 3 (1989), pp. 73–97.

Keen, F.G.B., 'The fermented tea (*miang*) economy of northern Thailand', in Peter Kunstadter, E.C. Chapman, and Sanga Sabhasri (eds), *Farmers in the forest: economic development and marginal agriculture in northern Thailand* (Honolulu: University Press of Hawaii, 1978).

Keen, F.G.B., 'Land use', in John McKinnon and Wanat Bhruksasri (eds), *Highlanders of Thailand* (Kuala Lumpur: Oxford University Press, 1983).

Keeton, Charles Lee, *King Theebaw and the ecological rape of Burma: the political and commercial struggle between British India and French Indo-China in Burma, 1878–1886* (Delhi: Manohar Book Service, 1974).

Kelly, Talbot R., *Burma: painted and described* (London: Adam and Charles Black, 1912).

Kemp, Jeremy H., 'Legal and informal land tenures in Thailand', *MAS* 15, 1 (1981), pp. 1–23.

Kemp, J.H., *Seductive mirage: the search for the village community in Southeast Asia* (Dordrecht: Foris Publications, 1988).

Kemp, Jeremy, 'Peasants and cities: the cultural and social image of the Thai peasant village community', *Sojourn* 4, 1 (1989), pp. 1–19.

Kemp, Jeremy, 'The dialectics of village and state in modern Thailand', *JSEAS* 22, 2 (1991), pp. 312–26.

Kerkvliet, Benedict J., *The Huk rebellion: a study of peasant revolt in the Philippines* (Berkeley: University of California Press, 1977).

Kerkvliet, Benedict J. Tria, 'Profiles of agrarian reform in a Nueva Ecija village', in Antonio J. Ledesma, Perla Q. Makil, and Virginia A. Miralao, *Second view from the paddy: more empirical studies of Philippine rice farming and tenancy* (Manila: Ateneo de Manila University, 1983).

Kerkvliet, Benedict J. Tria, *Everyday politics in the Philippines: class and status relations in a central Luzon village* (Berkeley: University of California Press, 1990).

Kerkvliet, Benedict J. Tria, 'Withdrawal and resistance: the political significance of food, agriculture and how people lived during the Japanese occupation in the Philippines', in L. Sears (ed.), *Autonomous histories, particular truths* (Madison: Center for Southeast Asian Studies, University of Wisconsin, 1993).

Keyes, Charles F., 'In search of land: village formation in the central Chi river valley, northeastern Thailand', *CAS* 9 (1976), pp. 45–63.

Keyes, Charles F., *The golden peninsula: culture and adaptation in mainland Southeast Asia* (New York: Macmillan, 1977).

Keyes, Charles F., 'Economic action and Buddhist morality in a Thai village', *JAS* 42, 4 (1983), pp. 851–68.

Keyes, Charles F., 'Peasant strategies in Asian societies: moral and rational economic approaches – a symposium', *JAS* 42, 4 (1983), pp. 753–68.

Khin Maung Kyi, 'Western enterprise and economic development in Burma', *JBRS* 53, 1 (1970), pp. 25–51.

Khin Maung Kyi, 'Problems of agricultural policy in some trade dependent small countries: a comparative study of Burma and Thailand', *KEM* 16, 1–2 (1979), pp. 55–73.

Khin Maung Kyi et al., 'Process of communication in modernisation of rural society: a survey report on two Burmese villages', *MER* 18, 1 (1973), pp. 55–73.

Khoo Kay Kim, 'Malay society, 1874–1920s', *JSEAS* 5, 2 (1974), pp. 179–98.

Khoo Khay Jin, 'Revenue farming and state centralisation in nineteenth-century Kedah', in John Butcher and Howard Dick (eds), *The rise and fall of revenue farming: business elites and the emergence of the modern state in Southeast Asia* (Houndmills: Macmillan, 1993).

Kiernan, Ben, 'Wild chickens, farm chickens, and cormorants: Kampuchea's eastern zone under Pol Pot', in David P. Chandler and Ben Kiernan (eds), *Revolution and its aftermath in Kampuchea: eight essays* (New Haven: Monograph Series No. 5, Southeast Asia Studies, Yale University, 1983).

Kikuchi, Masao, 'Recent changes in a Laguna rice village: a new generation of changes?', in Antonio J. Ledesma, Perla Q. Makil, and Virginia A. Miralao, *Second view from the paddy: more empirical studies of Philippine rice farming and tenancy* (Manila: Ateneo de Manila University, 1983).

Kikuchi, Masao, 'Growing impact of off-farm employment on a rural economy: changes in labour utilization and income earning structure in a Philippine rice village', in R.T. Shand (ed.), *Off-farm employment in the development of rural*

Asia (Canberra: National Centre for Development Studies, Australian National University, 1986).

Kikuchi, Masao, and Yujiro Hayami, 'Technological and institutional response and income shares under demographic pressure: a comparison of Indonesian and Philippine villages', in Geoffrey B. Hainsworth (ed.), *Village-level modernization in Southeast Asia: the political economy of rice and water* (Vancouver: University of British Columbia Press, 1982).

Kikuchi, Yasushi, *Mindoro highlanders: the life of the swidden agriculturalist* (Quezon City: New Day Publishers, 1984).

King, Victor T., *The peoples of Borneo* (Oxford: Blackwell, 1993).

Knaags, Walter, 'A visit to Perak', *Journal of Eastern Asia* 1, 1 (1875), pp. 26–37.

Knight, G.R., 'Capitalism and commodity production in Java', in Hamza Alavi et al., *Capitalism and colonial production* (London: Croom Helm, 1982).

Knight, G.R., 'Peasant labour and capitalist production in late colonial Indonesia: the "campaign" at a north Java sugar factory, 1840–70', *JSEAS* 19, 2 (1985), pp. 245–65.

Knight, G.R., 'Sugar, peasants and proletarians in colonial southeastern Asia, 1830–1940', *CrA* 9, 2 (1988), pp. 39–63.

Knight, G.R., 'The peasantry and the cultivation of sugar cane in nineteenth-century Java: a study from Pekalongan residency, 1830–1870', in Anne Booth, W.J. O'Malley, and Anna Weidemann (eds), *Indonesian economic history in the Dutch colonial era* (New Haven: Monograph Series No. 35, Yale University Southeast Asia Studies, 1990).

Knight, G.R., 'The Java sugar industry as a capitalist plantation: a reappraisal', in E. Valentine Daniel, Henry Bernstein, and Tom Brass (eds), *Plantations, proletarians and peasants in colonial Asia* (London: Frank Cass, 1992).

Koch, Margaret Lindley, 'Malay society in Temerloh, Pahang, under British colonial rule 1889–1948', PhD dissertation, Columbia University, 1982.

Koenig, William J., *The Burmese polity, 1752–1819: politics, administration, and social organization in the early Kon-baung period* (Ann Arbor: Michigan Papers on South and Southeast Asia No. 34, Center for South and Southeast Asian Studies, University of Michigan, 1990).

Koentjaraningrat, 'The village in Indonesia today', in Koentjaraningrat (ed.), *Villages in Indonesia* (Ithaca: Cornell University Press, 1967).

Koentjaraningrat, 'Population mobility in villages around Jakarta', *BIES* 11, 2 (1975), pp. 108–19.

Koizumi, Junko, 'The commutation of *suai* from northeast Thailand in the middle of the nineteenth century', *JSEAS* 23, 2 (1992), pp. 276–307.

Koppel, Bruce, and John Hawkins, 'Rural transformation and the future of work in rural Asia', in Bruce Koppel, John Hawkins, and William James (eds), *Development or deterioration? Work in rural Asia* (Boulder: Lynne Rienner, 1994).

Kratoska, Paul H., 'Rice cultivation and the ethnic division of labour in British Malaya', *CSSH* 24, 2 (1982), pp. 280–314.

Kratoska, Paul H., '"Ends that we cannot foresee": Malay reservations in British Malaya', *JSEAS* 14, 1 (1983), pp. 149–68.

Kratoska, Paul H., 'Land law and land tenure in British Melaka', in Kernial Singh Sandhu and Paul Wheatley (eds), *Melaka: the transformation of a Malay capital c. 1400–1980* (Kuala Lumpur: Oxford University Press, 1983).

Kratoska, Paul H., 'Penghulus in Perak and Selangor: the rationalization and decline of a traditional Malay office', *JMBRAS* 57, 2 (1984), pp. 31–59.

Kratoska, Paul H., 'The peripatetic peasant and land tenure in British Malaya', *JSEAS* 16, 1 (1985), pp. 16–45.

Kratoska, Paul H., 'The post-1945 food shortage in British Malaya', *JSEAS* 19, 1 (1988), pp. 27–47.

Kratoska, Paul H., 'The British Empire and the Southeast Asian rice crisis of 1919–1921', *MAS* 24, 1 (1990), pp. 115–46.

Krishnamurty, J., 'Handicrafts in India and Indonesia in the nineteenth century', *Itinerario* 11, 1 (1987), pp. 253–64.

Kristanto, Kustiah, 'The smallholder cattle economy in South Sulawesi', *BIES* 18, 1 (1982), pp. 61–85.

Kroeber, A.L., *Peoples of the Philippines* (repr. Westport: Greenwood Press, 1973) [1928].

Kuchiba, Masuo, and Yoshihiro Tsubouchi, 'Paddy farming and social structure in a Malay village', *Review of Agricultural Economics Malaysia* 2, 1 (1968), pp. 9–34.

Kuchiba, Masuo, Yoshihiro Tsubouchi, and Narifumi Maeda (eds), *Three Malay villages: a sociology of paddy growers in West Malaysia* (Honolulu: University of Hawaii Press, 1979).

Kumar, A., 'The peasantry and the state on Java: changes of relationship, seventeenth to nineteenth centuries', in James J. Fox (ed.), *Indonesia: Australian perspectives* (Canberra: Research School of Pacific Studies, Australian National University, 1980).

Kunstadter, Peter, 'Hill and valley populations in northwestern Thailand', in Peter Hinton (ed.), *Tribesmen and peasants in north Thailand: proceedings of the first symposium of the Tribal Research Centre, Chiang Mai, Thailand, 1967* (Chiang Mai: Tribal Research Centre, 1967).

Kunstadter, Peter, 'The Lua? and Skaw Karen of Maehongson province, northwestern Thailand', in Peter Kunstadter (ed.), *Southeast Asian tribes, minorities and nations*, vol. 2 (Princeton: Princeton University Press, 1967).

Kunstadter, Peter, 'Alternatives for the development of upland areas', in Peter Kunstadter, E.C. Chapman, and Sanga Sabhasri (eds), *Farmers in the forest: economic development and marginal agriculture in northern Thailand* (Honolulu: University Press of Hawaii, 1978).

Kunstadter, Peter, 'Subsistence agricultural economies of Lua' and Karen hill farmers, Mae Sariang district, northwestern Thailand', in Peter Kunstadter, E.C. Chapman, and Sanga Sabhasri (eds), *Farmers in the forest: economic development and marginal agriculture in northern Thailand* (Honolulu: University Press of Hawaii, 1978).

Kunstadter, Peter, and E.C. Chapman, 'Problems of shifting cultivation and economic development in northern Thailand', in Peter Kunstadter, E.C. Chapman, and Sanga Sabhasri (eds), *Farmers in the forest: economic development and marginal agriculture in northern Thailand* (Honolulu: University Press of Hawaii, 1978).

Kuntowidjojo, 'Economic and religious attitudes of entrepreneurs in a village industry: notes on the community at Batur', *Indonesia* 12 (1971), pp. 47–55.

Kurasawa, Aiko, 'Japanese occupation and leadership changes in Javanese villages', in J. van Goor (ed.), *The Indonesian revolution* (Utrecht: Utrechtse Historische Cahiers, 1986).

Lains, Alfian, 'West Sumatra: the road to Parasamya Purnakarya Nugraha', in Hal Hill (ed.), *Unity in diversity: regional economic development in Indonesia since 1970* (Singapore: Oxford University Press, 1989).

Larkin, John A., *The Pampangans: colonial society in a Philippine province* (Berkeley: University of California Press, 1972).

Larkin, John A., 'Philippine history reconsidered: a socioeconomic perspective', *AHR* 87, 3 (1982), pp. 595–628.

Lawless, Robert, 'Societal ecology in northern Luzon: Kalinga agriculture, organization, population, and change', *Papers in Anthropology* 18, 1 (1977), pp. 1–136.

Le May, Reginald, *An Asian arcady: the land and peoples of northern Siam* (repr. Bangkok: White Lotus, 1986) [1926].

Le Roy, James A., *Philippine life in town and country* (New York: Putnam's Sons, 1905).

Leach, E.R., 'Some aspects of dry rice cultivation in north Burma and British Borneo', *Advancement of Science* 6 (1949), pp. 26–8.

Leach, E.R., *Political systems of highland Burma: a study of Kachin social structure* (Cambridge, Mass.: Harvard University Press, 1954).

Leach, E.R., 'The frontiers of "Burma"', *CSSH* 3, 1 (1960–61), pp. 49–68.

Lebar, Frank M. (ed.), *Ethnic groups of insular Southeast Asia* (New Haven: Human Relations Area Files Press, 1972–5).

Lebar, Frank M., Gerald C. Hickey, and John K. Musgrave, *Ethnic groups of mainland Southeast Asia* (New Haven: Human Relations Area Files Press, 1964).

Leckie, Charles Stuart, 'The commerce of Siam in relation to the trade of the British empire', in Chattip Nartsupha and Suthy Prasartset (eds), *The political economy of Siam 1851–1910* (Bangkok: The Social Science Association of Thailand, 1981).

Ledesma, Antonio, 'Land reform in East and Southeast Asia: a comparative approach', *PS* 28 (1980), pp. 305–43, 451–81.

Lee, E.L.H., 'Rural poverty in West Malaysia, 1957–70', in Anon., *Poverty and landlessness in rural Asia* (Geneva: International Labor Office, 1977).

Lee, Y.L., 'Land settlement for agriculture in North Borneo', *Tijdschrift voor Economisch en Sociale Geografie* 52 (1961), pp. 184–91.

Lee, Y.L., 'The long house and Dayak settlements in British Borneo', *OG* 6, 1 (1962), pp. 39–60.

Lefevre, Dominique, 'Details respecting Cochin China', *JIAEA* 1 (1847), pp. 49–65, 109–18.

Legarda, Benito, 'Two and a half centuries of the galleon trade', *PhS* 3–4 (1955), pp. 345–72.

Legarda, Benito, 'The Philippine economy under Spanish rule', *Solidarity* 2, 10 (1967), pp. 1–21.

Legendre, Sidney J., *Land of the white parasol and the million elephants; a journey through the jungles of Indo-China* (New York: Dodd, Mead and Co., 1936).

Lehman, F.K., 'Burma: Kayah society as a function of the Shan-Burma-Karen context', in Julian H. Steward (ed.), *Contemporary change in traditional societies. Volume II. Asian rural societies* (Urbana: University of Illinois Press, 1967).

Lehman, F.K., 'Freedom and bondage in traditional Burma and Thailand', *JSEAS* 15, 2 (1984), pp. 233–44.

Leinbach, Thomas R., 'Rural transport and population mobility in Indonesia', *Journal of Developing Areas* 17, 3 (1983), pp. 349–64.

Lewis, Henry T., 'Landlord and tenant', *PSR* 20, 1–2 (1972), pp. 188–97.

Librero, Aida R., 'An overview of food production programs in the Philippines', *KEM* 16, 1–2 (1979), pp. 15–30.

Lieberman, Victor B., 'The political significance of religious wealth in Burmese history: some further thoughts', *JAS* 39, 4 (1980), pp. 753–69.

Lieberman, Victor B., *Burmese administrative cycles: anarchy and conquest c. 1580–1760* (Princeton: Princeton University Press, 1984).

Lieberman, Victor B., 'Reinterpreting Burmese history', *CSSH* 29, 1 (1987), pp. 162–94.

Lieberman, Victor B., 'Secular trends in Burmese economic history, c. 1350–1830, and their implications for state formation', *MAS* 25, 1 (1990), pp. 1–31.

Lieberman, Victor B., 'Local integration and Eurasian analogies: structuring Southeast Asian history, c. 1350–c. 1830', *MAS* 27, 3 (1993), pp. 475–572.

Likhit Dhiravegin, 'The Meiji restoration (1868–1921) and the Chakkri reformation (1868–1910): a case for a comparative study', in Chira Hongladarom and Meedhi Krongkaew (eds), *Comparative development: Japan and Thailand* (Bangkok: Thammasat University Press, 1981).

Lim, David, *Economic growth and development in West Malaysia, 1947–1970* (Kuala Lumpur: Oxford University Press, 1973).

Lim Teck Ghee, *Peasants and their agricultural economy in colonial Malaya, 1874–1941* (Kuala Lumpur: Oxford University Press, 1977).

Lim Teck Ghee, 'Reconstituting the peasantry: changes in landholding structure in the Muda irrigation scheme', in Gillian Hart, Andrew Turton and Benjamin White with Brian Fegan and Lim Teck Ghee (eds), *Agrarian transformations: local processes and the state in Southeast Asia* (Berkeley: University of California Press, 1989).

Lim Teck Ghee and Muhammad Ikmal Said, 'Malaysia: rice peasants and political priorities in an economy undergoing restructuring', in Gillian Hart, Andrew Turton and Benjamin White with Brian Fegan and Lim Teck Ghee (eds), *Agrarian transformations: local processes and the state in Southeast Asia* (Berkeley: University of California Press, 1989).

Lim Teck Ghee and Richard Dorall, 'Contract farming in Malaysia with special reference to FELDA land schemes', in David Glover and Lim Teck Ghee (eds), *Contract farming in Southeast Asia: three country studies* (Kuala Lumpur: Institute of Advanced Studies, University of Malaya, 1992).

Lindblad, J. Thomas, 'Economic change in southeast Kalimantan 1880–1940', *BIES* 21 (1985), pp. 69–103.

Lindblad, J. Thomas, *Between Dayak and Dutch: the economic history of south Kalimantan 1880–1942* (Dordrecht: Foris, 1988).

Lindblad, J. Thomas, 'Economic aspects of the Dutch expansion in Indonesia 1870–1914', *MAS* 23, 1 (1989), pp. 1–23.

Lineton, Jacqueline, 'Pasompe' ugi': Bugis migrants and wanderers', *Archipel* 10 (1975), pp. 173–201.

Little, Daniel, 'Rational-choice models and Asian studies', *JAS* 50, 1 (1991), pp. 35–52.

Lockard, Craig A., 'The Javanese as emigrant: observations on the development of Javanese settlements overseas', *Indonesia* 11 (1971), pp. 41–62.

Loeb, Edwin M., *Sumatra: its history and people* (repr. Kuala Lumpur: Oxford University Press, 1972) [1935].

Loekman Soetrisno, 'The sugar industry and rural development: the impact of cane cultivation for export on rural Java: 1830–1934', PhD dissertation, Cornell University, 1980.

Lopez-Gonzaga, Violeta, *Peasants in the hills: a study of the dynamics of social change among the Buhid swidden cultivators in the Philippines* (Quezon City: University of the Philippines Press, 1983).

Low, Hugh, *Sarawak: its inhabitants and productions* (repr. London: Frank Cass, 1968) [1848].

Low, James, *The British settlement of Penang* (repr. Singapore: Oxford University Press, 1972) [1836].

Luong, Hy Van, 'Agrarian unrest from an anthropological perspective: the case of Vietnam', *Comparative Politics* 17, 2 (1985), pp. 153–74.

Luong, Hy V., *Revolution in the village: tradition and transformation in North Vietnam, 1925–1988* (Honolulu: University of Hawaii Press, 1992).

Luton, Harry, 'American internal revenue policy in the Philippines to 1916', in Norman G. Owen (ed.), *Compadre colonialism: studies on the Philippines under American rule* (Ann Arbor: Michigan Papers on South and Southeast Asia No. 3, Center for South and Southeast Asian Studies, University of Michigan, 1971).

Ma Mya Sein, *Administration of Burma. Sir Charles Crosthwaite and the consolidation of Burma* (repr. Kuala Lumpur: Oxford University Press, 1973) [1938].

Mabry, Bevars D., 'Peasant economic behaviour in Thailand', *JSEAS* 10, 1 (1970), pp. 400–19.

MacAndrews, Colin, H. Benjamin Fisher, and Atar Siero, 'Regional development, planning and implementation in Indonesia: the evolution of a national policy', in Colin MacAndrews and Chia Lin Sien (eds), *Too rapid rural development: perceptions and perspectives from Southeast Asia* (Athens, Ohio: Ohio University Press, 1982).

Mackie, J.A.C., 'The changing political economy of an export crop: the case of Jember's tobacco industry', *BIES* 21, 1 (1985), pp. 113–39.

Mackie, J.A.C., and Djumilah Zain, 'East Java: balanced growth and diversification', in Hal Hill (ed.), *Unity in diversity: regional economic development in Indonesia since 1970* (Singapore: Oxford University Press, 1989).

Mackie, J.A.C., and W.J. O'Malley, 'Productivity decline in the Java sugar industry from an Olsonian perspective', *CSSH* 30, 4 (1988), pp. 725–49.

Mackie, Jamie, 'Plantations and cash crops in East Java: changing patterns', in Howard Dick, James J. Fox, and Jamie Mackie (eds), *Balanced development: East Java in the New Order* (Singapore: Oxford University Press, 1993).

Mackie, Jamie, 'The East Java economy: from dualism to balanced development', in Howard, Dick, James J. Fox, and Jamie Mackie (eds), *Balanced development: East Java in the New Order* (Singapore: Oxford University Press, 1993).

MacMicking, Robert, *Recollections of Manilla and the Philippines during 1848, 1849 and 1850* (repr. Manila: Filipiniana Book Guild, 1967) [1852].

MacPhail, Fiona, and Paul Bowles, 'Technical change and intra-household welfare: a case study of irrigated rice production in South Sulawesi, Indonesia', *JDS* 26, 1 (1989), pp. 58–80.

Mahoney, Timothy, 'Local political and economic structures', in Gary Hansen (ed.), *Agricultural and rural development in Indonesia* (Boulder: Westview, 1981).

Mai, Ulrich, 'Small-town markets and the urban economy in kabupaten Minahasa', *Indonesia* 37 (1984), pp. 48–58.

Makaliwe, W.H., and Ace Partadireja, 'An economic survey of east Nusatenggara', *BIES* 10, 1 (1974), pp. 33–54.

Makil, Lorna Pena-Reyes, and Patricia N. Fermin, *Landless rural workers in the Philippines: a documentary survey* (Quezon City: Institute of Philippine Culture, Ateneo de Manila University, 1978).

Malcolm, Howard, *Travels in south-eastern Asia* (London: Charles Tilt, 1839).

Manawia, M.D., 'The life of the Nueva Ecija peasant', *JEAS* 4 (1955), pp. 279–81.

Mangahas, Mahar, 'The political economy of rice in the New Society', *FRIS* 14, 3 (1975), pp. 295–309.

Manning, C., 'Public policy, rice production and income distribution: a review of Indonesia's rice self-sufficiency program', *Southeast Asian Journal of Social Science* 15, 1 (1987), pp. 66–82.

Manning, Chris, 'Rural economic change and labour mobility: a case study from West Java', *BIES* 23, 3 (1987), pp. 52–79.

Manning, Chris, 'Rural employment creation in Java: lessons from the Green Revolution and the oil boom', *Population and Development Review* 14, 1 (1988), pp. 47–80.

Manning, Chris, 'Survey of recent developments', *BIES* 28, 1 (1992), pp. 3–38.

Manning, Chris, and Ross Garnaut, 'An economic survey of West Irian, Part I', *BIES* 8, 3 (1972), pp. 33–65.

Manning, Chris, and Michael Rumbiak, 'Irian Jaya: economic change, migrants, and indigenous welfare', in Hal Hill (ed.), *Unity in diversity: regional economic development in Indonesia since 1970* (Singapore: Oxford University Press, 1989).

Mannsdorf, Hans, 'The hill tribe program of the Public Welfare Department, Ministry of Interior, Thailand: research and socio-economic development', in Peter Kunstadter (ed.), *Southeast Asian tribes, minorities and nations*, vol. 2 (Princeton: Princeton University Press, 1967).

Mansvelt, W.M.F., and P. Creutzberg (eds), *Changing economy in Indonesia. A selection of statistical source material from the early 19th century up to 1940. Volume 1. Indonesia's export crops 1816–1940* (The Hague: Martinus Nijhoff, 1975).

Marlowe, David H., 'Upland-lowland relationships: the case of the S'kaw Karen of central upland western Chiang Mai', in Peter Hinton (ed.), *Tribesmen and peasants in north Thailand: proceedings of the first symposium of the Tribal Research Centre, Chiang Mai, Thailand, 1967* (Chiang Mai: Tribal Research Centre, 1967).

Marsden, William, *The history of Sumatra* (repr. Kuala Lumpur: Oxford University Press, 1966) [1811].

Marshall, Harry Ignatius, *The Karen people of Burma: a study in anthropology and ethnology* (repr. New York: AMB Press, 1980) [1922].

Maurer, Jean-Luc, 'Agricultural modernization and social change: the case of Java over the last fifteen years', *MI* 11, 2 (1984), pp. 109–19.

Maurer, Jean-Luc, 'Beyond the sawah: economic diversification in four Bantul villages, 1972–1987', in Paul Alexander, P. Boomgaard and B. White (eds), *In the shadow of agriculture: non-farm activities in the Javanese economy, past and present* (Amsterdam: Royal Tropical Institute, 1991).

May, Glenn Anthony, *Social engineering in the Philippines: the aims, execution and impact of American colonial policy, 1900–1913* (Westport: Greenwood Press, 1980).

McCarthy, James, *Surveying and exploring in Siam* (London: John Murray, 1902).

McCawley, Peter, 'Survey of recent developments', *BIES* 9, 3 (1973), pp. 1–27.

McCawley, Peter, 'Survey of recent developments', *BIES* 12, 1 (1976), pp. 1–43.

McCawley, Peter, 'Survey of recent developments', *BIES* 21, 1 (1985), pp. 1–31.

McCawley, Peter, and Chris Manning, 'Survey of recent developments', *BIES* 12, 3 (1976), pp. 1–49.

McCoy, Alfred W., 'French colonialism in Laos', in Nina S. Adams and Alfred W. McCoy (eds), *Laos: war and revolution* (New York: Harper Colophon, 1970).

McCoy, Alfred William, 'Yli-ilo: factional conflict in a colonial economy, Iloilo province, Philippines, 1937–1955', PhD dissertation, Yale University, 1977.

McCoy, Alfred W., 'Introduction: the social history of an archipelago', in Alfred W. McCoy and Ed. C. de Jesus (eds), *Philippine social history: global trade and local transformations* (Sydney: Allen and Unwin, 1981).

McCoy, Alfred W., 'A queen dies slowly: the rise and decline of Iloilo city', in Alfred W. McCoy and Ed. C. de Jesus (eds), *Philippine social history: global trade and local transformations* (Sydney: Allen and Unwin, 1981).

McCoy, Alfred W., 'Sugar barons: formation of a native planter class in the colonial Philippines', in E. Valentine Daniel, Henry Bernstein and Tom Brass (eds), *Plantations, proletarians and peasants in colonial Asia* (London: Frank Cass, 1992).

McDonald, Peter, 'An historical perspective to population growth in Indonesia', in James J. Fox et al. (eds), *Indonesia: Australian perspectives* (Canberra: Research School of Pacific Studies, Australian National University, 1980).

McLennan, Marshall Seaton, 'Peasant and hacendero in Nueva Ecija: the socio-economic origins of a Philippine commercial rice-growing region', PhD dissertation, University of California at Berkeley, 1973.

McMillan, Robert T., 'Land tenure in the Philippines', *Rural Sociology* 20 (1955), pp. 25–33.

McNicoll, Geoffrey, 'Internal migration in Indonesia: descriptive notes', *Indonesia* 5 (1968), pp. 29–92.

McStocker, Robert, 'The Indonesian coffee industry', *BIES* 23, 1 (1987), pp. 40–69.

McVey, Ruth T., 'Local voices, central power', in Ruth T. McVey (ed.), *Southeast Asian transitions: approaches through local history* (New Haven: Yale University Press, 1978).

Mears, Leon A., 'A new approach to rice intensification', *BIES* 6, 2 (1970), pp. 106–11.

Mears, Leon, 'Problems of supply and marketing of food in Indonesia in Repelita III', *BIES* 14, 3 (1978), pp. 52–62.

Mears, Leon A., *The new rice economy of Indonesia* (Yogyakarta: Gadjah Mada University Press, 1981).

Mears, Leon A., and Saleh Afiff, 'A new look at the BIMAS program and rice production', *BIES* 10 (1968), pp. 29–44.

Mears, Leon A., Meliza H. Agabin, Teresa L. Anden, and Rosalinda C. Marquez, *Rice economy of the Philippines* (Quezon City: University of the Philippines Press, 1974).

Meyer, Hans, 'A trip to the Igorots in the interior', in William Henry Scott (ed.), *German travelers on the Cordillera (1860–1890)* (Manila: Filipiniana Book Guild, 1975).

Mink, Stephen D., Paul A. Dorosh, and Douglas H. Perry, 'Corn production systems', in C. Peter Timmer, *The corn economy of Indonesia* (Ithaca: Cornell University Press, 1987).

Mintz, Sidney W., 'A note on the definition of peasantries', *JPS* 1, 1 (1973), pp. 91–106.

Mitchell, B.R., *International historical statistics: Africa and Asia* (New York: New York University Press, 1982).

Mizuno, Koichi, 'The social organization of rice-growing villages', in Yoneo Ishii (ed.), *Thailand: a rice-growing society* (Honolulu: University Press of Hawaii, 1970).

Moerman, M., *Agricultural change and peasant choice in a Thai village* (Berkeley: University of California Press, 1968).

Moise, Edwin E., *Land reform in China and North Vietnam: consolidating the revolution at the village level* (Chapel Hill: University of North Carolina Press, 1983).

Monk, Paul M., *Truth and power: Robert S. Hardie and land reform debates in the Philippines, 1950–1957* (Clayton: Monash Paper No. 20, Centre of Southeast Asian Studies, Monash University, 1990).

Monke, Eric, and Scott Pearson, 'The international rice market', in Scott Pearson, Walter Falcon, Paul Heytens, Eric Monke, and Rosamund Naylor, *Rice policy in Indonesia* (Ithaca: Cornell University Press, 1991).

Montgomery, Roger, 'Employment generation within the agricultural sector', in Gary Hansen (ed.), *Agricultural and rural development in Indonesia* (Boulder: Westview, 1981).

Montgomery, Roger, 'Maize yield increases in east Java', *BIES* 17, 3 (1981), pp. 74–85.

Montgomery, Roger, and Toto Sugito, 'Changes in the structure of farms and farming in Indonesia between censuses, 1963–1973: the issues of inequality and near-landlessness', *JSEAS* 2 (1980), pp. 348–65.

Moor, J.H., *Notices of the Indian archipelago, and adjacent countries* (repr. London: Frank Cass, 1968) [1837].

Morrison, Philip S., 'Transitions in rural Sarawak: off-farm employment in the Kemena Basin', *PV* 34, 1 (1993), pp. 45–68.

Mote, F.W., 'The rural "Haw" (Yunnanese Chinese) of northern Thailand', in Peter Kunstadter (ed.), *Southeast Asian tribes, minorities and nations,* vol. 2 (Princeton: Princeton University Press, 1967).

Motooka, Takeshi, 'The conditions governing agricultural development in Southeast Asia', in Shinichi Ichimura (ed.), *Southeast Asia: nature, society and development* (Honolulu: University Press of Hawaii, 1976).

Motooka, Takeshi, 'Rice exports and the expansion of cultivation', in Yonei Ishii (ed.), *Thailand: a rice growing society* (Honolulu: University Press of Hawaii, 1978).

Mubyarto, 'The sugar industry: from estate to smallholder production', *BIES* 13, 2 (1977), pp. 29–44.

Murray, Francis J., 'Land reform in the Philippines: an overview', *PSR* 20, 1–2 (1972), pp. 151–68.

Murray, Martin J., *The development of capitalism in colonial Indochina (1870–1940)* (Berkeley: University of California Press, 1980).

Murray, Martin J., '"White gold" or "white blood"? The rubber plantations of colonial Indochina, 1910–40', in E. Valentine Daniel, Henry Bernstein, and Tom Brass (eds), *Plantations, proletarians and peasants in colonial Asia* (London: Frank Cass, 1992).

Mya Maung, 'Military management of the Burmese economy: problems and prospects', in Josef Silverstein (ed.), *The future of Burma in perspective: a symposium* (Athens, Ohio: Center for International Studies, Papers in International Studies, Southeast Asia Series No. 35, 1974).

Mya Maung, *The Burma road to poverty* (New York: Praeger, 1991).

Mya Than, 'A Burmese village – revisited', *Southeast Asian Review* 2, 2 (1978), pp. 1–15.

Mya Than, 'Little change in rural Burma: a case study of a Burmese village (1860–1980)', *Sojourn* 2, 1 (1987), pp. 55–88.

Mya Than and J.L.H. Tan, 'Introduction: optimism for Myanmar's economic transition in the 1990s?', in Mya Than and Joseph L.H. Tan (eds), *Myanmar dilemmas and options: the challenges of economic transition in the 1990s* (Singapore: ISEAS, 1990).

Mya Than and Nobuyoshi Nishizawa, 'Agricultural policy reforms and agricultural development in Myanmar', in Mya Than and Joseph L.H. Tan (eds), *Myanmar dilemmas and options: the challenges of economic transition in the 1990s* (Singapore: ISEAS, 1990).

Nag, Moni, Benjamin N.F. White, and R. Creighton Peet, 'An anthropological approach to the study of the economic value of children in Java and Nepal', in Hans P. Binswanger et al. (eds), *Rural household studies in Asia* (Singapore: Singapore University Press, 1980).

Napitupulu, B., 'Hunger in Indonesia', *BIES* no. 9 (1968), pp. 60–70.

Narongchai Akrasanee and Atchana Wattananukit, 'Comparative advantage in rice production in Thailand', *FRIS* 15, 2 (1976), pp. 177–212.

Nas, P.J.M., 'Town and countryside in Indonesia: a sceptic's view', *Sojourn* 4, 1 (1989), pp. 20–33.

Nash, Manning, *The golden road to modernity: village life in contemporary Burma* (Chicago: University of Chicago Press, 1965).

Naylor, Rosamund Lee, 'Rice and the rural labor market in Indonesia', PhD dissertation, Stanford University, 1989.

Naylor, Rosamund, 'Equity effects of rice strategies', in Scott Pearson, Walter Falcon, Paul Heytens, Eric Monke, and Rosamund Naylor, *Rice policy in Indonesia* (Ithaca: Cornell University Press, 1991).

Naylor, Rosamund, 'The rural labor market in Indonesia', in Scott Pearson, Walter Falcon, Paul Heytens, Eric Monke, and Rosamund Naylor, *Rice policy in Indonesia* (Ithaca: Cornell University Press, 1991).

Naylor, Rosamund, 'Culture and agriculture: employment practices affecting women in Java's rice economy', *EDCC* 42, 3 (1994), pp. 509–35.

Newbold, T.J., *Political and statistical account of the British settlements in the Straits of Malacca* (repr. Kuala Lumpur: Oxford University Press, 1971) [1839].

Ng Shui Menh, *The population of Indochina* (Singapore: ISEAS, 1974).

Ng, Ronald C.Y., 'Some land-use problems of north-east Thailand', *MAS* 4, 1 (1970), pp. 23–42.

Ng, Ronald, 'Man and land in northeast Thailand', in P.A. Stott (ed.), *Nature and man in Southeast Asia* (London: School of Oriental and African Studies, 1978).

Ngo Vinh Long, *Before the revolution: the Vietnamese peasants under the French* (Cambridge, Mass.: MIT Press, 1973).

Ngo Vinh Long, 'View from the village', *Indochina Issues* 12 (1980), pp. 1, 4–7.

Ngo Vinh Long, 'Some aspects of cooperativization in the Mekong delta', in David G. Marr and Christine P. White (eds), *Postwar Vietnam: dilemmas in socialist development* (Ithaca: Cornell University Southeast Asia Program, 1988).

Ngo Vinh Long, 'Vietnam: the real enemy', *BCAS* 21, 2–4 (1989), pp. 6–34.

Nguyen Tien Hung, *Economic development of socialist Vietnam, 1955–80* (New York: Praeger, 1977).

Nguyen Xuan Lai, 'Questions of agrarian structures and agricultural development in southern Vietnam', *Vietnamese Studies* (new series) 5 (1984), pp. 22–64.

Nibbering, Jan Willem, 'Crisis and resilience in upland land use in Java', in Joan Hardjono (ed.), *Indonesia: resources, ecology and environment* (Singapore: Oxford University Press, 1991).

Nibbering, J.W., 'Agricultural diversification in the Upper Konto region', in Howard Dick, James J. Fox, and Jamie Mackie (eds), *Balanced development: East Java in the New Order* (Singapore: Oxford University Press, 1993).

Nibbering, J.W., and A. Schrevel, *The role of additional activities in rural Java: a case study of two villages in the Malang Regency* (Utrecht: Geografisch Instituut, Rijksuniversiteit Utrecht, 1982).

Nipon Poapongsakom, 'Transformations in the Thai rural labor market', in Bruce Koppel, John Hawkins, and William James (eds), *Development or deterioration? Work in rural Asia* (Boulder: Lynne Rienner, 1994).

Nurge, Ethel, *Life in a Leyte village* (Seattle: University of Washington Press, 1965).

Nuttonson, M.Y., *The physical environment and agriculture of Thailand* (Washington DC: American Institute of Crop Ecology, 1963).

O'Malley, William Joseph, 'Indonesia in the Great Depression: a study of East Sumatra and Jogjakarta in the 1930s', PhD dissertation, Cornell University, 1977.

Ofreneo, Rene E., *Capitalism in Philippines agriculture* (Quezon City: Foundation for Nationalist Studies, 1980).

Oki, Akira, 'Social change in the west Sumatran village: 1908–1945', PhD dissertation, Australian National University, 1977.

Oki, Akira, 'The river trade in central and south Sumatra in the 19th century', in Tsuyoshi Kato, Muchtar Lutfi, and Narifumi Maeda (eds), *Environment, agriculture and society in the Malay world* (Kyoto: Center for Southeast Asian Studies, Kyoto University, 1986).

Onghokham, 'The residency of Madiun. Pryayi and peasant in the nineteenth century', PhD dissertation, Yale University, 1975.

Ooi Jin Bee, *Land, people and economy in Malaya* (London: Longmans, 1963).

Ooi Jin Bee, *Depletion of forest resources in the Philippines* (Singapore: ISEAS, 1987).

Oppenfeld, Horst and Judith et al., 'Labor force and utilization', in Socorro C. Espiritu and Chester L. Hunt (eds), *Social foundations of community development* (Manila: R.M. Garcia, 1964).

Osborne, Milton E., *The French presence in Cochinchina and Cambodia: rule and response (1859–1905)* (Ithaca: Cornell University Press, 1969).

Oshima, Harry T., 'The transition from an agricultural to an industrial economy in East Asia', *EDCC* 34, 4 (1986), pp. 783–809.

Otsuka, Keijiro, Violeta Cordova, and Cristina C. David, 'Green Revolution, land reform, and household income distribution in the Philippines', *EDCC* 40 (1992), pp. 719–41.

Ouchi, Tsutomu, Naomi Saeki, Akira Takahashi, Kenzo Horii, Manabu Tanaka, *Farmers and villagers in West Malaysia* (Tokyo: Faculty of Economics, University of Tokyo, 1977).

Owen, Norman G., 'On using the Philippine census', in Norman G. Owen (ed.), *Compadre colonialism: studies on the Philippines under American rule* (Ann Arbor: Michigan Papers on South and Southeast Asia No. 3, Center for South and Southeast Asian Studies, University of Michigan, 1971).

Owen, Norman G., 'Philippine economic development and American policy: a reappraisal', in Norman G. Owen (ed.), *Compadre colonialism: studies on the Philippines under American rule* (Ann Arbor: Michigan Papers on South and Southeast Asia No. 3, Center for South and Southeast Asian Studies, University of Michigan, 1971).

Owen, Norman G., 'The rice industry of mainland Southeast Asia, 1850–1914', *JSS* 59, 2 (1971), pp. 75–143.

Owen, Norman G., 'Colonialism, development and under-development in Burma', *JAS* 35, 1 (1975), pp. 115–9.

Owen, Norman G., 'Textile displacement and the status of women in Southeast Asia', in Gordon P. Means (ed.), *The past in Southeast Asia's present* (Ottawa: Canadian Council for Southeast Asian Studies, 1978).

Owen, Norman G., *Prosperity without progress: Manila hemp and material life in the colonial Philippines* (Quezon City: Ateneo de Manila University Press, 1984).

Owen, Norman G., 'A subsistence crisis in the provincial Philippines 1845–1846', *Kina Adman* 8 (1986), pp. 35–46.

Owen, Norman G., 'The paradox of nineteenth-century population growth in Southeast Asia: evidence from Java and the Philippines', *JSEAS* 18, 1 (1987), pp. 45–57.

Owen, Norman G., 'Towards a history of health in Southeast Asia', in Norman G. Owen (ed.), *Death and disease in Southeast Asia: explorations in social, medical and demographic history* (Singapore: Oxford University Press, 1987).

Owen, Norman G., 'Subsistence in the slump: agricultural adjustment in the provincial Philippines', in Ian Brown (ed.), *The economies of Africa and Asia in the inter-war depression* (London: Routledge, 1989).

Owen, Norman G., 'Economic and social change', in Nicholas Tarling (ed.), *The Cambridge history of Southeast Asia*, vol. 2 (Cambridge: Cambridge University Press, 1992).

Pahilanga-De Los Reyes, Romana, and Frank Lynch, 'Reluctant rebels: leasehold converts in Nueva Ecija', *PSR* 20, 1–2 (1972), pp. 7–78.

Palmer, Ingrid, 'Rural poverty in Indonesia with special reference to Java', in *Poverty and landlessness in rural Asia* (Geneva: International Labour Office, 1977).

Palmer, Ingrid, 'Technology and peasant production: a comment', *DC* 8, 3 (1977), pp. 368–70.

Palte, Jan G.L., *The development of Java's rural uplands in reference to population growth: an introductory essay in historical perspective* (Yogyakarta: Faculty of Geography, Gadjah Mada University, 1984).

Palte, J.G.L., *Upland farming on Java, Indonesia: a socio-economic study of upland agriculture and subsistence under population pressure* (Den Haag: CIP-Gegevens Koninklijke Bibliotheek, 1989).

Pannee Auansakul, 'Chinese rice traders in Thailand', in Hans-Dieter Evers and Heiko Schrader (eds), *The moral economy of trade: ethnicity and developing markets* (London: Routledge, 1994).

Papanek, Gustav F., 'Agricultural income distribution and employment in the 1970s', *BIES* 21, 2 (1985), pp. 24–50.

Partadireja, Ace, 'Rural credit: the ijon system', *BIES* 10, 3 (1974), pp. 54–71.

Partadireja, Atje, 'An economic survey of Central Java', *BIES* 5, 3 (1969), pp. 29–46.

Partadireja, Atje, 'An economic survey of South Kalimantan', *BIES* 6, 2 (1970), pp. 46–65.

Patten, Richard H., and Jay K. Rosengard, *Progress with profits: the development of rural banking in Indonesia* (San Francisco: ICS Press, 1991).

Pearson, Scott, 'Summary and conclusions', in Scott Pearson, Walter Falcon, Paul Heytens, Eric Monke, and Rosamund Naylor, *Rice policy in Indonesia* (Ithaca: Cornell University Press, 1991).

Pearson, Scott, Rosamund Taylor, and Walter Falcon, 'Recent policy influences on rice production', in Scott Pearson, Walter Falcon, Paul Heytens, Eric Monke, and Rosamund Naylor, *Rice policy in Indonesia* (Ithaca: Cornell University Press, 1991).

Peletz, Michael G., 'Moral and political economies in rural Southeast Asia: a review article', *CSSH* 25, 4 (1983), pp. 731–9.

Peletz, Michael Gates, *A share of the harvest: kinship, property, and social history among the Malays of Rembau* (Berkeley: University of California Press, 1988).

Peluso, Nancy Lee, 'The history of state forest management in colonial Java', *Forest & Conservation History* 35 (1991), pp. 65–75.

Pelzer, Karl J., *Pioneer settlement in the Asiatic tropics: studies in land utilization and agricultural colonization in southeastern Asia* (New York: American Geographical Society, 1945).

Pelzer, Karl J., *Planter and peasant: colonial policy and the agrarian struggle in east Sumatra 1863–1947* ('s Gravenhage: Martinus Nijhoff, 1978).

Pelzer, Karl J., 'Swidden cultivation in Southeast Asia: historical, ecological and economic perspectives', in Peter Kunstadter et al. (eds), *Farmers in the forest: economic development and marginal agriculture in northern Thailand* (Honolulu: University Press of Hawaii, 1978).

Pelzer, Karl J., *Planters against peasants: the agrarian struggle in east Sumatra 1947–1958* ('s Gravenhage: Martinus Nijhoff, 1982).

Pendleton, Robert L., *Thailand: aspects of landscape and life* (repr. Westport: Greenwood, 1976) [1962].

Penny, D.H., 'Hunger in Indonesia: comments', *BIES* 9 (1968), pp. 773–4.

Penny, D.H., and Masri Singarimbun, 'A case study of rural poverty', *BIES* 8, 1 (1972), pp. 79–88.
Perlin, Frank, 'State formation reconsidered', *MAS* 19, 3 (1985), pp. 415–80.
Perlin, Frank, 'Disarticulation of the world: writing India's economic history: a review article', *CSSH* 30, 2 (1988), pp. 379–87.
Pham Cao Duong, *The Vietnamese peasants under French domination 1861–1941* (Lanham MD: University Press of America, 1985).
Philippine Assistant on Community Development, 'The barrio in 1957', in Socorro C. Espiritu and Chester L. Hunt (eds), *Social foundations of community development* (Manila: R.M. Garcia, 1964).
Piker, Steven, 'The post-peasant village in Central Plain Thai society', in G. William Skinner and A. Thomas Kirsch (eds), *Change and persistence in Thai society: essays in honor of Lauriston Sharp* (Ithaca: Cornell University Press, 1975).
Piker, Steven, 'The closing of the frontier: land pressures and their implementation for rural social organization in the Thai central plain', *CAS* 9 (1976), pp. 7–26.
Pingali, Prabhu L., and Vo-Tong Xuan, 'Vietnam: decollectivisation and rice productivity growth', *EDCC* 40 (1992), pp. 698–718.
Pingali, Prabu, and Hans P. Binswanger, 'Population density and farming systems: the changing locus of innovations and technical change', in Ronald D. Lee et al. (eds), *Population, food and rural development* (Oxford: Clarendon Press, 1988).
Pitt, Mark M., and Mark R. Rosenzweig, 'Agricultural price, food consumption and the health and productivity of Indonesian farmers', in I. Singh, L. Squire, and J. Strauss (eds), *Agricultural household models* (Baltimore: Johns Hopkins University Press, 1986).
Pletcher, James, 'Public interventions in agricultural markets in Malaysia: rice and palm oil', *MAS* 24, 2 (1990), pp. 323–40.
Popkin, Samuel L., *The rational peasant: the political economy of rural society in Vietnam* (Berkeley: University of California Press, 1979).
Pornpun Futrakul, 'The environmental history of pre-modern provincial towns in Siam to 1910', PhD dissertation, Cornell University, 1989.
Potter, Jack, *Thai peasant social structure* (Chicago: University of Chicago Press, 1976).
Potter, Lesley, and Ali Hasymi, 'South Kalimantan: the Banjarese heartland', in Hal Hill (ed.), *Unity in diversity: regional economic development in Indonesia since 1970* (Singapore: Oxford University Press, 1989).
Potter, Sulamith Heins, *Family life in a northern Thai village: a study in the structural significance of women* (Berkeley: University of California Press, 1977).
Preston, David A., 'Too busy to farm: under-utilisation of farm land in central Java', *JDS* 26, 1 (1989), pp. 43–57.
Prill-Brett, June, 'The Bontok: traditional wet-rice and swidden cultivators of the Philippines', in Gerald G. Marten (ed.), *Traditional agriculture in Southeast Asia* (Boulder: Westview, 1986).
Purcal, J.T., 'Employment pattern in rice growing areas of West Malaysia', in David Lim (ed.), *Readings on Malaysian economic development* (Kuala Lumpur: Oxford University Press, 1975).
Raffles, Sophia, *Memoir of the life and public services of Sir Thomas Stamford Raffles* (London: John Murray, 1830).

Raffles, T.S., *Substance of a minute recorded by the honourable Thomas Stamford Raffles, lieutenant-governor of Java and its dependencies, on the 11th February 1814* (London: Black, Parry, 1814).

Raffles, Thomas Stamford, *A history of Java* (repr. Kuala Lumpur: Oxford University Press, 1978) [1817].

Rambo, A. Terry, 'Orang asli adaptive strategies: implications for Malaysian natural resource development planning', in Colin MacAndrews and Chia Lin Sien (eds), *Too rapid rural development: perceptions and perspectives from Southeast Asia* (Athens, Ohio: Ohio University Press, 1982).

Rambo, A. Terry, and Percy E. Sajise (eds), *An introduction to human ecology research on agricultural systems in Southeast Asia* (Los Baños: University of the Philippines at Los Baños, 1984).

Ramsay, Ansil, 'Modernization and reactionary rebellions in northern Siam', *JAS* 38, 2 (1979), pp. 283–97.

Ramsay, Ansil, 'Tenancy and landlessness in Thailand: how severe a problem?', *AS* 22, 11 (1982), pp. 1074–92.

Ramsay, James Ansil, 'Modernization and centralization in northern Thailand, 1875–1910', *JSEAS* 7, 1 (1976), pp. 16–32.

Ray, Rajat Kanta, 'Chinese financiers and Chetti bankers in southern waters: Asian mobile credit during the Anglo-Dutch competition for the trade of the eastern archipelago in the nineteenth century', *Itinerario* 11, 1 (1987), pp. 209–34.

Reed, Robert R., 'Corn', in Robert Huke (ed.), *Shadows on the land: an economic geography of the Philippines* (Manila: Bookmark, 1963).

Reed, Robert R., 'The tobacco industry', in Robert Huke (ed.), *Shadows on the land: an economic geography of the Philippines* (Manila: Bookmark, 1963).

Reid, Anthony, 'The Japanese occupation and rival Indonesian elites: North Sumatra in 1942', *JAS* 35, 1 (1975), pp. 49–61.

Reid, Anthony, *The blood of the people: revolution and the end of traditional rule in northern Sumatra* (Kuala Lumpur: Oxford University Press, 1979).

Reid, Anthony, *Southeast Asia in the age of commerce, 1450–1680. Volume I: the lands below the winds* (New Haven: Yale University Press, 1988).

Reid, Anthony, 'An "age of commerce" in Southeast Asian history', *MAS* 24, 1 (1990), pp. 1–30.

Reid, Anthony, *Southeast Asia in the age of commerce, 1450–1680. Volume II: expansion and crisis* (New Haven: Yale University Press, 1993).

Reid, Anthony, and Shiraishi Saya, 'Rural unrest in Sumatra, 1942: a Japanese report', *Indonesia* 21 (1976), pp. 115–33.

Renard, Ronald D., 'The role of the Karens in Thai society during the early Bangkok period, 1782–1873', *CAS* 15 (1980), pp. 15–28.

Resnick, Stephen A., 'The decline of rural industry under export expansion: a comparison among Burma, Philippines, and Thailand, 1870–1938', *JEH* 30, 1 (1970), pp. 51–73.

Rice, Robert C., and David Lim, 'Survey of recent developments', *BIES* 12, 2 (1976), pp. 1–29.

Rice, Robert C., and Hal Hill, 'Survey of recent developments', *BIES* 13, 2 (1977), pp. 1–28.

Richardson, Jim, 'Does grass-roots action lead to agrarian reform?', *PSR* 20, 1–2 (1972), pp. 143–50.

Richter, H.V., 'The high yield program in Burma', in R.T. Shand (ed.), *Technical change in Asian agriculture* (Canberra: Australian National University Press, 1973).

Richter, H.V., and C.T. Edwards, 'Recent economic developments in Thailand', in Robert Ho and E.C. Chapman (eds), *Studies of contemporary Thailand* (Canberra: Department of Human Geography, Research School of Pacific Studies, Australian National University, 1973).

Ricklefs, M.C., 'Some statistical evidence on Javanese social, economic and demographic history in the later seventeenth and eighteenth centuries', *MAS* 20, 1 (1986), pp. 1–32.

Rieffel, Alexis, 'The BIMAS program for self-sufficiency in rice production', *Indonesia* 8 (1969), pp. 103–33.

Rigg, Jonathan, 'The Chinese agricultural middleman in Thailand: efficient or exploitative?', *SJTG* 7, 1 (1986), pp. 68–79.

Rivera, Generoso F., and Robert T. McMillan, *An economic and social survey of rural households in central Luzon* (Manila: Philippine Council for United States Aid/United States of America Operations Mission to the Philippines, 1954).

Rivera, Generoso F., and Robert T. McMillan, *The rural Philippines* (Manila: Mutual Security Agency, 1952).

Riwanto Tirtosudarmo and Paul Meyer, 'Migration', in Howard Dick, James J. Fox, and Jamie Mackie (eds), *Balanced development: East Java in the New Order* (Singapore: Oxford University Press, 1993).

Robequain, Charles, *The economic development of French Indo-China* (London: Oxford University Press, 1944).

Roberts, Edmund, *Embassy to the eastern courts of Cochin-China, Siam and Muscat during the years 1832, 1833, 1834* (repr. New York: Harper, 1972).

Roekasah, E.A., and D.H. Penny, 'Bimas: a new approach to agricultural extension in Indonesia', *BIES* no. 7 (1967), pp. 60–9.

Rosenburg, David A., and Jean G. Rosenburg, *Landless peasants and rural poverty in selected Asian countries* (Ithaca: Rural Development Committee Monograph, Center for International Studies, Cornell University, 1978).

Rothstein, Frances, 'The new proletarians: Third World reality and First World categories', *CSSH* 28, 2 (1986), pp. 217–38.

Rousseau, Jerome, *Central Borneo: ethnic identity and social life in a stratified society* (Oxford: Clarendon Press, 1990).

Rudner, Martin, 'The Malayan quandary: rural development policy under the first and second five-year plans', in David Lim (ed.), *Readings on Malaysian economic development* (Kuala Lumpur: Oxford University Press, 1975).

Rudner, Martin, 'The state and peasant innovation in rural development: the case of Malaysian rubber', in David Lim (ed.), *Readings on Malaysian economic development* (Kuala Lumpur: Oxford University Press, 1975).

Rush, J., 'Social control and influence in nineteenth century Indonesia: opium farms and the Chinese of Java', *Indonesia* 35 (1983), pp. 53–64.

Rush, James R., 'Opium in Java: a sinister friend', *JAS* 44 (1985), pp. 549–60.

Rush, James, *The last tree: reclaiming the environment in tropical Asia* (New York: The Asia Society, 1991).

Rutherford, J., 'Double cropping of wet padi in Penang, Malaysia', *GR* 66 (1966), pp. 239–55.

Ruttan, Vernon W., 'Tenure and productivity of Philippine rice producing farms', *PEJ* 5 (1966), pp. 42–63.

Ruttan, Vernon W., A. Soothipan, and E.C. Venegas, 'Changes in rice production, area and yield in the Philippines and Thailand', *Economic Research Journal* 12 (1965), pp. 181–201.

Saefudin, Yusuf, and Faisal Kasryno, 'Structural changes in employment and income in low income rural households in west Java, Indonesia', in I.P. Getubig and A.J. Ledesma (eds), *Voices from the culture of silence: the most disadvantaged groups in Asian agriculture* (Kuala Lumpur: Asian and Pacific Development Centre, 1988).

Saito, Teruko, 'Farm household economy under paddy delivery system in contemporary Burma', *The Developing Economies* 19, 4 (1981), pp. 167–97.

Saito, Teruko, 'Agricultural labourers in Burma', in *Burma and Japan: basic studies on their cultural and social structure* (n.p.: n.d., 1987).

Sakurai, Yumio, 'Abandoned villages in the Red River delta in the 18th and early 19th century', in Akira Hayami and Yoshihiro Tsubouchi (eds), *Economic and demographic development in rice producing societies: some aspects of East Asian economic history, 1500–1900* (Tokyo: n.p., 1989).

Salleh, Mohamed B. Nik Mohd., 'Kelantan in transition: 1891–1910', in William R. Roff (ed.), *Kelantan: religion, society and politics in a Malay state* (Kuala Lumpur: Oxford University Press, 1974).

Sandee, Henry, and Hermine Weijland, 'Rural cottage industry in transition: the roof tile industry in kabupaten Boyolali, central Java', *BIES* 25, 2 (1989), pp. 79–98.

Sanga Sabhasri, 'Opium culture in northern Thailand: social and ecological dilemmas', in Peter Kunstadter, E.C. Chapman, and Sanga Sabhasri (eds), *Farmers in the forest: economic development and marginal agriculture in northern Thailand* (Honolulu: University Press of Hawaii, 1978).

Sangermano, V., *A description of the Burmese empire compiled chiefly from Burmese documents* (repr. London: Susil Gupta, 1966) [1833].

Sansom, Robert L., *The economics of insurgency in the Mekong delta of Vietnam* (Cambridge, Mass.: MIT Press, 1970).

Santoso, Amir, 'The working of rural co-operatives (KUD) in Malang, 1970–1984', in Howard Dick, James J. Fox, and Jamie Mackie (eds), *Balanced development: East Java in the New Order* (Singapore: Oxford University Press, 1993).

Satari, Gunawan, Faisal Karyno, and Chairil A. Rasahan, 'Rice policies in Indonesia: historical perspectives, features and performance', in A. Fujimoto and T. Matsuda (eds), *An economic study of rice farming in west Java* (Tokyo: Nodai Research Institute, University of Agriculture, 1986).

Sato, Shigeru, *War, nationalism and peasants: Java under the Japanese occupation 1942–1945* (Sydney: Allen and Unwin, 1994).

Savage, Victor R., *Western impressions of nature and landscape in Southeast Asia* (Singapore: Singapore University Press, 1984).

Saw Swee Hock, 'Patterns of urbanization in West Malaysia, 1911–1970', *MER* 17 (1972), pp. 114–20.

Sawit, M. Husein, and Ibrahim Manwan, 'The beginnings of the new Supra Insus rice intensification program: the case of the north coast of west Java and south Sulawesi', *BIES* 27, 1 (1991), pp. 81–103.

Sayogyo and William L. Collier, 'Adoption of new high yielding rice varieties by Java's farmers', in R.T. Shand (ed.), *Technical change in Asian agriculture* (Canberra: Australian National University Press, 1973).

Scheltema, A.M.P.A., 'De voeding van de inlandsche bevolking van Nederlandsch-Indië', *Koloniale Studiën*, 14, 2 (1930), pp. 368–94.

Scheltema, A.M.P.A., *Deelbouw in Nederlandsch-Indië* (Wageningen: H. Veenman, 1931).

Schlegel, S.T., *Tituray subsistence: from shifting cultivation to plow agriculture* (Quezon City: Ateneo de Manila University Press, 1979).

Schul, Norman W., 'A Philippine sugar cane plantation: land tenure and sugar cane production', *EG* 43 (1967), pp. 157–69.

Schulte Nordholt, Henk, 'The Mads Lange connection. A Danish trader on Bali in the middle of the nineteenth century: broker and buffer', *Indonesia* 32 (1981), pp. 16–47.

Schweizer, Thomas, 'Agricultural transformation? Rice production in a Javanese village', *BIES* 23, 2 (1987), pp. 38–70.

Schweizer, Thomas, 'Economic individualism and the community spirit: divergent orientation patterns of Javanese villagers in rice production and the ritual sphere', *MAS* 23, 2 (1989), pp. 277–312.

Scott, J.G. [Shway Yoe], *The Burman: his life and notions* (repr. New York: W.W. Norton, 1963) [1909].

Scott, J.G. [Shwe Yoe], *Burma from the earliest times to the present day* (London: T. Fisher Unwin, 1924).

Scott, James C., *The moral economy of the peasant: rebellion and subsistence in Southeast Asia* (New Haven: Yale University Press, 1976).

Scott, James C., *Weapons of the weak: everyday forms of peasant resistance* (New Haven: Yale University Press, 1985).

Scott, William Henry, *The discovery of the Igorots: Spanish contacts with the pagans of northern Luzon* (Quezon City: New Day Publishers, 1974).

Scott, William Henry, 'The Spanish occupation of the Cordillera in the 19th century', in Alfred W. McCoy and Ed.C. de Jesus (eds), *Philippine social history: global trade and local transformations* (Sydney: Allen and Unwin, 1981).

Scoville, Orlin J., 'Rebuilding Kampuchea's food supply', in David Ablin and Marlowe Hood (eds), *The Cambodian agony* (Armonk: M.E. Sharpe, 1987).

Seavoy, Ronald E., 'The transition to continuous rice cultivation in Kalimantan', *AAAG* 63 (1973), pp. 218–25.

Seavoy, Ronald E., 'The origin of tropical grasslands in Kalimantan, Indonesia', *JTG* 40 (1975), pp. 48–52.

Seavoy, Ronald E., 'Population pressure and land use change: from tree crops to sawah in northwestern Kalimantan, Indonesia', *SJTG* 1, 2 (1980), pp. 61–7.

Shamsul, A.B., *From British to bumiputra rule* (Singapore: ISEAS, 1986).

Shand, R.T., 'Income distribution in a dynamic rural sector: some evidence from Malaysia', *EDCC* 36 (1987), pp. 35–50.

Shand, R.T., and T.A. Chew, 'Off-farm employment in the Kemubu project in Kelantan, Malaysia', in R.T. Shand (ed.), *Off-farm employment in the development of rural Asia* (Canberra: National Centre for Development Studies, Australian National University, 1986).

Shand, R.T., et al., 'Conclusions', in R.T. Shand (ed.), *Off-farm employment in the development of rural Asia* (Canberra: National Centre for Development Studies, Australian National University, 1986).

Shanin, Teodor, 'Introduction', in Teodor Shanin (ed.), *Peasants and peasant societies: selected readings* (Harmondsworth: Penguin, 1971).

Shanmugam, Bala, 'Socio-economic development through the informal credit market', *MAS* 25, 2 (1991), pp. 209–25.

Shari, Ishak, and Jomo Kwame Sundaram, 'Malaysia's green revolution in rice-farming: capital accumulation and technological change in a peasant society', in Geoffrey B. Hainsworth (ed.), *Village-level modernization in Southeast Asia: the political economy of rice and water* (Vancouver: University of British Columbia Press, 1982).

Sharom Ahmat, 'The structure of the economy of Kedah: 1879–1905', *JMBRAS* 43, 2 (1970), pp. 1–24.

Sharom Ahmat, 'The Kedah sultanate in the nineteenth century: some economic aspects', in Asmah Haji Omar (ed.), *Darulaman: essays on linguistic, cultural and socio-economic aspects of the Malaysian state of Kedah* (Kuala Lumpur: University of Malaya Press, 1979).

Sharp, Lauriston, and Lucien M. Hanks, *Bang Chan: social history of a rural community in Thailand* (Ithaca: Cornell University Press, 1978).

Sherard, Sam H., 'Agricultural conditions in the province of Nueva Ecija', *Philippine Agricultural Review* 4 (1911), pp. 130–8.

Sherman, D. George, *Rice, rupees and ritual: economy and society among the Samosir Batak of Sumatra* (Stanford: Stanford University Press, 1990).

Sherman, George, 'What "green desert"? The ecology of Batak grassland farming', *Indonesia* 29 (1980), pp. 112–48.

Sibley, Willis E., 'Leadership in a Philippine barrio', *Philippine Journal of Public Administration* 1, 1 (1957), pp. 154–9.

Silcock, T.H., *The economic development of Thai agriculture* (Ithaca: Cornell University Press, 1970).

Silverman, Sydel, 'The peasant concept in anthropology', *JPS* 7, 1 (1979), pp. 49–65.

Simkins, Paul D., and Frederick L. Wernstedt, 'Growth and internal migrations of the Philippine population, 1948 to 1960', *JTG* 17 (1963), pp. 197–202.

Sinaga, Rudolf S., 'Implications of agricultural mechanisation of employment and income distribution: a case study from Indramayu, west Java', *BIES* 14, 2 (1978), pp. 102–11.

Singarimbun, Masri, 'Srihardjo revisited', *BIES* 12, 2 (1976), pp. 117–25.

Skinner, G. William, *Chinese society in Thailand: an analytical history* (Ithaca: Cornell University Press, 1957).

Skinner, G. William, 'Change and persistence in Chinese culture overseas: a comparison of Thailand and Java', *Journal of the South Seas Society* 16, 1–2 (1960), pp. 86–100.

Smith, Julius, *Ten years in Burma* (Cincinnati: Jennings and Pye, 1902).

Smith, Peter C., 'Crisis mortality in the nineteenth century Philippines: data from parish records', *JAS* 38, 1 (1978), pp. 51–76.

Smyth, H. Warington, *Notes of a journey on the upper Mekong, Siam* (London: John Murray, 1895).

Soejatno, 'Revolution and social tensions in Surakarta 1945–1950', *Indonesia* 17, 1974, pp. 99–111.

Soejono, Irlan, 'Growth and distributional changes of incomes in paddy farms in central Java 1968–1974', *BIES* 12, 2 (1976), pp. 80–9.

Soemardjan, Selo, 'Land reform in Indonesia', *AS* 1, 12 (1962), pp. 23–30.

Sompop Manarungsan, 'Demographic development and rice production in Thailand in the nineteenth century', in Akira Hayami and Yoshihiro Tsubouchi (eds), *Economic and demographic development in rice producing societies: some aspects of East Asian economic history, 1500–1900* (Tokyo: n.p., 1989).

Sophon Ratanakhon, 'Legal aspects of land occupation and development', in Peter Kunstadter, E.C. Chapman, and Sanga Sabhasri (eds), *Farmers in the forest: economic development and marginal agriculture in northern Thailand* (Honolulu: University Press of Hawaii, 1978).

Spate, O.H.K., 'The Burmese village', *GR* 35 (1945), pp. 523–43.

Speare, Alden, Jr, and John Harris, 'Education, earnings, and migration in Indonesia', *EDCC* 34, 2 (1986), pp. 223–44.

Spencer, J.E., *Land and people in the Philippines: geographic problems in rural economy* (Berkeley: University of California Press, 1952).

Spencer, Joseph E., *Shifting cultivation in Southeastern Asia* (Berkeley: University of California Press, 1966).

Spencer, J. E., 'Water control in terrace rice-field agriculture in southeastern Asia', in Theodore G. Downing and McGuire Gibson (eds), *Irrigation's impact on society* (Tucson: University of Arizona Press, 1974).

St. John, Horace, *The Indian archipelago: its history and present state* (London: Longman, Brown, Green, and Longmans, 1853).

St. John, Spenser, *Life in the forests of the Far East* (repr. Kuala Lumpur: Oxford University Press, 1974) [1862].

Steensgaard, Niels, 'The seventeenth-century crisis and the unity of Eurasian history', *MAS* 24, 4 (1990), pp. 683–97.

Steinberg, David I., *Burma's road towards development: growth and ideology under military rule* (Boulder: Westview, 1981).

Steinberg, David I., *Burma: a socialist nation of Southeast Asia* (Boulder: Westview, 1982).

Steinberg, David I., 'Neither silver nor gold: the 40th anniversary of the Burmese economy', in Josef Silverstein (ed.), *Independent Burma at forty years: six assessments* (Ithaca: Southeast Asia Program, Cornell University, 1989).

Sternstein, Larry, 'The distribution of Thai centres at mid-nineteenth century', *JSEAH* 7, 1 (1966), pp. 66–72.

Sternstein, L., 'Aspects of agricultural land tenure in Thailand', *MJTG* 24 (1967), pp. 22–9.

Sternstein, Larry, 'The growth of the population of the world's pre-eminent "primate city": Bangkok at its bicentenary', *JSEAS* 15, 1 (1984), pp. 43–68.

Stevenson, H.N.C., *The economics of the central Chin tribes* (Bombay: The Times of India Press, 1943).

Stifel, Laurence D., 'Patterns of land ownership in central Thailand during the twentieth century', *JSS* 64 (1976), pp. 237–74.

Stivens, Maila, 'The fate of women's land rights: gender, matriliny and capitalism in Rembau, Negeri Sembilan, Malaysia', in Haleh Afshar (ed.), *Women, work, and ideology in the Third World* (London: Tavistock, 1985).

Stockdale, John Joseph, *Sketches, civil and military, of the island of Java and its immediate dependencies* (London: S. Gosnell, 1812).

Stoler, Ann, 'Class structure and female autonomy in rural Java', in Michelle McAlpin et al. (eds), *Women and national development: the complexities of change* (Chicago: University of Chicago Press, 1977).

Stoler, Ann, 'Rice harvesting in Kali Loro', *AE* 4 (1977), pp. 678–98.

Stoler, Ann, 'Garden use and household economy in rural Java', *BIES* 14, 2 (1978), pp. 85–101.

Strange, Heather, *Rural Malay women in tradition and transition* (New York: Praeger, 1981).

Strout, Alan M., 'Managing the agricultural transformation on Java: a review of the survey agro ekonomi', *BIES* 21, 1 (1985), pp. 62–79.

Stuart-Fox, Martin, *Laos: politics, economics and society* (London: Frances Pinter, 1986).

Stuart-Fox, Martin, 'The French in Laos, 1887–1945', *MAS* 29, 1 (1995), pp. 111–39.

Sturgess, N.H., and Hesti Wijaya, 'Rice harvesting: a view from the theory of common property', *BIES* 19, 2 (1983), pp. 27–45.

Subrahmanyam, Sanjay, 'State formation and transformation in early modern India and Southeast Asia', *Itinerario* 12, 1 (1988), pp. 91–109.

Suehiro, Akira, *Capital accumulation in Thailand 1855–1985* (Tokyo: Centre for East Asian Cultural Studies, 1989).

Sukor Kasim and Mustafa Najimudin, 'Evolution of sources of income in the Muda Irrigation Scheme, Malaysia, 1972/73 to 1981/82', in R.T. Shand (ed.), *Off-farm employment in the development of rural Asia* (Canberra: National Centre for Development Studies, Australian National University, 1986).

Sullivan, Patrick, *Social relations of dependence in a Malay state: nineteenth century Perak* (Kuala Lumpur: MBRAS Monograph No. 10, 1982).

Supachit Manopimoke, 'Choice of rice production technique in Thailand, 1890–1940', PhD dissertation, University of Hawaii, 1989.

Surichai Wun' Gao, 'The significance of socio-political factors in Meiji economic development with comparative reference to the Thai case', in Chira Hongladarom and Meedhi Krongkaew (eds), *Comparative development: Japan and Thailand* (Bangkok: Thammasat University Press, 1981).

Sutherland, Heather, 'The transformation of the Trengganu legal order', *JSEAS* 11, 1 (1980), pp. 1–29.

Sutter, John O., *Indonesianisasi: politics in a changing economy, 1940–1955* (Ithaca: Data Paper No. 38, Southeast Asia Program, Cornell University, 1959).

Swift, M.G., 'The accumulation of capital in a peasant society', in T.H. Silcock (ed.), *Readings in Malayan economics* (Singapore: Eastern Universities Press, 1961).

Swift, M.G., 'Capital, saving and credit in a Malay peasant economy', in Raymond Firth and B.S. Young (eds), *Capital, saving and credit in peasant societies: studies from Asia, Oceania, the Caribbean and middle America* (London: George Allen and Unwin, 1964).

Swift, M.G., *Malay peasant society in Jelebu* (London: The Athlone Press, 1965).

Tabor, Steven R., 'Agriculture in transition', in Anne Booth (ed.), *The oil boom and after: Indonesian economic performance in the Soeharto era* (Singapore: Oxford University Press, 1992).

Tadem, Eduardo, 'Peasant land rights and the Philippine corporate farming program', *Philippine Social Sciences and Humanities Review* 42, 104 (1978), pp. 56–76.

Tadem, Eduardo C., *Grains and radicalism: the political economy of the rice industry in the Philippines: 1965–1985* (Quezon City: Third World Studies Center, University of the Philippines, 1986).

Taintor, Mavis Bunker, 'An ecological model of peasant revolution: the Indonesian communist experience 1952–1965', PhD dissertation, State University of New York at Buffalo, 1974).

Takahashi, Akira, *Land and peasants in central Luzon: socio-economic structure of a Bulacan village* (Tokyo: Institute of Developing Economies, 1969).

Takahashi, Akira, 'The peasantization of kasama tenants', *PSR* 20 (1972), pp. 129–33.

Takahashi, Akira, 'The Philippines: agrarian reform before and under martial law', in Zubeda M. Ahmad (ed.), *Land reform in Asia, with particular reference to Pakistan, The Philippines and Thailand* (Geneva: International Labour Office, 1976).

Takahashi, Akira, 'Thailand: growing land problems', in Zubeda M. Ahmad (ed.), *Land reform in Asia, with particular reference to Pakistan, The Philippines and Thailand* (Geneva: International Labour Office, 1976).

Takahashi, Akira, 'Rural labour and agrarian changes in the Philippines', in S. Harashima (ed.), *Hired labor in rural Asia* (Tokyo: Institute of Developing Economies, 1977).

Tanabe, Shigeharu, 'Land reclamation in the Chao Phraya delta', in Yoneo Ishii (ed.), *Thailand: a rice growing society* (Honolulu: University Press of Hawaii, 1975).

Tanabe, Shigeharu, 'Historical geography of the canal system in the Chao Phraya river delta, from the Ayutthaya period to the fourth reign of the Ratanakosin dynasty', *JSS* 65, 2 (1977), pp. 23–72.

Tate, D.J.M., *The making of modern South-East Asia* (Kuala Lumpur: Oxford University Press, 1979).

Taylor, Robert H., *The state in Burma* (Honolulu: University of Hawaii Press, 1987).

Teken, I.G.B., and H. Soewardi, 'Food supply and demand and food policies', in Mubyarto (ed.), *Growth and equity in Indonesian economic development* (Jakarta: Yayasan Agro-ekonomi, 1982).

Tem Smitinad, Sanga Sabhasri, and Peter Kunstadter, 'The environment of northern Thailand', in Peter Kunstadter, E.C. Chapman, and Sanga Sabhasri (eds), *Farmers in the forest: economic development and marginal agriculture in northern Thailand* (Honolulu: University Press of Hawaii, 1978).

Temple, Gordon, 'Migration to Jakarta', *BIES* 11, 1 (1975), pp. 76–81.

ten Dam, H., 'Cooperation and social structures in the village of Chibodas', in W.F. Wertheim et al. (eds) *Indonesian economics: the concept of dualism in theory and practice* (Van Hoeve: The Hague, 1966).

Terra, G.J.A., 'Mixed-garden horticulture in Java', *MJTG* 3 (1954), pp. 33–43.

The Siauw Giap, 'Urbanisatie problemen in Indonesië', *Bijdragen tot de Taal-, Land- en Volkenkunde* 115 (1959), pp. 249–76.

Thee Kian Wie, 'The impact of the colonial past on the Indonesian economy', in Anne Booth, W.J. O'Malley, and Anna Weidemann (eds), *Indonesian economic history in the Dutch colonial period* (New Haven: Monograph Series No. 35. Yale University Southeast Asia Studies, 1990).

Thiem Komkris, 'Forestry aspects of land use in areas of swidden cultivation', in Peter Kunstadter, E.C. Chapman, and Sanga Sabhasri (eds), *Farmers in the forest: economic development and marginal agriculture in northern Thailand* (Honolulu: University Press of Hawaii, 1978).

Thion, Serge, 'The Cambodian idea of revolution', in David P. Chandler and Ben Kiernan (eds), *Revolution and its aftermath in Kampuchea: eight essays* (New Haven: Monograph Series No. 5, Southeast Asia Studies, Yale University, 1983).

Thomas, Kenneth D., 'Shifting cultivation and production of smallholder rubber in a south Sumatran village', *MER* 10, 1 (1965), pp. 100–15.

Thomas, William L., 'The use of herbicides in south Vietnam: resultant economic stress and settlement changes', *PV* 16, 1 (1975), pp. 1–25.

Thompson, Virginia, *Thailand. The new Siam* (New York: Macmillan, 1941).

Thorbecke, Erik, and Theodore van der Pluijm, *Rural Indonesia: socio-economic development in a changing environment* (New York: New York University Press, 1993).

Tichelman, F., *The social evolution of Indonesia: the Asiatic mode of production and its legacy* (The Hague: Martinus Nijhoff, 1980).

Tichelman, F., 'Problems of Javanese labour: continuity and change in the nineteenth century (servitude and mobility)', *Itinerario* 11, 1 (1987), pp. 155–91.

Timmer, C. Peter, 'Choice of technique in rice milling in Java', *BIES* 9 (1973), pp. 57–76.

Timmer, C. Peter, 'Choice of technique in rice milling on Java: a reply', *BIES* 10, 1 (1974), pp. 121–6.

Timmer, C. Peter, 'The political economy of rice in Asia: Indonesia', *FRIS* 14, 3 (1975), pp. 197–96.

Timmer, C. Peter, 'The political economy of rice in Asia: a methodological introduction', *FRIS* 14, 3 (1975), pp. 191–6.

Timmer, C. Peter, 'The formation of Indonesian rice policy: a historical perspective', in Gary Hansen (ed.), *Agricultural and rural development in Indonesia* (Boulder: Westview, 1981).

Timmer, C. Peter, 'Rural bias in the East and South-east Asian rice economy: Indonesia in comparative perspective', *JDS* 29, 4 (1993), pp. 149–76.

Tin Soe and Brian S. Fisher, 'An economic analysis of Burmese rice-price policies', in Mya Than and J.L.H. Tan (eds), *Myanmar dilemmas and options: the challenges of economic transition in the 1990s* (Singapore: ISEAS, 1990).

Tjondronegoro, Sediono M.P., *Social organization and planned development in rural Java: a study of the organizational phenomenon in kecamatan Cibabak, west Java, and kecamatan Kendal, central Java* (Singapore: Oxford University Press, 1984).

Tomosugi, Takashi, *Changing features of a rice-growing village in central Thailand: a fixed-point study from 1967 to 1993* (Tokyo: The Centre for East Asian Cultural Studies for Unesco, 1995).

Trager, Frank N., William J. Koenig, with assistance of Yi Yi, *Burmese sit-tans 1764–1826: records of rural life and administration* (Tucson: University of Arizona Press, 1979).

Trullinger, James Walker, *Village at war: an account of revolution in Vietnam* (New York: Longman, 1980).

Trumbull, Charles P. (ed.), *Britannica Book of the Year 1995* (Chicago: Encyclopaedia Britannica, 1995).

Turton, Andrew, 'Northern Thai peasant society: twentieth-century transformations in political and jural structures', *JPS* 3, 3 (1976), pp. 267–98.

Turton, Andrew, 'Thailand: agrarian bases of state power', in Gillian Hart, Andrew Turton and Benjamin White with Brian Fegan and Lim Teck Ghee (eds), *Agrarian transformations: local processes and the state in Southeast Asia* (Berkeley: University of California Press, 1989).

Ueno, Fukuo, *Desa Cimahi: analysis of a village on Java during the Japanese occupation* (Rotterdam: CASP, Erasmus University, 1988).

Umehara, Hiromitsu, *A hacienda barrio in central Luzon: case study of a Philippine village* (Tokyo: Occasional Papers Series No. 12, Institute of Developing Economies, 1974).

Umehara, Hiromitsu, 'Green Revolution for whom? (An inquiry into its beneficiaries in a central Luzon village, Philippines)', in Antonio J. Ledesma, Perla Q. Makil, and Virginia A. Miralao, *Second view from the paddy: more empirical studies of Philippine rice farming and tenancy* (Manila: Ateneo de Manila University, 1983).

United Nations, *Field enquiries into the living conditions of selected social groups in less-developed areas* (New York: United Nations, 1950).

United Nations, Department of Social Affairs, *Enquiries into household standards of living in less-developed areas* (New York: United Nations, Department of Social Affairs, 1951).

Utrecht, Ernst, 'Land reform in Indonesia', *BIES* 5 (1969), pp. 71–88.

Valdepeñas, Vicente B., Jr, and Gemilino M. Bautista, *The emergence of the Philippine economy* (Manila: Papyrus Press, 1977).

Van Ark, Bart, 'The volume and price of Indonesian exports, 1823 to 1940: the long-term trend and its measurement', *BIES* 24, 3 (1988), pp. 87–120.

Van Baardewijk, F., 'Rural response to intensifying colonial exploitation: coffee, state and society in central and east Java, 1830–1880', in G.J. Schutte (ed.), *State and trade in the Indonesian archipelago* (Leiden: KITLV Press, 1994).

Van der Eng, Pierre, 'Survey of recent development', *BIES* 29, 3 (1993), pp. 3–35.

Van der Eng, Pierre, *Agricultural growth in Indonesia since 1880: productivity change and the impact of government policy* (Groningen: Universiteitsdrukkerij, Rijksuniversiteit Groningen, 1993).

Van der Eng, Pierre, *Cassava in Indonesia: a historical re-assessment of an underrated food crop* (Canberra: Working Papers in Economic History No. 176, Australian National University, 1993).

Van der Eng, Pierre, *Food consumption and the standard of living in Indonesia, 1880–1990* (Canberra: Economics Division Working Papers, Research School of Pacific Studies, Australian National University, 1993).

Van der Eng, Pierre, *Food supply in Java during war and decolonisation, 1940–1950* (Hull: Centre for South-East Asian Studies, Occasional Papers, University of Hull, 1994).

Van der Meer, C.L.J., *Rural development in northern Thailand: an interpretation and analysis* (Meppel: Krips Repro, 1981).

Van Laanen, Jan T.M., 'Between the Java Bank and the Chinese moneylender: banking and credit in colonial Indonesia', in Anne Booth, W.J. O'Malley, and Anna Weidemann (eds), *Indonesian economic history in the Dutch colonial period* (New Haven: Monograph Series No. 35, Yale University Southeast Asia Studies, 1990).

Van Niel, R., 'Economic and population changes in Java, 1750–1850', in Akira

Hayami and Yoshihiro Tsubouchi (eds), *Economic and demographic development in rice producing societies: some aspects of East Asian economic history, 1500–1900* (Tokyo: n.p., 1989).

Van Niel, Robert, *Java under the cultivation system: collected writings* (Leiden: KITLV Press, 1992).

Van Roy, Edward, *Economic systems of northern Thailand: structure and change* (Ithaca: Cornell University Press, 1971).

Van Schendel, Willem, 'Origins of the Burma rice boom, 1850–1880', *JCA* 17, 4 (1987), pp. 456–72.

Van Valkenburg, Samuel, 'Agricultural regions of Asia. Part III – Farther India', *EG* 9, 8 (1933), pp. 1–18.

Van Valkenburg, Samuel, 'Agricultural regions of Asia. Part VIII, Malaysia', *EG* 11 (1935), pp. 227–46, 325–37.

VanderMeer, Canute, 'Population patterns of the island of Cebu, the Philippines' 1500 to 1900', *AAAG* 57 (1967), pp. 315–38.

Vickerman, Andrew, *The fate of the peasantry: premature 'transition to socialism' in the Democratic Republic of Vietnam* (New Haven: Monograph Series No. 28, Yale University Southeast Asia Studies, 1986).

Vickery, Michael, 'Thai regional elites and the reforms of King Chulalongkorn', *JAS* 24, 4 (1970), pp. 863–81.

Vickery, Michael, 'Democratic Kampuchea – themes and variations', in David P. Chandler and Ben Kiernan (eds), *Revolution and its aftermath in Kampuchea: eight essays* (New Haven: Monograph Series No. 5, Southeast Asia Studies, Yale University, 1983).

Vickery, Michael, 'Refugee politics: the Khmer camp system in Thailand', in David Ablin and Marlowe Hood (eds), *The Cambodian agony* (Armonk: M.E. Sharpe, 1987).

Vickery, Michael, 'Cambodia (Kampuchea); history, tragedy, and uncertain future', *BCAS* 21, 2–4 (1989), pp. 35–58.

Vincent, Frank Jr, *The land of the white elephant: sights and scenes in south-eastern Asia* (New York: Harper and Brothers, 1874).

Vo Nhan Tri, *Vietnam's economic policy since 1975* (Singapore: ISEAS, 1990).

Von Benda-Beckmann, Franz, *Property in social continuity: continuity and change in the maintenance of property relationships through time in Minangkabau, west Sumatra* (The Hague: Martinus Nijhoff, 1979).

Vondal, Patricia J., 'The common swamplands of southeastern Borneo: multiple use, management and conflict', in Bonnie J. McCay and James M. Acheson (eds), *The question of the commons: the culture and ecology of communal resources* (Tucson: University of Arizona Press, 1987).

Voon Phin Keong, 'The rubber smallholding industry in Selangor, 1895–1920', *JTG* 24 (1967), pp. 43–9.

Walinsky, Louis, *Economic development in Burma 1951–1960* (New York: Twentieth Century Fund, 1962).

Walker, Anthony R., et al., *Farmers in the hills: upland peoples of north Thailand* (Taipei: Chinese Association for Folklore, 1981).

Wallace, Ben J., 'Technological impact and culture change among the pagan Gaddang', in Mario D. Zamora, Vinson H. Sutlive, and Nathan Altshuler (eds), *Culture change in the Philippines* (Williamsburg: Studies in Third World Societies No. 1, Department of Anthropology, College of William and Mary, 1976).

Ward, Barbara E., 'Cash or credit crops? An examination of some implications of peasant commercial production with special reference to the multiplicity of traders and middlemen', *EDCC* 8 (1960), pp. 148–63.

Ward, Marion W., and R. Gerard Ward, 'An economic survey of west Kalimantan', *BIES* 10, 3 (1974), pp. 26–53.

Warr, Peter G., 'Survey of recent developments', *BIES* 16, 3 (1980), pp. 1–31.

Warren, Carol, 'Class and change in rural Southeast Asia', in R. Higgott and R. Robison (eds), *Southeast Asia: essays in the political economy of structural change* (London: Routledge and Kegan Paul, 1985).

Warren, Carol, *Adat and dinas: Balinese communities in the Indonesian state* (Kuala Lumpur: Oxford University Press, 1993).

Watters, R.F., 'The nature of shifting cultivation: a review of recent research', *PV* 1 (1960), pp. 59–99.

Wells, R.J.G., and L.J. Fredericks, 'Food policies in Malaysia with particular reference to self-sufficiency and poverty reduction goals', *KEM* 16, 1–2 (1979), pp. 44–71.

Welsch, Delane E., and Sopin Tongpan, 'Background to the introduction of high yielding varieties of rice in Thailand', in R.T. Shand (ed.), *Technical change in Asian agriculture* (Canberra: Australian National University Press, 1973).

Wernstedt, F.L., and J.E. Spencer, *The Philippine island world: a physical, cultural and regional geography* (Berkeley: University of California Press, 1967).

Wharton, Clifton R., 'The Green Revolution: cornucopia or Pandora's box?', *Foreign Affairs* 47 (1968–69), pp. 464–76.

White, Benjamin, 'The economic importance of children in a Javanese village', in Moni Nag (ed.), *Population and social organization* (The Hague: Mouton 1975).

White, Benjamin, 'Population, involution and employment in rural Java', *DC* 7 (1976), pp. 267–90.

White, Benjamin, 'Political aspects of poverty, income distribution and their measurement: some examples from rural Java', *DC* 10, 1 (1979), pp. 91–114.

White, Benjamin, '"Agricultural involution" and its critics: twenty years after', *BCAS* 15, 2 (1983), pp. 18–31.

White, Benjamin, 'Problems in the empirical analysis of agrarian differentiation', in Gillian Hart, Andrew Turton and Benjamin White with Brian Fegan and Lim Teck Ghee (eds), *Agrarian transformations: local processes and the state in Southeast Asia* (Berkeley: University of California Press, 1989).

White, Benjamin, 'Economic diversification and agrarian change in rural Java, 1900–1990', in Paul Alexander, P. Boomgaard and B. White (eds), *In the shadow of agriculture: non-farm activities in the Javanese economy, past and present* (Amsterdam: Royal Tropical Institute, 1991).

White, Benjamin, and Gunawan Wiradi, 'Agrarian and nonagrarian bases of inequality in nine Javanese villages', in Gillian Hart, Andrew Turton and Benjamin White with Brian Fegan and Lim Teck Ghee (eds), *Agrarian transformations: local processes and the state in Southeast Asia* (Berkeley: University of California Press, 1989).

White, Christine Katherine Pelzer, 'Agrarian reform and national liberation in the Vietnamese revolution: 1920–1957', PhD dissertation, Cornell University, 1981.

White, Christine Pelzer, 'State, culture and gender: continuity and change in women's position in rural Vietnam', in Halef Afshar (ed.), *Women, state and ideology: studies from Africa and Asia* (Albany: State University of New York Press, 1987).

Wickberg, Edgar, *The Chinese in Philippine life, 1850–1898* (New Haven: Yale University Press, 1965).

Wickizer, V.D., and M.K. Bennett, *The rice economy of monsoon Asia* (Stanford: Institute of Pacific Relations, Food Research Institute, Stanford University, 1941).

Widjojo Nitisastro, *Population trends in Indonesia* (Ithaca: Cornell University Press, 1970).

Widya Utami and John Ihalauw, 'The relation of farm size to production, land tenure, marketing, and social structure – central Java, Indonesia', in Anon., *Interpretive analysis of selected papers from changes in rice farming in selected areas of Asia* (Los Baños: IRRI, 1978).

Wiegersma, Nancy, *Vietnam: peasant land, peasant revolution: patriarchy and collectivity in the rural economy* (London: Macmillan, 1988).

Wijaya, Hesti, and N.H. Sturgess, 'Land leasing in east Java', *BIES* 15, 2 (1979), pp. 75–93.

Wijeyewardene, Gehan, 'A note on irrigation and agriculture in a north Thai village', in *Felicitation volumes of South-East Asian studies presented to his highness Prince Dhaninivat Kromamun Bridhyakorn*, vol. 2 (Bangkok: Siam Society, 1965).

Wijeyewardene, Gehan, 'Hydraulic society in contemporary Thailand?', in Robert Ho and E.C. Chapman (eds), *Studies of contemporary Thailand* (Canberra: Department of Human Geography, Research School of Pacific Studies, Australian National University, 1973).

Wikkramatileke, R., 'Federal land development in West Malaysia 1957–71', in David Lim (ed.), *Readings on Malaysian economic development* (Kuala Lumpur: Oxford University Press, 1975).

Wilkes, Charles, 'Narrative of the U.S. exploring expedition', in Anon., *Travel accounts of the islands* (Manila: Filipiniana Book Guild, 1974).

Williams, Clement, *Through Burma to western China* (Edinburgh: William Blackwood and Sons, 1868).

Williams, Linda B., *Development, demography, and family decision-making: the status of women in rural Java* (Boulder: Westview, 1990).

Williams, Michael, 'Banten: "rice debts will be repaid with rice, blood debts with blood"', in Audrey Kahin (ed.), *Regional dynamics of the Indonesian revolution* (Honolulu: University of Hawaii Press, 1985).

Wilson, Constance M., 'Ethnic participation in the export of Thai rice, 1885–1890', in Karl Hutterer (ed.), *Economic exchange and social interaction in Southeast Asia* (Ann Arbor: Center for South and Southeast Asian Studies, University of Michigan, 1977).

Wilson, Constance M., 'The nai kŏng in Thai administration, 1824–68', *CAS* 15 (1980), pp. 41–57.

Wilson, Constance M., 'Revenue farming, economic development and government policy during the early Bangkok period, 1830–92', in John Butcher and Howard Dick (eds), *The rise and fall of revenue farming: business elites and the emergence of the modern state in Southeast Asia* (Houndmills: Macmillan, 1993).

Wilson, Peter, *A Malay village and Malaysia: social values and rural development* (New Haven: HRAF, 1967).

Wilson, Richard W., 'Reconciling universalism and relativism in political culture:

a view based on economic and psychological perspectives', *JAS* 50, 1 (1991), pp. 53–66.

Wilson, T.B., *The economics of padi production in north Malaya. Part I. Land tenure, rents, land use and fragmentation* (Kuala Lumpur: Department of Agriculture, 1958).

Winstedt, R.O., *Papers on Malay subjects. Life and customs. Part II. The circumstances of Malay life. The kampung, the house, furniture, dress, food* (Kuala Lumpur: The Government Printer, 1909).

Wolf, Eric R., *Peasants* (Englewood Cliffs, N.J.: Prentice Hall, 1966).

Wolf, Eric R., *Europe and the people without history* (Berkeley: University of California Press, 1982).

Wolters, Willem, 'A comparison between the taxation systems in the Philippines under Spanish rule and Indonesia under Dutch rule in the 19th century', *Asian Studies* 21 (1983), pp. 79–106.

Wolters, Willem, *Politics, patronage and class conflict in central Luzon* (Quezon City: New Day Publishers, 1984).

Wong Lin Ken, 'Singapore: it growth as an entrepot port, 1819–1941', *JSEAS* 9, 1 (1978), pp. 50–84.

Wong, David S.Y., *Tenure and land dealings in the Malay states* (Singapore: Singapore University Press, 1975).

Wong, Diana, *Peasants in the making: Malaysia's Green Revolution* (Singapore: ISEAS, 1987).

Worcester, Dean C., *The Philippines: past and present* (New York: Macmillan, 1914).

Wright, Arnold (ed.), *Twentieth century impressions of Siam: its history, people, commerce, industries, and resources, in which is incorporated an abridged edition of Twentieth century impressions of British Malaya* (London: Lloyd's Greater Britain Publishing Company, 1908).

Wurfel, David, 'The development of post-war Philippine land reform: political and sociological explanations', in Antonio J. Ledesma, Perla Q. Makil, and Virginia A. Miralao, *Second view from the paddy: more empirical studies of Philippine rice farming and tenancy* (Manila: Ateneo de Manila University, 1983).

Wyatt, David K., *The politics of reform in Thailand: education in the reign of King Chulalongkorn* (New Haven: Yale University Press, 1969).

Yengoyan, Aram A., 'Hierarchy and social order: Mandaya ethnic relations in southeast Mindanao, Philippines', in A. Terry Rambo, Kathleen Gillogly, and Karl L. Hutterer (eds), *Ethnic diversity and the control of natural resources in Southeast Asia* (Ann Arbor: Michigan Papers on South and Southeast Asia No. 32, Center for South and Southeast Asian Studies, University of Michigan, 1988).

Yoshihara, Kunio, *The rise of ersatz capitalism* (Singapore: Oxford University Press, 1988).

Yotopoulos, Pan A., and Kamphol Adulavidhaya, 'The green revolution in Thailand: with a bang or with a whimper', in Tan Bock Thiam and Shao-Er Ong (eds), *Readings in Asian farm management* (Singapore: Singapore University Press, 1979).

Young, Ken, *Islamic peasants and the state: the 1908 anti-tax rebellion in west Sumatra* (New Haven: Monograph 40, Yale Southeast Asia Studies, Yale University, 1994).

Young, Kenneth R., 'The late nineteenth-century commodity boom in west Sumatra', *Indonesia Circle* 22 (1980), pp. 64–9.

Young, Kenneth R., 'Transformation or temporary respite? Agricultural growth, industrialisation and the modernisation of Java', *RIMA* 22, 2 (1988), pp. 114–32.

Young, Kenneth R., 'The cultivation system in west Sumatra: economic stagnation and political stalemate', in Anne Booth, W.J. O'Malley, and Anna Weidemann (eds), *Indonesian economic history in the Dutch colonial period* (New Haven: Monograph Series No. 35, Yale University Southeast Asia Studies, 1990).

Yule, Henry, *A narrative of the mission to the court of Ava in 1855* (repr. Kuala Lumpur: Oxford University Press, 1968) [1858].

Yuon, Hou, 'The peasantry of Kampuchea: colonialism and modernization', in Ben Kiernan and Chantou Boua (eds), *Peasants and politics in Kampuchea, 1942–1981* (London: Zed Press, 1982).

Zaharah binti Haji Mahmud, 'Economic and demographic profiles of the rice production societies of peninsular Malaysia 1500–1900', in Akira Hayami and Yoshihiro Tsubouchi (eds), *Economic and demographic development in rice producing societies: some aspects of East Asian economic history, 1500–1900* (Tokyo: n.p., 1989).

Zaharah Mahmud, 'The population of Kedah in the nineteenth century', *JSEAS* 3, 2 (1972), pp. 193–209.

Zaharah binti Haji Mahmud, 'The evolution of population and settlement in the state of Kedah', in Asmah Haji Omar (ed.), *Darulaman: essays on linguistic, cultural and socio-economic aspects of the Malaysian state of Kedah* (Kuala Lumpur: University of Malaya Press, 1979).

Zimmerman, C.C., 'Some phases of land utilization in Siam', *GR* 27 (1937), pp. 378–93.

Index

Aceh, 16, 21, 36, 57
administration
  greater reach of, 67–8, 205–6
  machinery of, 48–9
  supra-village, 28
  see also state–peasant relations
age, division of labour according to, 12–13, 179–83
Agricultural Bank (Malaysia), 204, 205
Agricultural Land Reform Code (Philippines), 151
Agricultural Loans Act (Burma), 200
agricultural production, government development of, 63–5
agricultural research, 51–2, 56, 86–7
Agta, 130, 165
Akha, 32, 78
Anderson, John, 16
Annam, 130
Arakan, 42
Ata, 107
Ava, 11, 12, 18, 19
Ayta, 109–10
Ayutthaya, 42

Badan Kredit Kecamatan scheme (Indonesia), 204
Baguio, 103
Bali, 4, 11, 215
Ban Me Thuot, 46
Bangkok, 20, 32, 40, 41, 42, 44, 46, 49, 50, 55, 61, 62, 86, 115, 126, 166, 176, 188, 189, 192, 194, 196, 215, 231, 233
Banjarese, 99, 107, 131, 229
Banjarmasin, 236
Bank for Agriculture and Agricultural Cooperatives (Thailand), 205
Bank Rakyat Indonesia, 67, 204
Banten, 91
Barrio Charter (Philippines), 223
barter, 18, 70, 190, 189, 211
Batak, 110
Batavia/Jakarta, 23, 188, 229, 230
Batu, 103
Bayly, C.A., xviii
Bikol, 89, 98
Bimas programme (Indonesia), 65, 204
Bintulu, 240
Bisayans, 107, 130
Black Tai, 117
Bombay Burma Trading Corporation, 44
Borneo, 1, 3, 4, 7, 100, 107, 114, 130, 187, 221, 229
Bowring, John, 40, 41, 83
  Bowring Treaty, 40, 186–7
Britain, economic impact in Southeast Asia, 38–9
Brookes family, 47, 221
Brunei, 187
  see also Bintulu
Bugis, 32
Buhid, 106, 109
Bulacan, 11
Bullinger pool (Burma), 199
BULOG (National Logistics Agency) (Indonesia), 67
Burma, xvi–xvii, 1, 4, 5, 6, 7, 9, 10, 11, 16, 18, 19, 20, 22, 25, 26, 29, 30, 31, 32, 42–4, 46, 47, 49, 50, 53, 54, 55, 56, 57, 58, 59, 61, 70, 78, 83, 85, 87, 90, 105, 106, 109, 116, 117, 118, 120, 126–7, 131, 133, 134, 135, 136, 137, 139, 140, 141, 143, 145, 146, 147, 148–9, 151, 152, 153, 154, 161, 162, 166, 169, 176, 177, 187, 188, 189, 190, 194, 195, 199, 200, 202, 204, 205, 217–18, 219–20, 220–1, 223, 227, 229, 234–5
  see also Arakan, Ava, Irrawaddy river/delta, Mandalay, Pegu Yoma, Rangoon, Tenasserim
BUUD (rural coperative) (Indonesia), 224

Cagayan, 37, 45, 97, 189, 214, 229, 230
Cambodia, 25, 49, 66, 73–4, 96–7, 137, 150, 167, 217, 233
  civil war, 73, 97, 181
  see also Phnom Penh
Carter, A. Cecil, 160
cattle, 112
Cebu, 113
Chao Phraya river, 31, 97
Chettiars, 59, 135, 141, 195
Chiang Mai, 20, 49, 135, 176, 198
Chin, 15, 108
Chinese
  immigration to Siam, 39–40
  role as traders/creditors, 19, 39, 40, 44–5, 190, 191, 192–7, 198, 200, 201, 202, 205, 207–8
Cholon, 44
Chulalongkorn, King, 41, 42, 47, 126
citizens, development of, 225–6
cloth manufacture, *see* weaving
clothing, peasant, 4
Cochinchina, 4, 8, 11, 13, 20, 44, 50, 51, 58, 74–7, 83, 87–8, 92, 127, 132, 176, 195, 217
coconuts, expansion of smallholder production of, 101
Code of Agrarian Reform (Philippines), 152
coffee
  forced cultivation in Java, 21, 37, 98
  forced cultivation in Minangkabau, 37–8, 45, 48, 88, 216
collectivisation
  in Cambodia, 73
  in Laos, 72
  in Vietnam, 70–2
Collier, William L., 233
colonial land register, 131–2
commerce, 33, 82, 120, 185–212, 240
  commercial cultivation, 112–13
  commercial networks, 189–90, 196–7
  impact on peasant production, 21, 188 ff.
  impediments to, 21–3
  international, 20–2, 187
  role of local shop in, 193–4, 201–2
  traditional village, 17–21
  upland-lowland, 19–20, 195–6, 210
commercialisation, 81–2
  and land alienation, 132–3
Condominas, Georges, 7
conservation, in swidden agriculture, 106
consumerism, 202, 203–11, 236
cooperatives, 62, 67, 71, 138, 166–7, 180, 200–1, 205–6, 206–7
corvée labour, 28, 40, 41, 46, 48, 54, 162, 185, 186
craft, 14–16, 182
Crawfurd, John, 5, 6, 12, 16, 17, 22, 30, 31
credit, 53, 61, 143–4, 147–8, 190, 193–5, 197–200, 200–1, 204–9, 210–11
  government intervention in, 200–1
  government-provided, 53, 204–7, 208, 209, 210
  growth of, 143
  in Burma, 148, 194–5
  in Philippines, 200–1, 205, 207
  in Thailand, 200, 205, 206
  in Vietnam, 201
  land as security for, 132–3, 148
  local, 185
  saving, 199–200
  see also land, tenancy
crime, upsurge during Depression, 55
Crosthwaite, Charles, 218
Cultivation System, in Java, 37–8, 45, 50, 98, 124, 173, 180, 214, 216, 225, 235
cultural diversity of region, xvii
currency, 17–18, 189

Dalat, 46
debt, of tenants, 148
  see also credit
Demak, 23, 132
demography, 81–2
  see also population
Depression, 54–5, 86, 99, 141, 145, 199, 234, 235
Diem, Ngo Dinh, 69, 152
differentiation, social and economic, 226–7, 235–8

Dobby, E.H.G., 105, 222
double cropping, 11, 64, 90–2, 93, 94, 95, 97, 112, 163, 167, 169, 174, 237
dryland cultivation, 6, 13, 14, 83–4, 89–90, 91, 98, 102, 109, 113, 120
Dusun, 130
Dutch East Indies Company, 37
dwellings, 3, 236

East Nusatenggara, 112, 164
economic diversification, 174 ff.
employment, off-farm, *see* labour, wage labour
environment, damage to, 113, 235

FACOMA (Philippines), 205
Farmers' Association (Malaysia), 205, 206
Federal Land Development Authority scheme (Malaya), 63, 154
Feeny, David, 93
fertiliser, 10, 65, 87, 94, 104, 105, 120, 188, 205, 208, 234
Firth, R., xx
fishing, 5, 15, 66, 104–5, 109
food production, government control of, 82
food, peasant, 4–5, 33
forest foraging, 15, 109–10
forests, decline in, 83, 112–14
Freeman, J.D., 112, 179
frontier society, development of, 82–5
Furnivall, J., xvi, 218

garden cultivation, 4–5, 89, 103–4, 156
Geertz, C., xvi, xx
Gourou, Pierre, 15, 91, 92, 104, 118, 124, 125, 132, 138, 139, 140, 174, 190, 199, 202, 213, 229, 232, 233
Green Revolution, 63–6, 93–7, 102, 105, 133, 153, 167, 168, 172, 184, 204, 205, 234, 237
Grobogan, 132
Gunungkidul, 230

Hanoi, 87
Hanunóo, 161
Haw, 78
Hayami, Yujiro, 237
Hendry, James B., 165, 229
herbicides, 168
Hickey, Gerald C., 229
Hmong, 7, 32, 78, 109, 110, 111, 117, 195–6
Homan van der Heide, J., 52, 63, 116, 119
household, 3
  as production unit, 12, 160–1
Hue, 5
Hukbalahap, 57
Hulu Singai, 99, 236
hunting, 5, 15–16, 107, 109–10

Iban, 3, 5, 7, 8, 15, 17, 19, 29, 47, 70, 99–100, 111, 112, 130, 161, 179, 187, 221, 227, 230
Ifugao, 14, 107
Ilocos, 9, 97, 115, 135–7, 165, 229–30
Ilongot, 90
Indonesia/Netherlands Indies, 7, 37, 47, 48, 52, 53, 55, 56, 58–9, 60, 61, 63, 64, 65, 66, 67, 92, 94, 96, 99, 100, 101, 113, 118, 174, 175, 177–8, 181, 182, 200, 203, 204, 206, 215, 218, 223, 224, 225, 229, 236
  see also Aceh, Bali, Banjarmasin, Banten, Batavia/Jakarta, Batu, Borneo, Demak, East Nusatenggara, Grobogan, Gunungkidul, Hulu Sungai, Irian Jaya, Jambi, Java, Kalimantan, Kudus, Lampung, Malang, Maluku, Minahasa, Minangkabau, Pacitan, Palembang, Pasuruan, Sulawesi, Sumatra, Sumbawa, Surabaya, Yogyakarta
industry, peasant labour in, 178–7
Indian Cooperative Societies Act (Burma), 200
International Rubber Regulation Scheme, 54–5, 234
Irian Jaya, 155

Irrawaddy river/delta, 31, 42, 43, 83, 126, 134–5, 162
irrigation, 11, 50–1, 52, 61, 63–4, 85, 86, 91, 92, 93, 94, 120, 168
 see also water control

Jakarta, *see* Batavia/Jakarta
Jambi, 32
Japanese occupation, 54, 55–8, 149, 219, 222
 forced labour projects, 57
 impact on export base, 56
 impact on food production, 57
 social and structural changes caused by, 55–8
Java, 3, 6, 9, 10, 11, 16, 21, 22, 23, 25, 26, 28, 31, 32, 36, 37–8, 39, 41, 45, 48, 49, 50, 51, 53, 54, 57, 58, 59, 60, 61, 65, 66, 74, 81, 83, 89, 90–1, 92, 93, 96, 97, 98, 101, 102, 103, 105, 113, 115, 118, 120, 123, 124, 125, 133, 134, 135, 138, 150, 155, 156, 162, 164, 165, 167–8, 169, 170, 171, 172–3, 175, 176, 178, 180, 181, 182, 186, 188, 191, 192–3, 197, 199–200, 204, 211, 213, 214, 222, 224, 225, 228, 230, 233, 234, 235, 236
Johnston, David B., 236
Johor, 209

Kachin, 7, 109, 183, 220
Kahn, Joel S., 165
Kalimantan, 99, 107, 112, 131, 235–6
Kalinga, 107, 109, 115, 117, 183, 227
Karen, 6–7, 32, 46, 47, 106, 107, 108, 109, 128–9, 164, 165–6, 209, 210, 221
Kasimo plan (Indonesia), 63
Kayah, 106
Kedah, 31, 48, 50, 83, 93, 116, 133, 165, 192, 193, 203, 228, 229
Kelantan, 87, 146, 165, 201
Kemubu rice intensification project, 64, 93, 174
kenaf, expansion of cultivation in Thailand, 102
Khmer Rouge, 73
Khmu, 108, 176, 195
Kontum, 46
Korat, 233
KUD (Indonesia), 67
Kudus, 23
Kunstadter, Peter, 210

labour
 and village agriculture, 159–66
 cooperative, 13, 159–66, 183
 division by age, 179, 181–2
 division by gender, 179–83
 growth in need for, 119, 168
 growth in wages, 168
 impact of mechanisation on, 163
 in off-farm employment, 118, 148, 156, 173–9, 181, 183–4, 237, 240
 organisation of, 159
 recruitment, 171–3
 relations, 162
 revolution in, 159–84
 seasonal migration of, 165–6, 174, 175–6, 179, 181
 seasonal shortages of, 173
 socialist cooperativisation of, 166–7
 subsistence, 5
 technology and, 167–8
 under Japanese occupation, 57
 see also wage labour
Laguna, 135, 168
Lahu, 32, 78
Lakon, 20
Lamet, 7, 17, 29, 109, 161
Lampung, 155
land
 alienation, 131 ff., 148
 as commodity, 49, 123–9
 as security for credit, 132–3
 concentration, 131–4
 conflict over, 130–1
 exploitation of, 123
 fragmentation, 138–40
 inheritance of, 27, 30, 33, 138–40, 153, 228
 landlessness, 54, 134–8, 153, 173, 174, 225
 protective intervention, 137–8
 right to dispose of, 27
 role in peasant life, 123, 156, 240

land – *continued*
rotation in Java, 27
shortages, 134, 143
state control of, 123
swiddeners' rights to, 129–31
Land Code (Thailand), 129
land grants, in Burma, 127
Land Improvements Loans Act (Burma), 200
Land Nationalisation Acts (Burma), 152
Land Records Department (Burma), 127
land reform, 62, 148–54, 232
in Burma, 59, 151, 152–3
in Laos, 150
in Indonesia, 150
in Philippines, 151–2, 236
in Thailand, 151
in Vietnam, 72, 125, 149–50, 152–3
legislation for, 127–8
land registration, 126–9
impact on peasants, 129–31
Torrens system, 127
Land Rent Act (Thailand), 151
land resettlement, 154–5
in Borneo, 130
in Indonesia, 154–5
in Malaysia, 100–1, 154
in Philippines, 154
in Thailand, 155
in Vietnam, 69, 155
Land Tenure Administration (Philippines), 151
land use, 123–57
intensification of, 90–6
techniques, 6 ff.
landholding, 26–7, 30, 123–57
communal, 30, 124–6
in Burma, 26–7, 126–7, 136
in Java, 26–7, 123, 125
in Minangkabau, 27
in Thailand, 126
in Vietnam, 26–7, 126
polarisation of, 131
landlords, power of, 137, 144
Laos, 7, 13, 15, 16–17, 18, 22, 29, 47, 49, 53–4, 61–2, 69, 72, 75, 85, 88, 90, 92, 97, 105, 108, 109, 110, 112, 113, 114, 115, 117, 118, 137, 139, 147, 149, 150, 166, 167, 176–7, 181, 195, 196, 204, 207, 209–10
see also Luang Prabang, Vientiane
Lawa, 20
Leach, E.R., 24, 161, 220
leisure activities, 5
Leyte, 135
Lisu, 32, 78
longhouses, 3
move away from, 128, 129
Low, Hugh, 5
lowlands
spatial expansion of, 82–5
technology of expansion, 85–8
Lua', 106, 108, 160, 164
Luang Prabang, 88, 115, 176, 209
Luzon, 7, 9, 10, 12, 14, 17, 18, 36–7, 41, 44, 51, 58, 59, 74, 78, 83, 89, 92, 107, 109, 113, 115, 117, 130, 132, 135, 141, 144, 148, 154, 165, 169, 175, 186, 214, 229

maize, expansion of cultivation of in Thailand, 102
Malang, 103, 175
Malay Reservations Act, 52, 137–8
Malaya, 1, 2, 3, 6, 7, 10, 13, 15, 18, 19–20, 23, 28–9, 32, 42, 47, 49–50, 51, 52, 53, 54, 55, 58, 59, 60, 64, 66, 67, 77, 81, 83, 87, 88, 90, 92, 93, 94, 95, 96, 98–101, 103, 105, 112, 116, 127, 131, 132, 133, 135, 137–8, 139, 140, 144, 146, 152, 154, 163, 164, 165, 168, 169, 174, 179, 181, 182, 188, 189, 195, 197, 202, 206, 222–3, 228, 229, 234
Malayan 'Emergency', 59, 180
Malaysia, 106, 113, 114–15, 175, 204
see also Borneo, Brunei, Johor, Kedah, Kelantan, Kemubu, Krian, Malaya, Melaka, Muda, Negeri Sembilan, Pahang, Penang, Perak, Perlis, Sabah, Sarawak, Selangor, Sungei Kulim, Temerloh, Terengganu

Maluku, 101
Mandalay, 52
Mandayas, 107, 130
Mangyan, 107, 165
Manila, 23, 39, 45, 55, 188, 194, 230
Marcos, Ferdinand, 153
marketing, 60, 62, 65, 67, 71, 104, 117, 193, 196–7, 201, 203–6, 208, 211, 216, 224
Masagana 99 programme, 64–5, 205
material life, of peasants, 2–5
material wellbeing, *see* prosperity
McLennan, Marshall Seaton, 147
mechanisation, 94–5, 96
  see also technology
Mekong delta, 72, 94, 207
Melaka, 38, 169, 174
mercantilism, 35–8
Minahasa, 211
Minangkabau, 3, 10, 14, 21, 23, 27, 29, 30, 32, 37–8, 45, 48, 114, 116, 128, 144, 164–5, 180, 214–15
Mindanao, 2, 70, 107, 221, 230
Mindon, King, 43
Mindoro, 107, 230
Mnong Gar, 7
mobility, social, 30, 227–31
modern state, emergence of, 46
Moerman, M., xx, 160
Moi, 109, 129
Mon, 32
moneylenders, *see* credit
Mongkut, King, 115
Moro, 47
Mountain Province, 94, 107, 108
Muda irrigation scheme, 64, 93, 96, 146, 168, 170, 223, 234
Murut, 130

National Agricultural Credit Office (Vietnam), 62
National Padi and Rice Authority (Malaysia), 206
National Rice and Corn Corporation (Philippines), 53
National Tribal Welfare Committee (Thailand), 155
Naylor, Rosamund, 236
Negeri Sembilan, 100
Negritoes, 7, 18, 90, 107
Negros, 50, 107, 165
New Economic Policy (Malaysia), 64
New Management System (Vietnam), 71
New Order (Indonesia), 65
NGOs, growth in number of, 68
North Borneo Company, 128
Nueva Ecija, 45, 78, 97, 160, 165, 229

opium, 110–11, 196
Owen, Norman G., 199, 237

Pacitan, 91
Padi Centra programme (Indonesia), 63
Pahang, 1, 14, 29, 189
Palanan, 130, 165
Palawan, 100
Palembang, 191
Palmer, Ingrid, 233–4
Pampanga, 11, 74, 141
PANAMIN (Philippines), 70
Panay, 90, 113
Pangasinan, 140, 141, 165
Pasuruan, 97–8
Pattani, 31, 229
pawnbrokers, *see* credit
peasant, definition of, xix–xxiii, 238
Pegu Yoma, 46
Penang, 11, 38, 187
Perak, 88, 98, 127, 229
Perlis, 93
Philippines, 3, 10, 11, 14, 17–18, 19, 22, 36–7, 38–9, 47, 49, 51–2, 54, 55, 56, 57, 58, 61, 62, 64, 67, 74, 83–4, 86, 87, 90, 92, 93–4, 95, 96, 101, 103, 104, 106, 107, 109, 113, 118, 127, 128, 130, 131, 132, 135, 140, 141, 142, 143–4, 145, 146, 147, 148, 151–2, 153–4, 160, 165, 168, 169, 171–2, 174, 175, 177, 179, 187, 189, 192, 193–4, 200–1, 202, 203, 205, 206, 207, 208, 214, 218, 220, 223, 229, 232, 235

Philippines – *continued*
see also Baguio, Bikol, Bulacan, Cagayan, Cebu, Ilocos, Laguna, Leyte, Luzon, Manila, Mindanao, Mindoro, Mountain Province, Negros, Nueva Ecija, Palanan, Palawan, Pampanga, Panay, Pangasinan, Tarlac, Zamboanga
Phnom Penh, 73
Pol Pot, 167
population
density, 1, 123
growth, 74–8, 82, 89, 120, 134, 232
movement, 25, 31–3, 44, 45, 57, 69, 73, 74, 78, 81, 89–90, 123, 149, 162, 175–9, 207, 227–31
pressure, 109
sparseness, 1
rural–urban movement, 178–9, 231
poverty, 231–5
prosperity, 231–8

Raffles, Stamford, 26, 28, 39, 91, 120
railways, 49–50, 52, 56, 117, 188
see also transport infrastructure
rainfall, importance to swidden agriculture, 9
Rama II, King, 40
Rama III, King, 40
Rangoon, 43, 49, 54, 166, 188, 194, 199, 229
Rangsit, 42, 52, 86, 127, 141, 145, 146, 148
Red River delta, 74, 89, 90, 91, 139, 140, 165, 195–6, 202–3, 232–3
Reid, Antony, 239
Rejang river, 32
religious observance, 5
retailers, part-time, 189–90
rice, 6, 9–12, 108, 161, 107 ff.
decline in cultivation, 103
expansion of area for growing, 40–4, 64–5, 82 ff., 93 ff.
seed broadcasting, 11–12, 85–6, 95, 170
Rice Commission (Philippines), 53
Rice Share Tenancy Act (Philippines), 151
roads, *see* transport infrastructures
rubber smallholder, 53, 54–5, 58, 63, 69–70, 98–101, 103, 108, 111, 140, 235
ruler–patron relationship, 24–5
see also state–peasant relations

Sabah, 49, 94, 128
Saigon/Ho Chi Minh City, 44, 69, 153, 188
Sarawak, 46–7, 69–70, 100, 106, 112, 154, 240
Selangor, 127, 169, 229
Semang, 18
settlement patterns, 2
clumped settlement, 2
linear settlement, 2
Shan, 19, 47
Shanin, Teodor, xxi
Siam, *see* Thailand
Singapore, 39, 54, 174, 187, 192, 195
Skinner, G. William, 40
slavery, 41, 48, 162
Smallholder Replanting Scheme (Malaya), 100
social stratification, 227
state–peasant relations, 24–7, 33, 81–2, 213–27
concerning landholding, 27, 123–34, 137–8
for welfare, 52
increased control of village by state, 67
village agency and, 28–30
State Trading Corporation (Vietnam), 206–7
Stevenson scheme, 53, 100
Straits Settlements, 38
Subanu, 2, 70, 221
Suez Canal, 43
Sulawesi, 32, 100, 101, 105, 177, 179
Sumatra, 1, 3, 4, 6, 9, 10, 17, 19, 36, 37–8, 45, 50, 55, 59, 67, 81, 82, 86, 88, 92, 93, 100, 105, 111, 128, 201, 214, 216, 219, 228
Sumbawa, 109, 117, 183
Sungei Kulim, 92
Surabaya, 188

swidden cultivation, 6–9, 14, 15, 19, 46, 69, 88, 89, 104, 105–14, 130, 154, 161, 227
as supplementary work, 109
impact of land registration on, 129–30
increase in, 105–6

Tai Lu, 17
Tarlac, 165
taungya forestry system, 106, 110
taxation, 20, 22–3, 25, 28, 40, 47–8, 62, 123, 159, 189
technology in agriculture, 51, 85–8, 101, 120, 133–4, 163–4, 217, 218, 233–4, 236–7
impact in Burma, 169
impact in Philippines, 169
impact in Thailand, 169
impact on gender division of labour, 181–3
impact on labour, 167–8, 170
impact on peasants of, 133, 170
labour-saving, 94, 95–6, 168–70
spread of, 170
stagnation of, 86
Temerloh, 7, 131
tenancy, 140–8
as social form, 147–8
fragmentation of tenanted holdings, 146
growth of, 143–7
in Burma, 141, 143
in Malaya, 140, 145
in Philippines, 141, 142, 143–4
in Thailand, 141, 145
kin-structured tenancy, 145
reasons for increase in, 143–7
tensions regarding, 146
Tenasserim, 42
Terengganu, 229
textiles
decline of indigenous, 115–18, 233
impact of imports on, 116, 233
Thai Rice Company, 53
Thailand, 6, 7, 9, 10, 18, 21, 22, 23, 25, 28, 31, 32, 39–42, 43, 44, 46, 47, 48, 49, 51, 52, 53, 55, 56, 57, 60, 61, 62–3, 65–6, 67, 68, 69, 74, 75, 78, 81, 83, 85–6, 87, 88, 89–90, 92, 93, 95, 96, 97, 100, 102, 105, 108, 110, 111, 112, 113, 114, 115, 117, 118, 119, 126, 127, 128, 129, 131–2, 134, 135, 138, 139, 140, 141, 144, 145, 146, 147, 148–9, 151, 155, 160, 162, 164, 165, 166, 169, 174, 176, 177, 178, 180, 181–2, 186–7, 188, 192, 194, 196, 197, 200, 201, 202, 206, 208, 209, 210, 211, 212, 215, 218, 220, 221–2, 224, 225, 228, 230, 233, 236, 238
see also Ayutthaya, Bangkok, Chao Phraya river, Chiang Mai, Lakon, Pattani, Rangsit, Korat
Thieu, Nguyen Van, 152, 153
Tichelman, F., 232
tobacco
in east Sumatra, 50, 56
monopoly in Philippines, 36–8, 39, 45, 214
Tonkin, 104, 110, 114, 124, 138, 145, 174, 176, 192, 195, 202, 213–14, 217, 234
trade, *see* commerce
transmigration program, Indonesian, 154–5, 230
transport infrastructure, 22, 49, 52, 56, 58, 61–2, 66–7, 120, 185, 186, 188, 204, 209–10, 211

urbanisation, 175–7, 178–9, 229, 230–1

Van den Bosch, Johannes, 37
Vickery, Michael, 233
Vientiane, 62, 85, 88, 118, 119, 137, 145, 147, 166
Vietnam, 3, 5, 7, 9, 12–13, 25, 26, 27, 28, 29, 32, 44, 46, 48, 53, 57, 61, 70–2, 87, 91, 92, 94, 106, 108, 109, 115, 117–18, 123, 124, 125, 126, 131, 132, 138, 149–50, 152, 153, 154, 155, 160, 164, 165, 166–7, 175–6, 180, 190–1, 192, 201, 205, 206–7, 207–8, 209, 213, 220, 222, 224, 227–8, 229, 232

Vietnam – *continued*
see also Annam, Ban Me Thuot, Cholon, Cochinchina, Dalat, Hanoi, Hue, Kontum, Mekong delta, Red River delta, Saigon/Ho Chi Minh City, Tonkin
Vietnam War, 69
village
agency and state power, 28–30, 67
changes to role, 213–38
consolidation of village power, 223–5
development as community, 213–16
headship, 29
in Bali, 215
in Burma, 217–18, 219–20, 223
in Cambodia, 217
in Java, 213, 214, 216, 218, 219, 223
in Malaya, 222–3
in Philippines, 214, 220, 221, 223
in Sumatra, 214–15, 216, 219, 223
in Thailand, 215–16, 218, 220, 221–2
in Vietnam, 213–14, 217, 220, 224
independence, 29
sharing of resources in, 30
size and shape, 2–4, 213–15, 225–6
social structure, 213, 226
society, 30
village chief, power of, 28–9, 59, 67–8, 216–25, 227
Village Government Law (Indonesia), 223, 225
village industry
decline of, 114–15
new types of, 118, 119
see also crafts
Village Regulation (Burma), 218

wage labour, 23–4, 33, 159–66, 183, 237, 240
as replacement for cooperative labour, 164
control of, 171–3
development in Laos, 165
in Java, 172
in multiple cropping, 163
in Philippines, 165, 171–2
in Vietnam, 165
labour brokering, 171
labour contractors, 171
labour gangs, 171
opportunities, 210
recruitment, 171–3
trend towards, 163
see also labour
Wan Mat Saman, 50
canal, 83
water control, 51
mechanisms, 120
see also irrigation
weaving, 14, 16–17, 118, 233
see also textiles
White, Benjamin, xvii
Winstedt, R.O., 222
women, xvi, 5, 8, 88, 163–4, 170, 171, 172, 175, 177, 190–1
division of labour, 12–13, 179–83
increase in agricultural participation, 118
see also weaving, commerce

Yao, 32, 78, 111, 196
Yogyakarta, 11
Yunnan, 20, 78, 196

Zamboanga, 47